PRAISE FOR

Dancing in the Glory of Monsters

"He is a cracking writer, with a wry sense of understatement . . . Mr. Stearns has spoken to everyone—villagers, child soldiers, Mobutu's commanders, Kabila's ministers, Rwandan intelligence officers. In these conversations he found gold, bringing clarity—and humanity—to a place that usually seems inexplicable and barbaric. *Dancing in the Glory of Monsters* is riveting and certain to become essential reading for anyone looking to understand Central Africa."
—Douglas Rogers, *The Wall Street Journal*

"The best account [of the conflict in the Congo] so far; more serious than several recent macho-war-correspondent travelogues, and more lucid and accessible than its nearest competitor. . . . [Stearns] has lived in the country, and has done a raft of interviews with people who witnessed what happened before he got there . . . his picture is clear, made painfully real by a series of close-up portraits."
—Adam Hochschild,
The New York Times Book Review

"Enter Jason Stearns. One of Congo's most intrepid observers, he describes the war from the point of view of its perpetrators. He has tracked down and interviewed a rogue's gallery of them. The resulting book, *Dancing in the Glory of Monsters*, is a tour de force, though not for the squeamish."   —*The Washington Post*

"[Stearns] is probably the most widely travelled and the most meticulous and empathetic observer of the war there. This is a serious book about the social and political forces behind one of the most violent clashes of modern times—as well as a damn good read."

—*The Economist*

"A serious, admirably balanced account of the crisis and the political and social forces behind it, providing vivid portraits of both victims and perpetrators and eyewitness accounts of the main events ... perhaps the most accessible, meticulously researched and comprehensive overview of the Congo crisis yet."

—*Financial Times*

"[A] tremendous book. This is a very complicated, largely unfamiliar subject that's basically off the radar of the American media and he's managed to produce a genuinely readable and engrossing account. To the extent that it's possible to breeze through a book about a years-long bloody civil war I breezed right through it."

—Matthew Yglesias, ThinkProgress.org

" ... The subject he has tackled is vast and impossible to cover in one book. But for anyone interested in the Congo and the Great Lakes region this is a great read—one I highly recommend."

—Stephanie Wolters,
Mail & Guardian (Johannesburg)

"Perhaps the best account of the most recent conflict in the Congo."

—Foreign Policy

"A brave and accessible take on the leviathan at the heart of so many of Africa's problems ... Stearns's eye for detail, culled from countless interviews, brings this book alive ... I once wrote that the Congo suffers from 'a lack of institutional memory,' meaning that its atrocities well so inexorably that nobody bothers to keep an account of them. Stearns's book goes a long way to putting that right."

—*The Telegraph*

"This courageous book is a plea for more nuanced understanding and the silencing of the analysis-free 'the horror, the horror' exclamation that Congo still routinely wrings from Western lips."
—Michela Wrong, *The Spectator*

"Stearns's objective in his book is to pick apart the political causes behind this war, to make sense of the madness—and to select individuals, such as a father in Kisangani who helplessly watches his son bleed to death after a senseless battle, whose stories will make us care . . . Stearns succeeds. His book is engrossing, persuasive, copiously researched, well-organized, well-sourced, and viscerally disturbing."
—Jeffrey Gettleman, *The New Republic*

"Stearns has done a fine job of amassing vast amounts (of material), much of it based directly on interviews with the participants and victims, to bring to light details of a scandalously under-reported war . . . (T)his book succeeds in providing a vivid chronicle of this rolling conflict involving 20 rival rebel groups."
—*Sunday Times*

"Impressively controlled account of the devastating Congo war. . . . The book's greatest strength is the eyewitness dialogue; Stearns discusses his encounters with everyone from major military figures to residents of remote villages (he was occasionally suspected of being a CIA spy) . . . An important examination of a social disaster that seems both politically complex and cruelly senseless."
—*Kirkus*

"On the ground in Congo for a decade, he has written a compelling history of the turmoil, combining a deep sympathy for the people's plight and a sharp analytical eye on the reasons for the unfolding disasters. Stearns' great strength is his ability to tell the tortuous history of the past decade and a half by bringing on the Congolese people themselves as the central players in the drama. . . . Unsparing in his critique of the vanity and greed of Congo's political class, Stearns also gives an incomparable eye-witness account of a system that tries to suck everyone into a vortex of compromise and corruption."
—*The Africa Report*

Dancing in the Glory of Monsters

DANCING
IN THE
GLORY
OF
MONSTERS

THE COLLAPSE OF THE
CONGO
AND THE GREAT WAR OF
AFRICA

Jason K. Stearns

PUBLICAFFAIRS
New York

PublicAffairs books are available at special discounts for bulk purchases in the U.S.
by corporations, institutions, and other organizations. For more information, please
contact the Special Markets Department at the Perseus Books Group, 2300
Chestnut Street, Suite 200, Philadelphia, PA 19103, call (800) 810-4145, ext.
5000, or e-mail special.markets@perseusbooks.com.

Book design by Timm Bryson

Library of Congress Cataloging-in-Publication Data
Stearns, Jason K.
  Dancing in the glory of monsters: the collapse of the Congo and the great war of
Africa / Jason K. Stearns. — 1st ed.
    p. cm.
  Includes bibliographical references and index.
  ISBN 978-1-58648-929-8 (hardcover)
  ISBN 978-1-61039-107-8 (paperback)
  ISBN 978-1-61039-159-7 (e-book)
  1. Congo (Democratic Republic)—History—1997- 2. Political violence—Congo
(Democratic Republic) 3. Ethnic conflict—Congo (Democratic Republic) 4. War
and society—Congo (Democratic Republic) 5. Genocide—Congo (Democratic
Republic) 6. Massacres—Congo (Democratic Republic) I. Title.

DT658.26.S74 2011
967.5103'4—dc22

                              2010043075

10 9 8 7 6 5 4 3 2 1

For Lusungu

Contents

Acknowledgments

My thanks go to the many Congolese, Rwandans, Burundians, and Ugandans who helped me write this book and whose names appear in these pages. They were generous enough to sit with me for many hours and explain their experiences. Others I could not name so as not to get them in trouble—you know who you are, *asanteni*.

I owe a special debt to Kizito Mushizi, Raphael Wakenge, Christian Mukosa, and their families, whose warm support since I first arrived in Bukavu made me appreciate the complexities and beauty of their country. I am also grateful for the help provided by Remy Ngabo, Gandy Rugemintore, Balzac Buzera, Pascal Kambale, Willy Nindorera, Noel Atama, Adelar Mivumba, James Habyarimana, Soraya Aziz, Tshivu Ntite, Thomas Nziratimana, Mvemba Dizolele, Thomas Luhaka, and Michel Losembe in understanding the shifting sands of Congolese politics and in opening doors for me.

My research relied heavily on the hospitality of friends and strangers. To several generations of dedicated journalists in Kinshasa, thanks for the couch, the conspiracies, and insider advice—especially the Reuters crew of Dinesh Mahtani, David Lewis and Joe Bavier, but also Franz Wild, Arnaud Zajtman, Thomas Fessy, and Michael Kavanagh. James Astill and Marcos Lorenzana were important companions through the early stages of the book, and Wim Verbeken, Eddie Kariisa, and Jean-Jacques Simon provided wonderful hospitality. Federico Borello, Louazna Khalouta, Matt Green, Djo Munga, and Johan Peleman were also often on hand to help me out with support and expert advice.

Great Lakes politics is a minefield of stereotypes and misinformation. I was fortunate to have experienced scholars and researchers to help me navigate, including David and Catharine Newbury, Herbert Weiss, Peter Rosenblum, Anneke van Woudenberg, and Ida Sawyer. My friends Serge Maheshe and Alison

Des Forges saw me begin this project and encouraged me along, but, sadly, neither could see it finished. They will be sorely missed.

This was my first experience of writing and publishing a book. Many people helped me through the process. Thanks to my parents, my wife, and my brother for so patiently reading the various drafts and providing comments. Michela Wrong believed in this project from the beginning and provided moral and literary support, as did my agent, Robert Guinsler, and editor, Clive Priddle.

This book benefited from the support of the Rockefeller Foundation, whose generous fellowship allowed me to enjoy peace and quiet at the Bellagio Center for a month so I could make sense of my notes.

Acronyms

ADF	Allied Democratic Forces (Uganda)
ADM	Allied Democratic Movement (Uganda)
AFDL	Alliance of Democratic Forces for the Liberation of Congo-Zaire
AIDS	Acquired Immune Deficiency Syndrome
BBC	British Broadcasting Corporation
CIA	Central Intelligence Agency
COMIEX	Mixed Import-Export Company
COPACO	Collective of Congolese Patriots
DRC	Democratic Republic of the Congo
FAR	Rwandan Armed Forces
FAZ	Zairian Armed Forces
FDD	Forces for the Defense of Democracy (Burundi)
FDLR	Democratic Forces for the Liberation of Rwanda
FLEC	Front for the Liberation of the Enclave of Cabinda (Angola)
FNI	National and Integrationist Front (Congo)
FNL	National Liberation Forces (Burundi)
FRPI	Patriotic Resistance Forces of Ituri (Congo)
ICHEC	Catholic Institute of Higher Commercial Studies
IRC	International Rescue Committee
LRA	Lord's Resistance Army (Uganda)
MLC	Movement for the Liberation of the Congo
MPR	Popular Revolutionary Movement
MRC	Congolese Revolutionary Movement
NALU	National Army for the Liberation of Uganda
NATO	North Atlantic Treaty Organization

NGO	Non-Governmental Organization
NRM	National Resistance Movement (Uganda)
OECD	Organization for Economic Co-operation and Development
OSLEG	Operation Sovereign Legitimacy
RCD	Congolese Rally for Democracy
RCD-N	Congolese Rally for Democracy-National
RPA	Rwandan Patriotic Army (the armed wing of the RPF)
RPF	Rwandan Patriotic Front
SADC	South African Development Community
UMLA	Uganda Muslim Liberation Army
UNESCO	United Nations Educational, Scientific, and Cultural Organization
UNHCR	United Nations High Commissioner for Refugees
UNITA	National Union for the Total Independence of Angola
UNOSOM	United Nations Operation in Somalia
UPC	Union of Congolese Patriots (Congo)
UPDF	Uganda People's Defense Force
WNBLF	West Nile Bank Liberation Front (Uganda)

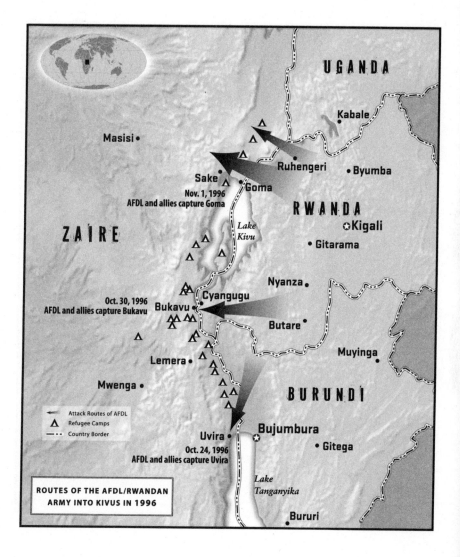

UGANDA

Kabale

Masisi •

Sake • 　 △
Nov. 1, 1996
AFDL and allies capture Goma

△
△
△

• Goma

Ruhengeri

• Byumba

RWANDA

☆Kigali

• Gitarama

Lake
Kivu

ZAIRE

△
△
△
△

Oct. 30, 1996
AFDL and allies capture Bukavu

△△
Bukavu △△△

Cyangugu

Nyanza
•

Butare
•

Muyinga
•

△

Lemera •

△
△
△

Mwenga •

△
△
△

BURUNDI

Uvira •
Oct. 24, 1996
AFDL and allies capture Uvira

Bujumbura
☆

• Gitega

Lake
Tanganyika

Bururi •

Attack Routes of AFDL
△ Refugee Camps
– · – · Country Border

**ROUTES OF THE AFDL/RWANDAN
ARMY INTO KIVUS IN 1996**

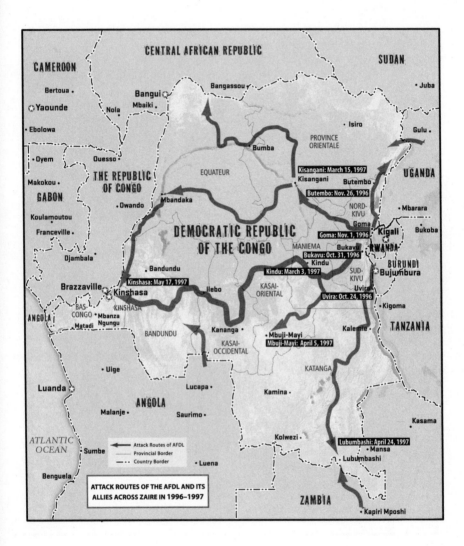

ATTACK ROUTES OF THE AFDL AND ITS
ALLIES ACROSS ZAIRE IN 1996–1997

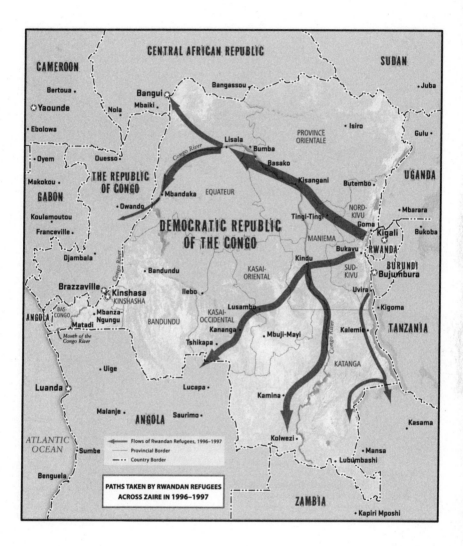

PATHS TAKEN BY RWANDAN REFUGEES
ACROSS ZAIRE IN 1996–1997

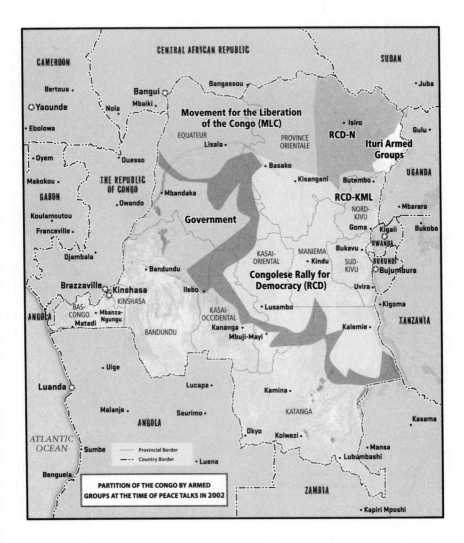

PARTITION OF THE CONGO BY ARMED
GROUPS AT THE TIME OF PEACE TALKS IN 2002

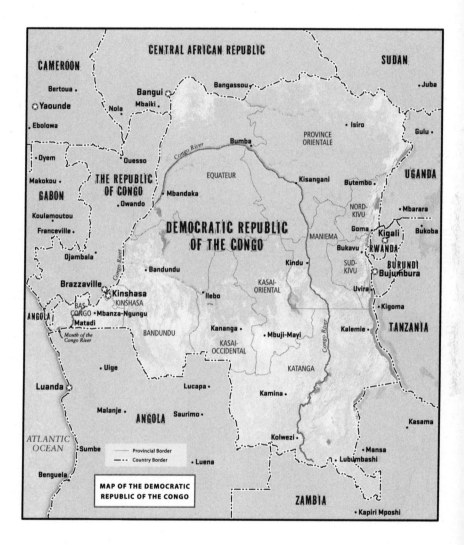

CENTRAL AFRICAN REPUBLIC

CAMEROON

SUDAN

Bertoua •

Bangassou

• Juba

○ Yaounde

• Nola

Bangui ○

Mbaiki •

• Isiro

Gulu •

• Ebolowa

Bumba

PROVINCE
ORIENTALE

Congo River

• Oyem

• Ouesso

EQUATEUR

Kisangani

Butembo •

UGANDA

Makokou •

THE REPUBLIC
OF CONGO

• Mbandaka

GABON

• Owando

NORD-
KIVU

• Mbarara

Koulamoutou •

DEMOCRATIC REPUBLIC

Goma •

Kigali •

Bukoba

Franceville •

OF THE CONGO

MANIEMA

Bukavu •

RWANDA

• Djambala

• Bandundu

Kindu •

SUD-
KIVU

BURUNDI

• Bujumbura

Congo River

Brazzaville

KASAI-
ORIENTAL

Uvira •

✗Kinshasa

• Kigoma

KINSHASA

• Ilebo

BAS-
CONGO

• Mbanza-Ngungu

Congo River

Matadi •

BANDUNDU

Kananga •

• Mbuji-Mayi

Kalemie •

TANZANIA

ANGOLA

Mouth of the
Congo River

KASAI-
OCCIDENTAL

KATANGA

• Uige

Kamina •

Luanda ○

• Lucapa

Kasama •

Malanje •

Saurimo •

ANGOLA

Kamina •

Kolwezi •

• Mansa

ATLANTIC
OCEAN

• Sumbe

Provincial Border

• Lubumbashi

Country Border

• Luena

Benguela •

ZAMBIA

MAP OF THE DEMOCRATIC
REPUBLIC OF THE CONGO

• Kapiri Mposhi

Preface to the Paperback Edition

Authors are bound unforgivingly to their written record. The Congolese wars are stories within stories. Once you put pen to paper, you tie yourself inextricably to one image and one narrative, excluding all others. We are bound to regret our lapses and omissions.

I returned to the eastern Congo twice since this book was first published, doing research and following preparations for the critical November 2011 elections. Traveling in the eastern part of the country, I was nagged by two different kinds of regret linked to my book. First, I was afraid that I had undersold the Congo's many virtues, highlighting the tragedy and bloodshed.

The Congo is not just blood and gore. It also has an incandescent, raw energy to it, a dogged hustle that can be seen in street-side hawkers and besuited ministers alike. This charm is not unlike that of America's mythical Wild West, full of gunslingers, Bible-thumpers, prostitutes, street urchins, and rogue businessmen. This is the paradox of the Congo: Despite its tragic past, and probably in part due to the self-reliance and ingenuity resulting from state decay, it is one of the most alive places I know.

This effervescence was on display on my most recent trip to the eastern border town of Bukavu. I was monitoring the elections and stayed with my friend Tshivu, who works as a human rights officer for the United Nations. In the evenings, on our way home through the muddy streets, we would pass a grim group of soldiers on the corner, with AK-47s and rocket-propelled grenades on display. Tshivu complained that just the other day they had run about, stopping traffic and threatening a mutiny if they didn't get their salaries and promotions. In the mornings, I was woken up at dawn by preaching and singing from the neighboring Pentecostal church. "If our economy depended on praying—*loud squawking*," Tshivu moaned, bleary-eyed, "we'd be like South Korea by now."

Congolese approached elections with similar wit. The race for the presidency had been reduced to two candidates. The incumbent president, Joseph Kabila, who had been in power since his father was assassinated in 2001, was running a campaign based on his Cinq Chantiers (Five Construction Sites): electricity and water, infrastructure, jobs, health, and education. His youthful face, with sunken eyes and chiseled features, was plastered all over the town, but his popularity had plummeted in Bukavu because of abuses by the security services and runaway corruption. Every time the electricity went out in town or we bounced down a pothole-ridden road, my Congolese friends quipped: *"Voilà: Cinq Chantiers!"* Some had even begun calling it Les Cinq Chansons—the five songs, all melody and no substance.

Speaking of songs, there were a lot of them. The Congo is music crazy, and President Kabila had been able to persuade most of the country's superstars to sing his praises. It was sad to see this kind of mercenary opportunism, but if you listened closely to the lyrics in Lingala, you wondered if the musicians were not trying to send an encrypted message. Take Koffi Olomide, the king of the Congolese rumba, famous for flamboyant outfits and racy dancing girls. "If someone gives you a cricket," he began his pro-Kabila campaign song cryptically, "take it! It's better than someone who promises you an elephant but never provides." My friend Serge laughed—"So we should take a shitty little cricket? I think I'll wait on that elephant." Spontaneously, over a bar table full of beer bottles, my friends decided to found their political party: *Batu ya nzoku.* The elephant people.

The only person who had a chance beating Kabila was Etienne Tshisekedi, a seventy-eight-year-old veteran opposition politician. He was, depending on whom you spoke with, the principled visionary who suffered torture and prison for his beliefs; or a stubborn firebrand who was out of touch with his country. Both of these qualities were on display during his campaign. Seeking medical treatment in South Africa (rumors abounded: was it diabetes? heart trouble?), he proclaimed himself president two weeks before his fellow Congolese had even gone to the polls. "We don't need to wait for the elections," he said. "In a democracy, whoever has the power is the majority of the people. And the people of Congo, in its majority, have chosen and trust Tshisekedi."

It was a strange declaration from a man who had been hauled off to jail numerous times for demanding the right to elect Congo's leaders. Tshisekedi then visited the East and continued his incendiary rhetoric, telling crowds that President Kabila was actually a Rwandan, a Manchurian candidate who had come to exploit them. This xenophobic tripe was supposed to make up for his low popularity in the East, where he isn't well known. In some places, he succeeded—the deep anti-Rwandan sentiment led a minority to latch onto his message. In rallies in border towns, he was greeted by people pointing toward Rwanda—"We will send him back to where he belongs." A Photoshopped picture that made the rounds on computers and cell phones showed Tshisekedi as a husky cop, schlepping a shackled Kabila off to Rwanda. "We want *elections*, not *erections*," some of Tshisekedi's rabble-rousers inveighed, poking fun at the Rwandan tendency to switch "l" for "r."

The elections had the Congo's best and worst on display. People stood for hours in long queues; I saw women with infants swaddled in blankets lining up hours before polling stations opened, and old men hobbling in from miles away to cast their votes. Above all, even in their deepest cynicism, Congolese could find humor and hope. But greed was also at work. Politicians distributed cash handouts, and soldiers in some areas warned peasants that it was President Kabila or war.

~:~

My second regret—or perhaps irritation is the right word—about the book was the desire in some quarters to pin "the essence" of the book, to boil it down to its elemental residue. "What is your book about?" many asked, quite reasonably, and then had to suffer my irritation.

The reason is simple. One of the main goals of the book is to tackle "Congo reductionism"—the tendency to reduce the conflict to a Kabuki theater of savage warlords, greedy businessmen, and innocent victims. To some, the war can be reduced to Rwandan meddling, to others to Western greed for raw minerals. One potential editor (thankfully, not my final one) urged me to cast the conflict as a result of "globalization." More recently, there has been a push by advocates to see the conflict through the sole prism of sexual violence and conflict minerals.

The Congolese conflict does not fit well in these straitjackets. I do not have a Unified Theory of the Congo War, because it does not exist. The conflict is complex and knotted, with dozens of different protagonists. The long history of state decay in the Congo—or, more accurately, the failure ever to build strong institutions—has meant that actors have proliferated, competing for power and resources in the absence of a strong government. At the height of the war, there were upwards of forty Congolese armed groups in the eastern Congo alone, while nine different African states deployed troops. This complexity has thwarted journalists and diplomats alike, but the book suggests: beware of over-simplification; it will get you into trouble. In this sense, I recommend the opposite of William of Occam's famous razor: We should *not* always try to simplify for the sake of theoretical clarity. Get into the grime and grit of the story, rub up against its intricacy.

This emphasis on the conflict's complexity provided the philosophical thrust of the book. How should we define responsibility and guilt in the Congo, when the violence is of a very different nature than, for example, the Nazi-led Holocaust? A majority of the Congolese victims died from hunger, starvation, and illness brought about as a side effect of the conflict. There was no industrial architecture of genocide, no master plan to exterminate the country's citizens. I do not say this to minimize the suffering or to excuse the many horrific crimes, some of which are described in these pages. But the kind of guilt may well be different.

An example: the role of international actors. After many dozen interviews with Congolese and Rwandan protagonists of the wars, I found little evidence for direct American military involvement in support of any parties during the wars, although their intelligence agents were certainly active. The Alliance of Democratic Forces for the Liberation of Congo-Zaire (AFDL) rebellion to overthrow Mobutu (1996–1997)—which has often been rumored to have received U.S. military support—had enough firepower coming from Rwanda, Uganda, Tanzania, Eritrea, and Angola. Nor could I find much support in my interviews for an international corporate conspiracy in support of any of the wars, although many foreign companies did make considerable profits during the war. They were guilty of criminal neglect, perhaps, but in most cases not intent to murder.

American and, in some cases, European policy has been sadly shortsighted on many occasions, in particular in its sympathy for Rwandan interference in the Congo in the name of self-defense. Overall, however, the greatest sins of Western governments have been ones of omission and ignorance, not of direct exploitation. We simply have not cared enough about a crisis that is too complex—and too marginal to geopolitics—to fit into a sound bite. This has led at times to one-dimensional policymaking and the search for simple heroes and villains when the roles are much more complex than that.

~:~

As I write this, Kinshasa prepares to find out who won the 2011 presidential elections. As ambassadors and journalists converge on the election commission headquarters, a weird mood has gripped this city of nine million, an opposition stronghold. In some neighborhoods, a rumor has caught on that Tshisekedi won the elections—raucous celebration and chanting have broken out. Elsewhere, people who think Kabila has won are sulking or celebrating in private. Late at night, the commission decides to yet again postpone announcing the results until the following day. Finally, on December 9, the results are announced—Kabila has won the election with 49 percent of the vote, his main rival trailing him with 32 percent.

The elections are a telling example of the ham-fisted international approach.

From the beginning, the process was steeped in controversy. In January 2011, Joseph Kabila's ruling coalition changed the constitution to get rid of a second-round, runoff vote. This meant that a candidate could win with just 30 percent of the vote, as long as he beat the next man (no women were running). It was a crafty move, and President Kabila figured it would pit his rivals against each other. Sure enough, the fractious opposition was unable to unite, dividing the anti-Kabila vote.

Several months later, Kabila's allies in parliament were able to change the electoral law, allowing them to name a majority of election commissioners. A close ally and spiritual adviser of the president, Daniel Ngoy Mulunda, became the head of the election body. With other allies of the president controlling the Supreme Court, which would deal with electoral disputes, and the Media Council, the incumbent had a clear advantage.

President Kabila's greatest asset, perhaps, lay in his deep pockets. In the run-up to elections, the government sold shares in mining concessions worth around $5.8 billion. The problem is, according to company and government documents since made public, the companies that bought stakes in these mines paid around one-tenth of that price, only to turn around and resell their shares on the international market for the full value, making a fortune. The beneficiaries were all unknown companies based in the British Virgin Islands, some of which had been created just months before the sales took place. Many of the companies were linked to Israeli businessman Dan Gertler, a close associate of President Kabila. Although it is impossible to prove profits from these sales benefited Kabila's campaign, a presidential aide confided to me that similar sales, also involving Gertler, had helped finance their 2006 campaign.

Despite these advantages, Kabila faced a stiff challenge. He had won the 2006 election by virtue of extremely high scores in the East, where the population was grateful for the unification of the country and the departure of Rwandan troops. Since then, however, the East has seen an escalation of violence and a peace deal with Rwanda that led its government to redeploy troops into the Congo with Kabila's permission. The president's popularity plummeted in many parts of the East. In addition, the return of the mercurial Etienne Tshisekedi injected adrenaline into the opposition. Crowds of tens of thousands of people gathered in Kinshasa and elsewhere to hear him speak.

As election day approached, it became increasingly clear that it would be almost impossible to hold a good vote within schedule. There had been too many delays; ballots were still being distributed, and the list of voters and polling stations was marred with mistakes. But the Election Commission was anxious to complete the vote, as the president's legal mandate expired on December 6. So it went ahead.

The commission deserves credit for being able to pull off the elections in 64,000 polling stations across the vast country. It was a huge accomplishment, involving hundreds of thousands of staff deployed in difficult conditions. But the haste came at a price: In some areas, voters couldn't find their names on the voting lists and spent hours wandering from station to station trying to find their names. Some just gave up and went home. Elsewhere, ballots didn't arrive until the day after elections, or they ran out before the vote was finished.

Many irregularities, however, could not be written off as logistical hiccups. In dozens of polling stations, voters accused election officials of illegally stuffing ballots; perhaps the most brazen case was that of the governor of Equateur Province, who chased opposition witnesses out of the polling station so he could vote, then spent an hour in the room, allegedly stuffing ballots. When the results still appeared to tilt against him, he threatened the election officials there to "correct" the result, leading them to seek protection from the United Nations.

In Katanga Province, the brother of the election commissioner declared on his brother's local radio station that, whether the population wanted him or not, he would be elected to parliament. After all, he said, it was his own brother who had organized the elections. There were hundreds of such incidents, including the disappearance of up to 1.6 million votes, mostly from opposition strongholds.

The Atlanta-based Carter Center has panned the results, saying they lacked credibility, and the European Union has come to a similar conclusion. Although it is unclear whether the fraud was widespread enough to have changed the outcome—Kabila was declared winner by three million votes—the reelected president does not have legitimacy in the eyes of many Congolese.

Throughout this process, the international community has taken a backseat, despite the $3 billion in aid the Congo receives each year and the several hundred million that donors provided for the elections. During the fire sale of mining assets, the World Bank and International Monetary Fund helped the country reach debt forgiveness worth $12 billion, and the IMF provided further loans of $551 million, with the specific demand that the government promote more transparency in the mining sector.

Perhaps most egregiously, despite massing evidence that voting should be delayed, the top UN official in the Congo and other diplomats backed the Election Commission's decision to hold elections on November 28. Even as polling stations were set on fire and ballot boxes stuffed, diplomats initially maintained in public that the process had been largely peaceful and proper. In private, they admitted that there had been fraud but said they didn't know how much. Afraid of becoming an arbiter of a "three-ring circus"—as one diplomat described the elections to me—they intoned the need for peace and respect for a process that had already gone off the rails. They gave the impression of doctors refusing to treat a dying patient for fear of a malpractice lawsuit.

A Congolese friend told me: "When Bush beat Gore by several hundred votes, everybody freaked out. And they are telling us not to get upset over the theft of several hundred thousand votes?"

I am being harsh—the Congolese government would have bristled at anything akin to "neocolonial meddling" by donors, and for the best of diplomats the Congo would have been a tough task. And I am not claiming that the salvation of the Congo lies in foreign hands; it doesn't. But the one chance the Congolese had to hold their leaders accountable and to determine their own future

Preface to the Paperback Edition

was being squandered, and diplomats could have done much better than hand-wringing. On the phone with diplomats, the words "mess" and "morass" often popped up, leaving me to wonder where responsibility lay. You couldn't really expect us to umpire a mess, mediate in a morass? My friend Tshivu put it better: "If you try to referee a cockfight, expect to get pecked." Nobody was in a mood to get pecked.

As I write this, it is unclear how the election dispute will pan out. Both Joseph Kabila and Etienne Tshisekedi have claimed victory. Hundreds of opposition supporters have been rounded up, and there have been many cases of arbitrary killings and torture, often by the presidential guard. Still, there has been little mass mobilization, and defeatism is slowly overcoming both diplomats and activists.

I will not make any predictions. If the past is anything to judge by, Congolese politics will continue to surprise and bewilder, frustrate and inspire. As Koffi Olomide sang: *Lokuta eyaka na ascenseur, kasi vérité eyei na escalier mpe ekomi.* Lies come up in the elevator; the truth takes the stairs but gets here eventually.

Bukavu, December 2011

Dancing in the Glory of Monsters

Understanding the Violence

Power is Eaten Whole.
—CONGOLESE SAYING

This is how it usually worked: I would call up one of the people whose names I had written down in my notebook, and I'd tell him I was writing a book on the war in the Congo and that I wanted to hear his story. Most people like to talk about their lives, and almost everybody—Congolese ministers, army commanders, former child soldiers, diplomats—accepted. We would typically meet in a public place, as they wouldn't feel comfortable talking about sensitive matters in their offices or homes, and they would size me up: a thirty-year-old white American. Many asked me, "Why are you writing this book?" When I told them that I wanted to understand the roots of the violence that has engulfed the country since 1996, they often replied with a question, "Who are you to understand what I am telling you?"

The look of bemusement would frequently appear in the eyes of interviewees. An army commander spent most of our meeting asking me what *I* thought of the Congo, trying to pry my prejudices out of me before he told me his story. "Everybody has an agenda," he told me. "What's yours?" A local, illiterate warlord with an amulet of cowries, colonial-era coins, and monkey skulls around his neck shook his head at me when I took his picture, telling me to erase it: "You're going to take my picture to Europe and show it to other white people. What do they know about my life?" He was afraid, he told me, that they would laugh at him, think he was a *macaque*, some forest monkey.

He had good reason to be skeptical. There is a long history of taking pictures and stories from Central Africa out of context. In 1904, an American missionary brought Ota Benga, a pygmy from the central Congo, to the United States. He was placed in the monkey house at the Bronx Zoo in New York City, where his filed teeth, disproportionate limbs and tricks helped attract 40,000 visitors a day. He was exhibited alongside an orangutan, with whom he performed tricks, in order to emphasize Africans' similarities with apes. An editorial in the *New York Times*, rejecting calls for his release, remarked that "pygmies are very low in the human scale. . . . The idea that men are all much alike except as they have had or lacked opportunities for getting an education out of books is now far out of date."

While not as shockingly racist, news reports from the Congo still usually reduce the conflict to a simplistic drama. An array of caricatures is often presented: the corrupt, brutal African warlord with his savage soldiers, raping and looting the country. Pictures of child soldiers high on amphetamines and marijuana—sometimes from Liberia and Sierra Leone, a thousand miles from the Congo. Poor, black victims: children with shiny snot dried on their faces, flies buzzing around them, often in camps for refugees or internally displaced. Between these images of killers and victims, there is little room to challenge the clichés, let alone try to offer a rational explanation for a truly chaotic conflict.

The Congo wars are not stories that can be explained through such stereotypes. They are the product of a deep history, often unknown to outside observers. The principal actors are far from just savages, mindlessly killing and being killed, but thinking, breathing Homines sapientes, whose actions, however abhorrent, are underpinned by political rationales and motives.

⁓:⁓

The Democratic Republic of the Congo is a vast country, the size of western Europe and home to sixty million people. For decades it was known for its rich geology, which includes large reserves of cobalt, copper, and diamonds, and for the extravagance of its dictator Mobutu Sese Seko, but not for violence or depravity.

Then, in 1996, a conflict began that has thus far cost the lives of over five million people.

The Congolese war must be put among the other great human cataclysms of our time: the World Wars, the Great Leap Forward in China, the Rwandan and Cambodian genocides. And yet, despite its epic proportions, the war has received little sustained attention from the rest of the world. The mortality figures are so immense that they become absurd, almost meaningless. From the outside, the war seems to possess no overarching narrative or ideology to explain it, no easy tribal conflict or socialist revolution to use as a peg in a news piece. In Cambodia, there was the despotic Khmer Rouge; in Rwanda one could cast the genocidal Hutu militias as the villains. In the Congo these roles are more difficult to fill. There is no Hitler, Mussolini, or Stalin. Instead it is a war of the ordinary person, with many combatants unknown and unnamed, who fight for complex reasons that are difficult to distill in a few sentences—much to the frustration of the international media. How do you cover a war that involves at least twenty different rebel groups and the armies of nine countries, yet does not seem to have a clear cause or objective? How do you put a human face on a figure like "four million" when most of the casualties perish unsensationally, as a result of disease, far away from television cameras?

The conflict is a conceptual mess that eludes simple definition, with many interlocking narrative strands. The *New York Times*, one of the few American newspapers with extensive foreign coverage, gave Darfur nearly four times the coverage it gave the Congo in 2006, when Congolese were dying of war-related causes at nearly ten times the rate of those in Darfur.[1] Even Nicholas Kristof, the *Times* columnist who has campaigned vigorously for humanitarian crises around the world, initially used the confusion of the Congo as a justification for reporting on it less—it is less evil because it is less ideologically defined. He writes:

> Darfur is a case of genocide, while Congo is a tragedy of war and poverty.... Militias slaughter each other, but it's not about an ethnic group in the government using its military force to kill other groups. And that is what Darfur has been about: An Arab government in Khartoum arming Arab militias to kill members of black African tribes. We all have within us a moral compass, and that is moved partly by the level of human suffering. I grant that the suffering is greater in Congo. But our compass is also moved by human evil, and that is greater in Darfur. There's no greater crime than genocide, and that is Sudan's specialty.[2]

~:~

What is the evil in the Congo? How can we explain the millions of deaths?

In 1961, the philosopher Hannah Arendt traveled to Jerusalem to witness the trial of a great Nazi war criminal, Adolph Eichmann, who had been in charge of sending hundreds of thousands of Jews to their deaths. Herself a Jewish escapee from the Holocaust, Arendt was above all interested in the nature of evil. For her, the mass killing of Jews had been possible through a massive bureaucracy that dehumanized the victims and dispersed responsibility through the administrative apparatus. Eichmann was not a psychopath but a conformist. "I was just doing my job," he told the court in Jerusalem. This, Arendt argued, was the banality of evil.

This book takes Arendt's insight as its starting point. The Congo obviously does not have the anonymous bureaucracy that the Third Reich did. Most of the killing and rape have been carried out at short range, often with hatchets, knives, and machetes. It is difficult not to attribute personal responsibility to the killers and leaders of the wars.

It is not, however, helpful to personalize the evil and suggest that somehow those involved in the war harbored a superhuman capacity for evil. It is more useful to ask what political system produced this kind of violence. This book tries to see the conflict through the eyes of its protagonists and understand why war made more sense than peace, why the regional political elites seem to be so rich in opportunism and so lacking in virtue.

The answers to these questions lie deeply embedded in the region's history. But instead of being a story of a brutal bureaucratic machine, the Congo is a story of the opposite: a country in which the state has been eroded over centuries and where once the fighting began, each community seemed to have its own militia, fighting brutal insurgencies and counterinsurgencies with each other. It was more like seventeenth-century Europe and the Thirty Years' War than Nazi Germany.

~:~

For centuries the Congo has held a fascination for outsiders. Lying at the heart of the African continent, and encompassing some of the continent's most impenetrable jungles, it has long been associated with violence and injustice. In 1885, during the scramble to divide Africa among colonial powers, King Leopold II of Belgium claimed the country as his personal fiefdom. He set up the Congo Free State, a private enterprise, and during the rubber boom of the 1890s the country became a key source of latex for car and bicycle tires. Colonial officers created a draconian system of forced labor during which they killed or mutilated hundreds of thousands and pushed millions of others to starvation or death from disease.

This brutality prompted the first international human rights campaign, led by missionaries and activists, including Mark Twain and Arthur Conan Doyle. Under pressure, King Leopold capitulated and handed the country over to the Belgian government in 1908. Although they established a much more elaborate administration with extensive primary education, the Belgians still focused on extracting resources and did little to encourage Congolese development. The upper echelons of the military and civil service were entirely white, pass laws kept Congolese from living in upper-class neighborhoods, and education was limited to the bare minimum.

By the time they were forced to hand over power, the Belgians had set the new nation up to fail. As the novelist Achille Ngoye vents through one of his characters: "I don't like these uncles mayonnaise-fries[3] for their responsibility in the debacle of our country: seventy-five years of colonization, one [Congolese] priest by 1917, five [Congolese] warrant officers in an army of sergeants and corporals in 1960, plus five pseudo-university graduates at independence; a privileged few chosen based on questionable criteria to receive a hasty training to become managers of the country. And who made a mess of it."[4]

One of those sergeants, Joseph Mobutu, a typist and army journalist by training, went on to rule the country for thirty-two years, fostering national unity and culture and renaming the nation Zaire[5] in 1971, but also running state institutions into the ground. Mobutu's rule, although initially popular, paved the ground for Zaire's collapse. By the 1980s, Mobutu (by then he had changed his name to Mobutu Sese Seko) was increasingly paranoid and distrustful of his government and army; fearing dissent from within the ranks of his single-party state, he cannibalized his own institutions and infrastructures. Political interference and corruption eroded the justice system, administration, and security services; Mobutu was only able to ward off military challenges by resorting to dependence on his cold war allies and mercenaries. With the end of the cold war, even those resources had become more difficult to muster.

~:~

Then, in 1994, came the trigger: The civil war in neighboring Rwanda escalated, resulting in the genocide of 800,000 Hutu and Tutsi at the hands of Hutu militia and the army. When the incumbent Hutu regime crumbled, the Tutsi Rwandan Patriotic Front (RPF) rebels, led by Paul Kagame, took power, and over a million Hutu fled across the border into Zaire, along with the soldiers and militiamen who had carried out the massacres. The defeated Rwandan army was not the only displaced group seeking refuge. In his Machiavellian bid to become a regional power broker, Mobutu had come to host over ten different foreign armed groups on his territory, which angered his neighbors to no end. By 1996, a regional coalition led by Angola, Uganda, and Rwanda had formed to overthrow Mobutu.

Finally, in addition to national and regional causes, there were local dimensions to the conflict, which resulted perhaps in the greatest bloodshed. The weakness of the state had allowed ethnic rivalries and conflicts over access to land to fester, especially in the densely populated eastern regions on the border with Rwanda and Uganda. During Mobutu's final years, he and other leaders cynically stoked these ethnic tensions in order to distract from challenges to their power and to rally support.

~:~

This book tells the story of the conflict that resulted from these regional, national, and local dimensions and that has lasted from 1996 until today. The war can be divided into three parts. The first Congo war ended with the toppling of Mobutu Sese Seko in May 1997. After a brief lull in the fighting, the new president, Laurent Kabila, fell out with his Rwandan and Ugandan allies, sparking the second Congo war in August 1998, which lasted until a peace deal reunified the country in June 2003. Fighting, however, has continued in the eastern Kivu region until today and can be considered as the third episode of the war.

The book focuses on the perpetrators more than the victims, the politicians and army commanders more than the refugees and rape survivors, although many of the protagonists oscillate between these categories. Rather than dwelling on the horror of the conflict, which is undeniable, I have chosen to grapple with the nature of the system that brought the principal actors to power, limited the choices they could make, and produced such chaos and suffering.

What is this system? As a Congolese friend and parliamentarian told me as I was finishing this book: "In the Congo, in order to survive, we all have to be a bit corrupt, a bit ruthless. That's the system here. That's just the reality of things. If you don't bribe a bit and play to people's prejudices, someone else who does will replace you." He winked and added, "Even you, if you were thrown into this system, you would do the same. Or sink."

There are many examples that bear out his sentiment. Etienne Tshisekedi, the country's former prime minister, insisted so doggedly that the government had to respect the constitutional order before he stepped back into politics and stood for election that he briefly moralized himself out of politics. Wamba dia Wamba, a former rebel leader who features in this book, was so idealistic about what a rebellion should be that he marginalized himself to irrelevance. It would have been an interesting experiment to drop a young, relatively unknown Mahatma Gandhi into the Congo and observe whether he, insisting on nonviolent resistance and civil disobedience, would have been able to change anything, either. The Cuban revolutionary Che Guevara spent almost a year in the Congo in 1965 fighting with rebels in the east before he abandoned the struggle. Malnourished and depressed, he concluded they "weren't ready for the revolution." The Congo has always defied the idealists.

Even Laurent Kabila, who as president would be stereotyped by many as the quintessential Congolese big-man politician, was acutely aware of how deeply entrenched in society the Congolese crisis had become. An inveterate lecturer, he often turned his speeches into morality lessons. "*Vous, Zairois . . . ,*" he would begin, a finger thrusting upward, berating the crowd for having put up with the country's moral decline for so long. "Who has not been Mobutist in this country?" he asked during one press conference. "Three-quarters of this country became part of it! We saw you all dancing in the glory of the monster."[6]

∿∶∾

Papy Kamanzi[7] is an example of how easy it is to be drawn into the deepest moral corruption. A thirty-year-old, mid-level army commander from the minority Tutsi community, he had fought for four different armed groups. I interviewed him almost a dozen times over two years to try to understand his experience. We became friends, and he took me home to meet his young wife and two children. Finally, in one of our last interviews, he broke down and started telling me about how he had worked for a Rwandan death squad in the eastern border town of Goma in 1997. Together with sixty other soldiers, they had been tasked with rounding up dissidents; often the definition of "dissident" was stretched to include any Hutu refugee. Papy could kill up to a hundred of these dissidents—sometimes old women and young children—a day, usually using a rope to crush their windpipes and strangle them.

"Why did you do it?"

"I had to. If I hadn't, it would have been suspicious," he replied, but then looked at me. "You know, you can't really explain these things. For us soldiers, killing comes easy. It has become part of our lives. I have lost five members of my family during the war. You have to understand that. You have to understand the history of my family—how we were persecuted, then favored by Mobutu, how we were denied citizenship and laughed at at school. How they spat in my face. Then you can judge me." But it was clear that he didn't think I could ever understand.

Nevertheless, this book is an attempt to do just that: to explain the social, political, and institutional forces that made it possible for a family man to become a mass murderer. Kamanzi, and all those like him, were not inherently predisposed to evil. Some other explanation is called for.

PART I

PREWAR

THE LEGACY OF GENOCIDE

Between April and June 1994, an estimated 800,000 Rwandans were killed in the space of 100 days. Most of the dead were Tutsis—and most of those who perpetrated the violence were Hutus.

—"RWANDA: HOW THE GENOCIDE HAPPENED," BBC

GISENYI, RWANDA, JULY 17, 1994

To the east of the Congo, in the heart of the African continent, lie the highlands of Rwanda. The country is tiny, the size of Massachusetts, and has one of the highest population densities in the world. This is not the Africa of jungles, corruption, and failed states portrayed in movies. Temperatures fall to freezing on some hilltops, cattle graze on velvety pastures, and the government maintains a tight grip on all aspects of society. On the thousands of hills—in between tea plantations and eucalyptus groves—millions of peasants eke out a living by farming beans, bananas, and sorghum.

The conflict in the Congo has many causes, but the most immediate ones came across the border from Rwanda, a country ninety times smaller. In 1994, violence unfolded there that was many times larger than anything the modern African continent had ever seen, killing a sixth of the population and sending another sixth into refugee camps. This genocide helped create the conditions for another cataclysm in neighboring Congo, just as terrible in terms of loss of life, albeit very different in nature.

≈

Paul Rwarakabije, a lieutenant colonel in Rwanda's police force, fled across the border into Zaire on July 17, 1994. He was dejected; after four years of civil war, the Hutu-led government had been defeated by soldiers of the Rwandan Patriotic Front (RPF). At the beginning of the war, he had sworn to himself that he would never surrender or accept defeat. Now he was sitting in an army truck, crossing the border into the Congo with his wife, children, and a few belongings. He was not alone: It was one of the largest population movements of modern times; over half a million people packed into a two-lane highway forty miles long. The air was filled with the rumble of thousands of flip-flops and bare feet on the hot tarmac.

While Rwarakabije and the elite moved in a fleet of hundreds of cars—they had taken with them every functioning vehicle they could find—the peasantry trudged sullenly with children strapped to their backs and bundles of clothes and mattresses on their head, moving in lockstep with panic written on their faces. Government trucks with loudspeakers brought up the rear, warning that "anybody who stays will be massacred by the RPF." Army soldiers fired salvos into the air to keep the crowds moving. The roadside was littered with the old and sick, unable to continue.

The masses were leaving one of the largest, quickest slaughters of humankind at their backs. On April 6, 1994, Rwandan president Juvénal Habyarimana's plane was shot down just before landing in the capital Kigali, ending the fragile cease-fire that had halted the civil war.[1] Preying on the population's fear of the Tutsi insurgents, Hutu extremists in the Rwandan government deployed killing squads and popular militias, who rallied others, saying they must kill or be killed.

The two largest and most notorious of these youth militias were the Interahamwe and the Impuzamugambi, ragtag bands made up mostly of unemployed young men, which were affiliated with two radical Hutu political parties. They drew up hit lists and manned roadblocks, checking identity cards for ethnic identity or just looking for stereotypical Tutsi features: a slender frame, high cheekbones, an aquiline nose. It mattered little that the Hutu and Tutsi identities themselves were historically as much class-based as morphological and that a rich, cattle-owning Hutu could be promoted to become a Tutsi. Or that there had been extensive intermarriage between the ethnicities, meaning that in many cases the physical stereotypes had little meaning.

In just one hundred days, between April and July 1994, over 800,000 Tutsi and moderate Hutu were killed. Unlike the holocaust of World War II, which had been carried out by a select group of state officials and army officers, largely away from the view of the population, Rwanda's genocide was organized by the elites but executed by the people. Between 175,000 and 210,000 people took part in the butchery, using machetes, nail-studded clubs, hoes, and axes.[2] The killing took place in public places: in churches, schools, and marketplaces, on roads, and in the fields. The entire population was involved in the drama, either as an organizer, a perpetrator, a victim, or a witness.

It was paradoxically the Hutu, who made up around 85 percent of Rwanda's population, who fled during the violence, even though the genocide mainly targeted the minority Tutsi community. This was because the genocide spelled the end of the government's resistance against the Tutsi-led RPF. It was one last, final paroxysm of violence as the government's army and police fell apart. A million Hutu civilians streamed across the border into Zaire, accompanied and driven along by 30,000 government soldiers and tens of thousands of militiamen.

The army's flight across the border did not end the civil war in Rwanda but constituted a hiatus in the hostilities. The Rwandan Armed Forces (FAR), as the Hutu-dominated army was called, used the protection provided by the border to regroup, rearm, and prepare to retake power in Kigali. One of their leaders, Colonel Théoneste Bagosora, said in an interview that they would "wage a war that will be long and full of dead people until the minority Tutsi are finished and completely out of the country."[3]

Crucially, they enjoyed the support of Zaire's ailing president, Mobutu Sese Seko, who had sent troops to support the FAR against the RPF, and who had been close friends with President Juvénal Habyarimana. In part, what was to play out over the next decade in the Congo was a continuation of the Rwandan civil war, as the new government attempted to extirpate the *génocidaires* and the remnants of Habyarimana's army on a much broader canvas.

~:~

Between 1994 and 2003, Paul Rwarakabije continued fighting the Rwandan civil war. He eventually took command of the remnants of those Rwandan soldiers

and militiamen who had fled to Zaire, commonly known as the ex-FAR and Interahamwe. Under Rwarakabije, they became one of the most feared militia in
the region.

I met Rwarakabije in Kigali in 2004. After spending a decade fighting a guerrilla war against the Rwandan government, he had surrendered and had been
given a high-ranking, if somewhat ceremonial, job in Rwanda's demobilization
commission.[4] Even though he had led a brutal insurgency that had claimed the
lives of thousands of Rwandan civilians, he had not been involved in the 1994
genocide, and the government had chosen not to press charges.

Over the years, I met the general a dozen times, always in his sparsely decorated office. He is a short, avuncular man with a proud gut undercut by his tight
belt, always available for a chat, always polite and friendly. He told me he had
diabetes, and he took short, deliberate steps when he walked, but otherwise
looked as if he were in good health; he had put on forty pounds since he had
deserted the rebellion and returned home. His reintegration into the army had
gone without problems, he said. He was a major general, the same rank as President Paul Kagame. He lived in a house provided by the government and had
an official car and guard (although it wasn't clear if they were protecting him or
keeping tabs on him). He now taught lessons on counterinsurgency and gave
advice on how to deal with the remaining Hutu rebels across the border.

When I asked him about the flight into Zaire after the genocide, all Rwarakabije could remember was "the confusion." There was little hint of remorse or
distress, just the military man's disdain for disorder. He was a career officer who
talked about past wars in terms of strategy, battle plans, and clinical figures. He
made it seem there was little ideology at play; he had fought against the RPF,
lost, and now here he was, taking orders from his former enemies.

"The anti-Tutsi propaganda was part of our military tactics," he said, smiling
affably. "We didn't believe it, but in a guerrilla war you have to motivate soldiers
and indoctrinate the population."

Even though the general had far less blood on his hands, his attitude reminded me of Hannah Arendt's description of Adolph Eichmann, the Nazi officer who ordered the transport of countless Jews to their death in concentration
camps, as someone who had never been a Jew-hater and had never willed the
murder of human beings. His guilt came from his obedience, his mindless desire
to please his hierarchy.[5] There were, however, far more differences than similar-

ities between Eichmann and Rwarakabije. In the case of the Rwandan commander, there was little formal law and no dehumanizing bureaucracy to justify his actions. Rwarakabije was not just a cog in a machine whose nature he did not question. So what drove him?

~:~

Rwarakabije was from the Kiga community in northern Rwanda, home of "the mountain people," who had fought annexation by the central Rwandan court and colonial rulers well into the twentieth century. Warrior folklore ran deep in his family, and he had grown up on tales of his ancestors' heroism and exploits. Rwarakabije's father had told him how, when he was a child growing up, their community had risen up numerous times against the German and then Belgian rulers who tried to impose forced labor and taxes on the peasants there. Later, colonial administrators sent Tutsi, considered by the European clergy and rulers as genetically superior, to replace the Kiga chiefs. Slowly, the Kiga were assimilated into Rwandan culture. On colonial identity cards, they were classified as Hutu, as they met the stereotype of short, broad-nosed farmers. Like the Hutu, their ambitions were stymied by the colonial government's ethnic prejudice.

All that changed with independence in 1962. Rebelling against Tutsi domination, a new Hutu elite took power in the wake of pogroms, in which tens of thousands of Tutsi and many others fled. Over 300,000 Tutsi refugees emigrated to neighboring Uganda, the Congo, and Burundi, where many lived as refugees and second-class citizens.

Given this political turbulence, Rwarakabije saw little sense in going to university. Power was in the hands of the army, a fact driven home by the 1973 military coup that brought Juvénal Habyarimana to power. Rwarakabije was twenty, and he promptly signed up for officer training in the prestigious High Military Academy. Immediately after graduating, he was sent to a special forces training run by Belgian officers in Kota-Koli, in the heart of Zaire's rainforest, where he was taught survival techniques, abseiling, and basic tactics. Upon his return to Rwanda, he was placed in the *gendarmerie*, a souped-up police force that dealt with internal security as well as matters of law and order. He was a career soldier who took pleasure in describing military tactics and logistics to me, but steered away from questions about politics.

"It is strange to think this given everything that has happened in this country," he told me, "but the army when I joined was a place of discipline and order, where people were not swayed so much by identity as by professionalism."

In late 1990, the political situation in the country deteriorated rapidly. A range of factors contributed to this: The price of Rwanda's main exports, tin and tea, had collapsed over recent years, leading to a contraction of the national budget by 40 percent. The same year, after seventeen years of one-party rule, Habyarimana decided to open his country to multiparty democracy, prompting a proliferation of political parties with affiliated radio stations and newsletters, some of which resorted to explicit ethnic hate-mongering.

The trigger for the conflict was the decision by the Tutsi diaspora—through the Rwandan Patriotic Front—to launch a civil war to reclaim their rights as Rwandan citizens. The war provoked many hardships, especially for the population in northern Rwanda, where the RPF was based. Up to a million people were displaced. The RPF's abuses of local villagers were reciprocated with virulent pogroms against Tutsi throughout the country, test runs for the cataclysm that would ultimately unfold. The peasantry was subjected to rumors of ghastly massacres committed by RPF troops, propagated by the new, rabid press, most famously the Hutu extremist Radio Télévision Libre Mille Collines.

All of these factors fueled the ethnic tensions, which Rwarakabije saw seeping into his barracks. "There were older officers who thought we had to blame the whole Tutsi community for the crimes of their soldiers. It was a throwback to independence, when similar Tutsi guerrillas had killed civilians and vice versa." He shook his head. "Indiscipline crept into the army."

It was, of course, not the first time Rwarakabije had experienced ethnic hatred. Although many families had intermarried with the other ethnicity, and they all shared the same language, culture, and traditional religious practices, the Hutu-Tutsi rift had grown steadily since independence. "In secondary school I was taught that Hutu come from Chad and Niger, while Tutsi are from Abyssinia, what is now Ethiopia. This was the ideology that was hammered into us, even at the military academy: Tutsi are more intelligent, more beautiful, but also tricksters, unreliable. But," he laughed, "they said it was the Hutu who had developed the country, who had farmed the fields!"

When Habyarimana was killed on the evening of April 6, 1994, Rwarakabije, then the operational commander for the *gendarmerie*, became part of a war council that was supposed to name new commanders to take the country forward. The commander of the army had been killed along with President Habyarimana, and a new leader needed to be named. Rwarakabije was in close contact with the acting commander in chief, who opposed the killing of Tutsi civilians. "He used to call me every day," he said, "telling me to make sure no *gendarmes* kill civilians."

Rwarakabije, in the meantime, concentrated on the civil war, pushing back the RPF rebels, who had launched a major attack on Kigali as soon as the president's plane was shot down. However, parallel chains of command permeated the security services, and his orders were often contradicted by extremists. The acting commander lost control of much of the army; Colonel Théoneste Bagosora, a close confidant of President Habyarimana, took control of the most important units and began orchestrating massacres. The presidential guard and the various youth militia began systematically killing Tutsi civilians. On one occasion, Rwarakabije's own officers, whom he had sent to evacuate a group of eight Tutsi who lived next to his house, were attacked by a mob of militiamen who accused them of conniving with the enemy.

"I knew that members of the police were also carrying out massacres, but what could I do to stop them?" When I asked the general whether he had given orders to stop the killings, he nodded, then put his hands in the air. "Of course. But what could we do? We were no longer in control." On his way to work every morning, Rwarakabije passed by roadblocks where Tutsi were picked out and hacked to death. The smell of rotting flesh hung in the air over Kigali; his children complained and cried in their beds at night. Crows circled in the skies, and packs of dogs roamed the streets, scavenging for dead bodies.

And yet Rwarakabije continued to go to the office every day, continued to do his job. Unlike other officers, who defected to the RPF, Rwarakabije was determined to win the war. He sent his family to his home village in the north and only fled Kigali when it was clear the fight was lost. When talking about the genocide, he emphasized the military, not the human dimension: "The army deployed most of its forces to massacre civilians, diverting trucks, ammunition, and manpower to slaughter them. The genocide caused our resistance to crumble. It was a *cafouillage*, a real mess."

The words "chaos," "mess," and "confusion" recurred in my discussions with the general. They contrasted with his refrain that all he tried to do during this time was obey orders and uphold discipline. They were two conflicting ways of absolving himself from responsibility, but also means of coping morally and psychologically with the killing around him.

According to everybody who knew him, Rwarakabije was not himself involved in the killing. In 2009, he stood trial in court for crimes of genocide, but his former neighbors and colleagues quickly came to his defense. "I was glad I was put on trial," he insisted, "so that once and for all, my reputation would be cleared." A Tutsi man whom he helped bring to safety testified for him; one of the officers whom he had sent to evacuate a group of Tutsi argued on his behalf.

He was, however, part of an organization that caused the deaths of over 800,000 people, and he was in a position to save lives. When I pressed Rwarakabije about his loyalty to the army, even when it became obvious that many of his superiors were involved in the massacres, he shook his head, exasperated: "You are much too logical about this! We were in the middle of a war. We didn't have time to think whether we were complicit in a genocide—we were just trying to survive!" He thought they still had a chance to win the war, he said. They thought their flight to Zaire was a tactical retreat, nothing more.

Many of his colleagues, however, did run, and called him from Canada and Belgium, urging him to join them in exile. He refused. One of his fellow police commanders, who had defected during the genocide and didn't want me to reveal his name, told me: "He was a disciplinarian to the core. He never really asked why he was fighting; that was for the politicians to decide. And when the politicians ran, he just kept on fighting, like a robot."

Even if he had decided to defect, it would not have been simple. Several of Rwarakabije's colleagues surrendered to the RPF but were never heard from again. There were stories of President Habyarimana's former officers turning themselves in only to be found the next day in a banana grove, their hands tied behind their back and their brains shot out.

"Don't forget that this was a war," the avuncular general repeated. "If I had deserted, I could have been killed by my own commanders *or* by the RPF." He paused and fiddled with his watch. "The genocide was terrible, of course," he said. "I thought it was a huge mistake." He saw the killing out of his office window, as it were, disagreed with it, and got on with his work.

Watching him seated behind his almost empty desk, I found it hard to imagine that this man had been the leader of one of the most notorious rebel groups in Africa. He explained with his steady, glued-on smile that he had never learned how to use a computer in the bush. Instead, he operated with pen and a stack of printer paper, on which he made random notes and diagrams, as if to illustrate his thoughts to himself as he spoke with me. He was writing his own history of the war, he told me, showing me a stack of worn notebooks. He flipped through their pages as we talked, to find dates and names he was uncertain of. He had highlighted important passages in yellow or circled them with a ballpoint pen. When I asked him when he would publish his own book, he smiled. "Not yet. The country is not yet ready for everything I have to say. It is too early."

～:～

Ethnic-based violence, the most extreme form of which was the genocide, is so often associated with the Congolese and Rwandan wars that it is worth trying to understand its causes. We tend to see the history of Rwanda as the history of a struggle between two ethnic groups, the agriculturist Hutu and the cattle-herding Tutsi. An honest interrogation of the past, however, would require us to throw most of these crude concepts out the window, or at least to deconstruct them. The Rwandan state in its current geographical and political form did not come into existence until the twentieth century, after centuries of fighting between competing kingdoms and princely states.

Ethnic identities behind the rift between Hutu and Tutsi are being constantly contested and redefined with the changing political, cultural, and economic landscape. Until the eighteenth century, for example, ethnicity was less important than class and clan-based identities, which themselves coexisted alongside several layers of regional and social identities. Thus, each of the twenty major clans in Rwanda includes both Hutu and Tutsi, and among each ethnic group one can find poor, landless peasants as well as wealthier princes. To label someone a Hutu and leave it at that neglects that she may, depending on the social context, see herself more as a southerner, a member of the Abega clan, or a follower of the Pentecostal church. This is not just hair-splitting; much of contemporary Rwandan politics has been shaped by these competing and overlapping identities.

The polarization of Rwandan society into Hutu and Tutsi increased with King Rujugira's consolidation of the Rwandan state in the eighteenth century. He expanded his armies and began subjugating much of what is today Rwanda, including areas where these ethnic distinctions previously had little traction.

His armies' long military campaigns required more revenues and deeper administrative penetration of society. The military, which was led by Tutsi, became the
basis for a bureaucracy that administered land and collected taxes. Progressively,
the loose distinctions between Hutu and Tutsi tightened and became more hi-
erarchical. By the late nineteenth century, when the first colonizers arrived, many
Hutu depended on Tutsi chiefs for land to farm and had to pay tithes as well as
provide free manual labor. Still, ethnic identity remained fluid, with intermar-
riages between ethnic groups and the possibility, albeit rare, for rich Hutu to
become "promoted" to Tutsi if they owned many cattle and had power in society.
At the local level, Hutu remained influential, in particular in the administration
of land. Still, social arrangements varied greatly between different regions, with
some, like Gisaka in eastern Rwanda, not showing much ethnic polarization
until much later.

The conquest of Rwanda—first by Germans, then Belgians—radically al-
tered social structures. A tiny group of white administrators was faced with ruling a complex, foreign country they barely understood. As elsewhere in Africa,
the new rulers chose to rule through what they thought were well-established,
existing structures. They thus empowered the Tutsi monarchy, which they saw
as the "natural" elite, abolished checks and balances on the royal family, and
streamlined the local administration by ousting Hutu chiefs and vesting all
power in a Tutsi-dominated administration. At the same time, they helped the
royal court double the territory under its control, conquering kingdoms and
princely states around its periphery.

The delicate social balance between the farmers and the pastoralists, the royal
elite and the peasantry, the rich and the poor was brutally disrupted. Whereas
Hutu peasants had previously been able to appeal to their relatives in case of
abuses by the government, or at least play different chiefs off against each other,
now they were left at the mercy of a Tutsi administration.[6]

The European rulers grounded their rule in an ideology and ethnography
heavily influenced by racial theories popular in the United States and Europe
at the time. John Hanning Speke, one of the first British explorers in the region,
had written in 1863 about a distinct "Asiatic" sophistication among some of the
people, presumably Tutsi, he encountered. "In these countries," he wrote, "government is in the hands of foreigners, who had invaded and taken possession of
them, leaving the agricultural aborigines to till the ground." Speke, dabbling in

history and religion, conjectured a link between these tribes and Ethiopia and proposed a "historical" basis for what he claimed to observe: "The traditions of these tribes go as far back as the scriptural age of King David."

Speke's theory was not a mere flight of fancy. Since the Middle Ages, Europeans had studied Africa through the lens of the Bible, trying to find divine design in nature and human society. One of the passages of most interest was from Genesis 9 and 10. Just before a description of how Noah's sons peopled the earth after the flood, the text tells the story of when Noah, drunk from wine, falls asleep naked. His sons Shem and Japheth avert their eyes and cover him, but their brother, Ham, stares at his naked body. When he awakes, Noah is furious at Ham and condemns Ham's son, Canaan, to slavery: "a servant of servants shall he be unto his brethren."

Although the Bible remains vague about Ham and Canaan's destiny, well into the nineteenth century biblical scholars and scientists alike categorized the nations of the world as the descendents of Noah's sons: the Semitic races of the Middle East, the Japhetic races of Europe, and the Hamitic races of Africa. Turned on its head, this theory explained the advanced civilizations found in Africa: Rock-cut wells, complex political organization, and irrigation systems were all creations of a Hamitic race that traced its lineage back to the Middle East. In Speke's view, this explanation placed the continent's Negroid races firmly where they belonged: on the bottom of the racial hierarchy, incapable of advanced civilization, and open game for slavery. Elsewhere, in the Muslim world, leaders also used the Hamitic theory to justify the enslavement of black Africans.

The first German governor of Rwanda, Count von Goetzen, theorized "the Tutsi are Hamitic pastoralists from Ethiopia, who have subjugated a tribe of Negro Bantus," while Catholic prelate Monsignor Le Roy put it differently: "Their intelligent and delicate appearance, their love of money, their capacity to adapt to any situation seem to indicate a Semitic origin." Armed with rulers and measuring tape, craniometric Belgian administrators went about rigidifying with physical measurements the previously more fluid boundaries between Tutsi and Hutu identities.

These colonial fantasies soon became engraved on the consciousness of the colonized, as well. The Tutsi elite, long favored under the Belgians, seized on the myths to justify their continued superiority, imbibing the stereotypes of Hutu—as espoused by a Belgian priest—as "the most common type of black, brachycephalic and prognathous, with agronomic taste and aptitudes, sociable and jovial . . . with thick lips and squashed noses, but so good, so simple, so loyal."[7] Hutu dissidents, in the meantime, appropriated the stereotypes of Tutsi as a race of crafty herders from Ethiopia to rally support against "the foreigners."

∾∶∾

Where loyalty and power stirred General Rwarakabije, the masses were moved more by fear, ideology, and local politics. In the popular imagination, the RPF had been cast as subhuman, as demons. By the time the genocide began, the civil war had been raging for almost four years. Over a million people, mostly Hutu, had been displaced from the north of the country, and many of them had moved toward Kigali, where they spread the word of the rebels' abuses. Hutu extremists preyed on this paranoia in their radio broadcasts. A Tutsi officer, having seized a village, was asked by one of the few Hutu who had stayed to lift up his shirt so the villagers could see if he had a tail, so sure were they that he was a devil.[8] Even the sick and frail marched hundreds of miles to the border to escape the sure death they thought awaited them under the RPF. In the camps, refugees' reluctance to return came at least as much from their fear of the RPF. The intimidation had become internalized.

Recent studies of the genocide have also revealed the importance of local politics in determining whether an area carried out genocide or not. Seasonal laborers and the landless, for example, were more likely to be manipulated by rural elites who stood to lose if the Hutu regime lost power.[9] The local strength of more extremist political parties reinforced pressure to carry out killings, as did the presence of Burundian Hutu refugees who had fled violence in their home country. In total, some 200,000 probably took part in the killing for many reasons:[10] Some were forced to do so by authorities; others sought economic gain; still others participated out of a mixture of social pressure and the belief that they would be killed themselves if they did not comply.[11]

In southwestern Rwanda, the Hutu flight was stalled by the deployment of a UN-mandated French military mission, dubbed Operation Turquoise, intended to protect the few remaining Tutsi in that region as well as aid workers. It was one of the many absurdities of the Rwandan crisis: The French government and its contractors had made thirty-six shipments of weapons to Habyarimana's government between 1990 and 1994, worth $11 million, and had deployed seven hundred fifty French troops, who helped with military training, planning, and even interrogation of RPF prisoners.[12] Just months after they had finished helping to train the Interahamwe, the French, wolves turned shepherds, announced a humanitarian intervention to bring an end to the killing.

The French troops did save Tutsi lives. They also, however, refused to arrest the Habyarimana government and army officials in their territory who were known to have organized massacres. Hate radio continued broadcasting unhindered from the area controlled by the French, exhorting the population to continue the extermination of Tutsi. Meanwhile, across the Zairian border in Goma, the base of French operations, at least five shipments of weapons from France were delivered to the ex-FAR leadership who had fled from Kigali.[13] To add insult to injury, French president François Mitterrand personally authorized a donation of $40,000 to Habyarimana's wife, one of the most extremist members of the president's inner circle, when she arrived in Paris fleeing the violence in country. The donation was labeled as "urgent assistance to Rwandan refugees."[14]

∾∾

When Rwarakabije crossed into Zaire and arrived in Goma in July 1994, he spent a few days wandering about, disoriented and deflated. Goma, a town of 300,000, was inundated with goats, cars, and a teeming mass of people that surged in various directions, confused, without bearings. Rwarakabije had arrived in a truck with fellow officers, but everybody had dispersed to tend to their families. He finally managed to rent a house on the edge of town from a traditional chief for his wife and four children. Like all officers, he had benefited from the looting of state coffers before leaving Rwanda. They needed the extra cash, as the influx of refugees had sent prices in the markets skyrocketing. A kilo of meat was almost $10, five times the normal price.

Whereas the price of food had peaked, the value of weapons and ammunition had plummeted because of their abundance. At the border crossing, within sight of French troops, the fleeing Rwandan soldiers were supposed to give their weapons over to Mobutu's presidential guard. Machine guns and rocket launchers piled up.

Behind the customs offices, however, an arms market had spontaneously sprung up, where ex-FAR officers negotiated to buy back their arms. An AK-47 went for $40 to $50, a Russian-made rocket launcher for just under $100.

Other weapons were never handed over to the Zairians. Rwarakabije saw tons of ammunition smuggled through in trucks, hidden under bags of rice and maize. "We gave the border guards some money to look the other way. All they wanted was money."

Located on the northern tip of Lake Kivu, which forms most of the border between the Congo and Rwanda, and underneath the towering Nyiragongo volcano, Goma had been a prime tourist destination in its heyday. The local Belgian elite, Mobutu's coterie, and adventurous backpackers filled its colonial-style hotels, which featured ceramic tiling, whitewashed exteriors, and lush, manicured gardens. The fertile hinterlands had provided a cheap supply of vegetables—including such Belgian favorites as broccoli, sweet peas, and leeks—and the dairies created by Belgian priests had produced famous cheese rounds that were exported throughout the region. Travel agencies had organized guided tours to Virunga National Park to the north, habitat of the rare mountain gorilla. A beer and soft drinks factory just across the border in Rwanda kept the numerous bars and nightclubs supplied with a steady stream of lager, Coke, and Fanta.

The decay of the Zairian state and the influx of refugees drew a somber curtain over those days. Now the hotels hosted guests of a different caliber. The defeated Rwandan army commanders and politicians began checking into Hotel des Grands Lacs and Nyiragongo, Karibu, and Stella hotels and renting sumptuous villas on the lake. Journalists, fresh from the death-strewn camps, sat with politicians and army officers in their mansions on fake leather couches behind bougainvillea-draped walls.

~:~

After several months of confusion, Rwarakabije attended a meeting of the former Rwandan army's top brass in a Pentecostal church in Goma. Sitting with him in the church's sacristy, under a large cross, were the dour faces of his remaining army staff. Morale had hit rock bottom. Most of the officers present had evacuated their families on chartered flights to Nairobi, Yaounde (Cameroon), and Paris. "We had lost the war," Rwarakabije remembered. "Anyone who had enough money eventually left." Rwarakabije himself was not so fortunate.

The exiled war council took urgent measures. It swiftly reorganized the armed forces into two divisions of 7,680 and 10,240 men, based in camps on the northern and southern end of Lake Kivu, respectively. Support units of 4,000 soldiers pushed their total to 22,000 soldiers. Rwarakabije became the commander of the several thousand soldiers who made up the Fourth Brigade.

The quality of the soldiers varied. The officers came from regular army units, and many had trained in Belgium and France; they set up rigid administrative structures with carefully typed budgets and circulars. But some troops had no military experience. Hundreds of prisoners were recruited; since they were among the only people who benefited from the mayhem, they tended to have high morale. Primary and secondary students, some as young as nine, were coaxed and coerced into training camps, forming the Twenty-Sixth Reserve Brigade.

When I prodded Rwarakabije about the feared Interahamwe and Impuza-mugambi militias, who had carried out much of the genocidal killing, he scoffed, deriding their lack of discipline. "They drugged themselves on marijuana and cheap liquor, robbed the population. They were thugs," he remembered. "Many of them eliminated themselves in the war. They would stagger onto the battlefield like zombies, high and drunk, and get picked off by the enemy." For him, there was a world of difference between the FAR's discipline and objective of overthrowing the new government in Rwanda and the Interahamwe's ethnic vendetta.

To raise spirits, the war council authorized the immediate payment of June and July salaries for all state employees and soldiers. They had brought with them the entire treasury of Rwanda, $30–40 million in Rwandan francs, which they stashed in a bank in downtown Goma. According to some reports, they were able to transfer over $100 million dollars in the early days of the genocide into private accounts; they had just collected the yearly taxes, and the coffers were flush with money.[15] Most importantly, the commanders agreed on immediately launching guerrilla warfare against the new regime in Kigali. The expectations of the population were now especially palpable—the hopes of a million people, who were dying slow deaths in the camps, weighed on them. Since the Tutsi forces were known as *inyenzi*, or cockroaches, this offensive was dubbed Operation Insecticide.

~:~

Rwarakabije found pleasure, perhaps solace, in reciting troop strengths, names of commanding officers, and dates of battles, but he was reluctant to talk about the more human side of history: feelings, motivations, morality. The tragedy of the past decade was reduced to desiccated statistics.

Going through my notes later, the vision of two generals clashed in my head. One was of the pleasant old man who always had time for me and my many questions, who never seemed troubled or bothered by my probing. This was also the man his soldiers knew. In my interviews with the former Hutu troops under his command in demobilization camps in Rwanda, they painted a picture of a respected, caring commander who had become a father figure to many of the officers. They remembered him as a judicious leader, always conferring with his fellow leaders before making decisions.

The other Rwarakabije I had to infer through human rights reports and interviews with victims. While he was commander of the Hutu rebels between 1996 and 2003, his troops were guilty of massacres, mass rape, and routine pillage in both the Congo and Rwanda. Given the tight discipline that reigned, it was difficult to imagine that the general did not know about his soldiers' behavior. At the very least, he failed to punish them.

During my first journey to the eastern Congo in 2001, to work for a local human rights group, Héritiers de la Justice (Heirs of Justice), in the border town of Bukavu, I heard daily the stories of people who had been raped or tortured or had their family members killed by the ones they called Interahamwe, the catch-all term for Rwarakabije's rebels. Individual cases were then entered into a hardcover blue ledger in clipped terms:

> On 10/08/2000, Mr. Nono Marandura, from Nkono village in the territory of Bunyakiri, was shot to death in his house by Interahamwe. The victim left behind a widow and six children who until now suffer from a lack of support.

> On 19/09/2000, Mr. Papayi wa Katachi was killed by Interahamwe. The victim was 17 years old. He lived in Kaloba, in Bunyakiri territory. His brother was injured by bullets and their belongings were stolen. According to the information collected, the authors of these acts targeted the victim for unknown reasons.

The ledger contained hundreds of such entries.

I turned back to my own notes to reread Rwarakabije's answers to my questions. I had scrawled "Abuses?" on the top of one page with an arrow pointing at his answer:

At the beginning we didn't have many abuses. We even taught courses in international humanitarian law to our soldiers; some of our officers had done that training. But the troops got tired and hungry and started taking food by force from the population. We called it "pillage operations"—you would attack a village and take all of its cows and steal money.

When I pushed him, Rwarakabije conceded: "You have to remember that we had 10,000 soldiers and their families to feed. And once the pillage started, soldiers lost control and raped and even killed sometimes. If we caught them, we punished them. At the beginning, we executed several soldiers for murder, but that gave us problems, so we started caning. I remember we gave one rapist 300 strokes of a stick on his naked buttocks and expelled him from the troops. But how did you know who raped? The villagers were afraid of us; they didn't tell us. So most of the criminals went unpunished."

~:~

By October 1994, the Inzirabwoba—"those who are not afraid"—were infiltrating Rwanda from the refugee camps every week. Rwarakabije began leading nocturnal raids across the border. "We destroyed administrative buildings and killed local officials," Rwarakabije explained, showing no sign of remorse. "It was a war; they were collaborators."

As during the genocide, every Tutsi was seen as an accomplice of the RPF. In October 1994, rebels infiltrated across the hills at 3 AM, surrounding a village just yards from the border. They massacred thirty-seven people, mostly children. "Some killed out of hatred for Tutsi, others to prevent the survivors of the genocide from speaking out against them," Rwarakabije remembered. Monitors from the United Nations tallied hundreds of killings of Tutsi in the first two years after the RPF drove the FAR from Rwanda.

It was not just Tutsi who suffered. If Hutu refugees dared to return home from the camps, they were considered traitors. Anatole Sucyendore was a Hutu doctor who had fled to Goma with the other refugees but had returned to Rwanda several months later to work in the Gisenyi hospital, despite numerous death threats. On February 25, 1995, Hutu rebels broke into his house, shot the doctor, stabbed his two-year-old infant to death, and severely injured his wife and other child.

Anonymous pamphlets distributed by Hutu militias in the camps give a taste of the rhetoric of the day:

> You Hutu fools, who keep giving money which is used to buy weapons to kill your fellows. You say you are studying. Don't you know where those who studied are? How many studies did Kagame undertake, he to whom you give your money, who leads all the massacres?
>
> And You Tutsi, you have stretched your noses and necks because you think you have protectors! And you support your Inyenzi [RPF] fellows in their extermination of the Hutu, instead of fighting [us]. We will kill you until you are no longer contemptuous, and understand that you must cohabit with others.[16]

The general knew, however, that guerrilla attacks alone were never going to work. "We were nettling them, harassing them, but not really challenging their hold on power," Rwarakabije remembered. They needed to resort to a stronger weapon: blackmail.

A leader of the former government boasted to journalists from the comfort of his villa in Goma: "Even if the RPF has won a military victory, it will not have the power. It has only the bullets, we have the population."[17] Failing to beat the enemy, they would use blackmail, holding the million refugees in Zaire for ransom to force Kigali to negotiate.

The exiled leaders resorted to similar organizational models to those they had used in their homeland. The Rwandan administration had been a tightly woven mesh that reached from Kigali to the provincial authorities, down to the commune, sector, and cell, a chain of command that had made possible the mass murder of 800,000 people in just a hundred days. They grafted this grid onto the camps, regrouping refugees by their places of origin in Rwanda and placing trusted officials in charge, often the same ones who had been involved in the killings back home.

~:~

When I asked Rwarakabije about these practices, he shook his head.

"It is true. We were brainwashed. And there were a lot of extremists there who preyed on people's fear."

"Did you ever use this kind of language?" I asked.

"Yes, but we never did what the tracts said. We needed to scare them. There were extremists who wanted to kill Tutsi, but that was wrong. We had Tutsi with us in the camps! There were officers who had been in the Rwandan army and had fled with us. One of my bodyguards was Tutsi. We had to tell them not to stray too far from the barracks or the population could kill them."

"Did you ever order the killing of civilians?"

"No, never."

"But civilians were killed."

Rwarakabije sighed and fidgeted with his loose watch again. "Chain of command . . . I'm not sure you can apply that to our rebellion."

"You didn't control some of your own commanders?"

"My troops, yes. But the civilian ideologues, the extremists, no. Many of the army commanders did not support the genocide. It was something that had been organized by the civilians along with some extremist commanders."

Rwarakabije ducked and weaved, denying responsibility, blaming massacres on others, using ends to justify means. "Where elephants fight," he said, "the grass is trampled." It was a convenient metaphor. Almost every commander I met in the region used it when I asked them about abuses against civilians.

In his calm serenity, Rwarakabije was a counterpoint to the images of hate-driven killers. According to everyone who knew him, he didn't have any apparent hatred for Tutsi. One of his battalion commanders in the insurgency was Tutsi, and he was more comfortable being called Kiga than Hutu. Apparently he hadn't joined and led the so-called Hutu rebellion out of ethnic chauvinism, even if the movement was deeply bigoted. He had joined because this is where he had ended up and what made sense for him to do when the civil war broke out; he could have tried to change it, but it would have been too difficult, too risky. Back to the description of Eichmann's trial: "Evil comes from a failure to think. It defies thought for as soon as thought tries to engage itself with evil it is frustrated because it finds nothing there. That is the banality of evil."[18]

The same went for many rank-and-file soldiers I met. Many had joined because they were poor and unemployed or because they wanted "to be a man"; a gun and a uniform were among the best tools of social empowerment. Ethnicity was fundamental in this dynamic. I can't count the number of times I've heard "Tutsi aggression" invoked as the reason for the war in the Congo, but it is not the origin of the conflict, as the quote from the BBC at the beginning of this chapter might have you believe. By limiting ourselves to the simplistic "Hutu militia killed half a million Tutsi," we are suggesting that there is a reason for that violence implicit in those identities, that something about being Hutu and Tutsi caused the violence. While ethnicity is probably the strongest form of social organization in the region, we need to scratch behind that surface, to see what its history is, who is using it or being used by it, and for what reasons.

✦ 2 ✦

AIDING AND ABETTING

INERA REFUGEE CAMP, ZAIRE, OCTOBER 1994

Beatrice Umutesi was one of the million Rwandans who had fled to Zaire. She was more fortunate than most. Born in 1959 to a Hutu peasant family in northern Rwanda, she had been a good student, obtaining a scholarship to study sociology in Belgium before returning to work in a rural development cooperative. When fighting broke out in Kigali in April 1994, she fled with her ailing mother and members of her family, and after several weeks of walking, she crossed the border into Zaire and made herself at home in Inera, a camp on the shores of Lake Kivu. There a slum of 55,000 refugees living in squalid huts had sprung up overnight on the muddy silt.

Beatrice drew on her professional experience, quickly becoming a leader in a network of nonprofit groups working in the camps. She organized a small microcredit program to allow refugees to make a living in the camps, and she helped publish two newsletters for refugee women to express themselves and explain their problems.

Although Beatrice had a small salary, she lived in one of the *blindés*, the tiny, doghouse-size tents where the refugees lived. Each family was given one tarpaulin, four meters by five, with the insignia of the UN refugee agency: a laurel wreath protecting a family inside. They tied it over a lean-to made out of eucalyptus saplings. If they were lucky, they had enough tarp left over to cover the cold, wet ground. They got some scratchy fleece blankets, pots and pans, and a yellow jerry can to haul water from the wells.

Beatrice was thirty-five when she fled Rwanda. She was unmarried, and she crossed the border with her sixty-seven-year-old mother and four sisters. Other people joined her family: Virginie, Assumpta, and Marcelline, three young, abandoned girls she met in the camps and took in as nieces; and Bakunda, a thirteen-year-old boy she had taken in when the RPF rebels had invaded northern Rwanda in 1993, displacing thousands of people. Beatrice slowly gathered under her wings a motley bunch of seven ragged children who had lost their own families during the war and the flight to Zaire.

~:~

The refugee camps were set up in July 1994 and stayed in place for over two years. Some would swell to contain more than 400,000 inhabitants, becoming the largest refugee camps in the world and larger than any city in eastern Zaire. Together they housed over a million people. In a perverse way, they provoked a mobilization of international resources that the genocide never had. Within days of the first arrivals, aid workers detected a cholera outbreak; the virulent parasite spread fast in the unhygienic and cramped quarters. Without proper health care, the disease killed the weak refugees within days, emptying their bodies of liquids through violent diarrhea and vomiting until their organs failed. By July 28, 1994, a thousand bodies were being collected a day and dumped unceremoniously into chalk-dusted pits by the dump-truck load.

Foreign television crews who had not been able to reach Rwanda during the genocide now set up camp in Goma; the pictures of hundreds of chalk-dusted bodies tumbling into mass graves suggested a strange moral equivalency to the recent genocide, except that this catastrophe was easier to fix: Instead of a complicated web of violence in which military intervention would have been messy and bloody, here was a crisis that could be addressed by spending money. Over the next two years, donors spent over $2 billion on the refugee crisis in eastern Zaire, more than twice as much as they spent on helping the new Rwandan government.[1] The RPF was furious. Vice President Paul Kagame lamented, "Personally, I think this question of refugees is being overplayed at the expense of all our other problems. We no longer talk about orphans, widows, victims [in Rwanda]. We're only talking about refugees, refugees, refugees."[2]

In the camps the living stretched out next to corpses, which nobody had the strength or the means to remove. Medical workers ran from patient to patient, jabbing intravenous liquids in their arms as fast as possible, often failing to find veins. Diarrhea stained people's clothes and rags; everywhere, the smell of shit and death clogged the air. After one month, 50,000 people had died.

~:~

Beatrice arrived in a smaller refugee camp to the south of Goma and was spared some of the worst of the cholera epidemic. She had to face other challenges, however. Her days were made up of long stretches of waiting for the next food distribution, punctuated by meetings of her women's group and visits to the health clinics. "Feeling useless is the worst," she later wrote.[3] Men would try to make extra money working in local fields or transporting sugarcane and cassava to the market, while women busied themselves washing the few pans and clothes they had taken with them from Rwanda.

On the outskirts of the camps, bustling markets appeared, where looted goods from Rwanda were available along with the usual assortment of Chinese-made toothbrushes, soaps, cheap acrylic clothes, and bootleg tapes of Zairian, Rwandan, and western music. A UN official catalogued the amenities available in five camps around Goma: 2,324 bars, 450 restaurants, 589 different shops, 62 hairdressers, 51 pharmacies, 30 tailors, 25 butchers, 5 blacksmiths and mechanics, 4 photographic studios, 3 cinemas, 2 hotels, and 1 slaughterhouse.[4] Market stands advertised bags of generic, often expired or useless drugs, next to jars with traditional medicinal powders, roots, and concoctions. The camps were so well stocked that they became a hub of attraction for locals. Zairians from Bukavu and Goma trekked out to the camps to buy looted cars, stereos, and televisions. Youths from Bukavu went drinking on the weekends in the outdoor bars entrepreneurial refugees set up overlooking the lake, making sure they were home before night to avoid the hoodlums who roamed about looking for easy prey. Men in Bukavu still reminisce about the *mishikaki*, shish kebabs of sizzling goat and beef introduced by the refugees, that were downed with the local Primus beer.

Most refugees, however, like Beatrice, had fled Rwanda with little more than the clothes on their back and could not afford such luxuries. They ate once a day from the rations they received: a handful of U.S.-surplus maize meal, a cup of beans, a few drops of vegetable oil, and a pinch of salt.

Around Beatrice, refugee life gnawed away at the social fabric. A camp newsletter reported an alarming increase in child marriages, a rare phenomenon back home in Rwanda. Youths and older men married girls as young as thirteen and fourteen, sometimes taking them in as their third or fourth wives. Some youths had brought with them pillaged goods and money from Rwanda and were able to afford the dowries of several girls. Often families had broken up, and marriage allowed youths to rebuild their fractured world. In some cases, wives had to share their tiny shack with several other women. These marriages were often short-lived and produced many fatherless children, adding to the hungry and sick in the camps.[5] Beatrice, who traveled from camp to camp holding women's rights workshops, heard story after story of women suffering abuses. Many young girls were forced into prostitution, often selling themselves for the price of a plate of beans or a couple of *mandazi*, fried dough balls. As refugees were not, at least in theory, allowed to farm fields or move about freely outside the camps, boredom and inactivity became huge problems, especially for the thousands of unemployed. Men often resorted to drinking banana beer and homemade liquor. Alcoholism, domestic abuse, and violence were added to the long list of refugees' woes.

For Beatrice, as for many others, life was dominated by fear and distrust. She and other women had denounced the RPF's abuses in newsletters and statements. She thought that her name was on a blacklist in Kigali and that she would be arrested or worse if she tried to return. On several occasions, the RPF staged raids into the camps by Lake Kivu, killing scores of suspected militiamen and refugees. On the other hand, because she tried to organize women into self-help groups, the Hutu extremists in the camps also saw Beatrice as a challenge. Soon she was accused of being *pro*-RPF and of having Tutsi features. Thugs attacked several of her friends for their alleged sympathies with the new government across the lake, although the real motive was probably just to steal their meager belongings. In her diary she wrote, "Such is the human being: when he is afraid, he sees enemies everywhere and thinks the only chance to stay alive is to exterminate them."

The war had created a new class of thugs and delinquents. Gangs roamed the camps, harassing women and stealing to survive. A Rwandan priest who had come to visit his family was bludgeoned to death and left on the edge of the camp; a woman and her five-year-old child were killed by a grenade thrown into their tent.[6]

The mere suspicion that someone was a spy was enough to rally a mob with sticks, hoes, and machetes. On October 25, 1994, in Kituku camp, refugees caught four men by the water reservoir and accused them of trying to poison the wells; three escaped, but one was stoned to death. Several days later, in a nearby camp, five Tutsi were chased by a mob and killed. One of them made it to a Doctors Without Borders health center, where he was beaten to death in front of the medical staff. According to another aid organization, "fresh bodies [were found] in Mugunga camp every morning in September."[7] A study estimated that a total of 4,000 refugees were killed in the camps, often at the hands of the various militias employed by the former government.[8]

The camps were pressure cookers. A thousand people lived in the space of a soccer pitch. All intimacy was banished, as several dozen people could easily overhear the lovemaking, quarrels, and gossip of each *blindé*'s occupants. The tents were too small to stand up in and, during the nine-month-long rainy season, were caked with mud inside and out. At night, temperatures sometimes plummeted to 10 degrees Celsius. Beatrice only had one light blanket and a few *kikwembe* that she used for clothes, swaddling children, and lying on. In the morning, she would wake up with condensation dripping on her.

Women had other problems, as well. The aid organizations running the camps didn't provide sanitary napkins, and women had to use rags or tear up sheets to use instead. As there was little soap, these scraps of cloth became hard and caked with blood. To their humiliation, women had no choice but to try to wash these in the same pots they used for cooking. "The bloodied water snaked in rivulets between the tents and little puddles of blood formed here and there."[9]

One of Beatrice's neighbors was the tiny, malnourished Muhawe, a three-year-old orphan whose mother had died in childbirth on the trek to Zaire. When she first saw him, he was little more than a shriveled body with an over-sized head, unable to walk more than a couple of feet before collapsing. The health center had given him nutritional milk, but he couldn't keep the liquid down, and his grandmother, who was taking care of him, didn't have money to buy more substantial fare. Beatrice began to buy morsels of beef and potatoes that she would mash into porridge and feed him. Somehow, after her two-hundred-mile trek to Zaire and the hardships of the camps, Muhawe's suffering was the last straw for Beatrice. Disgusted and outraged by her life, she began writing at night in her *blindé*. "What had Muhawe and the thousands of other Rwandan children dying in the camps done? Was he, too, a *génocidaire* to have deserved this fate?" She began writing her own story, the horrors of the massacre of Tutsi, often crying herself to sleep.

~:~

For the humanitarian organizations, the dilemma was excruciating. The former government officials had set up administrative structures in the camps through which aid workers were forced to operate. With 5,000 people dying a day, they had to act, but unless the innocent civilians were separated from the soldiers and ex-government officials, aid groups were left little option other than to work with people guilty of genocide, bolstering and financing them in the process. Aid groups launched one of the largest humanitarian operations the continent had seen, bringing forty-five organizations and over 1,600 relief workers to Goma alone. In late 1994, the UN High Commissioner for Refugees (UNHCR) spent $1 million each day on operations in the camps. Its effort was effective: Within weeks of deployment, mortality dropped steeply, saving thousands of lives. At the same time, however, it became obvious that the aid was also sustaining the perpetrators of the genocide. As Alain Destexhe, the secretary-general of Doctors Without Borders, put it: "How can physicians continue to assist Rwandan refugees when by doing so they are also supporting killers?"

And they were supporting killers. Camp leaders refused to allow UNHCR to count the refugees for over half a year, inflating their numbers so as to pocket the surplus food, blankets, and clothes for themselves. In Ngara, Tanzania, food for 120,000 "ghost refugees" was being skimmed off the top, while in Bukavu leaders pocketed aid for 50,000 refugees over six months.[10] Even after censuses were carried out, leaders stole the food of those most in need, pushing thousands of children into severe malnutrition. "We never had to worry about food," Rwarakabije told me. "The United Nations supplied us with plenty." As families starved, desperate mothers abandoned their infants at night at camp orphanages, where they were sure to get fed.

The abject suffering inverted the moral standing of the refugees and even soldiers—they became victims, not killers. Aid workers and local groups, who spent months living with and talking to the refugees, became influenced by the revisionist concept of a double genocide—that the Habyarimana government and the RPF had both killed in equal proportions. Caritas, a Catholic aid group, provided food to FAR military camps in Bulonge and Panzi, protesting that the soldiers "have to eat, they are not all murderers." Groupe Jeremie, a Congolese human rights group affiliated with the Catholic church, published a collection of works that includes statements and reports by the government-in-exile.[11]

Camp leaders resorted to more subtle measures, as well, to make money. They taxed the thousands of refugees who worked with humanitarian organizations in the camps. An aid worker estimated that they made $11,000 per month from staff of one organization in one camp alone.[12] They also charged rent for land; controlled markets, bus routes, and hair salons; and ran a lucrative black market in Rwandan currency.

⌒:~

Between 1994 and 1996 the international community, Rwanda, and Zaire missed their best opportunity to nip the crisis in the bud. After failing to act to prevent a genocide in 1994, they now failed to separate the soldiers from the refugees, despite repeated threats from Kigali's government, starting in February 1996, that they would take military actions against the camps. A UN official recalled: "It was like watching a train wreck in slow motion."[13]

In retrospect, the only solution would have been to separate the military and civilians by force. Early on, in August 1994, the UN secretary-general, Boutros Boutros Ghali, began researching various options for securing the camps. The first proposal, drafted by military experts, suggested transporting 30,000 ex-FAR and their families to Zairian military camps hundreds of miles from the Rwandan border, thereby detaching them from the refugees. This relocation would have likely encountered resistance from the ex-FAR leadership and would have required at least 8,000 international troops deployed under a UN mandate, costing $90–$125 million. Once again, however, the initiative foundered on a lack of will: Boutros Ghali's request was turned down. Find alternative solutions, Security Council members told him, even though the cost of such an operation pales in comparison with the billions the international community has spent on the conflict since the renewed outbreak of hostilities in 1996.[14]

What could have been done to solve the situation? A glimpse was provided on August 17, when, under pressure from the international community and domestic opposition, Zaire's prime minister, Kengo wa Dondo, took matters into his own hands. The day before, donors had just lifted the arms embargo against Rwanda, and Kengo anticipated what was to come. He told diplomats that he was left with no choice but to begin the forceful repatriation of refugees. Over four days, Zairian soldiers brought 12,000 Hutu refugees to the border. The exercise went surprisingly well: Many refugees, glad to have an excuse to break free from the ex-FAR's grip, voluntarily joined the convoys. Zairian local authorities, eager to see the troublesome guests go, helped ensure the operation went smoothly. Instead of a violent backlash by soldiers in the camps, 20,000 refugees, mostly youths thought to be militia members, fled into adjacent forests, fearing arrest by Zairian authorities. Against all expectations, there was no armed resistance. After four days, however, under pressure from Mobutu and diplomats, who denounced what they perceived as forced repatriation and a violation of international law, the operations ground to a halt.[15]

What constituted forceful repatriation was, however, up for debate. After all, given the ex-FAR's control of the camps, was voluntary return even an option? Even the United Nations' legal advisors, usually risk-averse, began asking whether the exceptional circumstances merited "bending the rules." In April 1996, Denis McNamara, the UNHCR director of international protection, suggested that a forced return had become necessary as a result of pressure from Zaire, as well as a lack of money. He said, "We expect it to be highly criticized. But it's a fact of life because it is unavoidable."[16]

~:~

The response, as so often in the region, was to throw money at the humanitarian crisis but not to address the political causes. The spectacle was perverse, especially given the international community's inaction during the genocide. The United States, which had refused to intervene in the Rwandan massacre and had even blocked the United Nations from doing so, sent 3,000 soldiers whose mandate was strictly limited to assist with the relief effort; France, who had helped train and arm the Rwandan army and had received an official delegation from the Rwandan government at the height of the genocide, also had several thousand soldiers in eastern Zaire left over from their humanitarian intervention in Rwanda, Operation Turquoise. Fiona Terry, the head of Doctors Without Borders in the Tanzanian refugee camps, put it eloquently: "[It was] a dramatic, well-publicized show of human suffering in which the enemy was a virus and the savior was humanitarian aid. Paralyzed during the political crisis, military forces were suddenly mobilized for the 'humanitarian' disaster, transforming the genocide into a 'complex emergency' in which there was no good and bad side, only victims."[17]

After the first year, during which both the new and the old Rwandan governments were busy taking stock and consolidating their power, the situation deteriorated rapidly. While the international community categorized the situation as a humanitarian crisis, in reality the Rwandan civil war continued to smolder underground, on the verge of exploding to the surface once more. By July 1995, Rwanda had launched three targeted strikes against refugee camps in Zaire, an open provocation.

Mobutu had no interest in disbanding and separating the exiled government's various armed forces from the refugees. When the new Rwandan government demanded that Kinshasa hand over the state assets that Habyarimana's government had fled with, Mobutu gave them a few containers of rusty ammunition, two unusable helicopters, and heavy artillery in equally irreparable condition.[18] The refugee crisis had injected new life into his ailing regime. The French, who, having "lost" Kigali to English-speaking rebels, were eager to maintain their influence over Africa's largest French-speaking country, needed Mobutu's permission to launch Operation Turquoise, while the United Nations courted Kinshasa to set up their huge humanitarian operation along the Rwandan border. On September 15, the UN Special Representative to Rwanda called on him to discuss the refugee crisis; on November 8, Mobutu arrived in Biarritz for the Franco-African summit. The dictator had leveraged his way back into the favor of his western allies.

Mobutu's relations with the Rwandan exile government were even more cordial. He had been a close friend of President Habyarimana, sending a battalion of Zairian troops to help defend Rwanda against the initial RPF invasion in 1990, and had quickly evacuated the dead president's body to his hometown of Gbadolite. The dead president's widow, Agathe Habyarimana, who had been a shadowy power behind the president, joined Mobutu in Gbadolite as well, using the jungle palace as her base during the genocide. In October 1994, she and her brother Seraphin Rwabukumba accompanied Mobutu on a state visit to Beijing; press reports suggest they secured $5 million in arms shipments from the Chinese government, circumventing the arms embargo by shipping the weapons to the Zairian government.[19] The body of her husband lay refrigerated in Mobutu's palace. Her host promised her that one day he would be buried in Rwanda.

~:~

Between July 1994 and November 1996, the UN Security Council issued ten statements and resolutions regarding the refugee camps in Zaire, "strongly condemning," "expressing grave concern," and making other remarks of diplomatic vacillation that stopped short of committing the world body from doing anything. Numerous UN planning teams visited the camps, with Canadian military advisors taking the lead on a possible intervention. The proposed force was jokingly called "the 'No' force" among staff in New York headquarters. "They would not go into the camps and would not disarm the militia by force," Peter Swarbrick, an official at the Department of Peacekeeping Operations, told me. "It was a fig leaf." By the end of 1995, Boutros Ghali had given up on military intervention and focused on alleviating the humanitarian situation.

The U.S. Congress had, in the wake of their botched deployment in Somalia in 1993, enacted legislation that forbid U.S. troops to be placed under UN command. In the run-up to elections in November 1996, President Bill Clinton did not want to engage troops in a complicated, unpopular quagmire in central Africa. A State Department official involved in the decision-making process, who wanted to remain anonymous, told me: "Securing the camps was just too difficult; there was no stomach here for that kind of operation. In retrospect, could more have been done? Definitely." After all, more was done in Bosnia, where the United States and its European allies dispatched 60,000 troops in 1995.

Moreover, the U.S. government was at loggerheads with the French government on the issue. Leading members of the French government saw conflict in the Great Lakes[20] as pitting their sphere of influence against an Anglo-Saxon one. Hadn't the RPF, an English-speaking rebel movement, taken power in Kigali from a French ally, Juvénal Habyarimana, and wasn't it now trying to overthrow another, Mobutu Sese Seko? As a senior French official was quoted anonymously as saying: "We cannot let anglophone countries decide on the future of a francophone one. In any case, we want Mobutu back in, he cannot be dispensed with . . . and we are going to do it through this Rwanda business."[21] The French and Americans battled it out in the Security Council: Whenever Madeleine Albright pushed to get tough on Mobutu, France would threaten to veto; whenever Paris wanted to include strong language on human rights abuses committed by the RPF in Rwanda, the United States would soften it up.

The RPF, who were already disgusted by international inaction during the genocide, watched in despair. "By early 1996, it was clear to us that the international community would not take action," Patrick Karegeya, Rwanda's intelligence chief, remembered. In August 1996, Vice President Paul Kagame visited Washington, DC, where he spoke with the secretary of defense and the head of the National Security Council, warning them that he would be forced to act if the international community did not. A State Department advisor who attended the meetings said: "We didn't fully grasp what he was trying to tell us. We didn't realize they would invade." Despite their remonstrations, it is difficult to believe that Washington officials, who had deployed a military training and de-mining team to Kigali to provide nonlethal assistance to the new government, were in the dark. "We knew what was up," Rick Orth, the U.S. defense attaché in Kigali, said. "But I don't think we ever gave the Rwandan government the thumbs-up."

Finally, in October 1996, the Rwandan army invaded in force under the guise of a homegrown Congolese rebellion in order to stave off criticism. Journalists and aid workers deployed in the refugee camps along the eastern Congo border began to report attacks by "Banyamulenge rebels," Congolese Tutsi who had been in conflict with Mobutu's government. Their first targets were the refugee camps in the Rusizi plain, a broad, hundred-mile-long expanse of savannah and rice paddies where the borders of Congo, Rwanda, and Burundi meet. Some 220,000 refugees were in camps there, protected by a few hundred soldiers on hire by the United Nations from Mobutu's army. The invading troops quickly broke up these camps, driving some refugees into Burundi, while probably a majority fled further in the Congo. By October 22, the town of Uvira at the tip of Lake Tanganyika fell without much fighting to the Rwandan-backed coalition. The troops then marched northwards along the Great Rift Valley that connects Lake Tanganyika to Lake Kivu and that separates the Congo to the west from Rwanda and Burundi. By the end of October, they had taken control of Bukavu at the southern end of Lake Kivu, dispersing some 300,000 refugees, who had no choice but to flee into the hills, away from Rwanda.

Humanitarian officials were alarmed as the sickly refugees they had been feeding for the past two years fled into the inhospitable hinterlands. Emma Bonino, European Commissioner for Humanitarian Aid, warned that, "500,000 to a million people are in danger of dying."[22] Diplomats rekindled the idea again of sending in an international force to create "humanitarian corridors" to allow refugees to return home and to protect aid workers. However, the debate soon got bogged down in a new diplomatic, Franco-Anglo spat. French foreign minister Hervé de Charette pushed for the deployment of the force, focusing on the plight of Hutu refugees: "We are looking after our national interests ... but there are people in danger, there are a million."[23] The French exhorted the United States to "stop dragging its feet." The British minister for Overseas Development, Lynda Chalker, called the French position "daft."[24] Among French government officials, the rumor mill was in full gear, with senior policy advisors suspecting there was an Anglo-Saxon plot to delay intervention to allow the Rwandan-backed invasion to make headway.

In Goma, on the northern end of Lake Kivu, the Rwandan army crossed the border on November 2, pushing over 600,000 refugees into the Mugunga camp, located a dozen miles away from the border on the lakeside, making the makeshift camp into the largest city in the region. The Canadian government said it would take the lead of a multinational task force to help protect the refugees and aid workers; the United Kingdom put a special forces battalion on stand-by.

Finally, on November 16, as the Rwandan army and the rebels prepared to attack Mugunga, the United States agreed to pass a UN Security Council resolution authorizing 3,000 to 4,000 international troops to deploy in the Kivus, the eastern region of the country that borders on Rwanda, Uganda, and Burundi.

The following day, Rwanda attacked Mugunga from the west and the lake, corralling most refugees toward the eastern road back to Rwanda. Half a million people returned home in just three days. At the UN headquarters on the western shore of the East River in Manhattan, Peter Swarbrick wryly recalled the reaction of Canadian general Maurice Baril, who had just been named to lead the military intervention: "It was relief, absolute relief. The international community was off the hook."

Meanwhile, as the Canadian and American military reconnaissance teams began to pack their bags, anywhere between 400,000 and 600,000 refugees were fleeing into the jungles of the eastern Congo.

A COUNTRY IN RUINS

Africa has the shape of a pistol, and Congo is its trigger.
—FRANTZ FANON

KIGALI, RWANDA, JULY 1994–SEPTEMBER 1996

The few visitors to Rwanda in the months after the genocide found a smoldering, destroyed landscape. A third of the country had fled to Tanzania, Zaire, and Burundi, running from the Rwandan Patriotic Front—the Tutsi rebellion led by Paul Kagame—and shepherded on by the army and militia that had carried out the genocide. In Kigali, the capital, the insides of houses had been gutted, spilling clothes, toilet paper, stuffed animals, and trash onto the sidewalks. Not knowing when they would come back, or perhaps out of spite for the advancing rebels, fleeing militiamen and civilians had stripped doors off their hinges, removed glass panes from windows, and unearthed sewage pipes and miles of electric cable. Empty bullet casings littered the streets, which were patrolled by UN cars—the only ones apart from a few RPF pickups and civilian cars still on the roads.

In the countryside, crops rotted in the field for want of workers to harvest them, and thousands of bodies choked the country's waterways, filling the air with the cloying stench of rotting flesh for months. Red Cross and aid workers trekked the hills on foot, dousing the corpses with lime to prevent disease, pending burial.

The new rulers of the country drearily inspected the shell-pocked government buildings. In the ministry of justice, filing cabinets floated in a soup of sewage and documents. The hallways of Parliament were littered with debris, bricks, and dangling electrical wires. For the meantime, the RPF's offices were located in the Meridien Hotel, where the plumbing didn't work and sandbags still lined the lightless reception area and the poolside, and RPF officials, UN workers, and journalists worked side-by-side.

The new government faced bleak days ahead. Not a cent was left in the Central Bank. There were no cars, computers, or telephones left for the new government to use; even the stationery and paper clips were gone. There was no electricity or running water in much of the country; generators in the hospitals were turned on just several hours a day for surgery and emergency operations. An estimated 114,000 children had been orphaned by the genocide and needed looking after; 150,000 houses had been destroyed.

The most striking absence was people. Kigali had turned into a ghost town: 40 percent of the population was dead or in exile. In the capital, the numbers had shrunk from 350,000 to 80,000, and many of those were the RPF and their families or members of the Tutsi diaspora returned after decades in exile.

Amid the rubble, the new rulers tried to craft a sort of normalcy. The RPF named a government with a diverse cabinet. The president and prime minister were both Hutus, and many ministers were from political parties other than the RPF, although the military and Vice President Paul Kagame still wielded the most power. All across the country, teams of civil servants and volunteers set about cleaning up the debris, burying bodies, and rebuilding key installations.

No family was spared by the violence. Over 90 percent of children and youths had witnessed violence and believed they would die; only slightly fewer had experienced a death in their family. A study published in a psychiatric journal estimated that one-fourth of all Rwandans suffered from posttraumatic stress syndrome.[1] They called these people *ihahamuka*, "without lungs" or "breathless with fear." They would walk through town, catatonic, jumping when a bus honked or someone came up behind them unannounced. Many families adopted orphans of the genocide or took in distraught relatives. Paul Kagame himself took in five children.[2]

The genocide formed the grim backdrop to the preparations for the RPF's invasion of the Congo. It was the starting point for everything that followed in Rwanda: politics, culture, the economy—everything. It transfixed society and dominated the government's vision for the future. More importantly, the empty houses and abandoned villages reminded the country's leaders that the war was not yet over. On the radio in the west of the country, on the border with Congo, one could hear the government in exile broadcasting from the refugee camps, claiming to be Rwanda's legitimate government. For the survivors of the genocide, many of whom lost members of their families, the *génocidaires'* presence in the camps was a living insult.

~:~

Rwanda's unquestionable ruler was Paul Kagame. Officially, the thirty-sevenyear-old was vice president and minister of defense, but he had led the RPF since the early days of the rebellion and had firm control over the government. A gaunt, bony man with wire-rimmed spectacles and a methodical style of speaking, Kagame left an impression on people. He didn't smoke, drink, or have much time for expensive clothes or beautiful women. He wasn't given to flowery speech or elaborate protocol. His wardrobe apparently only contained drab, double-breasted suits that hung loosely from his thin frame, plain polo shirts, and combat fatigues. The only entertainment he apparently indulged in was tennis, which he played at the Sports Club with RPF colleagues and diplomats. Passersby would be alarmed by the soldiers standing guard with machine guns.

Kagame's obsessions were order and discipline. He personally expropriated his ministers' vehicles when he thought those public funds could have been used for a better purpose. He exuded ambition, browbeating his ministers when they didn't live up to his expectations. He complained to a journalist: "In the people here, there is something I cannot reconcile with. It's people taking their time when they should be moving fast, people tolerating mediocrity when things could be done better. I feel they are not bothered, not feeling the pressure of wanting to be far ahead of where we are. That runs my whole system."[3]

This asceticism had been forged in the harsh conditions of exile. Kagame's first memories were of houses burning on the hills and his panicked mother scrambling into a car as a local mob ran after them. This was in 1961, when anticipation of independence from Belgium had led to pogroms against the Tutsi community, which had been privileged by the colonial government. Around 78,000 Tutsi had fled to Uganda, with another 258,000 going to other neighboring countries.[4] Like many RPF leaders, Kagame grew up as a refugee in Uganda, living in a grass-thatched hut while attending school on a scholarship.

"You will always hear me talking about the importance of dignity," he later commented.

> It is really the key to people's lives, and obviously for me it relates back to the refugee camp, the lining up for food every day, the rationing. When we started primary school, we used to study under a tree. We used to write on our thighs with a piece of dry, hard grass, and the teacher would come over and look at your thigh, and write his mark with another piece of dry grass. You develop some sense of questioning, some sense of justice, saying, "Why do I live like this? Why should anybody live like this?"[5]

The squalid conditions of the refugee camps and the animosity of their Ugandan neighbors were constant reminders that this was not his real home. His mother was from the royal family in Rwanda—his great-aunt had been the queen—and their stories of royal grandeur and authority were a far cry from the UN handouts they lived on in the camps. When his schoolmates went to play, he preferred to sit with former Tutsi guerrilla fighters and listen to stories about their battle against the Hutu-dominated regime in the 1960s.[6]

After he finished high school, Kagame ventured across the border to see for himself what his fabled homeland had become. He was harassed for being a Tutsi, but he felt exhilarated by being among his people on his land. He sat in bars, sipping a soft drink and listening to conversations. He spent several afternoons walking by the presidential palace in Kigali, drawn magnetically to the seat of power that was at the root of his exile in Uganda, until security guards got suspicious and told him to scram.

Back in Uganda, fellow refugees told him about a Ugandan rebellion that was being formed in Tanzania to overthrow the dictator Idi Amin, who had discriminated against the refugees for years. Led by Yoweri Museveni, the National Resistance Movement (NRM) recruited heavily among the Tutsi refugees. It seemed perfect for the twenty-two-year-old Kagame, who was itching to rise up out of the squalor of the camps. His stern and disciplined temperament drew him to work in military intelligence, a branch that shaped his outlook on politics. He received training in Tanzania, in Cuba, and, much later, at Fort Leavenworth in the United States.

When the NRM took power in 1986, Kagame's fierce discipline earned him a position at the head of the military courts, investigating and prosecuting soldiers' breaches of discipline. Among detractors and supporters alike, he became known as "Pilato," short for Pontius Pilate, because of the harsh way he dealt with any violation of the military code. Soldiers who stole from civilians or embezzled fuel from military stocks would be locked up; more serious violations could earn a place in front of a firing squad. "He can't stand venality or indiscipline—it provokes an almost physical reaction of disgust in him," a Ugandan journalist who knew him during this time, remembered.[7]

Kagame was soon promoted to become the head of Ugandan military intelligence, a position that provided a perfect vantage point from which to pursue his true ambition: overthrowing the Rwandan government. He plotted together with other Rwandan refugees who had risen to leadership positions in the Ugandan army, positioning stocks of weapons and secretly recruiting other Rwandans to their cause.

In 1990, they attacked.

The guerrilla struggle in Rwanda was marked by self-sacrifice and harsh conditions. In the early years of the rebellion, the RPF was beaten back into the high-altitude bamboo forests of the volcanoes in northwestern Rwanda, where temperatures at night dropped to freezing and there was little food or dry firewood. Kagame enforced draconian discipline, executing soldiers suspected of treason or trying to desert.[8] He perfected his hit-and-run guerrilla tactics, harrying the enemy, attacking convoys, but never engaging in large, conventional battles.

People who met Kagame and his RPF colleagues during this time were impressed by the rebels' dedication. The refugee camps and years in exile had steeled them and made them rely on each other. This ethic was not new to their culture. The precolonial Rwandan kingdom had been forged over centuries of warfare, leading to a central, Tutsi-led royal court with large standing armies. Stories of great Tutsi warriors were embellished and passed down through the generations. The most famous Rwandan dance, *intore*, was a war dance that the RPF themselves sometimes practiced around the campfire, stamping their feet and mimicking cows' horns with their arms.

Kagame's exploits and discipline earned him praise from around the world. General John Shalikashvili, the American chairman of the Joint Chiefs of Staff, studied Kagame's military tactics and praised him as one of the best guerrilla leaders in decades.[9] "Kagame is an intellectual figure. I would rate him as a first-rate operational fighter," a former director of the U.S. Army School for Advanced

Military Studies said. "He understands discipline. He understands speed. He understands mobility."[10]

~:~

After the overthrow of the Habyarimana regime, RPF leaders celebrated victory in Kigali; Ugandan *waragi*—a strong gin made out of millet—was a favorite. Mixed with Coca Cola, it was dubbed "Kigali Libre" by RPF officers.

Kagame, however, was typically reserved. The war was not yet over, he told his army colleagues. There was merely a truce enforced by an international border with Zaire. A third of the population was still living in camps outside the country, and rebels were regularly caught with grenades and disassembled weapons in the main market in Kigali. Every month brought assassinations of local officials and attacks on army camps.

In the meantime, Rwandan frustrations with international donors stewed. Not only had they failed to intervene during the genocide, but they were now feeding the *génocidaires* and allowing them to rearm. Despite an arms embargo on the government-in-exile, arms traders flew over $8 million in weapons to the defeated Rwandan army in Goma and Bukavu in the months just after the genocide. Hundreds of new recruits were being trained on soccer pitches next to the refugee camps, often within sight of Zairian soldiers. Despite the hand-wringing and horror at the Rwandan genocide that had finally gripped western capitals, the international community was once again abandoning Rwanda. Kagame fulminated to the press: "I think we have learned a lot about the hypocrisy and double standards on the part of people who claim that they want to make this world a better place."[11]

In early 1995, Kagame, usually known for his cool, deliberate style, began to lose his temper. "Whenever we brought up the issue of the refugee camps, he would raise his voice and bang his fist on the table," a former government advisor recalled.

Kagame was briefed every day by his intelligence services on the situation in Zaire. Rwandan operatives had infiltrated the camps and Mobutu's army, providing blow-by-blow details about arms shipments, troop movements, and political developments.

In February 1995, Kagame traveled to his home commune of Tambwe, where he told gathered villagers, "I hope with all of my heart that they do attack! Let them try!" Several weeks later, he told journalists in Kigali that his government would pursue any criminals who attacked Rwanda by attacking the country where they were found.[12]

"We had told Mobutu publicly to move the camps from the border. He refused. We told the UN to move the camps. They refused. So we told them we would find a solution ourselves," Ugandan president Yoweri Museveni said.[13]

~:~

Within a year of the genocide, Kagame began planning military action against the camps. But he knew that he would have to proceed carefully, and he couldn't go it alone. In a region where international donors supply on average half of government budgets, and where the legacy of French, U.S., and Russian power politics was apparent, blatant violations of sovereignty had to be planned carefully.

Fortunately for Kagame, it wasn't difficult to find allies. Mobutu had angered enough governments to spawn a broad alliance of African states against him. By 1995, an alphabet soup of rebel movements had taken advantage of Zaire's weak security services and Mobutu's willingness to support his neighbors' enemies, creating a complex web of alliances and proxy movements in the region that could confuse even close observers:

REBEL GROUPS BASED IN ZAIRE

Angolan

National Union for the Total Independence of Angola (UNITA)	2,000–15,000
Front for the Liberation of the Enclave of Cabinda (FLEC)	1,000–3,000

Ugandan

West Nile Bank Liberation Front (WNBLF)	1,000–2,000
Uganda Muslim Liberation Army (UMLA)	100–1,000
Allied Democratic Movement (ADM)	100–1,000
National Army for the Liberation of Uganda (NALU)	100–1,000

Burundian

Forces for the Defense of Democracy (FDD)	1,000–3,000
National Liberation Forces (FNL)	N/A

Rwandan

Ex-Rwandan Armed Forces (ex-FAR)	30,000
Interahamwe and other militias	20,000–40,000

Unfortunately for Mobutu, he had become ideologically outdated. The political leadership of Africa was changing as a new generation of leaders, most of whom had themselves once been rebels, came to power. Between 1986 and 1994, ideologically inspired rebels ousted repressive regimes in Ethiopia, Eritrea, Uganda, and Rwanda. Coded cables sent to European and American capitals from embassies spoke of a new breed of African leaders, apparently different from the corrupt and brutal dictators who had ruled much of Africa since independence. Although they all had begun their careers as socialists, after coming to power they initially endorsed the principles of free markets and liberal democracy and were enthusiastically greeted by western leaders. U.S. Secretary of State Madeleine Albright swooned: "Africa's best new leaders have brought a new spirit of hope and accomplishment to your countries—and that spirit is sweeping across the continent. . . . They share an energy, a self-reliance and a determination to shape their own destinies."[14]

~:~

Kagame's most obvious ally was Uganda. He had fought side-by-side with President Museveni for seven years, and then had served as his chief of intelligence for another four. The two had attended the same high school in southern Uganda, and Kagame had stayed with Ugandan military officers when he took leave from the front lines during the Rwandan civil war. Many other Rwandan commanders had also been born and raised in Uganda.

More than just personal links were involved, however. By the early 1990s, President Museveni was becoming embroiled in a low-scale proxy war with his neighbor to the north, Sudan. In 1993, Museveni had begun providing military support to Sudanese rebels, known as the Sudan People's Liberation Army, as part of a regional strategy (endorsed by the United States) to destabilize the Sudanese government. The government in Khartoum reciprocated by funding and arming half a dozen Ugandan rebel groups, as well as the Rwandan ex-FAR.[15] In addition, Museveni, who was celebrating his first decade in power, had been looking around the region for economic opportunities for his government. For years, he had been dreaming about fostering business between northwestern Zaire and Uganda—much of the lucrative timber, diamonds, and palm oil from that region had to pass through Uganda to get onto the international market, and the burgeoning Ugandan manufacturing sector could peddle its soap, mattresses, and plastics to the millions of Zairians living there.

Kagame began to talk to his colleagues and friends about taking action. He traveled frequently to State House in Kampala and to safari lodges in southern Uganda to speak to his former mentor and boss, Museveni. The Ugandan president, more used to the intrigues and pitfalls of international politics than Kagame, warned him not to act brashly. He worried particularly about the French government, which still had ties to the Rwandan government-in-exile and could use its power to undermine their attack. The older man warned Kagame: You need to have the backing of the world powers—the United States, South Africa, the United Kingdom—to succeed in dramatically changing the constellation of power in Africa. As both Museveni and Kagame had learned in their own insurgencies, the international community was inherently hostile to foreign invasions but turned a blind eye to domestic rebellions that called themselves liberation struggles.

Go look for Congolese rebels, he told Kagame, who could act as a fig leaf for Rwandan involvement. He introduced him to a veteran Congolese rebel leader based out of Dar es Salaam, Tanzania's business capital on the Indian Ocean, whom he had met in the 1980s, a talkative and corpulent man called Laurent Kabila.[16]

~:~

Next on the list was Angola. This former Portuguese colony to the south of Zaire had been fighting an insurgency backed by the United States and South Africa for over two decades: the National Union for the Total Independence of Angola (UNITA), led by Jonas Savimbi. Since the end of the cold war, U.S. support for Savimbi had disappeared, but he continued his rebellion, sustained by huge diamond mines close to the Zairian border. Mobutu was Savimbi's main remaining lifeline. He had allowed the Angolan rebels to traffic diamonds through Zaire for many years, skimming handsomely off the deals. When the international community imposed an arms embargo against UNITA in 1993, Mobutu provided fake paperwork to military providers in eastern Europe to allow Savimbi to buy weapons.[17] The bearded rebel appeared regularly in Kinshasa, landing his aircraft at the international airport and meeting with Mobutu in full military regalia.

The war with UNITA was understandably an obsession for the Angolan government. In 1996, there were 1.2 million displaced people in the country, amounting to 10 percent of the total population, and the government was spending over half of its budget on the military.[18] Jonas Savimbi was making millions of dollars in diamond sales a year, and he had his own impressive, illegal networks for selling gems and purchasing weapons.[19] Although both sides had signed a peace deal in 1994, neither side believed it would hold. A previous agreement had resulted in bloody clashes in the capital, Luanda, after Savimbi rejected elections won by his rivals.

In the fall of 1996, Kagame sent his intelligence chief to Luanda to negotiate the government of Angola's participation in his plans. The response was cautious. The Angolan government couldn't afford to get bogged down in a protracted war in eastern Congo while it faced Savimbi's threat at home. "They weren't sure; they needed a lot of convincing," a member of the delegation later recalled.[20] Angola was heavily dependent on loans from the International Monetary Fund and the World Bank; an overt intervention in a foreign country could have jeopardized its international standing.[21]

Angolan president Dos Santos offered a compromise. They would send the Katangan Tigers and some logistical help. The Tigers—or *diabos*, the Devils, as they liked to call themselves—were troops from southern Congo who had fought for the secession of Katanga Province in 1960. After their defeat, thousands of these troops had fled into northern Angola, where, over the years, they fought first for the Portuguese colonial government and then, after independence in 1975, for the Angolan government.

∾

By mid-1996, Museveni and Kagame had stitched together an impressive alliance of African governments behind their drive to overthrow Mobutu. The war that started in Zaire in September 1996 was not, above all, a civil war. It was a regional conflict, pitting a new generation of young, visionary African leaders against Mobutu Sese Seko, the continent's dinosaur. Never had so many African countries united militarily behind one cause, leading some to dub the war Africa's World War. Unlike that war, however, the battle for the Congo would not be carried out in trenches over years, leading to millions of military casualties. Here, the battles were short and the number of soldiers killed in the thousands, figures dwarfed by the number of civilians killed. Unlike World War II, the African allies banded together not against aggressive expansionism, but against the weakness of the enemy.

The leader of this coalition was its youngest, smallest member: Rwanda. It was typical of the RPF, who had played David to Goliath several times before and would do so again later. At the outset, it seemed to be the perfect embodiment of a just war: Kigali was acting as a last resort based on legitimate security concerns.

What seems obvious in hindsight—that Mobutu's army had been reduced to a mockery of itself, that Mobutu's hold on power had crumbled—was a vague hypothesis in RPF intelligence briefings at the time. When Kagame told his officers that they would go all the way to Kinshasa, they nodded politely but in private shook their heads. That was a journey of over 1,000 miles, through unknown terrain, similar to walking from New York to Miami through swamps and jungles and across dozens of rivers. They would have to fight against 50,000 of Mobutu's soldiers as well as perhaps 50,000 ex-FAR and Interahamwe. It seemed impossible. "We never thought we could make it all the way to Kinshasa," Patrick Karegeya, the Rwandan intelligence chief, told me.

It is easy to forget, now that greed and plunder claim the headlines as the main motives for conflict in the region, that its beginnings were steeped in ideology. The Rwandan-backed invasion was perhaps the heyday of the African Renaissance, riding on the groundswell of the liberation of South Africa from apartheid, and of Eritrea, Ethiopia, and Rwanda from dictatorships. It was an alliance motivated in part by the strategic interests of individual governments, but also by a larger spirit of pan-Africanism. Not since the heyday of apartheid in South Africa had the continent seen this sort of mobilization behind a cause. For the leaders of the movement, it was a proud moment in African history, when Africans were doing it for themselves in face of prevarication from the west and United Nations. Zimbabwe provided tens of millions of dollars in military equipment and cash to the rebellion. Eritrea sent a battalion from its navy to conduct covert speedboat operations on Lake Kivu. Ethiopia and Tanzania sent military advisors. President Museveni recalled: "Progressive African opinion was galvanised."[22]

The optimism of the day was summed up by South Africa leader Thabo Mbeki, who just months before the beginning of the war had made his famous endorsement of pan-Africanism:

> I am African.
> I am born of the peoples of the continent of Africa.
> The pain of violent conflict that the peoples of Liberia, Somalia, the Sudan,

Burundi and Algeria is a pain I also bear.

The dismal shame of poverty, suffering and human degradation of
my continent

is a blight that we share. . . .

Whatever the setbacks of the moment, nothing can stop us now!

Whatever the difficulties, Africa shall be at peace!

However improbable it may sound to the sceptics, Africa will
prosper![23]

Absent from these talks, however, were the Congolese. Their country was to be liberated for them by foreigners who knew little to nothing of their country. And of course, these foreigners would soon develop other interests than just toppling Mobutu.

Within several years, the Congo was to become the graveyard for this lofty rhetoric of new African leadership as preached by Mbeki, Albright, and many others. Freedom fighters were downgraded to mere marauding rebels; self-defense looked ever more like an excuse for self-enrichment. Leaders who had denounced the big men of Africa who stayed in power for decades began appearing more and more like the very creatures they had fought against for so many decades.

In 1996, however, the future remained bright.

♦ 4 ♦

SIX DAYS

All Banyamulenge remember October 8, 1996. On that day, Lwasi Lwabanji, the vice governor of the province, made his way to the governor's office in Bukavu in a motorcade, accompanied by a pickup bristling with soldiers. The town was alive with rumors of the impending Rwandan invasion.

Bukavu is a border town in the eastern Congo, built on five hilly peninsulas on the southern end of Lake Kivu, separated only by a narrow river from Rwanda. From the main street, one could see the Rwandan army positions in the hills to the east, low camouflaged bivouacs with soldiers milling about. A few weeks before, the Zairian army had exchanged artillery fire with these positions, provoking mortar and machine gun fire into Bukavu's residential areas. Travelers arriving from the south brought stories of nightly infiltrations from Rwanda across the Rusizi River and fighting between Zairian troops and rebels there.

Lwabanji was of medium build, with an urbane manner he had cultivated during his studies in Kinshasa. With the military governor a thousand miles away in the capital Kinshasa, the task of dealing with the day-to-day administration of the province had fallen to him. The threat of an attack did not daunt him; on the radio, he had boasted of the Zairian army's prowess. "We will crush Rwanda if they try something," he promised, bolstered by the anti-Rwandan sentiment simmering in Bukavu's streets. No one imagined that Rwanda, a country ninety times smaller, could seriously challenge Zaire—in terms of size, it would be like Switzerland trying to conquer all of western Europe.[1]

At the governor's office, a crowd of local and international journalists awaited him, as well as several dozen legislators in suits and ties. The building's conference room, like much of Zaire's infrastructure, had fallen into disrepair. Windows were cracked or nonexistent, the yellow paint was peeling, and corridors smelled faintly of sewage. The vice governor had come to address the issue on everybody's minds and lips: the approaching rebels, referred to by most as "the Banyamulenge."

The Banyamulenge are a small community of Tutsi, the minority ethnic group in Rwanda, who emmigrated from Rwanda and Burundi to the Congo between the eighteenth and nineteenth centuries, settling in the remote highland pastures to the south of Bukavu. Only a few years earlier, most people in Bukavu had never heard of them. The war, however, catapulted them to national ignominy; it came to be known as the Banyamulenge's war.

Lwabanji resorted to the kind of anti-Tutsi hyperbole typical of many Congolese politicians: "In some villages of the highlands in which the Banyamulenge regularly exterminate civilian population, the latter are already defending themselves with their bare hands, knives and sometimes they capture firearms from the Banyamulenge." He cleared his throat. "I demand the population in the highlands to descend to the shores of the lake. We will consider everybody who stays in the high plateau as rebels." Striding out through the hallway afterwards, a journalist accosted him. How much time would they give the Banyamulenge to pack their belongings and leave? "I think a week will be enough," he said. "Six days."[2]

In times of tension, radios were almost like an appendage for many Zairians, the only means of getting reliable information. The first sound in villages, before even the cock's crow, is often the crackle of a shortwave receiver, as people tune in to the 5 o'clock Radio France International or BBC Swahili Service broadcast, which is relatively static-free in the early morning hours. In Bukavu, on their way to work, pedestrians typically walk with their radios in front of them or clasped close to their ear, listening to the news.

Many Banyamulenge heard Lwabanji's speech huddled around radios. Others heard of it by word of mouth, the details distorted with every retelling. Within several days, the news had spread that the vice governor had tendered a six-day ultimatum for all Banyamulenge to leave for Rwanda or be attacked. Lwabanji later protested that the regrouping of the Banyamulenge community was for their own protection, and in villages in Zaire, not in Rwanda. His explanation was to little avail; for the Banyamulenge, his name was henceforth tied to eviction from their country.[3]

∾⁞∾

Lwabanji was not alone in singling out the Banyamulenge community. Ask a random Congolese what the root of the war was, and he or she will usually answer, "Rwanda," or "the Banyamulenge." As the war dragged on, their notoriety grew, spreading far afield from their home in the highlands of the eastern Congo. This despite their size: The Banyamulenge make up only several decimal points of the entire Congolese population, between 100,000 and 300,000 people out of 60 million. However, given the Banyamulenge's close ethnic ties to the new Rwandan government—both belong largely to the Tutsi community—the war catapulted their leaders to the front of the political scene. From complete obscurity, they became arguably the country's most hated group, attracting venom from church leaders, human rights activists, and politicians alike.

Benjamin Serukiza emerged as a leading figure in the Banyamulenge community during the war. He was vice governor of South Kivu throughout the war, representing the community at the highest level in their home province. When I saw him in his apartment in downtown Kinshasa in November 2007, he was unemployed, having left politics. Dressed in an untucked pink shirt and plastic flip-flops, he told me he was tired of politics—"that never helped us much"—and was trying to leave the Congo to get a job in an international organization.[4]

Serukiza's features conformed with the stereotypes many Congolese have of Banyamulenge. He was over six feet tall, with high cheekbones, a thin and hooked nose, and slightly protruding teeth. In Congolese French, some words are known to illiterate farmers that educated Belgians and French rarely use. *Morphologie* was one of them; Banyamulenge would learn it as children, knowing that it connoted a vulnerability, a danger. "His morphology is suspicious," one sometimes heard people saying when they suspected someone of being Tutsi. As if you could tell someone's subversion by his bone structure or the slant of his nose.

The postwar housing of the former rebels can be revealing. Serukiza's three-bedroom flat next to the justice ministry was bare and run-down, a far cry from the gaudy interiors of some of his former colleagues. The windows were draped with slightly dirty voile curtains, the tables covered in cheap plastic spreads. The toilet—to my embarrassment—did not flush, and the doors were loose on their hinges, sticking in their frames. Most tellingly, in a country where importance can be measured in the number of cell phones and frequency of calls, he only had one phone, which remained silent throughout our three-hour meeting.

When I asked Serukiza about the war, he seemed weary of the subject, like a witness interrogated a dozen times but with little faith in justice. Instead of beginning in 1996, however, he started four generations earlier, with his ancestors' arrival in the country. Like other persecuted minorities, the Banyamulenge have an obsessive sense of history, clinging to names and dates. "The truth is, we have no idea when we left Rwanda. According to historians, it was in the mid-nineteenth century. All I know is that my great-grandfather was born in the Congo. But they still call us Rwandans! Imagine calling Americans British."

~:~

The controversy surrounding the Banyamulenge focuses on when they arrived in the Congo. Their detractors dismiss them as recent immigrants who are more Rwandan than Congolese. They often refer to colonial maps of tribes, pointing out that no "Tutsi" or "Banyamulenge" marker is to be found until after independence in 1960. Most academics, not to mention thousands of Banyamulenge, disagree. Isidore Ndaywel, a leading Congolese historian, writes in his *General History of the Congo*: "[The Rwandan immigration] is confirmed by oral sources from Rwanda that evoke the departure of lineages from Kinyaga (Rwanda) in the 19th century to install themselves in Mulenge. The reasons for this movement was reportedly the search for better pastures, but in particular also the flight from attacks by King Kigeri Rwabugiri (1853–1895), who was determined to bring an end to Kinyaga's autonomy."[5]

It is likely that roaming pastoralists had been visiting the high plateau for centuries, fleeing the frequent fighting between different clans in densely populated Burundi and Rwanda and trying to find new pastures for their cattle to graze. The nineteenth-century wars in Rwanda just fueled these migrations.[6] Other factors probably contributed to their exodus, including a devastating rinderpest epidemic that killed up to 90 percent of cattle in some parts of Rwanda, as well as the arrival of Europeans with smallpox and other diseases around the same time.[7] Most Banyamulenge have only a vague idea, passed on through their elders, of when their ancestors first came to the Congo. Before the war, almost none had known relatives in Rwanda.

The Banyamulenge's original exodus took the cattle herders across the Rusizi plain into what is today Congolese territory. There the immigrants and their cattle fled the malaria that is endemic at lower altitudes and scaled the Itombwe mountain range. They settled in the town of Mulenge, from which they derive their name. Tensions with their neighbors soon arose. The Tutsi are pastoralists, and their cows trampled their neighbors' fields. The newcomers also ate different food, had their own myths, and adhered to particular conjugal habits. The Banyamulenge poet Muyengeza distilled these tensions, along with his community's defiance, into a stanza:

> They came across
> They came across the shores of Lake Tanganyika
> They were swallowed by a python
> It found them too strong to crush.[8]

As in much of Africa, land in the eastern Congo was managed by traditional chiefs. While initially the local ruler from the Fuliro tribe was happy to lease land to the newcomers in return for cows, relations deteriorated when the traditional chief hiked up their tribute in the 1920s, prompting Banyamulenge to move to higher, less accessible pastures away from his control. The Banyamulenge's resentment was also stoked by the Belgian colony's refusal to give them their own administrative entity for fear of alienating neighboring communities.

The hunger for land rights became a central concern in Banyamulenge politics and religion. During the upheaval of the 1960s, several evangelical prophets came forward, all claiming that they had received prophecies about a promised land, their own Canaan. In 1972, a prayer group received divine instruction that they should go to a place called Nyabibuye, where they were told by God to look to the west, the east, the north, and the south—"the land surrounded by horizons that your eyes are seeing, I will make it your dwelling place."[9]

∾∶∾

The postindependence period was a tumultuous time for the Congo, as the country crumbled into chaos following the assassination of its independence leader and first prime minister, Patrice Lumumba. In April 1964, the rebellion reached the eastern Congo, led by Lumumba's followers and fueled by local communal grievances against the central state. One of the leaders sent to mobilize the locals from neighboring Burundi was Laurent-Désiré Kabila, a hitherto little-known youth leader from Katanga province. Black-and-white pictures show a grinning twenty-five-year-old Kabila with long sideburns and a budding afro, his chubby face somehow too big for his still relatively trim frame, accentuated by bell-bottomed jeans.

It was into this tense environment that Serukiza was born in 1964. He remembers his mother telling him stories about rebels streaming through their villages armed with bamboo, machine guns, and machetes and shouting "*Mai!*" invoking the ritual water, or *mai*, they believed made them invincible to bullets. She also told him about a group of white soldiers who spoke a foreign language and were only known by the order they arrived in the country: *moja, mbili, tatu* (one, two, three in Swahili), and so on. Serukiza smiles. "It was only much later that she found out that these were Cubans and that *tatu*, the third to arrive in the country, was Che Guevara." In the cold war world of international proxy warfare, the mountains of Mulenge had become a battleground between Cuba and the United States.

The rebellion exacerbated the tensions between the communities, as Kabila's rebels began to prey on the Banyamulenge's cattle. "It was some sort of bizarre Marxist approach," Serukiza said, "anyone with cattle was rich and therefore bourgeois and close to Kinshasa. But we were peasants!" Thousands of Banyamulenge fled to the shores of Lake Tanganyika, where they thought they could find protection and aid, but many died of malaria and malnutrition, unaccustomed to the hot climate. Desperate, the Banyamulenge sent a delegation, including one of Serukiza's uncles, to convince Mobutu's army to come to their rescue.

The Banyamulenge's siding with Mobutu marked their entry into regional politics and the origin of open hostilities with the neighboring communities. In 1966, Kabila's rebels attacked a Banyamulenge village, forcing dozens into a church and massacring them, prompting hundreds of Banyamulenge to join Mobutu's Forces Armées Zairoises (FAZ) and beat back the rebels from their pastures in the high plateau.[10] Kabila's troops' abuses led Banyamulenge, who attach great value to cows, to dub him "the one who cuts cows' teats." Serukiza's mother told him that no milk would flow where Kabila had been.

"There are many ironies in our history," Serukiza philosophized as a cool breeze blew in off the Congo River. "Who would have thought that Kabila would lead us many years later to overthrow Mobutu?"

~:~

When asked about discrimination, many Tutsi in the Congo immediately bring up schoolyard taunts. As everywhere, schools were places of socialization, where the ground rules were laid out. The most common insult was *bor*, which was local slang for "thing" as well as "penis." "For them, we were no better than objects," Serukiza remembered. Across the border, in Burundi, where many Banyamulenge fled, they were call *kijuju* after a local plant that looked like cassava but couldn't be eaten—a useless, treacherous substance. "They had songs they used to sing about us," Serukiza said. "They were all variations on 'Banyamulenge, go home to Rwanda.' They also called us 'RRR': 'Rwandans Return to Rwanda,' or *kafiri*, uncircumcised—that was a huge insult for us. We aren't Rwandans." For many communities in the eastern Congo and elsewhere in Africa, elaborate circumcision rituals mark the graduation to manhood; Banyamulenge are usually not circumcised.

Most Banyamulenge live in the remote villages of the high plateau, where the discrimination is less obvious and biting. But since they do not have good high schools, hospitals, or administrative offices, all Banyamulenge have to conduct regular pilgrimages to the lakeside towns of Uvira, Baraka, or Kalemie, where they are treated with disdain. "When you want to obtain a birth certificate, take a national exam, or get an ID, you had to walk three days to town," Serukiza said. "There, they threw stones at us and called us names."

A sociologist from the Bembe tribe (the neighboring community and the majority in the area), Kimoni Kicha, distilled this prejudice succinctly: "Bembe consider the Tutsi as no-gooders, weaklings, uncircumcised, an inferior people who do not do anything but drink milk all day long, and who do not cry over their dead brethren but over their deceased cows."[11]

~:~

Sitting on his beige, faux-leather sofa, Serukiza sought out dates like rosary beads, fingering them for reassurance and circling back to them as the conversation went on. April 24, 1990: That was a big one, he nodded. Mobutu, a deeply superstitious man who employed at different points in time West African marabouts (Muslim religious mystics), Indian gurus, and Catholic priests, chose the date because it contained the number four, a lucky number for him. He had been born on October 4, 1930; his first coup d'état took place on September 14, 1960, his second on November 24, 1965.

This date, as opposed to the others, was a black day for Mobutu. After twenty-five years of autocratic misrule, his grip on power had slipped. The cold war—in which he had masterfully positioned himself as an ally of the west, garnering billions of dollars in aid—had come to an end. Several months before, his friend the Romanian president Nicolae Ceaușescu was accused of abuse of power and put in front of a firing squad with his wife, an event that deeply affected Mobutu. Shocked, he watched on television as Romanian soldiers manhandled the dictator's limp, bloody body. Pressure was already coming from the United States, Belgium, and France, which had all supported him for many years, to reform. The economy had stagnated. Congolese wages were lower than at independence thirty years earlier. Inflation had climbed to over 500 percent.

"*Comprenez mon emotion*," went his now legendary appeal to the country on national television, wiping a tear from beneath his glasses. A rumble went through the rows of his loyalists who had lined up in the Nsele Party headquarters: They could not believe their ears. After twenty-three years of one-party rule—every man, woman, child, and even corpse was constitutionally required to be a member of the Popular Revolutionary Movement (MPR)—he legalized other political parties and stepped down from the helm of his own. Several months later, under continued domestic and international pressure, he bowed to the demand for a national conference of civic leaders that would name a prime minister and draft a new constitution, paving the way for elections.

"You know, for westerners democracy is a good thing. But I don't think for you and us that wonderful word means the same thing," Serukiza said. As his power slipped in the late 1980s, Mobutu began to pit different communities throughout the country against each other in order to distract from opposition against his regime. The advent of democracy saw mass mobilization, often along ethnic lines, and the autocrat tried to take advantage of these communal cleavages to divide his opposition. For the Banyamulenge, this divide-and-rule gambit focused on their citizenship and thus their eligibility for taking part in elections. Already in 1982, their candidates were barred from running for office in the

MPR's central committee because of their "dubious citizenship." Serukiza laughed. "Oh God, that term has plagued us!"

The transition to a multiparty democracy only made things worse for the Banyamulenge population. In 1989, playing to anti-Tutsi sentiment in the East, Mobutu promised to settle the citizenship question once and for all by conducting an "identification of citizens" in the East. This despite the existence of dozens of other cross-border communities elsewhere in the country—the Kongo people, for example, regularly cross back and forth into the Congo from Angola, and the Nande migrate back and forth from Uganda.

The 1989 census ended in disaster. While Tutsi in Kinshasa and in some villages in the Kivus were given identification cards, others were turned back. Thousands of Banyamulenge in Uvira were refused citizenship.[12] According to Serukiza, the authorities tried to force a special identification card on his village, which left them with an ambiguous status. "It didn't say we were foreigners, but it wasn't the usual ID either." At the time a fresh graduate from the University of Lubumbashi with a degree in international relations, he rallied fifteen Banyamulenge leaders to boycott the registration. The authorities called in the army and arrested the chiefs, while Serukiza only barely escaped, jumping from an army truck and hiding in the houses of local family members. He then fled to neighboring Burundi.

The National Sovereign Conference, widely hailed as a success for stemming Mobutu's authoritarianism, was another setback for Congolese Tutsi. Under pressure from other communities in the Kivus, all Tutsi delegates were banned from participating in the conference, where over 3,000 delegates convened to discuss the country's future. A special subcommission was created to deal with citizenship. The opposition, initially sympathetic to the Tutsi's entreaties, backpedaled to gain the support of the large and important Kivu delegation.

∾:∾

The Tutsi's woes may have gone unaddressed if not for developments in Zaire's two tiny neighbors to the east. Since independence, the fates of Rwanda and Burundi had diverged. Both countries were former Belgian colonies inhabited by a Hutu majority and a Tutsi minority, but in Burundi the Tutsi elite had held power since independence, while in its neighbor to the north a Hutu government had ruled. In Rwanda, Hutu governments had led pogroms against the Tutsi.

In Burundi military juntas organized the mass killing of Hutu in 1972 and 1988. These dynamics reinforced each other: For the Rwandan Hutu, the killings of their brethren to the south was a portent of what might happen if Tutsi came to power there; the opposite mind game was occurring among the Tutsi leaders of Burundi.

In October 1993, Burundi's first elected Hutu president, Melchior Ndadaye, was assassinated just months after his inauguration, prompting a spate of ethnic violence that drove tens of thousands of Hutu into Zaire. Less than a year later, the Rwandan genocide sent another million Hutu into camps across the border.

"Life became unbearable for us," Serukiza recalled. "The Rusizi plain [forming the border between Zaire, Burundi, and Rwanda] became white like snow with United Nations High Commissioner for Refugees tents. The refugees' slogan was: 'They are still alive?'" The sizable Banyamulenge population in Uvira was harassed and threatened. He recalled his mother not being able to leave the house to go to the market and being forced to ask neighbors to buy food for them.

With over half a million Tutsi massacred in Rwanda, the threat to the Congolese Tutsi was not hypothetical. Hutu militia posted a sign at the Cyangugu/ Bukavu border as a reminder: "Attention Zaireans and Bantu people! The Tutsi assassins are out to exterminate us. For centuries, the ungrateful and unmerciful Tutsi have used their powers, daughters and corruption to subject the Bantu. But we know the Tutsi, that race of vipers, drinkers of untrue blood. We will never allow them to fulfill their dreams in Kivuland."[13]

The influx of refugees further poisoned relations between the Tutsi and other communities, while politicians in Kinshasa cynically drew on anti-Tutsi sentiment to boost their popularity. After sending a commission to the Kivus to figure out what to do about the refugee camps, Mobutu's government voted on simultaneous resolutions on April 28, 1995, regarding citizenship and the refugee crisis.[14] The resolutions demanded "the repatriation, without condition or delay, of all Rwandan and Burundian refugees and immigrants."[15] In case there was any misunderstanding, Uvira's mayor issued a circular to his officers, responding to a Banyamulenge letter of protest: "I have the honor to transmit the memorandum of a certain ethnicity unknown in Zaire called Banyamulenge.... I should also add that at the latest by 31.12.1995, they will all be chased from the national territory."[16]

Kinshasa asked administrative officials to catalogue all property and real estate belonging to this group of "refugees and immigrants"—clearly understood in the Kivus to include the Banyamulenge—in view of their expropriation. In Bukavu, officials drew up lists of all Tutsi living in their respective neighborhoods.

Anti-Tutsi sentiment was exacerbated by a small group of Banyamulenge youths who, seeking adventure and responding to the call of their kin across the border, left in the early 1990s to join the RPF rebellion in neighboring Rwanda. Between 300 and 1,000 Banyamulenge joined this insurgency, although most did so surreptitiously, even stealing money from their families before quietly sneaking across the border at night.[17] To many Congolese the Banyamulenge's participation in the RPF war smacked of treason and reinforced their belief that, in their heart of hearts, the Banyamulenge were Rwandan.

In 1994, with the town of Uvira teeming with Hutu refugees from Rwanda and Burundi, Serukiza decided to leave for Rwanda with his wife and sister-in-law. He smiled, "We had to give my sister a different name for the bus manifest." He laughed: "Her real name was Nyira Batutsi—that wouldn't pass." They changed her name to Chantal. At the border in Bukavu, Mobutu's soldiers stopped him and stripped him of his Zairian ID and his briefcase, which contained his only copy of his university dissertation on Banyamulenge history. "You are no longer Zairian. You don't need this anymore," they told him.

5

ONION LAYERS

Like layers of an onion, the Congo war contains wars within wars. There was not one Congo war, or even two, but at least forty or fifty different, interlocking wars. Local conflicts fed into regional and international conflicts and vice versa. Teasing out origins can be a tail-chasing exercise. In my interviews, I often made the mistake of asking the interviewee to start from the beginning. "The beginning?" A look of bemused condescension would follow—what does this young foreigner know about our beginnings? "Good idea. Well, in 1885, at the Conference of Berlin. . . ." Others would start with Mobutu's coup d'état in 1965 or independence in 1960.

Deogratias Bugera offered a rough date: October 1993.[1] That month—he could not remember the exact date—in the muddy market town of Mushaki, in the eastern highlands, he loaded up ten truckloads of young Tutsi and sent them to join the rebellion in Rwanda to topple President Habyarimana's regime. Three years later, Bugera and the young Congolese Tutsi he mobilized would become the vanguard in a second rebellion, the Alliance of Democratic Forces for the Liberation of Congo-Zaire (AFDL). After liberating Rwanda, they now wanted to do the same with their homeland, with the strong backing of their Rwandan allies.

Bugera was one of the four founders of the AFDL, which was formed in Kigali in the dry season of 1996. "The only surviving founder," he reminded me when I met him in the Sandton luxury shopping mall, one of the well-protected gated communities around which the Johannesburg upper-class social scene is based. He laughed: "The last of my cofounders was killed in January 2001." Several years after the creation of the AFDL, Bugera had fallen out with both Laurent Kabila and the Rwandans and left for a cozy exile in South Africa, where he reverted to his previous profession as an architect. Now balding and in his early fifties, he was wearing a blue polo shirt with a beige cardigan draped over his shoulders. He spoke slowly and deliberately, and had a dazed look about him.

For Bugera, as for many Congolese Tutsi, politics had not been his chosen vocation; he had been born into it. "It was a fact of life for us; you were involved, whether you liked it or not." His grandfather, a traditional chief in North Kivu Province, had died during a hunger strike in 1924, protesting the resettlement policies of the Belgian colonizers. When Bugera was five years old, at the time of Congolese independence, his father was killed during a bout of communal violence, as people from neighboring communities rebelled against Rwandan immigrants. Bugera remembered seeing his father bludgeoned to death and thrown into a lake. He and dozens of other children were rushed to the nearby swamps, where their parents hoped the reeds and water would muffle the infants' cries and hide their smell. "They used dogs to hunt us down," Bugera said. "I can still remember the sound of the dogs barking and howling."

He initially tried to escape the turmoil of North Kivu, traveling to Kinshasa, a thousand miles away, to study architecture at the national university. Even there, however, he discovered he could not escape politics. In 1982, a group of Mobutu loyalists from the Kivus launched Operation R-B, targeting people they said were students from Rwanda and Burundi. Many Tutsi were forced to hide or be beaten by a crowd of angry students. Sympathetic friends smuggled Bugera out of his house on the floor of a car's backseat.

Bugera returned to the Kivus in the mid-1980s and tried once again to leave politics and pursue his career as an architect. He received a grant from a Canadian charity to begin a cattle ranching project with peasants in Masisi, and he became the real estate advisor to one of the large banks in Goma. One of Bugera's former colleagues told me, "Bugera was never a politician. He was a businessman who was forced into politics. But he didn't have the acumen for it. Politics in the Congo doesn't work like a business ledger, where you can add up the pluses and minuses and get a logical result. You have to be able to understand political intrigue and outplay your opponent." Bugera, his former colleague told me, thought that he could force reconciliation on the Congolese. "How can you stick a gun to someone's head and tell them to love you? It doesn't work."[2]

∼:∼

"Do you really think you can get this right?" Bugera asked me over the dinner table, pointing at the notes I was scribbling into my notebook. Like many of the people I interviewed, Bugera was skeptical that I could represent the complexity of his history.

"It is true that the Tutsi killed," Bugera told me at one point. "But we all had brothers, schoolmates, uncles who had been killed. It's all part of a whole. Can you portray that to your readers in Arizona or Berlin? Can you make them understand why someone would kill?"

∼:∼

The history of the Tutsi community in North Kivu is drastically different from that of the Banyamulenge in South Kivu, although both groups are labeled "Tutsi" by other Congolese. Both communities, despite their tiny size, played prominent roles in the Congo wars.

The problems in North Kivu can be dated to 1908, when the new Belgian colonial government took over the reins from Congo Free State. Under this new administration, thousands of Belgians escaped the industrial drudgery of their homeland to set up cattle ranches and plantations in the province's highlands. In 1928, the government created the National Committee of the Kivus, a charter company that granted itself "all vacant lands" in the region. In practice, this meant that any piece of land that was not being farmed belonged to the state. In a region where traditional chiefs owned all land, including forest, fallow farmland, and empty fields, this was tantamount to mass theft. The newcomers got much of the best farm and cattle land, expropriating a chunk of land larger than all of Belgium.[3]

The Belgians were then confronted with a lack of labor. The local Hunde and Nyanga communities wanted to farm their own fields, and the Belgians were wary of peasant revolts if they began exacting too much labor from locals. In 1937, they found the solution: By bringing in tens of thousands of Rwandans, whom they had long admired as industrious, the Belgians would create a large pool of loyal workers. It would also alleviate overpopulation and periodic famine in Rwanda. Over the next twenty years, the Mission d'Immigration des Banyarwanda imported around 175,000 Rwandans—mostly Hutu, but also many Tutsi—to the Kivu highlands.[4]

∾:∾

Unrest in Rwanda around its independence prompted a further 100,000 Rwandans to flee to the Congo between 1959 and 1964. They were settled initially by the United Nations but eventually integrated into local communities. This second wave of immigrants around independence included many affluent and well-educated Tutsi who came to form an important part of the Goma elite. The 1970 census found 335,000 Rwandans living in the Congo, mostly in the territory of Masisi, where they made up over 70 percent of the population.[5] By 1990, an estimated half million descendants of Rwandan immigrants were living in North Kivu.[6]

This massive influx caused bitter tensions with the local Hunde community, which had been living in Masisi for centuries. The Belgians leased land from the local traditional chief for a pittance and created the independent but short-lived chiefdom of Gishali, which was ruled by a Tutsi immigrant. The lease of land became permanent, and Hutu farmers and Tutsi ranchers came to dominate the local economy.

The newcomers constituted a strong lobby with considerable influence over Mobutu, who in turn found them to be useful allies. From 1969 to 1977, Barthélémy Bisengimana, a Rwandan immigrant and the president's influential chief of staff, played an important role in promoting his community's interests. Mobutu adopted a law in 1971 that granted blanket citizenship to all Rwandans and Burundians who had been in the Congo since 1960. Perhaps most importantly, when Mobutu expropriated all foreign businesses in 1973, it was the Tutsi elite in North Kivu who benefited. In Masisi, 90 percent of all large plantations—almost half of all the land—came to be owned by these immigrants or their descendants. By contrast, in South Kivu, the Banyamulenge were largely rural, uneducated, and relatively poor.

The ascendance of the Tutsi in North Kivu helps explain the virulent backlash against them. A diligent student of Machiavelli—*The Prince* could often be seen on his bedside table—Mobutu had mastered the art of divide-and-rule politics. In 1981, Mobutu reversed the citizenship law, decreeing that citizenship had to be obtained upon individual application and was only available for those who could trace their Congolese ancestry back to 1885. In theory, this not only stripped most Hutu and Tutsi in Masisi of their citizenship but also expropriated much of their property, since only Congolese could own such large concessions under the new law.[7] For the "immigrants," although most did not lose their land, this legal back and forth only underlined how tenuous their status was.

~:~

As with the Banyamulenge, the democratization process put the citizenship question front and center in North Kivu politics. In March 1993, goaded on by local politicians who reminded their communities of the land expropriation by the Rwandan immigrants, Hunde and Nyanga mobs launched attacks against Hutu and Tutsi, who fought back with their own militia and by buying protection from the national army. Somewhere between 3,000 and 7,000 people had been killed by the end of the year.[8]

Deogratias Bugera had by this time become a member of the local Tutsi elite and helped coordinate its armed resistance. The Rwandan Patriotic Front (RPF) was involved in a major offensive against Habyarimana's regime in neighboring Rwanda. As opposed to the Banyamulenge, who had mostly lost contact with relatives in Rwanda, the Tutsi in North Kivu still had family across the border. As Zaire became increasingly hostile toward them, the allure of joining a Tutsi liberation army grew. Bugera became involved in helping to recruit young Tutsi to join the RPF, hoping that they could create a safe haven in Rwanda and—perhaps—return to do the same in North Kivu.

The RPF recruitment was a slick, well-organized operation. Since the early days of their rebellion, the RPF Radio Muhabura ("Radio Beacon") broadcast on shortwave throughout North Kivu, providing the RPF's version of the war and encouraging young men to take up arms to overthrow Habyarimana. At the village level in Rwanda and the Congo, they created *umuryango* ("family") cells to mobilize new recruits and finances for their rebellion. "Each of our families gave whatever they could give to sponsor the movement. We held folk dances for fundraising and listened to RPF tapes smuggled across the border with songs and speeches on them," Bugera remembered, smiling.

Bugera had his first contact with the RPF through an affluent friend, whose family had helped fund the rebels since their creation. In 1993, Bugera sent the first batch of 172 recruits across the border along with enough money to pay for uniforms and weapons. He traveled with the convoy to the border, where he bribed the Zairian soldiers with $11,000 to allow the recruits through. He laughed when he told the story: "They arrested me on the way back! One of the soldiers hadn't gotten his cut. It was all about money, just money for them."

Every Friday, the highland town of Mushaki held a large market where many Tutsi brought their cows, milk, and cheese to sell. With the RPF recruitment drive, this market also became the assembly point for young Tutsi who wanted to join the rebellion. Every week, Bugera loaded two or three trucks full of young men and sent them on their way across the border.[9]

~:~

In Kinshasa, I was eventually able to track down Papy Kamanzi, one of hundreds of young Tutsi Bugera had helped recruit for the Rwandan rebellion in 1993 and who had later joined the AFDL.

Papy had come to Kinshasa to be integrated into the national army, and I met him on the second-floor terrace of a bar in a busy, popular neighborhood. "Do they know you are Tutsi?" I asked, motioning toward the waiters milling around. He smiled conspiratorially. "No, they don't know. People here can't tell. They think all Tutsi look like Paul Kagame, tall with thin noses." By 2007, when I met him, there had been several bouts of anti-Tutsi violence in the capital, and I was surprised at how relaxed he was moving about the bustling markets and backstreets. Then again, he did not conform to the received Tutsi stereotypes: He was short with a broad nose and spoke relatively fluent Lingala, the language of Congo's capital. Nonetheless, he grew quiet when the waiter came close to us, pausing until he had finished pouring our soft drinks. When Papy did speak, he turned his face slightly away from me, toward the bubbling street noise to make sure the other tables didn't hear him.

Papy's family had come from Rwanda to the highlands of North Kivu in the 1950s, brought by a Belgian Trappist monk, whose Flemish name tripped up his tongue: Jean de Bertersfeld. Papy's father looked after the monks' cattle and plantation and married a local Tutsi woman. Being part of a minority community in such a turbulent area means living in a pressure cooker in which family loyalty means everything; Papy could recite his clan genealogy six generations back.

The initial tensions were between the "immigrants"—both Hutu and Tutsi— and the indigenous Hunde people. Every harvest, Papy's family had to pay a tithe to the Hunde customary chief, and most tax collectors and land surveyors were Hunde. Papy's father and relatives had been well taken care of by the Trappist monks and were wealthier than many Hunde peasants. Papy remembered being called "snake" and "dirty Tutsi" by kids at the market and in school.

By contrast, until the 1990s, relations with the Hutu community were warm. As a child, Papy had attended a boarding school fifty miles away from his home. When he walked home for long weekends, he would often be taken in and fed by Hutu. "Back then, we were all one community; we all speak Kinyarwanda, the common language of all Rwandans. It was politics that got us into this mess." He wrinkled his nose. "Bad politics." Relations between the Hutu and Tutsi only started to sour with the eruption of civil war in Rwanda in 1990. The hysteria there contaminated the Kivus, driving a wedge between the communities in North Kivu. Hutu youngsters, in particular those close to the border, rallied to Habyarimana's side, while the Tutsi joined up with the RPF.

Papy remembered the RPF mobilization with a smile. "It was a great time," he said. "We organized dances and big parties to raise money. Even the white priests would come and donate for the cause." I wondered how he could have such fond memories when there was so much violence, but he shook his head. "There's nothing like having your own country. *Il fallait tupate adresse.* We needed to have our own address." Abruptly, he began to hum a melody; the words came back to him slowly:

> *Humura Rwanda nziza, humura ngaho ndaje!*
> Don't be afraid good Rwanda, don't be afraid I am coming!
> *Isoko y'ubumwe na mahoro.*
> The source of unity and peace.

Papy remembered with a smile: "I tried to leave in 1991, but I was only thirteen, so the recruiters turned me back—I was too young."

Every family was supposed to provide one male child over fifteen to join up and fight. He had four older brothers who had already joined the RPF, and was eager to go himself. His father berated him constantly that he would never find a girl to marry, that he would be considered impotent, if he didn't join his brothers in the rebellion. Frustrated, Papy continued his studies but joined the local Boy Scout troop that was being run as a premilitary education course by a local

Tutsi leader. He and other Tutsi adolescents learned how to build bivouacs, give first aid, and dismantle and load an AK-47. In his free time, he baked *mandazi*, fried dough balls, and took them to the local market to raise money for the cause—a Congolese version of a neighborhood bake sale.

Finally, when Papy was sixteen, he joined the RPF. His parents rejoiced, and his father sold several of his cows to give him some cash to take along. His mother hugged and kissed him, telling him how proud she was of him and his brothers. "We knew that we were leaving to eventually come back and free our country." Sitting in the bed of a truck with several dozen other youths, he traveled by night to Goma, sailing through the roadblocks, where Mobutu's soldiers had been bribed to let them through. When they were out of earshot of the villages, the youths sang RPF songs *sotto voce* to bide the time.

The beginnings of his military career were bittersweet. He was elated, surrounded by like-minded youths, all humming with purpose and ideals. He had studied and could read and write, gaining him preferential treatment among the other youngsters. But the hard side of war also became apparent. He learned of the death of two of his older brothers, who had died in the RPF's final push to take Kigali in 1994. Then there was the genocide, when the countryside was filled with stinking corpses, when you couldn't even drink the water in the wells because bodies had been thrown into them and contaminated the groundwater. Everybody seemed to be a killer or a victim or both.

It was a world full of fury and pain; there didn't seem to be anything pure left. When the RPF sent him and a friend back to school in Rwanda—they wanted some of their young soldiers to catch up on the education they had missed—his friend attacked the Hutu teacher one night, strangling him with a rope, saying that he was a *génocidaire*. Papy sought solace briefly in a Pentecostal church, where he and other soldiers would speak in tongues and sing all night, but he left soon afterwards, finding it hard to relate with members of the congregation.

⁓

Bugera stayed in Goma, preparing for an RPF invasion, even when the town was teeming with ex-FAR and Interahamwe. "As long as you didn't go out at night and didn't go into the rural areas, it was actually relatively safe," he remembered.

Bugera had a construction company, and with the influx of aid organizations, he managed to win several lucrative contracts. Beginning in August 1994, when the RPF took control of the last ex-FAR holdout in northwestern Rwanda, Bugera used his company as a front to set up an elaborate network of RPF spies. "As soon as the RPF conquered Rwanda," he told me, "they set their sights on invading Zaire, much sooner than most people realize." Overnight, he replaced thirty of his bricklayers with Hutu RPF soldiers. Other RPF officers took up jobs as motorcycle taxi drivers, ferrying ex-FAR officers and exiled politicians around the province and collecting intelligence, or worked in the markets in the refugee camps. Bugera remembered one of his friends exclaiming in disbelief when she saw her brother, an officer in the Rwandan army, on TV posing as a trader in a refugee camp. "The RPF could tell you with topographical precision where all of their enemy's troops were located," he said with admiration. "It was like having GPS." By 1995, young Tutsi soldiers had started infiltrating Goma, armed with maps on which they drew ex-FAR positions and strategic targets. "It was like Mossad," Bugera said, smiling proudly. "These guys were good."

The RPF's daredevil efficiency was in stark contrast with the decay of the Zairian state. Bugera attended nightly meetings in the house of General Yangandawele Tembele, Mobutu's regional military commander, where he would receive information regarding troop movements and political developments. Tembele, whom a UN official remembered as "famous for being afraid of his own soldiers" and stealing cars from the refugees, had been bribed by the Rwandans and even provided Bugera with one of his lieutenants as a liaison officer, institutionalizing his treason.[10] In 1996, with Tembele's help, Bugera boarded a plane for Kinshasa, where he bought weapons and ammunition from corrupt officers. He packed the goods into a chest freezer, put dinner plates on top to conceal them, and wrote "Gen. Tembele, Goma," on the lid. The porters at the airport groaned under the weight, complaining: "What is in here, boss? Rocks?" Bugera laughed.

∾:∽

By 1995, Papy and his fellow Zairian soldiers in the RPF were getting restless. The arrival of refugees had led to a drastic escalation of the violence. Until then, there had been a fragile alliance between Hutu and Tutsi in Masisi, as both communities had immigrated there from Rwanda during the colonial period and faced similar discrimination. With the arrival of the ex-FAR, Zairian and Rwandan Hutu allied together against the Tutsi, in order to loot their thousands of head of cattle. Still, some Tutsi families were holding out in Goma and in clusters in the surrounding hills. "The decision to abandon the soil on which your father and mother are buried is not an easy one," Papy told me.

Based on the intelligence they were gleaning through their network of spies and moles, the RPF realized the ex-FAR were preparing a major attack.[11] In early 1996, Vice President Kagame gave orders to set up two camps in Rwanda's western provinces of Gisenyi and Cyangugu to regroup the Zairian Tutsi soldiers, including Papy, and train them as crack troops to form the vanguard of the impending invasion. "I had never seen so many soldiers in one place," he remembered. It was during the training that he learned that ex-FAR and local Hutu militias had attacked his hometown of Ngungu, in Southern Masisi.

"I was sitting around the camp in the evening, eating from a pot of plantains and beans with some other soldiers, when a friend of mine from Ngungu came up crying," he remembered. "'They attacked Ngungu, they attacked Ngungu,' was all he said. I knew my family had been butchered." Two of Papy's brothers and several cousins were among several dozen Tutsi who were killed.

Between 1995 and 1996, a total of 34,000 Tutsi fled to Rwanda from North Kivu. Barred by the RPF from owning radios, Papy and his friends gleaned bits and pieces of information about their families from refugees who managed to make it across the border.

~:~

I never knew what to make of Papy. He was friendly and open, but rarely laughed or showed much emotion. His voice was a steady monotone, his body lacking the gesticulations typical of many Congolese. "The war sucked the life out of me," he told me.

He told the story of the wars by way of scars on his body—a shiny splotch on the back of his head from a piece of Zimbabwean shrapnel in 1999, a long thick scar that bunched up the flesh on his lower thigh from an ex-FAR bullet in 1996. He lifted up his T-shirt to show me a welt on his ribcage where a bullet had perforated his lung. Still, he smoked. "I'm not going to live long anyway, no need talking to me about cancer."

Papy had left the army and come to Kinshasa looking for a job in 2007, even though many of his fellow Tutsi had refused to leave North Kivu and had continued to fight against the central government. Money and war fatigue had lured him out, he told me. When I asked him about his former comrades who remained rebels, he said, "We Tutsi have problems. We will do anything to protect our community, and it is true that many people want to destroy us. But there are also manipulators in the Tutsi community, who will use that fear in their own interest. 'Oh, we must fight or the Hutu will kill us! Oh, take up your guns or Kabila will exterminate us!' But you discover later that it isn't true. We can't spend the rest of our lives fearing other communities. We have to make that first step." Then he shook his head. "But the stupid thing is that the Congolese government doesn't seem to want us. There, too, there are opportunists who use the Tutsi threat to mobilize people. So we are stuck in the middle, between extremists."

~:~

It is amazing to what extent the ethnic stereotypes and conflicts that were born in Rwanda have contaminated the rest of the region. No other image plagues the Congolese imagination as much as that of the Tutsi aggressor. No other sentiment has justified as much violence in the Congo as anti-Tutsi ideology. Again and again, in the various waves of conflict in the Congo, the Tutsi community has taken center stage, as victims and killers. This antagonism is fueled by struggles over land tenure, citizenship, and access to resources, but also and most directly by popular prejudice and a vicious circle of revenge.

The wars that began in the eastern Congo in 1993 acted as a vector to these prejudices, as Tutsi soldiers and politicians took lead roles in every Rwandan-backed insurgency since then. Whereas previously anti-Tutsi resentment was a phenomenon limited to small areas of North and South Kivu, it has now spread across the region. Its expressions crop up everywhere, from pillow talk to bar banter to televised debates. When I first lived in Bukavu, in 2001, I spent a lot of time with a local family. The mother of the family, a soft-spoken twenty-seven-year-old who was studying development at a local university, was, like most of the town, bitterly opposed to what she called the "Tutsi occupation of the eastern Congo." It was in the middle of the war, and Bukavu and the surrounding areas were heavily militarized. It was difficult to avoid some sort of harassment—taxation, verbal abuse, torture, or worse—by Rwandan troops or their local allies. One day, when I was arguing that you had to understand Tutsi paranoia, as it had its roots in the massacre of up to 800,000 Tutsi in Rwanda during the genocide, she replied, "Eight hundred thousand? Obviously it wasn't enough. There are still some left."

In the meantime, the towns were bombarded by anonymous tracts, political one-pagers photocopied on cheap machines intended to rally the population against the Tutsi occupiers. They would be handed around in universities, at the markets, at the crowded port. One from October 2000 reads in part:

ATTENTION! ATTENTION! ATTENTION!

Population of South Kivu,
Following the barbarous crimes committed in KAVUMU, MAKOBOLA, BURHINYI, MWENGA and BUNYAKIRI, massacres against our peaceful population of Bukavu are already being prepared by KAGAME, MUSEVENI and BUYOYA. . . .

   History does not contradict us. The terrible atrocities committed shortly before the beginning of the 20th century by the Tutsi kings prove sufficiently to what extent you are descended from CAIN. Just imagine: A Tutsi king, every time he wanted to stand up, had to lean on a spear that was plunged into the leg of a Hutu subject. The point was very sharp and covered with poison. What cruelty!

THE STRUGGLE CONTINUES AND
THE VICTORY IS CERTAIN!
OUR CAUSE IS NOBLE:
PATRIOTISM AND SELF-DEFENSE![12]

These tracts tried to outdo each other in their extremism. The Congolese imagination, flailing around for clarity and trying to understand the violent upheaval the country has experienced, has latched onto the most basic building block of society: ethnicity. Instead of disabusing it of these stereotypes, successive leaders on both sides of the ethnic divide have only cynically fanned these flames.

6

MZEE

Laurent Kabila's presence is hard to miss in Kinshasa. In the middle of town, he towers as a forty-foot statue (thanks to North Korean sculptors, experts in state-sponsored hagiography), his finger pointing to the sky, admonishing the Congolese for straying from the path he had envisioned for the country. His head is mounted on countless billboards around the city, dressed in his characteristic collarless brown safari suit. His eyes are turned upwards, "to the dazzling future," according to supporters. In the center of the government neighborhood, ensconced in a marble mausoleum, his shiny grey coffin is on display, lined with garish fake flowers and ribbons. On many afternoons, schoolchildren in blue and white uniforms parade by, chattering irreverently, impervious to the irritable presidential guards with machine guns.

Despite his omnipresence, however, it is difficult to penetrate Kabila's myth. His real character has been shrouded by both vilification and idolatry. For some of his former comrades—those responsible for the statue, posters, and mausoleum—it was his perseverance that helped liberate the country first from Mobutu's dictatorship and then from Rwanda's control. For many others, Kabila's image morphed into a stereotype of African leaders: the thuggish, authoritarian "big man," willing to do anything to preserve his power, a mold cast by Jean-Bedel Bokassa and Idi Amin, the military strongmen of neighboring Central African Republic and Uganda, respectively.

~:~

Kabila had been a rebel since his youth in rural, pre-independence Congo. The son of a disciplinarian civil servant, Kabila distinguished himself as a precocious but difficult student. His father insisted on speaking French with his children at home, which left his son with the smooth, urbane accent of an *évolué*, an African accepted into the exclusive colonial clique. His schooling was often interrupted, probably as a result of the turbulence in the country as well as in his household, where his father's polygamy caused tensions with his mother. Before the age of ten, his parents separated, and he divided the rest of his youth between his mother's and father's houses. It is not clear whether he even finished high school, but according to childhood friends, he could often be found in public libraries in Lubumbashi, the capital of the southern, mineral-rich Katanga Province, his nose buried in books. French Enlightenment philosophers such as Descartes and Rousseau appear to have been favorites.[1]

According to the few accounts from that period, his blinkered ambition appeared at an early age. Despite a slight limp that he developed when he was a child, he earned himself the nickname Chuma (made of iron) for his strength. A friend's description of his behavior on the soccer pitch reminds the reader of future traits: "Laurent Kabila was very authoritarian. When he said you weren't playing, he wouldn't change his opinion. In soccer, we respected him because he didn't fool around. Kabila didn't accept defeat, he was resolute and determined, he was above us. We feared him."[2]

Kabila began his political career during the upheaval that rocked his home province of Katanga in 1960. The province harbored some of the richest mineral deposits in Africa, prompting Belgian businessmen to back a bid for secession of the province when the Congo became independent. The province, however, split in two when the north, dominated by Kabila's Lubakat tribe, rejected secession. It was one of the many uprisings that broke out across the country following independence, sparked by both Prime Minister Patrice Lumumba's assassination and local ethnic power blocs, now free from the shackles of a strong central state, that were trying to stake out their own interests. Kabila quickly immersed himself in this wave of violence, becoming a commander in a youth militia at the age of twenty.

Politics provided a feeling of purpose and belonging that he couldn't find in his sprawling family of nineteen siblings and half-siblings and at least five parents-in-law. The rebellion also pitted him against his father, the diligent colonial administrator. In late 1960, as Lubakat youths across the north of the province rebelled, they captured dozens of former colonial officers, including Kabila's father. The sixty-year-old was kidnapped, beaten, and finally lynched by the same militia that his son belonged to. When word of his father's death reached him, Kabila is said to have reacted calmly.

The young revolutionary spent the next years on the move, after South African and Belgian mercenaries put down the rebellion. He traveled as part of a socialist delegation to Moscow and then Belgrade, where, according to some, he briefly enrolled at the university. Finally, in January 1964, the leaders of the rebellion sent Kabila to Burundi to make contact with the Chinese government and to launch a rebellion in the highlands of the Kivus, close to the homeland of the Banyamulenge. There, commanders from the local community had been fighting against the government for several years, using bows and arrows, colonial-era Mausers, and a few AK-47s.

The rebels purported to be nationalists fighting against colonialism and the exploitation of their country's natural resources. Marxist ideology, however, was having a hard time grafting itself onto the Congolese insurgencies that proliferated across the country after independence. With over 80 percent of the population living off subsistence agriculture, and with a tiny, unpoliticized, and largely uneducated industrial labor force, the Congolese rebellions had little truck with Marxist arguments of surplus labor and the exploited proletariat. Most importantly, the kinds of urban and rural social networks that communism was able to mobilize elsewhere through labor unions and peasants' associations were largely nonexistent in the Congo. After conquering half of the country by early 1964, the rebel groups quickly fractured and succumbed to corruption and ill-discipline.

The Chinese were not the only ones to misjudge the strength of socialism. Che Guevara led an expedition to support Kabila's insurrection in the eastern Congo in 1965. Fidel Castro's government, newly in power, had immediately embarked on exporting their revolutionary and anti-imperialist ideology elsewhere. The Congo was an obvious target in many ways. Not only had the CIA helped in Lumumba's assassination, but the United States and South Africa had helped assemble a contingent of white mercenaries to put down the various rebellions that had seized almost half the country in 1964.

The mercenaries' racism and brutality, as described by an Italian journalist, further stoked Guevara's determination: "Occupying the town meant blowing

out the doors with rounds of bazooka fire, going into the shops and taking anything they wanted that was movable. . . . After the looting came the killing. The
shooting lasted for three days. Three days of executions, of lynching, of tortures,
of screams, and of terror."[3] Pictures of white mercenaries smoking cigarettes and
laughing, as behind them rebels' bodies dangled loosely from trees, filtered out,
although only an African American newspaper would print them.[4] An added
affront to Castro was the CIA's hiring of Cuban exile pilots to provide air support to the mercenaries.

Che took on the Congo campaign as a personal challenge. For him, it was
not just a matter of freeing the country from imperialists. "Our view was that
the Congo problem was a world problem," he wrote in his diary.[5] During a three-
month tour of Africa in early 1965, Che was pressed by other rebel movements
for support, but he kept on coming back to the Congo. "Victory [in the Congo]
would have repercussions throughout the continent, as would defeat," he wrote.
As he described an exchange he had with rebels from other countries, "I tried
to make them understand that the real issue was not the liberation of any given
state, but a common war against a common master."[6]

Nevertheless, Che's experience, as well as the insurrection, ended in disaster.
The beginning words of his Congo journal were: "This is the history of a failure."
Suffering from internal divisions, lack of organization, and little military expe-
rience, the rebel offensives against the national army fell apart amid numerous
Cuban and Congolese casualties. After seven months, Che was forced to with-
draw, sick and dejected, his feet swollen from malnutrition.

Throughout this period, Kabila proved himself a wily and sometimes ruthless politician, deftly riding the political currents around him. In the conclusion
of his diaries from that time, Guevara had mixed feelings about the Congolese
leader:

> The only man who has genuine qualities of a mass leader is, in my view,
> Kabila. The purest of revolutionaries cannot lead a revolution unless he
> has certain qualities of a leader, but a man who has qualities of a leader
> cannot, simply for that reason, carry a revolution forward. It is essential
> to have revolutionary seriousness, an ideology that can guide action, a
> spirit of sacrifice that accompanies one's actions. Up to now, Kabila has
> not shown that he possesses any of these qualities. . . . I have very great

doubts about his ability to overcome his defects in the environment in which he operates.[7]

⁓⁚⁓

Between Guevara's departure and Kabila's rebirth at the helm of the coalition that toppled Mobutu, there were three decades of obscurity. Kabila never stopped talking about the revolution, sporadically mobilizing fighters and making the rounds of regional embassies and government for support. But the élan of his early years had waned; the charismatic revolutionary had lost his shine and began to look more and more like a common bandit. The nadir was perhaps reached in 1975, when Kabila's forces snuck into Jane Goodall's chimpanzee research camp in western Tanzania and kidnapped four American and Dutch students. They subjected their captives to lectures on Marxism and Leninism while demanding a ransom of $500,000. This was the last straw for Tanzanian president Julius Nyerere, who had been tolerating the rebels out of disdain for Mobutu. At one point, he had complained to the Cuban ambassador about their behavior: He described their emissaries as "always drunk, with women, partying all the time, going frequently to Cairo."[8]

Back in the Congo, Kabila's activities were hardly more popular. In the late 1970s, Kabila tried to consolidate his power by launching a campaign against witch doctors, whom he considered a bad influence and a challenge to his rule. He ordered a strong herbal drink to be concocted, a sort of truth potion that would trigger dizziness and nausea in wizards. Of course, the herbs themselves were so strong that they elicited this response from almost anybody. According to eyewitnesses, hundreds of elderly men and women were tied to stakes and burned.[9]

With his prospects of rebellion dwindling and his reputation tarnished, Kabila retreated to Dar es Salaam, where he had good contacts with the Tanzanian intelligence service. They provided him with a house and a diplomatic passport and allowed him to take on a more laid-back lifestyle. He had a vintage typewriter, on which he would bang out letters to regional leaders and his commanders in the field. The few writings that remain from this time indicate his attempts to establish himself as a revolutionary intellectual, using ornate prose and Marxist jargon.

It was this role of political operative that he felt most comfortable in, traveling throughout the region, exaggerating his military exploits and prowess, writing letters to friendly leftist governments in Africa and abroad. He spent little time in the bush, preferring to hopscotch through the socialist world in search of support for his rebellion. He traveled to China for seven months and made visits to Cairo, Nairobi, and Belgrade.

At home, his family life was complicated by his fondness for women. He had affairs with his two live-in Congolese maids, Vumilia and Kessia, who "were promoted" to wives, and squabbles between them and his first wife, Sifa, sparked tensions in the household. In total, Kabila would have at least twenty-four children with six women, creating endless family intrigue and drama, especially after he became president. He had behaved similarly in the field. According to accounts that filtered out from his commanders, Kabila would resort to a Mobutist subterfuge, regularly sleeping with his commanders' wives as a display of power and humiliation.[10]

~:~

In the summer of 1995, Kabila's stars aligned. He was restless, following the BBC news broadcasts from Rwanda and eastern Zaire several times a day and pestering his friends in the Tanzanian intelligence service with phone calls about what they might know. No Congolese rebellion could ever succeed without outside help, he often told these friends. The last such support had come from the Chinese and the Cubans in the 1960s. Now it seemed that Rwanda and others were gearing up to make the push.

Then, one afternoon, the Rwandan intelligence chief, Patrick Karegeya, turned up at Kabila's house in the leafy Oyster Bay neighborhood of Dar es Salaam in the company of several Tanzanian officials. The veteran Congolese rebel was in a talkative mood, his spirits lifted by the possibility of renewed support. He explained that he still had several thousand troops he could mobilize in the Fizi area of South Kivu. "He was just happy that somebody was visiting him and asking him about his ideas," Karegeya remembered. The aging rebel, perhaps thinking he was speaking to someone from the same bloodline, invoked his anti-imperialist struggle and lambasted Mobutu's links to the west. He dug among his chest of papers to come up with some of his revolutionary pamphlets, and he even talked military strategy, proposing flanking maneuvers of the refugee camps and tactical feints.

To Karegeya, who, like most of his RPF colleagues, had by then endorsed the maxims of free-market capitalism, the "old man seemed like a relic of the past." Kabila didn't convince Karegeya, but then again, "we weren't looking for a rebel leader. We just needed someone to make the whole operation look Congolese."

Karegeya later sent emissaries to Fizi to find Kabila's rebels. His men spent weeks climbing mountains and trekking through forests on promises by their guides that the following day the rebels would appear. After several months, they gave up. And yet Karegeya persisted with Kabila. Many Congolese, especially those close to veteran opposition leader Etienne Tshisekedi, now accuse Rwanda of having deliberately chosen a weak and marginal figure in order to manipulate him. The Rwandan government did, however, try to reach out to other leaders, including Tshisekedi, without much luck.[11]

Karegeya laughed at me when I questioned their choice of a rebel leader. "You act like we had a lot of options! By 1996, Mobutu had co-opted or locked up almost all of his opposition, with the possible exception of Tshisekedi. Kabila might have been old-school, but he had not been bought off. We gave him some credit for that."

~:~

Kabila arrived in the Rwandan capital, Kigali, from Dar es Salaam in July 1996 with almost nothing. He shacked up in a safe house in the affluent Kiyovu neighborhood of downtown Kigali, with a couple of suitcases. His only companions were his son, Joseph Kabila, who followed him everywhere, and several of his old rebel commanders, who "came in and out of the house, looking like janitors who had lost their brooms," as one Rwandan officer commented.

The Rwandans had picked four strange bedfellows to lead the rebellion. Besides Kabila, there was Deo Bugera, the architect from North Kivu; Andre Kisase Ngandu, a bearded and aging commander who was leading a rebellion in the Ruwenzori Mountains, on Congo's border with Uganda, and like Kabila traced his roots back to the rebellions of the 1960s, although he at least could still count several hundred active rebels under his command; and Anselme Masasu, a taciturn twenty-some-year-old from Bukavu who had a Rwandan mother and at the time was a sergeant in the Rwandan army. Years later, Bugera laughed when he heard Masasu's name. "You know he ended up being a popular commander, very popular. But then, he was a kid! They said he had a political party, but he was the only member in it."

Bugera remembered his first meeting with Kabila: "He was wearing sandals and one of those safari suits. He had uncut, blackened—I tell you, blackened!—toenails that stuck out over the end of his sandals. What a strange man, I thought! He didn't look you in the eyes when he talked." Bugera, who seemed privately to have hoped to become the rebellion's leader, had heard about Kabila in the 1980s but nothing about him since then. According to Bugera, Kabila was so cash-strapped that Bugera bought him some shoes and a safari suit at the local market.

These four men—two overhauled, aging guerrilla commanders, a twenty-something sergeant, and an architect—were meant to lift the Congo up out of its political morass.

∼:∼

In Kigali, the Rwandans embarked on some much-needed bonding exercises with their newly recruited rebel leaders.

"The Rwandans are weird," Bugera said. "They made us stay in a house together for three or four whole days, sleeping there, eating there, and preparing the war. They wanted us to become a team."

It must have been a strange few days. Bugera remembered Kabila as a largely silent man, listening to and observing his new comrades. Like an outmoded professor, Kabila distributed green pamphlets printed on cheap paper with his seven lessons of revolutionary ideology. Masasu skulked about in his neatly pressed fatigues, speaking mostly with the Rwandan officers who came in and out of the house, and keeping his distance from the two rebels thirty years his senior. Bugera huddled with other Tutsi leaders, who muttered bitterly about Kabila's massacres of Banyamulenge in the 1960s. The alliance had gotten off to a shaky start.

After several days, they finally came up with the one-page founding document the Rwandans had asked them to draft. They shared it with Colonel James Kabarebe, the commander of the Rwandan presidential guard who was preparing the Congo mission. He helped them polish it and added a Congolese dateline to mask Rwanda's involvement in their movement; the paper became known as the Lemera Agreement.[12] Kabila's outdated verbosity shines through the text: It speaks of the "imperious necessity" for their four political parties to come together to liberate Zaire and names Laurent Kabila as their spokesman. It laments the economic situation, marked by "doldrums, financial muddle, corruption and the destruction of the means of production."

The four leaders met three times with Vice President Kagame, who was constantly involved in the war preparations and seemed well-informed of the complexities of Congolese politics. The RPF strongman seemed more enthusiastic about the rebellion than the leaders themselves, exhorting the Congolese to understand their responsibilities in the struggle, but also to understand that the RPF and others were helping them liberate their country. He said, "If we win the war, we will all win! It's *our* victory!"

~:~

Thus was born the Alliance of Democratic Forces for the Liberation of Congo-Zaire (AFDL). A grandiose name for a group that initially had little political or military significance other than providing a smoke screen for Rwandan and Ugandan involvement.

At the beginning, Kabila felt awkward and marginalized. He had worked with Tutsi rebels in the 1960s, when some had fled the pogroms in Rwanda into the Congo, but he had not been in touch with this new, younger, cosmopolitan generation of rebels. They worked with laptop computers and satellite phones and organized their soldiers on the model of the British army. Even their marching style was different, he noticed.

He also felt a sense of entitlement. After all, he was at least twenty years older than the Rwandan officers milling about; he had been a guerrilla leader in the Congo when they were still in diapers.

Kabila was also smarter than most gave him credit for. He realized there was little he could do at the moment other than bide his time and try to position himself. After all, the Rwandans' ambitions were initially strictly military, and they had given little thought to the government they would set up once they controlled the conquered territory. Given Kabila's seniority, the Rwandans allowed him to become the movement's spokesperson and to begin setting up a political directorate for it.

He got his hands on a satellite phone himself and began calling members of the Congolese diaspora whom he had worked with in the past. Without his own soldiers on the battlefield, he would need to rally loyal advisors around him. He contacted one of his former comrades from the 1960s, who was a nightclub owner in Madrid. Another one was a lawyer in Belgium, while a third had been with him in Tanzania. As the rebellion became more visible, and Kabila began making appearances on radio and television, other diaspora figures contacted him, and his political clout grew.

Laurent Kabila emerged as an accidental leader of the AFDL movement and eventually as the president of a liberated Congo. In an example of Rwandan hubris, the RPF planners desperately tried to foist ideology and sincerity upon the Congolese they had handpicked. As ingenious as Kagame's military planners were, their political strategy ended up being simplistic and short-sighted. For many Congolese who had labored long—and ultimately unsuccessfully—to overthrow Mobutu peacefully, Kabila was a living symbol of foreign meddling in their country. It is one of the Congo's historical ironies that the same man came to be seen as a bulwark of patriotism and resistance against Rwandan aggression.

PART II

THE FIRST WAR

MANY WARS IN ONE

On August 30, 1996, the first battle of the Zaire war took place. Leaving their training camps in Rwanda, a small group of seventy Banyamulenge soldiers crossed the river into Zaire just south of the customs post where Burundi, Zaire, and Rwanda meet. It hadn't rained in weeks—the short dry season was the perfect time to launch the assault, as the roads were in decent shape—and the group made its way quietly through the waist-high elephant grass. On the other side of the plains, they could see the outline of the Itombwe Mountains rising into the clouds, cradling the highland pastures where they had grown up.

At dawn, they hid in a banana grove close to the small village of Kiringye. As they were resting, a woman on her way to farm her cassava field stumbled into their makeshift camp and began screaming at the sight of Tutsi soldiers armed to the teeth with Kalashnikovs and rocket launchers. They were tempted to kill her, but then let her go. She ran to the nearby military base, where she alerted Mobutu's army. They surrounded the rebels and opened fire, killing ten and capturing five others. It was one of the few battles of the war that Mobutu would win. The war, still at the planning stage in Kigali, had been jump-started.[1]

The army's ambush accelerated the spiral into outright conflict. The captured soldiers were paraded in front of television screens across the country. Five haggard-looking young men in military uniforms were placed under spotlights, with camera flashes illuminating their sunken eyes. This was the enemy. For many Zairians, it was the first time they put the Tutsi name to their distinctive features. "Rwanda invades!" read the September 1 headline in *Le Potentiel*, Kinshasa's most read daily newspaper.

In Bukavu, the state radio read out an editorial titled "A Historic Chance for Zaire." The broadcaster exhorted listeners not to believe the Tutsi's lies about citizenship, using a metaphor that has since become routine when arguing that the Banyamulenge can never become Zairian: "A tree trunk does not turn itself into a crocodile because it has spent some time in the water. In the same way, a Tutsi will forever remain a Tutsi, with his or her perfidy, craftiness and dishonesty."[2]

By now, it was obvious that more and more Banyamulenge troops were infiltrating into the high plateau, where the rebels began stockpiling weapons and preparing for another attack. Farmers and traders hid in the bushes by the side of mountain paths, as bands of rebels with metal boxes of ammunition on their heads climbed up the mountainside. A movement in the other direction was also visible: More and more Banyamulenge youths began crossing the Rusizi River into Burundi at night, where they were met by guides who would take them to training camps in Rwanda.

～:～

Most Congolese refer to the 1996 invasion as the War of Liberation. The population had had enough of Mobutu; despite the suspicions regarding Rwanda's involvement, crowds across the country welcomed the rebels as liberators. At the local level, however, this image of heroic patriots does not hold water. In the east, the advancing rebels became embroiled in bitter feuds between communities over power, land, and identity. Anti-Tutsi demagogues whipped up mobs to kill innocent civilians; the Banyamulenge rebels retaliated, blaming entire communities for their victimization. Thousands were killed.

A prime example of this was Anzuluni Bembe, the vice president of Zaire's national assembly, who had created a youth militia called, modestly, Group to Support Anzuluni Bembe. The short, pudgy firebrand held rallies along the shores of Lake Tanganyika, calling on people to take up arms against the invaders. At a meeting at a local school in Fizi, he called out: "Children of Fizi, are you sleeping? The Banyamulenge are taking our country! I want you to get weapons and attack them, attack the Banyamulenge!"[3]

In Uvira, Banyamulenge leaders were rounded up and put in jail, while the mayor mustered gangs of youths to kick their families out of their houses. Several days after the first clashes with the infiltrators, local authorities told the

Banyamulenge to regroup in camps "for their own safety." A local Banyamulenge leader later wrote about the experience of being arrested: "They beat us up and took us to jail. . . . Minute after minute, they brought in more Banyamulenge in that minuscule cell where there was a hellish stench due to the urine and feces and no oxygen. [Several days later] they took out the late Rukenurwa who they beat like a snake. His sobs made us all cry."[4]

Hundreds of Tutsi in eastern Zaire, but also in Kinshasa and Lubumbashi, were harassed and beaten. The hysteria reached a fever pitch, in which anyone who had a thinnish, hooked nose and high cheekbones was targeted. At a border post with Rwanda, youths attacked and hacked to death a Malian businessman.[5]

By 1996, social conditions in Zaire were ripe for youth-led violence. Due to Mobutu's predation and disastrous economic policies, the country's infrastructure and industry had collapsed. By 1996, the country had been through seven years of economic contraction. Zairians earned just over half of what they had been making in 1990. According to the United Nations, a full 27 million people, or 60 percent of the population, were undernourished. Even when people were paid, the money was worth little: Inflation soared to 5,000 percent in 1996.

This misery provided fertile terrain for ethnic prejudice. In the crowds, youths were able to channel their anger against a visible, known enemy. Leaders like Anzuluni provided added incentives, such as free alcohol and modest wages for some of their organizers. The Banyamulenge, while poor, had attractive and inflation-free assets: cows. Soldiers and youths rustled thousands of head of cattle in the early days of the war.

~:~

How can we explain this kind of brutality? It is difficult to describe the impact of abuse and dysfunctional government on the psyche of people in war-torn areas.

In March 2008, I traveled to various massacre sites in the region. Everywhere I stopped, people eyed me suspiciously, and local officials demanded to see my papers. Even though the war had officially come to an end years earlier, the region was still very tense; Rwanda and the Congo continued to fight a proxy war in the Kivus, each supporting different militia groups.

One morning, I was packing to leave for Makobola, perhaps the most notorious massacre site, when a friend from a local human rights group called me on my cell phone.

"Stop packing and turn on the radio," he said.

I quickly tuned into a debate show on a local Protestant radio station to hear the member of a local political party say, "I wanted to draw your attention to President George Bush's visit to Rwanda." Bush was visiting Kigali as part of his whirlwind Africa tour. "Is it a coincidence that his visit comes at the same time as Nkunda withdraws from the peace process? At the same time as there is an American mercenary by the name of Johnson who is here in Bukavu, recruiting youths for the next Rwandan invasion?" He got my name wrong, but it was clear by his following description that he meant me. He said he had proof of my activity and that he would provide it.

Friends in local civil society helped debunk this rumor, and the analyst retracted his allegations. Nevertheless, I needed a good justification to prevent harassment in the remote areas. A nonprofit group agreed to provide me with a "mission order," a hangover from the colonial era confirming that your employer takes responsibility for the trip. Local officials saw the piece of paper, with its letterhead and stamp, as a possible indication that I was not, as some apparently believed, working for the CIA.

I had taken a second, more important, precaution: I traveled with Remy Ngabo, a local human rights activist who was from the area and who organized interethnic soccer games as a way of reconciling youths from the Bembe and Banyamulenge communities. Once a month, the Banyamulenge players would walk five hours down the mountain to face off with a local Bembe team. The players paired up and spent the night at their rivals' houses. Some of the Banyamulenge players were survivors of the 1996 massacres, and Remy hoped they would open up and tell their story.

᪑

Our plans were cut short before the soccer game could start. Alerted by the presence of a foreigner in her small village, the local intelligence official arrested me and Remy for suspicious behavior.

"Don't you know it's International Women's Day today and I had to abandon my important activities in town to come climbing hills, running after you?" The woman huffed, leading us to her office, a bench under a mango tree. "All activities here have to be approved by me!" She chided us as we slalomed down through cassava fields.

In negotiating bribes, the local official's main leverage is time. Prudence, as her name turned out to be, had no real reason to detain us, other than the fact that she was in charge of security in town. With nothing on her hands—except, apparently, a Women's Day celebration—she could easily wait us out. Back in town, she sat us down underneath a mango tree and subjected us to a long lecture on the Rwandan threat and the superpower conspiracy against the Congo.

"You yourself say you are from the United States," she glared at me. "Is it not the United States who supported Rwanda during the war to get at our mineral wealth? Don't think just because we are black that we haven't studied! Well—say something, speak!" She was clearly infuriated by my silence, which she interpreted as condescension. "Didn't you hear that George Bush was in Rwanda the other day?" she said to her colleague, who nodded his head. "We have to be vigilant!" I feebly pointed out that I didn't work for the U.S. government and showed her my documentation. "That's what you say!" she retorted.

We had almost agreed on "a fine" or "a recompense for her hike"—the two different euphemisms for the bribe—of around five dollars, when a local village chief turned up.

As he came to shake my hand, I could feel the fetid smell of the local alcohol on his breath. His eyes were glazed over and specks of spittle hit my face as he spoke. *Kotiko*, as it is called in this area, is a palm wine that is tapped from the trunk of a decapitated tree in the morning and grows stronger as the day goes on and the sugars are fermented into alcohol. Although it was only eleven o'clock, much of the village was already falling under *kotiko's* sway.

"*Hapana, hapana*," he slurred in Swahili, shaking his head. No, no, no. "What is this white man doing here? Don't you know that I'm the chief here? Why are you talking to this woman?!" The situation got worse. "Haven't you heard that Bush was in Kigali last week? Is this a coincidence?" The chief played with his digital watch, which was much too large for his boney wrist and had apparently stopped working a long time ago. "And just after the earthquake destroyed our towns!" Bukavu lay close to a continental rift and had been hit by a series of bad earthquakes several weeks before. The chief leaned over and whispered: "The United States is using earthquakes as a weapon of war to destabilize the province!"

～:～

An hour later and around twenty dollars lighter, we finally found ourselves in front of two soccer teams on benches in front of a school. Our run-in with the authorities had attracted attention, and our meeting was being attended by several people whom Remy identified as intelligence agents. It was obviously not the venue for the Banyamulenge, lined up on one bench across from us, to tell their stories of massacres and abuse at the hands of their neighbors. Remy deftly changed the angle, announcing that I had come to inspect the success of his soccer project in promoting reconciliation. He whispered to me: "Take it easy with the questions."

After several platitudes about ethnic reconciliation, I asked the Bembe soccer team what they felt when they saw a Munyamulenge (singular of Banyamulenge) on the street. The captain of their team answered, "We are afraid. During the war, we didn't know who is a civilian and who is a soldier. For us, every Tutsi man was a soldier. Whenever violence broke out, they pulled the guns out from underneath the beds."

Alex, a Munyamulenge boy in an Arsenal T-shirt and jeans, demurred: "I don't know why we have to inherit the sins of our fathers and brothers. For them, we are all guilty." He paused, then added, "We are all targets."[6]

I asked Alex whether he had heard of the massacres committed by Rwandan or Banyamulenge soldiers against the Bembe in the region. He nodded carefully, glancing at the eavesdroppers. "Of course, we all hear these allegations."

"Do you think they are true?" I prodded.

He paused. "I wasn't there. I don't know."

His answer provoked some rumbling on the other bench. "These are not just rumors," the one with the Tanzanian accent said. "We all have family members who have been killed or raped by Banyamulenge."

"Have *you* heard of massacres committed *against* the Banyamulenge?" I asked the captain.

"Against them?" He looked around at his teammates, who shook their heads. "No, we've never heard about that."

~:~

After the meeting, Remy offered to drive the Banyamulenge back to the road-block, from where the path leads into the mountains. He politely but firmly told the village chief and the intelligence agent that we didn't have enough room for them in our car. The Banyamulenge piled seven-deep into the backseat and trunk of our jeep.

"Our problem is with leadership," Remy said in the car. "Imagine that we were CIA agents trying to start a new rebellion here. We would have bought them all off for twenty dollars."

Remy found an excuse to stop along the way to buy some drinks for the players, leaving me in the car with Alex. From the backseat, squeezed in between his teammates, in a whisper, Alex told me that he was twenty-five, which made him around thirteen at the time the war began. Several teenagers pressed their faces against the jeep's windowpanes, giggling at the sight of a white man talking to the Munyamulenge, but Alex continued in a steady tone, his eyes focused on the dashboard in front of me. I didn't want the villagers outside the car to overhear our conversation, so I rolled up the windows, which soon had both of us sweating in the midday heat, as the car didn't have air conditioning. Alex started off by telling me not about himself or his family, but about Mariam Kinyamarura.

Mariam was a famous Christian prophet, a legend in the Banyamulenge community and an unlikely casualty of the war. Mariam, Alex explained, had grown up as a young Munyamulenge peasant in a small village one day's walk into the hills from where we had parked the car. In 1956, when she was still a young woman, she fell sick and lost the function of her lower body. She nonetheless stayed married to her husband and later gave birth to several children. Shortly afterwards, she started having visions. She was a member of the Methodist Church but had not felt a particular religious vocation before her paralysis. Soon, her visitors began telling stories. She could read your mind, tell you what you were thinking, and even recount your sins. Before you even arrived at the house, she would know who you were and what you were thinking. The Methodist Church, worried about superstition in their midst, put her under observation. After a month, they proclaimed that she was indeed an oracle and asked several ministers to live with and assist her.

"She would lie in her bed all day, her head propped up against her hand," Alex said. His parents had visited her, taking him along once when he was a child. He remembered her magical aura and the people milling around in a small, dark room to hear her speak. By the mid-1970s, the church had built a center around Mariam, complete with guesthouses, gardens, and a small chicken farm. At times, hundreds of visitors from all across the region and from all ethnic groups would visit to hear her prophecies and advice.

As with everything in the eastern Congo, it is difficult to separate Mariam's myth from reality. Sometime in the late 1970s, she is said to have stopped eating, drinking, and passing waste. She also stopped sleeping, a fact that Alex testified to, as his parents stayed up all night talking to her while Alex slept on a banana-leaf mat on the floor.

In 1996, when the provincial authorities began calling for the Banyamulenge to return to Rwanda, the Methodist Church asked Mariam's followers, most of whom lived in the highlands, to come down to the lakeside for protection, thinking that together they would be safe. As they were deliberating what to do, Zairian soldiers rounded up Alex's family in their clay house in the mountains at dawn, before they had left to take the cows to the pasture.

"They told us they were taking us to Rwanda," Alex remembered. They weren't given time to pack their belongings and had to leave with bare essentials: a gourd of cow milk that Alex carried on his head, a bag of clothes, their family Bible.

He left with his parents and seven siblings, joining a caravan of around five hundred Banyamulenge, escorted by soldiers down to Lake Tanganyika. On September 17, they arrived at a small, makeshift camp in a town called Lweba. They were told a boat would pick them up the next day and take them "home," to Rwanda. Alex had never been to Rwanda and didn't have any family there. He remembered feeling very hungry. They had run out of food on the road and slept without eating dinner, drinking muddy water from the lake.

At 3 o'clock at night, shots began ringing out in the camp. "I think they wanted to get rid of us before the boat came," Alex said matter-of-factly. "They never wanted us to reach Rwanda." There was almost no moon, and they hadn't brought a flashlight. Alex remembered people screaming and running. A body fell against their shelter, and his father made them all hold hands and pray. The body just lay there, like a fallen branch, against their tight tarp. Even if they had run, they wouldn't have known where to go—better to stay and confront whatever was going to happen together. So they prayed, raising their voices above the screams. "Outside, in the light of lanterns we could see the other villagers watching. Some took part in the killing. Others just watched. But nobody did anything to help us."

According to Alex, a total of 153 people were killed that night.[7] Alex's immediate family was fortunate. They all survived. Similar massacres took place along the lakeshore that day. In Baraka, fourteen miles to the south, several hundred Banyamulenge were forced into the compound of a cotton factory and attacked. Remy's daughter, who was ten at the time, remembered people running after Banyamulenge in the streets, armed with knives and machetes, hacking them as they ran: "She still has nightmares about this."

The Prophetess Mariam was not spared. That same night, in her own village not far away, she and her followers were rounded up and separated into two groups: men and women. Setting upon the men with sticks, stones, and machetes, the mob killed most of them, including Mariam's disciples and relatives. The crowd then began to attack the women and children, but some of Mariam's Bembe followers implored them not to kill her. She escaped, badly wounded. "She said that she was not meant to die in the Congo; she had had this prophecy," Alex shook his head. "They killed most of her children and her husband. She was right: She didn't die of her wounds until she reached Rwanda."

I asked Alex where the bodies of the Banyamulenge were buried, and he shook his head again. "Who knows? They didn't give us time to bury our dead." He had heard that Mariam had a tomb in Rwanda, but he didn't know where it was. His voice cracked slightly, and he looked at his feet. "We don't even have tombs to go and mourn our dead, we carry the grief around with us."

Reluctantly, Alex circled back to his own story. The following day a long ship with an outboard motor pulled into the harbor and took the remaining Banyamulenge along the lake toward Rwanda. There was no awning on deck, and the sun beat down heavily for the four-hour journey. That night, they arrived at Mboko, a small fishing village with a long, white sand beach. At dawn, Mobutu's soldiers separated the men from the women and children. "We didn't understand," Alex said. "If they wanted to kill us, why did they give it to us bit by bit? Kill one person at a time? Why not just do it all at once?" The soldiers loaded their guns and shouted that all men over the age of fourteen had to come to one side.

As a tall thirteen-year-old, Alex was a borderline case. Picking him out of a lineup, where he was standing next to his brother, a soldier took pity on him and pushed him brusquely toward where his mother and sisters were waiting, knotting their skirts up between their fingers. They watched together as his father and older brother were bound with sisal ropes, their arms tied behind their back and their legs together. The soldiers dumped them "like sacks of cassava" into the boat, which they then paddled out into the lake. It was a big vessel; Alex estimated there to be around thirty or forty captives onboard. At around two hundred meters from shore, still within sight of their frantic families, the men were thrown into the water. Alex could see splashes of water where the men flopped and struggled in vain to keep their heads above water before they drowned. Some managed to keep afloat by wiggling their bodies for several minutes. On the beach, their families screamed out and cried but couldn't do anything. His mother fainted. The soldiers watched, their rifles on their shoulders.

The remaining group of children and women was taken to Kamanyola, on the border with Rwanda, where they joined up with hundreds of other Banyamulenge. The military escort brought five to six hundred "refugees" in trucks to the border. They were joined by thirty haggard Banyamulenge leaders, who had spent the past month in prison in Uvira. At dusk, once again the women and children were separated from the men and taken to a thirty-meter-long cement bridge that separated the two countries. The Rwandan Patriotic Army (the armed wing of the RPF) had deployed its troops to the iron gate that blocked the road, and the women and children ran toward the silhouettes of soldiers and tanks.

Alex was less fortunate this time; after a brief debate over his age, a soldier tousled his unkempt hair and kept him on the Zairian side of the border with the other men. They were pushed into a makeshift prison close to the border, where they were strip searched and beaten again. Around forty men pressed together in a small room, some beaten so badly that they couldn't walk. A youth who looked feverish and faint asked a soldier for some water to drink. The soldier shook his head in disgust, telling him he was being disrespectful. He yanked him outside, leveled his AK-47, and, as Alex watched in horror, blew his brains out.

The heat in the small room became unbearable. The air was getting heavy; in the distance they could hear a thunderstorm moving down the floodplain from Rwanda. The storms from the east were the worst; Congolese used to quip that "all bad things come from Rwanda."

The soldiers had left a light guard, including a young intelligence officer from Mobutu's home region in Equateur Province who had become friends with many Banyamulenge in Uvira. As the storm approached, he whispered to the prisoners that they would be shot at dawn; this was their only chance. Alex remembered the thunder cracking over them, unleashing a torrential downpour. "It was a miracle," he said. "We had never seen anything like it." The guards outside the houses sought shelter, and the Equateurian youth popped the bolt on the door, ushering them out and telling them to hurry and get to the border. "The rain was so heavy you couldn't even see the road in front of you," Alex remembered. Seeing their prisoners flee, the Zairian soldiers ran out in pursuit.

At the border, the Rwandan guards saw the commotion and advanced toward the bridge, over the border, guns at ready. Through the rain, the Zairian soldiers saw a phalanx of hostile troops blocking the road and retreated. Back at the prison, they found the prisoners who had been too weak to flee, including the president of the Banyamulenge community, and killed them.[8]

~:~

After the sweaty car meeting with Alex, Remy and I continued on to Baraka, a humid port town on the shores of Lake Tanganyika. I wanted to hear the other side of the story. Remy had told me that the massacre that Alex had lived through had been triggered when Banyamulenge infiltrators had killed a large group of people in a nearby village. Could we find some witnesses of that massacre?

Remy hit himself on his forehead. "Ah! Of course," he sucked his teeth loudly. "How could I forget? We have to go and see Malkia wa Ubembe." When I told him I had never heard of that name, a smile twitched across his lips, "No? Well, you should have. He's the physical reincarnation of Jesus Christ."

Religion is alive and well in the Congo. Colonialism and Mobutism eroded traditional authority and created uncertainty in everyday life. Various churches vigorously proselytized in the Congo throughout the nineteenth and twentieth centuries; white missionaries still abound in remote corners of the country, puttering about in battered Land Rovers, fluently bantering in the local language or dialect.

Malkia wa Ubembe is a different kind of church, a small utopian movement that shies away from politics. Its head and spiritual center is Prophet Wahi Seleelwa, a bouncy fifty-year-old man who founded the church in 1983. The name of the church means "the queen of the Bembe," the ethnic group that the prophet belongs to. Years before, a prophecy had gone out from members of the Catholic Church that a virgin saint would arise among the Bembe. Instead of a virgin girl, they got Wahi Seleelwa.

We drove into his compound late on a Friday afternoon, as the sun was going down through the palm trees that sprout everywhere in Baraka's sandy soil. The community's villages are identical to each other, each built after a common blueprint. Matching houses, made out of mud bricks and then whitewashed, line a long avenue that leads up to the prophet's house, which forms the center of the community. Behind the houses, communal vegetable plots stretch out into the surrounding palms.

The Prophet, as Wahi Seleelwa likes to be called, greeted us on the steps of his house wearing a white T-shirt with an imprint of his own picture and a black felt Stetson hat. Three large glass doors took up the front of the house, set into whitewashed walls and underneath a corrugated iron roof. The house seemed very open; in contrast with most buildings in the region, there were no bars on the windows or doors.

The prophet formed the physical and spiritual center of the community. Their founding belief is that Wahi Seleelwa is the reincarnation of Jesus Christ, a distinction he inherited from his predecessor. As Seleelwa explained, after the death of their previous leader, whose picture hung on the wall behind him as he spoke to us, he was possessed by the spirit of Christ. Over the following years, he received the revelations of Christ, which his followers wrote down in their drably named "Communication Notebook," which contains the main teachings of the church. Some of the passages would raise eyebrows among mainstream Christians: They allow polygamy (the prophet has three wives), have their own calendar with twelve-day months, and are governed by a conclave of elders dubbed the Four Living Beings.

Seleelwa was eager to speak with us about the beginning of the war. "Nobody has ever come to hear our story," he lamented. "Not the United Nations, not our own government, nobody." He pulled out sheaths of handwritten letters he had sent to various presidents and UN secretaries-general. "Nobody ever answers," he said, shaking the papers.

On the wall behind him hung a black-and-white picture of a group of people posing together in front of a white church with thatched roofing. In the middle of the group of around sixty people is a smiling Seleelwa, his Stetson hat tipped backwards, looking like a halo; many other men are also wearing the hats, a sign of "the coming kingdom," Seleelwa said. Children make up around half the congregation, kneeling and peering sullenly into the camera from the bottom of the picture.

"Of all the members of that church there," he said, pointing at the picture, "only a dozen survived. I'll show you the survivors." Seleelwa called for an assistant and gave him the names of several people.

There was no doubt that Seleelwa commanded respect from his congregation. Minutes later, we heard the voices of a dozen people milling around on the steps outside. Three males and eight females, some of them still children, had gathered to talk to us. The prophet grinned: "Here they are!"

The leader of the group was a forty-eight-year-old man called Neno Lundila. He was wearing an oversized green blazer and felt hat that was considerably shabbier than Seleelwa's.

∾

Neno's church had been located in Abala, a town in the foothills of the Itombwe Mountains, a two-day walk away. It was a corn- and cassava-farming village inhabited mostly by Bembe who had moved down to the main road that linked the lakeshore with the high plateau. Before the war, Banyamulenge had sent their children to primary school in Abala, and the lively trade had brought the two communities together in markets, churches, weddings, and funerals.

By the end of October 1996, the war that had begun two months before had reached Abala. Ragtag local militias skirmished with Banyamulenge troops, who advanced steadily down the road toward Baraka, prompting a mass exodus of the local population. In Abala, the entire village fled, except for the Malkia wa Ubembe congregation. "We weren't involved in politics," Neno said. "We were preaching the good word, nothing else. Why leave?"

On October 28, the congregation gathered in their church for morning prayers. As usual, they brought their whole families with them. The aisles were more crammed than usual that morning. "The troubled situation had given us good reason to pray," Neno recalled. After an hour, just before dawn, as they were singing the last song—"We will not run, we will not be afraid, we are with Prophet"—they saw soldiers surround the church. Their preacher told them to stop singing and went outside to talk to the soldiers. Through the windows, in the half-light, Neno could see the features of a Munyamulenge who had grown up just two hours away from Abala and was well-known to the community as a courteous, polite man. That day, however, he was aggressive.

"Why didn't you leave, like everybody else?" he barked at the preacher.

"We are people of God," Neno remembered the preacher saying. "We didn't have anywhere to go."

"Then you have to come away with us!"

The preacher refused, saying they didn't know anybody where the Banyamulenge lived and didn't have a church there.

The commander lost patience. Words were exchanged, and a scuffle ensued. Through the narrow window, Neno saw another soldier pull out his rifle, shove it into the preacher's nostril, and pull the trigger. In the church, people started screaming as the soldiers advanced on the doors and windows and opened fire. A grenade hit the ground not far from where Neno was, ripping into several people's bodies. Women took babies off their backs and huddled over them, praying. They tried to hide between the benches and under the altar, and Neno felt bodies falling on top of him. "They saved my life: I felt bullets going into their bodies; they shielded me." After several minutes, the soldiers stopped shooting. Neno could hear them debating outside. Then, the sound of tinder crackling broke the silence. "It was still dark outside, but all of a sudden there was a bright light I could see between the bodies."

The soldiers had set fire to the thatched roof, in order to kill survivors and get rid of evidence. When Neno heard the soldiers say, "Let's go," he climbed out from underneath the bodies. The whole roof was on fire, and clumps of burning thatch and crossbeams were falling down. Neno managed to drag himself and seventeen other survivors out of the burning church. A hundred and three others died, including Neno's two wives and six children.

We went back outside to the front steps, where the other survivors were still sitting. The women were sullen but hitched up their worn *kikwembe* to show me their wounds. One of the girls, now around seventeen, had grabbed her baby brother and put him on her back to try to flee when a bullet went through both of them. Twelve years later, she has a shiny welt on her lower back, matching his scar across his stomach. "They are tied together by their injury," Seleelwa told me. Blushing, the girl pulled up her T-shirt to show me. Another girl had had her leg amputated.

"The other bodies are still there, buried under the collapsed church," Neno told me as we got ready to leave. "Nobody has even so much as put a memorial plaque there. You can still see the charred remains." He shook his head. "We have nowhere to mourn our dead."

I asked him if he had ever heard of Banyamulenge who had been massacred. He looked surprised. "Banyamulenge? No. Never."[9]

~:~

It was not just in South Kivu that the war brought calamity. Throughout the country, the invading forces pillaged. The killing, however, was largely confined to the east, where the Tutsi communities had long-standing quarrels with other groups. In North Kivu, the invading Rwandan troops systematically rounded up and killed thousands of Hutu villagers, accusing them of supporting the *géno-cidaires*. Many prominent Hutu businessmen and traditional chiefs were also killed. Tutsi communities, of course, nurse their own memories of persecution and decimation at the hands of others.

None of the killings has led to prosecutions or even a truth commission that could ease the heavy burden of the past. Skeletons can still be found, stuffed into septic tanks, water cisterns, and toilets, reminders of the various tragedies. In Bukavu, mass graves dating back to this period are now covered with the cement of shopping centers. Every new bout of violence summons these spirits up and manipulates the past into a story of victimization, ignoring the wounds of the other communities. Peace, many diplomats and locals say, is more important than justice, especially when the government is full of yesterday's military leaders. Prosecute those leaders, and they will start the war again, the prevailing wisdom goes. Plus, some Congolese leaders say, war is nasty, and people die. One erudite politician reminded me: "Didn't General Ulysses Grant give an amnesty for Confederate soldiers after the American Civil War? Didn't the Spanish do the same for crimes committed under Franco? Why should it be different for us?" Unfortunately, the impunity has thus far brought little peace, and the criminals of yesterday become the recidivists of tomorrow.

THE DOMINOES FALL

Yo likaku, obebisi mbuma, bilei na ya moko!
You monkey, you are destroying the seeds, that will be your food!

—KOFFI OLOMIDE

BUKAVU, ZAIRE, OCTOBER 1996

Lieutenant Colonel Prosper Nabyolwa was sent in October 1996 to Bukavu, on the border with Rwanda, to be the commander of operations for Mobutu's army. "Naby," as his friends called him, knew the town well: He had been born in the hills just outside of Bukavu and had gone to the Jesuit secondary school perched on a hill in the middle of the lakeside town. The provincial capital of half a million people was enjoying the end of its three-month dry season; for once, its hilly roads were not clogged with mud and puddles, although a slight haze of dust hung over the whitewashed buildings, getting into clothes and food. At a mile above sea level, the nights were cold, while the cloudless days were scorching hot.

The experienced paratroop commander, who had been trained at military academies in Belgium and Oklahoma, surveyed the situation. It didn't look good. The Rwandan infiltrations across the Rusizi River south of Bukavu were continuing; intelligence reports told of Rwandan troops and their AFDL allies massing on the other side of the border to attack the refugee camps that sprawled out on either side of town. Naby had been taught how to deal with similar guerrilla threats during his training courses. His task would have been feasible for a disciplined army with adequate resources. But that was not what Naby had at his disposal.

Over the past twenty years, Mobutu had cannibalized his own state, particularly his army. Not surprisingly for a leader who had taken power through a coup, Mobutu feared his own officers the most, and he made sure that they would not have the wherewithal to contest his power. He gutted his regular army, depriving it of resources and salaries, while he invested millions in separate, paramilitary units—the presidential guard and the *garde civile*—which he then pitted against each other. Throughout these various units, he named close associates, often members of his own Ngbandi tribe, as commanders and allowed them to get rich off extortion rackets, gun-smuggling, and illegal taxation. A similar situation prevailed in the intelligence services, which proliferated and spied on each other. "We didn't have an army; we had individuals," Nabyolwa remembered.[1]

When he arrived in Bukavu, Nabyolwa took stock of the situation. There were 800 presidential guards, 1,000 *guardes civiles*, and 200 paratroopers in town who answered to different chains of command. The paratroopers had gone to seed, abandoning their positions to moonlight for private security companies in order to make a living. The presidential guards told Nabyolwa that they were deployed to protect the refugees under a deal they had negotiated with the United Nations. Despite Nabyolwa's entreaties that they had sworn an oath to protect Zaire with their lives, they refused to send any of their troops to the front lines.

The lack of intelligence further confused matters. Commanders in Bukavu received exaggerated, contradictory information about the security situation to the south of town in the Rusizi plain and in the High Plateau, where Rwandan vanguard parties began skirmishing with Nabyolwa's units in August and September. "I didn't know whether it was it 300 or 3,000 enemy troops active there," he remembered. He sent reports to the army command in Kinshasa but received little response. Politicians in the capital were too busy feuding with each other to pay much attention to the situation in Bukavu, a thousand miles away. When Nabyolwa radioed Kinshasa to tell them he urgently needed one battalion of special forces, the commander of the presidential guard answered, "We have problems in Kinshasa, too, you know. We need the soldiers here." Mobutu had been in power for so long, Nabyolwa remembered, that no one could conceive of him failing, least of all to a Lilliputian neighbor like Rwanda.

The Rwandan attacks to the south of town sent thousands of refugees and Zairian civilians spilling into Bukavu, where they sparked alarm and protests. On September 18, the Catholic Church and civil society groups rallied tens of thousands of people in the streets of Bukavu in protest of the "aggression by the Tutsi invaders." Waving banners and singing songs, they streamed down Avenue Lumumba, the main thoroughfare. They demanded that the government in Kinshasa "mobilize the means . . . to kick the invaders out of the national territory and to resolve, once and for all, the issue of citizenship."[2]

This firebrand rhetoric was, of course, not well received on the other side of the border. Thousands of Banyamulenge had been seeking refuge in Rwanda from the abuses of Mobutu's army and armed gangs. A week after the demonstration, Nabyolwa tuned into Radio Rwanda to hear Prime Minister Pasteur Bizimungu give a speech. "There is no difference between the Interahamwe and the Zairian authorities," he thundered. "Each time they mistreat us, Rwanda will get revenge. . . . If their gambit is to chase out those who have lived in the country for four hundred years, the only Banyamulenge we will welcome are the children and old women. The others must stay there to correct and give a lesson to those who want to chase them out."[3]

~:~

It was not long before it became clear to Nabyolwa that he was in serious trouble. Perhaps the first sign was the Lemera hospital massacre. The clinic was perched on the steep hills overlooking the Rusizi plain, forming an ideal military outlook. It had been founded in the 1930s by Swedish Pentecostal missionaries and by the time of the war was the largest hospital in the province, with 230 beds, several foreign doctors, and advanced medical equipment. Given its proximity to the fighting, it had received dozens of wounded soldiers, both Hutu militiamen and Zairian troops. The hospital had asked the Zairian government for protection in exchange for providing treatment, and a company of around a hundred men had been deployed there.

At dawn on October 6, nurses at the hospital were woken by gunfire from the military camp. The generator had been switched off for the night, but the almost full moon provided some light. The Rwandans were known to infiltrate vanguard units while the rear guard shot volleys into the air; it was possible that the rebels had already reached the hospital. Nurses saw fleeting shadows moving through the nearby banana groves. Havoc broke out in the rows of hospital beds, as those wounded soldiers who could move tore intravenous tubes out of their arms and ran, hobbled, or crawled for safety. The nurses barricaded themselves into their rooms and waited.

A few villagers ventured down to the hospital the following afternoon. The scene they saw turned their stomachs. Seventeen patients, mostly soldiers, lay dead in their beds and sprawled on the floor in the wards, bayoneted and shot to death. Broken glass, Mercurochrome, and intravenous fluids lay spilled around them. The attackers had looted the stock of medicines, spilling cartons of syringes and bandages on the floor. In the private quarters, they found the bodies of three nurses—Kadaguza, Simbi, and Maganya—in their white aprons, all shot by AFDL and Rwandan troops. At the nearby Catholic parish, several bodies of Zairian soldiers lay twisted in the courtyard. Inside, they found the bodies of two Catholic priests in their habits, also shot dead.[4]

Similar attacks took place across the Rusizi plain, following the same pattern: infiltrators from Rwanda attacking army positions and refugee camps, scattering the Zairian army and Hutu militia and killing civilians. Soon, 220,000 cowering refugees were flooding into Bukavu, bringing with them word of more massacres and spreading panic.

Nabyolwa decided to go to the Rusizi plain himself to rally the troops. He drove his Land Rover pickup to Luvungi, the Zairian army's most advanced position, only to find his soldiers piling into a truck, with their belongings and guns stacked up over the cabin. "Colonel," one of the men told him, hurriedly saluting him, "You are on your own."

Retreating back to town, he reported to his commanding officer, telling him they urgently needed reinforcements. "He couldn't have agreed more," Nabyolwa remembered, laughing. "When he heard what had happened, he succumbed to a sudden stomach ailment. He packed his suitcase and said he was going to Kinshasa to get more troops. He was on the next plane out."

The following day, Nabyolwa's mood was lifted briefly when he got word that a plane was arriving with the promised reinforcements. He hurried to the airport to receive the troops, only to see a cargo plane landing with a company of *garde civile* troops disembarking with their wives, children, and belongings. "There were two hundred shabbily dressed soldiers with pots and pans on their heads. Goats were running around the airstrip. They asked me where they could set up camp." He moaned in dismay, holding his head in his hands. "Goats!"

Nabyolwa called headquarters in Kinshasa three times, urging it to deploy more troops and more resources. Nothing came. Finally, as the enemy troops were just a few miles from Bukavu, Naby rang the army chief of staff one final time: "General, if you wait any longer you will have to pick us up as prisoners of war from the Red Cross!"

~:~

If the Rwandan genocide and the exodus of the *génocidaires* and refugees to Zaire were the immediate causes of the Congo war, the decay of Mobutu's state and army provided the equally important context. By 1996, Zaire was a teetering house of cards—as the *Economist* quipped, "They call it a country. In fact it is just a Zaire-shaped hole in the middle of Africa."[5]

The army that Nabyolwa joined in 1973 was a jumble of contradictions. Like the rest of the state apparatus, it was present everywhere, harassing and taxing the population, but effective nowhere. On the one hand, the Zairian Armed Forces (FAZ) received hundreds of millions of dollars of military assistance from western countries in their effort to make Zaire a bulwark against the so-cialist states—Angola, the Republic of Congo, and Tanzania—that surrounded it. On the other hand, despite their partners' profligacy, Mobutu's army was rarely able to deal effectively with even the most amateurish challenge. On numerous occasions, Mobutu had to call on his foreign allies or mercenaries to prop up his floundering army.

The roots of the army's weakness lie in the Belgian colonial state. The Force Publique, as the army was then called, was formed to maintain law and order and suppress any challenge to colonial rule. It conflated military and policing functions, and control of military units was strongly decentralized to serve the needs of the territorial administrators, who used the army for civilian tasks as well as to suppress dissent. The Belgian authorities never thought to create a strong army; up until the late 1950s, they thought that independence was still decades away and that they would continue to control the state and its security forces. They did not allow Congolese to advance beyond the rank of noncom-missioned officers, leaving a thousand white Belgians to make up the officer corps. Mobutu himself was a sergeant, a trained typist and journalist, at the time of independence. Within two months he was chief of staff of the newly independent Congo's army.

When the Belgians left, the brash and inexperienced new authorities sacked all Belgian officers, suspicious that they wanted to keep running the country even after independence. It would have been difficult to form a new army under the best of circumstances, but no one had expected the turmoil that followed. Almost immediately, parts of the provinces of Kasai and Katanga seceded, supported by western economic and political interests. When Belgium and the United States connived with Katangan secessionists to assassinate Prime Minister Patrice Lumumba in January 1961, the postindependence government and army split, and a new rebellion broke out in the eastern Congo. To get these various uprisings under control, Colonel Mobutu relied on foreign assistance, first from 20,000 United Nations peacekeepers and then from white mercenaries, Belgian paratroopers, and the U.S. Air Force.

Mobutu brought an end to this tumultuous period through a coup in November 1965 and set about reorganizing the army. The military became the centerpiece of his administration, and he consistently allocated over 10 percent of his budget to defense. Despite his meager training, he promoted himself to field marshal and minister of defense. He succeeded in attracting outside support by presenting himself as the bulwark against communism in the region. He hosted several Angolan rebel groups on his territory and allowed the United States to funnel money and weapons to them. Between 1960 and 1991, the United States provided $190 million in military assistance to Zaire and trained 1,356 officers.[6] France, Israel, and Belgium also provided military aid to the autocrat, despite the evidence that he himself had done little to improve the performance of his security services. The dictator knew that he was too important to the west to be allowed to fail.

As a result, there was no shortage of technically proficient and competent military officers. Nabyolwa was a good example of this. He was trained as a paratrooper by Belgians and then traveled to Brussels for artillery training at the royal military academy. Several years later, he studied for six months at Fort Sill in Oklahoma. At the same time, Zaire became a burgeoning African military power, with cadets from other countries undergoing paratroop, naval, and artillery training at various Zairian academies. Mobutu sent thousands of troops to help put down the Biafran secession in Nigeria, a Libyan-backed incursion in Chad, and rebel insurgencies in Burundi, Rwanda, and Togo.

While he courted outside support, however, Mobutu was deeply afraid that his army would actually become a professional, cohesive fighting force. Paradoxically, it was Mobutu's fear of dissent that weakened his security forces. Having risen through a coup, he knew the danger that independent poles of power represented, and he sidelined or eliminated competent officers he deemed to be a threat. The military's decline began in 1975, when Mobutu court-martialed a slew of U.S.-trained officers, including three generals and his own military advisor, Colonel Omba Pene, accusing them of planning a putsch in connivance with the American embassy. Three years later it was the turn of officers trained at the Belgian Royal Military Academy. Despite scant evidence regarding the alleged Belgium-linked plot, the officers were quickly sentenced and executed by firing squad. At the same time, Mobutu dismissed all Kinshasa-based officers from ethnic communities deemed disloyal, in particular those from Kasai, Maniema, Bandundu, and Katanga provinces. The commander in chief reorganized the army, placing members of his own, small Ngbandi tribe in key command positions. Loyalty, in this case cemented by ethnicity, trumped competence.

Nabyolwa, from the restive Kivu Province, was barred from important positions, despite his training abroad. "They thought people from the Kivus were rebels," Nabyolwa remembered. He was forced to receive orders from officers who, in some cases, had never even graduated from military academy. "If you weren't from Equateur, you were nobody."

Driven by his deeply paranoid fantasies, Mobutu proceeded to balkanize the army, creating a multitude of military units and intelligence services with different chains of command and overlapping mandates. He gave the command of most of these units to relatives. In 1982, he promoted his nephew Nzimbi Ngbale from captain to general and made him the command of his newly formed presidential guard. Several years later, General Philemon Baramoto, who had married Mobutu's sister-in-law, was placed at the head of the *garde civile*, which was supposed to protect the country's borders but ended up as a bloated paramilitary unit deployed throughout the country. Mobutu's son Kongolo, who had the rank of captain but was not part of the official armed forces, set up his own private security company "Eagle Service" that he used to extort money from diamond traders and customs officials. The national security advisor Honoré

Ngbanda, who was nicknamed "Terminator" for his brutality, created two private militias to target enemies of the regime.

By the 1990s, half of the sixty-two generals in the armed forces came from Mobutu's home province of Equateur and a third from his small Ngbandi ethnic group. In the ministry of defense, reportedly 90 percent of the staff was from Equateur.[7] Instead of loyalty, however, these poorly thought-out promotions created discord in the army. The various military and paramilitary services spent much of their time fighting among each other and building mafia-like networks throughout the country. Mobutu's own security advisor later described the farcical infighting among generals: "All the ministers of defense and army generals had, within the military or in Mobutu's entourage, a rival that they had to fight or defend against. General Bumba suffered attacks from General Molongya; Singa battled with Lomponda; Likulia backstabbed Eluki; Mahele gave Eluki a hard time; meanwhile Singa, back at the ministry of defense, was subjected to Likulia's plotting. The list is long."[8]

As loyalty was more important than probity, Mobutu allowed his protégés to enrich themselves. Officers competed for influence, juicy procurement deals, and patronage. Almost all high-ranking officers were involved in business, and the lines between public and private became completely blurred as they used state assets to further personal interests. The army's chief of staff, General Eluki Monga, siphoned fuel from military stocks for his fleet of taxis; General Baramoto rented his soldiers out as private security guards in Kinshasa; General Nzimbi, the commander of the presidential guard, used army trucks to smuggle copper from Katanga to Zambia.[9]

⁓∶⁓

As Mobutu's hold on state and economic power declined in the 1980s, his army, too, fell apart. Aside from the presidential guard, who were much better equipped, paid, and fed, most of the country's 70,000 soldiers rarely or never received salaries. Mobutu famously declared in a speech to the army, "You have guns; you don't need a salary."[10] It was another manifestation of his famous "Article 15," a fictitious clause in an obsolete constitution that called for the population to do anything they needed to do to survive. Débrouillez-vous ("improvise" or "get by") became the modus operandi for Zairians of all classes, in particular the armed forces.

It is difficult to overstate the impact these policies had on the security services. As early as 1979, a scholar traveling in the northeast came across soldiers in "tattered uniforms, the victims of long deferred pay. A number were reduced to begging for food." In order to survive, they were forced to hire themselves out to local farmers to work in the fields.[11] In military camps throughout the country, soldiers had turned training grounds into vegetable plots, and chickens and goats strayed about the dilapidated compounds.

Most soldiers resorted to less gallant means to earn their living. By the 1990s, impromptu roadblocks at which soldiers would extort money had become ubiquitous features of the Zairian countryside. Soldiers became known as *katanyama*, a Lingala term meaning "meat cutters," because they would come into the market and seize the choicest morsels of meat from the butchers. Mobutu himself, in one of his periodic bouts of "self-criticism," admitted that, "The truth is simply that these cadres seem to have lost the rigor of military life and discipline in favor of all sorts of commodities: commerce, beautiful cars, beautiful villas, bourgeois life."[12]

In Bukavu, Nabyolwa arrived to find the officers had become businessmen. "They would come to staff headquarters wearing gold rings and chains, sometimes even sunglasses, smelling of cologne," he told me, shaking his head. Most commanders had several wives; one of Nabyolwa's deputies had a clothes shop on the main road, while another ran a smuggling racket with local businessmen, sending trucks through the Burundian border at night.

~:~

As with a bankrupted business, when the army ceased functioning, its leaders began disassembling it and selling it off—weapons, vehicles, airplanes, generators, and anything else that could get a decent price on the international arms market or on the black market. In June 1994, General Nzimbi and General Baramoto sold the air force's last remaining fighter jets to arms dealers. Several months later, General Eluki gave orders to the air force commander to sell the last C-130 transport aircraft to South African dealers. So many spare parts were bartered away that, by the end of the 1980s, only 70 percent of the tanks of the country's main armored brigade were functional. A similar statistic applied to the Zairian air force.[13] The Zairian army was unable through its own means to transport troops or goods anywhere in a country 1,000 miles wide and with barely any paved roads. They had to resort to using commercial planes. At the end of the war, the defunct state allegedly owed local businessmen over $40 million in debts for air travel alone.[14]

The arrival of the displaced Rwandan army of the Habyarimana regime and the refugees also provided a good business opportunity for the generals. When Mobutu's security advisor inspected the arsenal of confiscated weapons in a Goma military camp, it took him a whole day to see all the equipment: "The whole courtyard was covered with heavy and modern machinery. Many of these had never been used. I was even surprised to see very modern amphibious tanks. Entire hangars were full of hundreds of thousands of rifles of all kinds, while three buildings were full of ammunition."[15] Most of these weapons were bartered away by the various generals involved in arms trafficking. The destination of the weapons revealed the officers' extreme cynicism: some were sold back to the Rwandan army in exile, while others were supplied to the RPF across the border. The Zairian army supplied its enemy with some of the bullets and guns it would use to kill them with later.

After decades of nepotism and mismanagement, it was clear that the only loyalty most commanders felt was to their own pocketbooks. General Tembele, Mobutu's commander on the eastern front, met regularly with RPF commanders across the border to brief them on the military situation.[16] Patrick Karegeya, the Rwandan external intelligence chief, spoke with Mobutu officers in Kinshasa and in the east in the run-up to the war. "We had extensive infiltration, we used money, we used friends. It wasn't hard."[17]

⁓∶⁓

Nabyolwa was in downtown Bukavu when the rebels finally reached town, entering across the Rwandan border and from the south at the same time. He raced in his pickup to Hotel Residence, a large monolith on the main strip where the army high command had rented apartments. His commanding officer had barricaded himself there, swearing that he would not abandon his position. Nabyolwa rushed into his room, urging him to order a tactical retreat. His commander refused, saying that they would still be able to hold the town. Exasperated, Nabyolwa took him out to the balcony, from where they could see Rwandan troops swarming into town. As they stood on the balcony, a rocket-propelled grenade hit the wall just meters away from them, knocking them both to the ground. Convinced, the general informed his staff to prepare a hasty withdrawal to a suburb on a hill adjacent to Bukavu, from where they would be able to prepare a counterattack.

The army high command piled into their military jeeps and screeched out of town, only to find that most of the army had already fled to the military barracks to the north. The situation, however, was not favorable for a counterattack. In the barracks, the terrified soldiers milled about with their wives and children. Their belongings—and also pillaged goods, Nabyolwa suspected—lay strewn about the parade grounds. It was impossible to envision a counterattack in these conditions, he thought. Nonetheless, and against his advice, his commander gave orders for the soldiers to line up in preparation for an attack. They finally got the unit commanders to present themselves at the front of the parade grounds, but their soldiers balked, leaving their officers standing alone, looking sheepish in the middle of the pitch. "My general was convinced that we had an army— we didn't," Nabyolwa recalled.

They beat a further retreat to the Kavumu airport eighteen miles to the north of town, where Kinshasa had promised to send them reinforcements. There they found one of the most formidable pieces left in Mobutu's arsenal, a fifteen-meter-long BM-30 Smerch rocket launcher with twelve barrels. His commander grinned and told Nabyolwa, much to his dismay, "We will use this to bomb Bukavu." Nabyolwa, who still had relatives and family members in town, retorted: "That doesn't make any sense. We will just kill civilians and destroy houses!" An order is an order, the general insisted, and they prepared a column to drive toward Bukavu to find an appropriate place from which to bomb the town.

Halfway into town, the general pulled up alongside Nabyolwa, who was driving in the middle of the convoy in a pickup, and ordered him to lead the offensive. "You want your operational commander to be the first to die in battle?" Nabyolwa fulminated. That was it: He stopped his vehicle and handed the keys over to his general. "I wasn't going to die like that," he remembered. He did not want to cross the line between bravery and stupidity. "If he wanted to lead the offensive, he was more than welcome."

Nabyolwa began walking back toward the airport on foot. He found the bulk of his troops at a crossroads together with hundreds of Rwandan refugees, debating whether to head north toward the airport or west into the equatorial rainforests. After some deliberation, they headed over the mountains into the inhospitable jungles. Naby joined them, climbing into a jeep belonging to a presidential guard commander.

In the meantime, the BM-30's electrical system short-circuited, and the hapless general fled toward the airport. Instead of taking the road westward into the jungles, however, he decided to head northward along Lake Kivu to Goma, where he thought he might still be able to join other units to resist the Rwandan invasion. Over his radio, Nabyolwa heard of his commander's decision and felt a pang of remorse. He was sure that Goma would soon fall as well and the general would then be stuck between two enemy contingents. In a small village sixty miles into the jungle, Nabyolwa told the presidential guard unit that they needed to return to get the general. It was the last straw for the soldiers, who thought it was suicidal to go back. They turned their guns on him.

"They didn't make any sense," Nabyolwa remembered. "First they accused me of deserting—which was strange coming from a bunch of deserters. Then they said I wanted to kill them by going back. Finally, an officer said, 'We think you are a traitor. Every time you send us into battle, we get attacked!'

"'But that's what war is about!'

"'You are a sadist!'"

Faced with this kind of logic, all Nabyolwa could do was to persuade them that, instead of killing him, it would be wiser to arrest him and take him to their commanding officer.

~:~

On the other side of the battlefield, the troops were being led by men a generation younger than the Zairian generals.

On the face of it, the Rwandan-led invasion was an amalgam of different nationalities, chains of command, and military cultures. There were Ugandan artillery units, Eritrean speedboats, Tanzanian military advisors, and Congolese soldiers. When it came down to it, however, the people calling the shots were Rwandans, at least for the first half of the war. The thirty-three-year-old in charge of operations on the ground was Colonel James Kabarebe, the former commander of Kagame's guard.

Kabarebe's reputation is legendary in the region, to the extent where people only refer to him by his first name, "James" or "Jamesi." Just a second lieutenant when the RPF invaded the north of Rwanda in 1990, he had risen to the rank of lieutenant colonel by the time they captured Kigali in 1994.[18] According to Congolese officers who worked with him, he led by example, often eating with his officers and going to the front line to lead offensives. In tactical meetings, he would typically defer to his colleagues for their opinions, and he was thus able to cultivate a loyal following among young Congolese army officers.

At the beginning of operations, Kabarebe asked Laurent Kabila whether his son Joseph could join him at the front. Joseph was the one family member the old revolutionary had brought with him to Kigali, and the twenty-five-year-old began popping up on the periphery of officials' vision in 1996. An academic re-members being driven from Kigali by a monosyllabic Joseph to meet his father in Goma; a Kenyan security officer recalls drinking with Joseph in a bar in Kampala along with other military officers.

Kabarebe now wanted Joseph to accompany him to witness military operations in the Congo. "I told Kabila that Joseph had to learn the military profession and that the AFDL was the best school. He finally accepted."[19] According to Kabarebe, his young disciple did not take readily to soldiering. When he heard gunfire, he would panic. "He had the hardest time learning how to fight."

Life at the front was different from Laurent Kabila's more languid existence in Dar es Salaam. The Rwandan-led troops had some tents and tarpaulins and would bivouac their troops wherever they could find cover. But the fighting had started in September, at the beginning of the rainy season. There were down-pours almost every evening, drenching the soldiers and infusing a fetid dampness into their clothes and belongings. Blow flies and jiggers deposited maggots under their skin, leading to infected, suppurating wounds.

The rain made it almost impossible to pass along the roads. Troops spent days getting trucks unstuck and over faulty bridges, and soldiers were forced to carry most of their belongings on their heads. Most threw their socks away after a few weeks and marched on, barefoot in Wellington boots, accumulating blisters and calluses. At night, they lashed together lean-tos out of banana leaves and sticks or occupied abandoned buildings.

There was little to eat. The troops had to rely largely on what they could find locally, and their path had been ravaged by several hundred thousand Congolese and Rwandan people fleeing the fighting. The fields had been uprooted, the fish ponds emptied, and the houses plundered. When they were lucky, they would stumble on stocks abandoned by humanitarian workers, in particular the UN

High Commissioner for Refugees. Then, for several weeks the staple diet of the soldiers became U.S., FDA-approved surplus cornmeal, vegetable oil, and kidney beans. For officers, dessert might be nutritional milk for infants mixed with sugar and coffee, along with some energy biscuits.

Most fighting along the eastern border at the beginning was carried out by Rwandan army troops along with Congolese Tutsi who had joined in the run-up to the rebellion. By October 1996, however, the first batch of new Congolese recruits had graduated from the two training camps the AFDL had set up in Nyaleke, North Kivu, and Kidote, South Kivu. Thousands of teenagers joined the rebellion, outfitted in neatly pressed green uniforms with Wellington boots. They advanced almost solely on foot—airplanes were expensive and used mostly by officers and elite units—singing songs and balancing ammunition boxes on their heads. *Mobailo*, they called it, the forced march that could cover forty or more miles in a day. They borrowed names they heard on the radio for feared fighters: "*Biso toza ba Taliban*" (we are Taliban), they told villagers. Several of them gave themselves nicknames of international bad guys; Ghadaffi was a popular one. Later in the war, Osamas began popping up. Years later, some Congolese villagers told me that the leader of the AFDL troops in their area had been Rambo or Chuck Norris.

In February, the troops were joined by over a thousand Katangan Tigers, old and young, flown in on cargo planes from Angola. The mention of the Katangan Tigers provokes a great deal of hilarity with Rwandan officers. "Eh! Tigers! Those guys caused us a lot of trouble," the member of the Rwandan command told me. "They were old men who fought with all kinds of magic amulets, believing they would be made invincible to bullets." Despite the Rwandans' jokes, however, not all Tigers were geriatric and useless. Many of the second-generation Tigers had been given thorough training in the Angolan army and were in their twenties and thirties at the beginning of the war.[20] It was these Portuguese-speaking exiles that the Angolan government planned on sending to join Kagame's alliance.

～:～

There were few memorable battles for the rebels as they crossed the country. Bukavu was one of the fiercer ones, as the Zairian army tried to put up some resistance; later, they knew better. Goma fell quickly as a result of treason, as

Mobutu's officers sold equipment and intelligence to their enemies in the months prior to the invasion and then did little to defend the town. Simultaneously, Ugandan troops had crossed the border to the north and taken the town of Mahagi with only thirty soldiers. A rebel commander told me that three of his men on a motorcycle defeated two hundred Mobutu soldiers in another town in the northeast.

Where there was resistance, it was often because of foreign troops. Rwandan ex-FAR were fighting alongside the Zairian army, trying to protect the retreating refugees. In Kindu, along the upper reaches of the Congo River, over a thousand ex-FAR joined Mobutu's troops, although they were poorly coordinated and soon scattered.[21] Mobutu's officers, however, had not given up. They decided to make a stand in Kisangani, the country's third largest city and the gateway to the east, located at a bend in the Congo River. The city had a long airstrip and was a major river port. The army's high command flew in reinforcements and also mined the airport and the main roads leading to town from the east. Diplomats speculated that Mobutu would be history if the town fell.

Mobutu's generals began frantically organizing other foreign support. Using their contacts in Belgrade and Paris, they managed to hire around 280 mercenaries, mostly French and Serbs, under the command of Belgian colonel Christian Tavernier, along with some attack helicopters and artillery.[22]

It was too little, too late. The area they had to cover was too large, and the Zairian army too disorganized for them to have much impact. The soldiers of fortune were also perhaps not of the best quality. A French analyst described them as a mixture between "Frederick Forsyth's 'dogs of war' and the Keystone Kops." He went on to disparage the Serbs' performance in particular: "They spent their days getting drunk and aimlessly harassing civilians. They did not have proper maps, they spoke neither French nor Swahili, and soon most of them were sick with dysentery and malaria."[23]

Tavernier chose as his operational base Watsa, a remote town in the northeast that had little strategic importance, but where he had obtained mining rights. The colonel himself was seen more often in the upscale Memling Hotel in Kinshasa than on the battlefield, haranguing foreign correspondents, boasting of his feats, and complaining of government ineptitude.

Internal tensions also hampered operations. The French, mostly former soldiers from the Foreign Legion, were better connected and paid up to five times as much as the Serbs—up to $10,000 per month for the officers. But the Serbs controlled most of the aircraft and heavy weaponry, old machines leased at inflated prices from the Yugoslav army. The French accused their counterparts of amateurism; the Serbs retorted that the last time the French had won a serious battle was at Austerlitz in 1805.

On the battlefield, everything fell apart. The Serbs never provided the air support the French demanded, complaining of missing parts and a lack of fuel. On several occasions, they even bombed Mobutu's retreating troops, killing dozens. Mobutu's security advisor remembered the episode: "We had two different delegations from Zaire recruiting mercenaries separately. What was the result? We had mercenaries from different countries who spoke different languages. . . . We bought weapons from different countries that didn't work together. It was a veritable Tower of Babel."[24]

The mercenaries behaved abysmally toward the local population. Even today, residents of Kisangani remember the deranged Serbian commander Colonel Jugoslav "Yugo" Petrusic, driving about town in his jeep, harassing civilians. He shot and killed two evangelical preachers who annoyed him with their megaphone-blasted prayers. He was sure that AFDL rebels had infiltrated Kisangani, and he arrested civilians for interrogation, subjecting them to electroshocks from a car battery and prodding them with a bayonet.[25]

⁓∷⁓

Colonel James Kabarebe remembered the battle for Kisangani as probably the hardest one they had to fight. Surrounded by thick jungle, the Rwandan troops faced off with the enemy across a narrow bridge over a tributary to the Congo River. They tried advancing but were met with a hail of bullets and well-calibrated mortar fire. They searched the banks of the Congo River but could not find any fishermen who could ferry them across to flank the enemy.

Again, it is difficult to tell how well war stories separate fact from fiction. "Laurent Kabila had strange notions of military tactics," James Kabarebe remembered. "In Kisangani, when we were blocked by the mercenaries, he came to me, urging me to put soldiers up in the trees and, on command, to start shooting in all different directions at once. He said it would confuse the hell out of the enemy!" From then on, every time Kabarebe was confronted with heavy resistance, his colleagues jokingly told him to put soldiers in the trees.

Other tales about the battle remain popular with the Rwandans. Blocked by heavy fire and the Congo River, the Rwandans decided to let the newly arrived Katangan Tigers have a try. According to the Rwandans, the Tigers rubbed their bodies down with magic salves and put amulets around their necks to protect them from bullets. Then they advanced on the enemy. One by one, they were picked off by sniper fire. Some jumped into the water and drowned. Others ran. "It was a massacre," Kabarebe remembered.[26]

It is unlikely that the Katangan Tigers, professionally trained by the Angolan army and no kamikazes, behaved in such a fashion. The more likely story is one provided by some of the AFDL soldiers who participated in the offensive: They were finally able to outflank Mobutu's forces by traveling several days upstream, crossing the river, and hitting them from the rear. At the same time, Ugandan tanks had arrived along the jungle roads and provided cover fire for the rebels.[27]

Kisangani fell in March 1997, sounding the death knell for Mobutu's government. It was the last real battle of Mobutu's war, with the possible exception of Kenge, some one hundred and twenty miles east of Kinshasa, when Angolan UNITA rebels rallied to his defense, along with several thousand unemployed and desperate youths from Kinshasa who had been given a hundred dollars each and sent to the front.

Mbuji-Mayi, the country's diamond hub, fell on April 5, 1997. The fact that Mobutu's army hardly mounted a defense of the town, whose state-run diamond company, Société Minière de Bakwanga, had been the last reliable source of cash for Mobutu, indicated that the government had pretty much given up. For Laurent Kabila, the capture of the town was a godsend, as it provided him with much-needed cash to pay the invoices for fuel and airplane rental, the two biggest expenses the rebels had. He asked the Lebanese diamond traders to pay him $960,000 in back taxes and seized a large shipment belonging to De Beers, the South African diamond giant, claiming the company was operating illegally. They reportedly had to pay $5 million to get the gems back.[28]

The next domino to fall was Lubumbashi, the country's copper capital, a week later. Soldiers from Mobutu's Twenty-first Brigade tore up bedsheets, tying white bandanas around their heads and waving white flags to greet the AFDL. Restaurant and hotel owners opened their doors, offering officers free beers and soft drinks. This was the town where Laurent Kabila had been raised, and he quickly set about recruiting new soldiers from local youth groups. The old flag of the Congo Free State, yellow stars set against a peacock-blue background, was resurrected and unfurled at government buildings in town. Painters were hired to quickly replace the ubiquitous "Zaire" with "Congo," and the flaming torch, symbol of Mobutu's party, was erased from public monuments.

Perhaps the true sign that Mobutu's era was coming to an end was the arrival in Lubumbashi of several executive jets full of officials from international mining and banking corporations. Goldman Sachs, First Bank of Boston, and the Anglo American Mining Corporation all met with Laurent Kabila.[29] An American congressional delegation led by Georgia congresswoman Cynthia McKinney arrived shortly afterwards.[30]

~:~

It is easy to make a mockery of Mobutu's army and government, to reduce the events that led to his demise to a comedy of errors carried on by a bunch of incompetent, bumbling generals in Kinshasa. But it was not for lack of training or expertise that the Zairian army lost the war. The security forces included a legion of intelligent officers trained at some of the world's best military academies. The problem was the decaying, corrupt structures within which they worked. Lacking proper institutions since independence, Mobutu had corroded his own state in order to prevent any challengers to his power from emerging, eroding that very power in the process.

This dry rot that beset the army also had a serious impact on soldiers' morale. Soldiers who were rarely paid and could barely feed their wives and children were unlikely to risk their lives for their corrupt, thieving commanders. "The real challenge in the Congo," Nabyolwa told me, "is not how to reform the army, but how to reform the men in the army! There is a serious problem with *Homo congoliensis!*"

It is this legacy of institutional weakness that for many Congolese is almost as depressing as their physical suffering. Since the 1970s until today, the Congolese state has not had an effective army, administration, or judiciary, nor have its leaders been interested in creating strong institutions. Instead, they have seen the state apparatus as a threat, to be kept weak so as to better manipulate it. This has left a bitter Congolese paradox: a state that is everywhere and oppressive but that is defunct and dysfunctional.

A THOUSAND MILES
THROUGH THE JUNGLE

BUKAVU, ZAIRE, OCTOBER 1996

Beatrice Umutesi, the Rwandan refugee and social worker, was in Bukavu when the fighting started in October 1996. She had come to wait for money that a Belgian nonprofit organization was sending to help her and her colleagues evacuate their families before the fighting began. The town was on edge; all morning, the thunder of mortar fire had been audible in the distance. She waited desperately at the Indian-run wholesale store where the money transfer was supposed to arrive. The shop had been closed for the past three days out of fear of looting; today seemed to be no different. Around 10:30, the automatic machine-gun rat-a-tat joined the mortars, although this was not necessarily cause for panic. For the past few days, the town had been exchanging fire with the Rwandan positions across the border. The streets were full of people trying to find food at the market. A group of men with cardboard biscuit boxes on their heads was walking briskly from the Red Cross warehouse that had just been ransacked.

Suddenly, Beatrice saw a group of soldiers running down the hill, tearing off their uniforms as they ran. Somebody screamed, "They are at the ISP!" The ISP was a technical school barely half a mile from where she was standing. Pandemonium erupted, as people streamed out of their houses with baskets on their heads and babies strapped to their backs. Beatrice had enough time to grab her adoptive children, Bakunda and Assumpta, and run after the fleeing soldiers. She had to leave her other relatives, as well as her few belongings, behind. All she had was seventy dollars and her Rwandan ID card. Mortar shells passed over their heads, whistling and then exploding off to the side of the road. Everywhere there were wounded people, moaning, some alone, others with anxious family members or friends watching over them. She pinned her hopes on a refugee camp fifteen miles away, where she had friends and family members. She thought she might be able to find protection there as the international community tried to find a solution for the refugees.

~:~

Her hopes were misplaced. As Beatrice was running into the hills, diplomats around the world tried to wish the Rwandan Hutu refugees out of existence. After the initial invasion had brought hundreds of thousands of refugees back to Rwanda, the U.S. ambassador to Rwanda, Robert Gribbin, concurred with his hosts' view that those "still with the ex-FAR and *Interahamwe* ... were family or sympathizers who had no intention of returning to Rwanda," and the remaining "refugees appear to be in the tens to twenties of thousands rather than in vast numbers."[1] In reality, between 300,000 and 600,000 Hutu refugees had fled into the jungles and were at risk of starvation and disease. None of the refugees around Bukavu had the choice of returning to Rwanda—it would have entailed heading into the advancing troops.[2]

On November 20, U.S. military officers presented pictures of aerial reconnaissance to aid groups in Kigali. They had been flying over the country in PS Orion aircraft, taking pictures of refugee flows and settlements. In the photos were clearly visible around half a million people distributed in three major and numerous smaller agglomerations. It was not clear how many of these people were displaced Zairians and how many were refugees. Just three days later, the U.S. military claimed that they had located only one significant cluster of people, which "by the nature of their movement and other clues can be assumed to be the ex-FAR and militias."[3] All the other groups had magically vanished. The aid group Oxfam cried foul, accusing the U.S. military of "losing" refugees on purpose. "We feel bound to conclude that as many as 400,000 refugees and unknown numbers of Zairian displaced persons have, in effect, been air-brushed from history."[4]

～:～

After Beatrice fled from Bukavu, she ran with Bakunda for a day until she could not run anymore. Fearing the advancing rebels, she stayed away from the main roads and followed a line of cowed, silent refugees through the banana groves that covered the hillsides. They spent the first night in a school that was being protected by members of Mobutu's youth organization, who had banded together to protect their community. They checked Beatrice's ID but were skeptical about one of the children who had joined her on the way, a child with Tutsi features. Beatrice finally convinced them that he was her son; they grudgingly allowed her to spend the night in the house of a local family. That family, she later wrote, "was part of that chain of Zairians, who, throughout my long journey, shared with me their roof and the little food they had."[5]

The only road of escape was toward Kisangani, Zaire's third largest town at the bend in the Congo River, more than three hundred miles to the northwest. Hundreds of thousands of Hutu refugees were on the move now through the forests of the eastern Congo, accompanied by tens of thousands of scared Congolese. First, they had to climb the hills of the Kahuzi-Biega National Park, in more peaceful times famous for its lowland gorillas and highland elephants. On the narrow footpaths, Beatrice ran into a traffic jam of people. It was the beginning of the rainy season, and every evening heavy rains would gush down over them, turning the soil into a muddy, slippery torrent. Tens of thousands of people filled the forest; at times, Beatrice had to stand on the path and wait for the single-file line to start moving again. The humid, cool air under the canopy echoed with the sound of thousands of tired feet slapping through the mud.

Not only was this one of the longest mass treks in modern history, but it was also one of the most outlandish. The refugees walked through some of the densest rain forest on the planet, under layered canopies two hundred feet high. Beatrice walked for days without seeing direct sunlight. Elsewhere, they had to ford deep rivers or cut new paths through the forest. Wasps laid larvae under their skin, long leeches plastered their bodies after they passed through streams, and several of Beatrice's companions were killed by snakes. Once in the middle of the night, Beatrice was awakened by screams when her group was attacked by millions of driver ants. They tried, with some success, to use fire to chase the ants away, but eventually they had to move.

The basic need to survive overcame the many taboos inherent in Rwandan society. Forced to eat raw roots and leaves, Beatrice developed sores in her mouth and a bad case of diarrhea. First, she tried to hide herself behind bushes to ease her discomfort, but eventually, when she no longer had the strength, she would just squat down next to the path and look the other way as others plodded by. Lacking soap, she began to stink, and fleas and lice infested her clothes. Rwandan women, who are known for their modesty, were forced to bathe topless next to men in rivers.

Death surrounded them. Chronic diseases, such as diarrhea, malaria, and typhoid, were the biggest killers. Others died of diabetes or asthma, having run out of medicine to treat their chronic illnesses. The smell of rotting bodies filled the air. "In this race against the clock, if anyone fell, it was rare to see someone reach out a hand to help her or him. If, by chance, they were not trampled, they were left lying by the side of the road."[6] Beatrice saw flurries of white and blue butterflies alight on fresh corpses, feeding off their salt and moisture. Further on, she saw a woman who had just given birth forced to bite through her own umbilical cord and continue walking. In one town, locals by the side of the road held up a malnourished baby they had found lying by the side of the road after her mother died and her father was unable to feed her. People passed by in silence, unwilling to take on another burden.

After two hundred and fifty miles and five weeks of walking, Beatrice reached Tingi-Tingi, "the camp of death," as she calls it. Mobutu's soldiers had blocked their advance westward, saying the refugees' arrival would help the rebels infiltrate. Too weak to fight the soldiers, the refugees settled down and prayed for help to arrive.

The name for the town meant "swamp," and it lived up to its name; mosquitoes and dirty groundwater plagued the refugees. Beatrice had lost over thirty pounds by the time she arrived there; her skin was leathery and stiff, her muscles were sore, and she was so hungry that the sight of food made her salivate. To the refugees' dismay, no humanitarian organization was there to help them; there were few latrines and no clean water. A dysentery epidemic broke out shortly after their arrival, followed by cholera. Soon, aid workers did arrive, but they were overwhelmed by the needs of 80,000 people. Every day, bodies, partially covered by white sheets, would be carried away on stretchers. The refugees looked as if they had aged twenty years—their eyes sunk deep into their skulls, skin hanging loosely from their bodies, and their feet swollen from malnutrition and hundreds of miles of walking. Children, in particular, were affected by the lack of vitamins and protein: Their hair thinned and turned beige or blond. Beatrice described women suffering from dysentery as "old fleshless grandmothers even though they weren't even thirty.... They had lost all their womanly attributes.... We only knew they were women because they looked after the children." Beatrice joked with her newly acquired family that they should take a good look at her feet and toenails so they could recognize her when she was carted away in a shroud, her feet protruding.

During the two months Beatrice spent there, aid workers registered 1,800 deaths, about half of them children.[7]

~:~

A decade later the town where the camp was located is still not easy to reach. I had to fly into Kisangani, a hundred and fifty miles away, and rent a motorcycle. In some places the road was completely overgrown by the surrounding forest. Here and there deep, muddy pits had replaced the asphalt for several hundred feet. About twenty miles before Tingi-Tingi, the wrecks of armored cars belonging to Mobutu's fleeing army sat abandoned on their naked axels, rusting on the side of the road, their heavy-caliber machine guns pointing into the rainforest.

An old yellow highway sign reading "Tingi-Tingi" was still standing by the side of the road, a reminder of when truckers could travel from Kisangani to Bukavu in two days. Now it takes two weeks if the truck doesn't break down. A rickety vehicle I saw there had taken a whole month to reach Tingi-Tingi from Bukavu, two hundred fifty miles distant. In the town itself, the tarmac was in good shape, and villagers showed me the stretch of road around which the refugees had built their camp, boasting that airplanes had used it as a landing strip to supply the refugees with food and medicine.

The whole village remembered the two months the refugees had spent there in 1996. It had become a reference point—"he got married two years after the refugees left," or "I bought my house before the refugees came." When asked how many refugees were there, some villagers said, "a million"; others, "it was a city of Rwandans." Now Tingi-Tingi has reverted to being a village of several dozen huts scattered through undergrowth on either side of the road. Locals live by farming cassava and beans, supplementing their diet by hunting monkeys and small antelope in the nearby forest.

The local traditional chief was not there, so the villagers took me to the Pentecostal minister, a fifty-one-year-old named Kapala Lubangula. He was wearing plastic flip-flops, pleated dress pants, and a plain cotton shirt. When I told him I wanted to talk to him about the refugees, he nodded grimly and called a group of four other elderly men from his church. It was dangerous speaking to a foreigner alone in your house; people could accuse you of anything afterwards. We sat on rickety wooden chairs in a small mud house with a low ceiling. Despite the stewing heat, he insisted on sitting inside; he didn't want people to see us talking.

"Why do people always talk about the refugees?" He blurted out almost immediately, to my surprise. "The local population also suffered! Imagine 100,000 people arrive in this small town. They ate everything we had. Their soldiers raped our women and shot dead our traditional chief. Nobody talks about us!" The other men nodded.

The elders described successive waves of soldiers and refugees intruding on their small village. First, a wave of fleeing soldiers had come to town—Mobutu's soldiers mixed with ex-FAR. They had terrorized the local population, taxing people going to the market, breaking into their houses, and stealing their livestock. Then the refugees arrived, "like a band of walking corpses." They were starving. Instead of talking, they just stared and cupped their hands. They pulled up cassava roots and peanuts from the fields and picked raw mangos from the trees. As dire as their situation was, if the villagers shared the little they had with this horde of foreigners, they knew they would all die of starvation. The men from the church helped organize vigilante groups to guard the village and the fields. They patrolled with machetes and sticks. If they found someone stealing, they would beat him to death. There were no prisons and no courts. Justice was swift and decisive.

The minister remembered vividly new colleagues who arrived with the refugees. Two Catholic priests as well as Adventist and Pentecostal ministers set up churches made out of UN tarps. Wooden planks set on rocks served as benches. They gave sermons almost every day during which they talked about the genocide. "They said the Tutsi wanted to dominate everything, to take the land away from the Hutu. So when Habyarimana was killed, they sought revenge for his death and killed. They admitted they had killed! What kind of priests were these?"

When the white people's aid groups came, he said, they only thought about the Rwandans. If a Congolese fell sick, he would be treated last. Reverend Kapala's voice rose. "First the white people bring the refugees here; then they refuse to help us!" When I reminded them that it had been the civil war in Rwanda that had brought the refugees, not the United Nations, Kapala sucked his teeth. "The international community has all the power. You can't tell me that the United States, the biggest superpower in the world, could not stop all this if they had wanted to. They didn't stop it because they didn't want to."

Another elder chimed in: "Do you think that Rwanda, this peanut of a country, could defeat the Congo alone? No way."

For a while, it seemed that Tingi-Tingi had become the capital of the world. Three weeks after the arrival of the first Rwandans, aid groups began arriving with helicopters, large and small planes, and, eventually, convoys of trucks with food. Doctors and logisticians from the United States, India, France, South Africa, and Kenya set up shop in the local hospital and health centers. Emma Bonino, the EU aid commissioner, arrived, as did Sadako Ogata, the UN High Commissioner for Refugees. Agathe Habyarimana, the wife of the former Rwandan president, also visited from her exile at Mobutu's palace in Gbadolite to deliver bags of cornmeal, rice, and beans. The planes landed in the middle of the camp, sending people scurrying for cover. In one case, a woman, dizzy and disoriented from hunger and thirst, didn't move out of the way quickly enough and was decapitated by a plane's propellers.

～:～

Laurent Kabila's improvised army, the AFDL, arrived in Tingi-Tingi on February 28, 1997. Many sick or weak refugees did not manage to flee. Dozens were crushed to death or drowned following a stampede on a nearby bridge. Some 2,000 survived the attacks and were airlifted back to Rwanda by aid organizations.

Others were killed. A worker for the local Red Cross, who, ten years later, was still too afraid to tell me his name, said he had returned several days afterward to find bodies bludgeoned to death in the camp's tented health centers. Others had fallen, intravenous needles still in their arms, in the forests nearby. A local truck driver, who had been commandeered by the AFDL to help clean up the town after the attack, told me there were dead bodies everywhere, refugees who had been too weak to flee and had then been bayoneted by the soldiers. "They didn't use bullets on the refugees—they used knives," he told me. His eyes glazed over as he remembered the image of an infant sucking on his dead mother's breast, trying in vain to get some sustenance from her cold body. Reverend Kapala, who had fled into the forest for one night and then returned, told me, "They killed any male refugee over the age of twelve. They slit their throats. Not the women or children. Just the men."

However, when I separately asked the truck driver, the minister, and the Red Cross worker how each had felt about the AFDL, they all quickly responded, "It was a liberation! We were overjoyed."

I was amazed. I pressed Reverend Kapala: "What about their killing of refugees? How can you call them liberators?"

He shrugged. "That was a Rwandan affair. It didn't concern us." He told me the story of a brave local man, who, during a public meeting shortly after the AFDL's arrival, asked the local commander why they killed so much. "He answered, 'Show me the Congolese we killed. There are none.' And it was true. They didn't kill any Congolese."

This is one of the paradoxes of the first war. The population was so tired of Mobutu that they were ready to welcome their liberator on whatever terms. The Hutu refugees hadn't been welcome in the first place; any massacre was their own business. For the local population, this paradox was resolved by separating the rebels into two groups: the aggressive Tutsi killers and the Congolese freedom fighters.

~:~

After their flight from Tingi-Tingi, the refugees marched toward Kisangani, only to find their path blocked again by the Zairian army at Ubundu, a small town sixty miles south of Kisangani. After several days, the local commander allowed Beatrice's group to pass, in return for five hundred dollars. Leaders went around to the thousands of refugees, collecting tattered and soiled banknotes from different currencies until they had the sum. Most of the refugees, however, stayed behind, too tired or afraid to continue.

In the meantime, the AFDL had already conquered Kisangani, the country's third largest city. Some 85,000 refugees were stuck in the camps along the train line between Ubundu and Kisangani. They knew that if the international community did not come to their rescue, they would be forced to follow Beatrice and the others, crossing the mighty Lualaba River and plunging once again into the inhospitable jungle, where there were no villages or food for dozens of miles.

Humanitarian organizations followed the refugee stream, hopscotching from one camp to the next, packing their bags every time the AFDL approached. They set up shop in various camps around Ubundu in early April, providing elementary health care and nutrition to the despondent refugees. The conditions they found were terrible: In some camps, mortality rates were five times higher than the technical definition of an "out-of-control emergency."[8] Nevertheless, by this time the AFDL soldiers had arrived in the camps and began regulating humanitarian access. Foreign health workers were only allowed into the camps for a few hours during the day.

Finally, on April 20, the AFDL soldiers made their move. Without warning, Rwandan soldiers shut down all humanitarian access to the camps south of Kisangani. When diplomats and aid workers asked, they were told the security situation had suddenly deteriorated. Then, several planeloads of well-equipped Rwandan soldiers arrived at Kisangani's airport and immediately headed toward the camps. The next day, the Rwandan soldiers attacked them. Congolese workers in the camps reported well-armed soldiers in uniforms participating in the attack, lobbing mortars and grenades into the dense thicket of tents and people during the nighttime attack.[9] One nurse working for Doctors Without Borders recalled: "One day, they dropped bombs on the camp; everybody fled, leaving everything behind and scattering in the equatorial forest—there were many dead. The AFDL put the cadavers into mass graves and burnt them."[10] When journalists and humanitarian organizations were allowed back to the camps three days later, they found them ransacked. The thousands of refugees who were there had all disappeared. Doctors Without Borders had been providing medical treatment to 6,250 patients who were too weak even to walk short distances. When they didn't find any trace of them after one week, they assumed they had died, either violently or from disease and malnutrition.

~:~

How many of the Rwandan Hutu refugees who fled Rwanda during the genocide died in the Congo? From the beginning, the refugee crisis was bogged down in number games. One major problem was the lack of a starting figure: Rwandan officials challenged the United Nations' figure of 1.1 million refugees in the camps before the invasion, arguing that aid estimates err on the high side so that no one is deprived of food or medicine. The ex-FAR and former government officials in the camps had refused to allow a census, themselves inflating their population in order to receive more aid. Doctors Without Borders' estimate was 950,000, although Rwandan officials sometimes place it even lower. In the early days of the AFDL invasion, between 400,000 and 650,000 refugees returned to Rwanda, and a further 320,000 refugees were either settled in UN camps or repatriated over the course of 1997, a total of 720,000 to 970,000 refugees. As the starting figure is not clear, this number is not very helpful: Anywhere between zero and 380,000 refugees could still have been missing.[11] Also, just because refugees were missing, they weren't necessarily dead. Some had repatriated spontaneously, without UNHCR help; many others were hiding in the mountains of the eastern Congo, and others had settled with friends and relatives in villages and cities across the region.

It is more fruitful to base estimates on eyewitness accounts. When in July 1997, after eight months of walking, a group of refugees arrived on the other side of the Congo River in neighboring Republic of Congo, Doctors Without Borders conducted a survey of 266 randomly selected people, asking them how many members of their families had survived the trek. The result was disturbing: Only 17.5 percent of people in their families had made it, while 20 percent had been killed and a further 60 percent had disappeared, meaning they had been separated from them at some point in the journey. Over half of those killed were women; it wasn't just ex-FAR being hunted down. If that survey was representative of the rest of the refugees—the sample size is too small to be wholly reliable—then at least 60,000 refugees had been killed, while the whereabouts of another 180,000 were unknown.

Reports by journalists and human rights groups confirm this magnitude of the killings. Although the AFDL repeatedly denied access to international human rights investigators, making it difficult to confirm many reports issued by churches and civil society groups, there is no doubt that massacres took place. The UN human rights envoy, the Chilean judge Roberto Garreton, received reports from local groups that between 8,000 and 12,000 people were massacred by the AFDL in the eastern Congo, including Congolese Hutu who were accused of complicity with the ex-FAR. In the Chimanga refugee camp forty miles west of Bukavu, eyewitness reports collected by Amnesty International tell of forty AFDL soldiers separating about five hundred men from women and children and murdering them. Close by, a Voice of America reporter found a mass grave containing the remains of a hundred people who, according to villagers, were refugees massacred by the rebels. Rwandan Bibles and identity cards were scattered amid human remains and UN food bags.[12] In the Hutu villages I visited north of Goma a decade later, villagers consistently spoke of RPF commanders calling meetings and then tying up and executing dozens of men. They showed me cisterns and latrines with skeletal remains still showing.

Finally, more than a decade after the massacres, a UN team went back to investigate some of the worst massacres of the Congo wars, including those against the Hutu refugees. They interviewed over a hundred witnesses of the refugee massacres, including people who had survived and some who had helped bury the victims. They concluded that Rwandan troops and their AFDL allies killed tens of thousands of refugees, mostly in cold blood. These were not people caught in the crossfire: The report details how the invading troops singled out and killed the refugees, often with hatchets, stones, or knives. "The majority of the victims were children, women, elderly people and the sick, who posed no threat to the attacking forces."[13] Controversially, the report concludes that the Rwandan troops may have been guilty of acts of genocide against the Hutu, given the systematic nature of the killing.[14]

~:~

One of the few places where refugees were killed in plain sight of hundreds of Congolese eyewitnesses was in Mbandaka, where the Congo River separates the Democratic Republic of the Congo from the smaller, former French colony, the Republic of the Congo. The Rwandan army and its Congolese allies had by this time pursued the refugees for over 1,000 miles over mountains, through jungles and savannahs. At Mbandaka, the refugees were blocked by the expanse of the Congo River, which is over a mile wide at that point.

A curious sight greeted the Rwandan troops and the AFDL: Throngs of locals waved palm fronds and sang joyously, while thousands of refugees made a run for the river, trying to board a barge. Others threw themselves into the river, trying to swim across the swiftly moving water, preferring to face crocodiles and hippos than RPF soldiers. The welcoming committee watched in horror as their "liberators" drove the refugees off the boat, made them kneel on the embankment with their hands behind their heads, and executed over a hundred of them. Many were bludgeoned to death with rifle butts or clubs. A local priest saw AFDL soldiers kill an infant by beating its head against a concrete wall. In Mbandaka and another nearby town, Red Cross workers buried some nine hundred bodies. "The alliance fighters told us they only killed former soldiers guilty of murdering many Tutsi people in Rwanda," a Red Cross worker told another journalist. "Yet with my own hands I buried small children whose heads were crushed by rifle butts. Buried those poor little ones and women, too."[15] Bodies of others who had probably drowned were seen snagged in the floating clumps of water hyacinth in the Congo River. In total, between 200 and 2,000 were killed on the banks of the river.

The inescapable truth is that tens of thousands of refugees were killed, while more probably died from disease and starvation as they were forced into the inhospitable jungles to the west. No thorough investigation has ever been carried out. Most of the victims don't have graves, monuments, or even a simple mention in a document or a report to commemorate them.

～:～

Why did the Rwandan soldiers kill so many refugees? There were certainly some individual cases of revenge, as there had been in Rwanda when the RPF arrived. After all, many RPF soldiers had lost family members and wanted payback.

The Rwandan army, however, was known for its strict discipline and tight command and control. It is very unlikely that soldiers would have been able to carry out such large-scale executions as in Mbandaka, for example, without an order from their commanders. Attesting to that possibility, a Belgian missionary told a journalist: "The soldiers acted as if they were just doing their job, following orders. They didn't seem out of control."[16] In other words, even if these were revenge killings, they were carried out systematically, with the knowledge and complicity of the command structure. UN investigators also concluded that in many cases the massacres were carried out in the presence of high-ranking Rwandan officers and by those following orders from above.

Other scholars—such as Alison Des Forges, one of the foremost chroniclers of the genocide—believe that the RPF was trying to prevent another Rwandan refugee diaspora from being created that would one day, much like the RPF in its own history, return to threaten its regime.

Papy Kamanzi, the Tutsi who had joined the RPF in 1993, was deployed in the "clean-up operations" against the ex-FAR to the north of Goma. He recalled: "Thousands returned to Rwanda on their own. But there were some remaining in the area, those who couldn't flee and couldn't return home. The sick and weak. We lied to them. We said we would send them home; we even cooked food for them. But then we took them into the forest. We had a small hatchet we carried on our backs, an *agafuni*. We killed with that. There was a briefing, an order to do so." He showed me the place at the back of the skull, just above the nape of the neck.

Shortly afterwards, Papy was deployed to Goma, where he worked for the Rwandan army's intelligence branch. He considered it an honor. It was an elite group of sixty young soldiers, mostly Congolese Tutsi, who were charged with hunting down "subversives."

They were put under the command of the Rwandan intelligence chief Major Jack Nziza, a discreet, sinister character. His definition of "subversive" was broad: people who were known to have supported Habyarimana's government; members of any of the various Hutu militias; people known to oppose the AFDL; people who had personal conflicts with Rwandan officers. Sometimes, just being a Rwandan refugee—women and children included, Papy specified—was enough. They would take them to two sites they used, a house belonging to Mobutu's former Central Bank governor and a quarry to the north of Goma. There they would interrogate them and then kill them.

"We could do over a hundred a day," Papy told me. I had a hard time believing him; it seemed so outrageous. "We used ropes, it was the fastest way and we didn't spill blood. Two of us would place a guy on the ground, wrap a rope around his neck once, then pull hard." It would break the victim's windpipe and then strangle him to death. There was little noise or fuss.

I asked Papy why he did it. It was an order, he replied. Why did your commander want to do it? He shrugged. That was the mentality at the time. They needed to fear the AFDL. They had committed genocide. It was revenge, he said. But it was also a warning: *Don't try to mess with us.*

∾∶∽

Beatrice spent fourteen months crossing the Congo, forced to hide for months in jungle villages where Congolese families took her in. Finally, at the end of 1997, a Belgian friend who had been looking for her for over a year managed to find her with the help of a local Congolese organization. In early 1998, four years after she had fled Rwanda, she arrived in Belgium. She had lost many of her friends and family. It took years for her body to recover, although she would never be free from the nightmares that plagued her. "I still dream of what happened sometimes. I feel guilty for having survived, for leaving my friends behind."[17]

Sixteen years after the Rwandan genocide, it remains difficult to write about Rwandan history. For many, the moral shock of the Rwandan genocide was so overpowering that it eclipsed all subsequent events in the region. Massacres that came after were always measured up against the immensity of the genocide: If 80,000 refugees died in the Congo, that may be terrible but nonetheless minor compared with the 800,000 in Rwanda. The Rwandan government may have overstepped, but isn't that understandable given the tragedy the people suffered?

In addition, many argued that accountability would destabilize Rwanda's fledgling RPF government, so it was better to sweep a few uncomfortable truths under the carpet than undermine its fragile authority. This kind of logic would crop up again and again throughout the Congo war: War is ugly, and you can't build a state on diplomacy alone. If we push too hard for justice, we will only undermine the peace process. An American diplomat asked me, "Did we have prosecutions after the American Civil War? No. Did the South Africans ever try the apartheid regime? Not really. Why should we ask them to do it here?"

The dour shadow that the genocide cast over the refugee crisis was evident already in April 1995, when RPF soldiers opened fire on a camp of displaced Hutu peasants in Kibeho, Rwanda, killing between 1,500 and 5,000 people. At the time, the American defense attaché in Kigali remarked, "The 2,000 deaths were tragic; on the Rwandan scene the killings were hardly a major roadblock to further progress. Compared to the 800,000 dead in the genocide, the 2,000 dead was but a speed bump."[18] A similar logic drove the U.S. ambassador in Kigali to write a confidential coded cable to Washington in January 1997, with the following advice regarding the Tingi-Tingi refugee camp: "We should pull out of Tingi-Tingi and stop feeding the killers who will run away to look for other sustenance, leaving their hostages behind. . . . If we do not we will be trading the children in Tingi-Tingi for the children who will be killed and orphaned in Rwanda."[19]

When I met her in Belgium, Beatrice seemed tired of this kind of reasoning. "Why do they have to measure one injustice in terms of another?" she asked. "Was the massacre of thousands of innocent people somehow more acceptable because hundreds of thousands had been killed in Rwanda?"

THIS IS HOW YOU FIGHT

BUKAVU AND LEMERA, ZAIRE, OCTOBER 1996

Kizito Maheshe was one of the thousands of children who made up the bulk of Laurent Kabila's Congolese fighters.[1] When the war began, he was sixteen years old and lived in the Panzi neighborhood of Bukavu, a muddy suburb of bumpy streets and loud bars. Like most of his friends, he had dropped out of high school because his father couldn't afford the five-dollar monthly fee. In any case, he didn't see the point in studying. In 1996, Bukavu was a town of 300,000 people with only a few thousand jobs that required a high school diploma. If you were lucky, you could get a job in either the nonprofit sector, which worked mainly in the refugee camps and had the best-paying jobs; the private sector, including the beer factory and the quinine plant, where antimalarial medicine was produced; or the civil service, perhaps the largest employer but where workers relied on bribes and embezzlement to make a decent living.

Kizito had listlessly followed his friends' path, without much hope for a decent future. After he dropped out of school at sixteen, he wandered around town, looking for work but mostly just hanging out with friends at soccer games, in neighborhood bars, and at church. He had six siblings at home, and his father, a low-level accountant, was deep in debt. The power company had cut their electricity because of nonpayment, and the pipes in their neighborhood had burst, so he helped his sisters and mother carry jerry cans of water for cooking and washing several hundred yards from the pump to his house.

When the AFDL rebellion arrived in Bukavu in October 1996, Kizito hid at home like everyone else. Through their windows and cracked doors they saw Mobutu's soldiers stripping off their uniforms in the streets and running for the hills. "For us, soldiers had been like gods. They had all the power; they were terrible," he told me. "When we saw them running like that, we were amazed."

A week after the battle for Bukavu, Laurent Kabila arrived in town. Over the radio, the soldiers called the population to the post office, a run-down, four-story, yellow building that filled up a whole block in the city center. Thousands of people turned out to see Kabila, a man most had only heard vague rumors about. After a long wait, he stepped up to the podium, dressed in his signature safari suit and sandals, and spoke in a mixture of Tanzanian-accented Swahili and French. Kizito remembered him as fat, with a big smile and sweat pouring down his neck. One of his bodyguards, a Rwandan, carried a white towel to wipe off the perspiration.

He spoke about the need to get rid of Mobutu and to allow the Congolese people to benefit from the riches that lay beneath the soil. Then he spoke to the question that was on everyone's mind: Was this a foreign invasion or a Congolese rebellion?

"If you see me here with our Rwandan allies," he told the crowd, "it's because they agreed to help us overthrow Mobutu." His podium was being guarded by a mixture of Tutsi and other soldiers, all well-armed and wearing Wellington boots. "But now we have a chance to build our own army. Give me your children and your youths! Give us 100,000 soldiers so we can overthrow Mobutu!"

Anselme Masasu, a twenty-four-year-old half-Tutsi from Bukavu, was in charge of mobilization and was popular among the youth. New recruits would get a hundred dollars a month to overthrow Mobutu. A hundred dollars a month! Kizito remembered. That was five times the monthly rent for their house. A few months with that salary and you could even buy a decent dowry and get married. Masasu began buying off youth leaders to mobilize young men and bring them to recruitment centers. He approached Boy Scout leaders, karate instructors, and schoolteachers, giving them money if they agreed to help enlist youths in the rebellion. Hundreds of street children, unemployed youths, and pupils heeded Kabila's call.

"It was obvious for me," Kizito told me. "I had no future in Bukavu. They were offering me a future."

Like most youths and children who joined the AFDL, he didn't tell his parents. He and a group of friends went to Hotel Lolango, a run-down building close to the post office where the rebels had set up a recruitment office. A soldier used a naked razor blade to shave *A*, *B* or *C* into the recruits' heads to mark which brigade they would join. Kizito was put into the *B* group; his scalp burned from the scrapings. He handed over all of his belongings—a watch, a few Nouveau Zaire banknotes, and his ID—to a recruitment officer for safekeeping and got into a waiting truck. "It was like a dream," he remembered. "I was so excited."

~:~

The AFDL's first training camp was in Kidote, a hamlet in the hills overlooking the Rusizi plain, just a few miles away from the Lemera hospital where the rebels had carried out the first massacre of the war. In March 2007, I convinced Kizito to take a day off from his job as a driver for a local development organization and take me to the place where he had been trained.

He hadn't been back since he had finished boot camp there. As we crossed the ridge and the parish came into view, he rolled down the car window and looked around in a daze. "This whole hill was full of sentries," he said, reliving the moment of his first arrival there. "You wouldn't have been able to approach— they kept the whole area blocked off."

Kidote wasn't even a village. A cluster of school buildings and an abandoned church, all with rusted, corrugated-iron roofs, were set into hills dotted with banana groves and eucalyptus trees. The buildings were surrounded by a flat area, perhaps the size of four football fields, with shoulder-high, dense elephant grass. There were no more than a dozen huts and no sign of movement in the school buildings. "We cut down all that grass. They gave us machetes, and we spent the first week just clearing the pitch. This whole plain was a training ground," he said. "The hills behind the school were all full of bivouacs made out of banana leaves that we slept in."

We parked the car and walked down to the church. It had been abandoned for a decade. Even the benches had been pillaged, probably for firewood. One of its walls had been sprayed repeatedly with bullets. Did they execute people here? I asked Kizito. "No," he said; he didn't think so. He pointed at a lone eucalyptus sapling in the middle of the meadow to our left. "It was down there."

~:~

After being recruited, Kizito's initial excitement waned quickly. The living conditions were harsh. The new recruits slept in the open for a week until they were
given tarps with UN logos—they had been taken from the dismantled refugee
camps—to build small lean-tos they could crawl into and sleep. They weren't
given uniforms, and the heavy labor tore their clothes. After several weeks, fleas
infested the camp, and many soldiers preferred to burn their clothes than to stay
awake at night, itching. "We would throw our rags into the fire and listen to the
fleas pop," Kizito said, smiling and imitating the popping sound. Kidote is
around 6,000 feet high, and even huddling together in their tiny huts at night,
the youths froze.

There were over 2,000 recruits in Kizito's training camp. They were the first
graduating class, he remembered proudly, almost all under twenty-five, with
some as young as twelve. "Some kids were shorter than their guns," he recalled,
laughing. They came from different social and ethnic backgrounds but were
mostly poor, unemployed, and uneducated. Morale, however, was high at the
beginning. "They told us that we would finish the training and get money and
have beautiful girls," Kizito remembered, laughing. "What did we know about
beautiful girls? We were very young."

Their diet consisted almost solely of *vungure*, a tasteless mix of cornmeal and
beans that often didn't have any oil or salt. Soldiers cooked the mixture over
firewood in large steel vats that had been used for boiling clothes at the nearby
hospital. The food made their stomachs knot up; many suffered from diarrhea.
They ate once a day, at 11 o'clock, placing banana leaves in holes in the ground
to use as plates. In the evening, they were given some tea with a little bit of
sugar.

The commander of the camp was a tall, light-skinned Rwandan officer called
Afande Robert,[2] who spoke accented Swahili mixed with English. He was quiet
but ruthless and feared by the recruits. They called him Mungu ("God"). After
clearing the bush for the camp, Robert began the "introduction." Kizito recalled,
"If you lived through that, it was by God's will."

The introduction was a hazing ceremony that consisted of three days of gru-
eling exercises on the training pitch. The recruits, or *bakurutu* in the local slang,
were divided into groups of twenty-five and surrounded by circles of Tutsi sol-

diers with long canes. Robert would then yell out "Roll around!" or "Snake forward!" and the soldiers would descend on them and begin beating them. *Viringita* was one of the worst exercises. Next to the pitch was a waist-deep swamp, thick with reeds. The recruits were ordered to get into the water and do somersaults as fast as they could as the soldiers beat them and insulted them. Kizito saw youths have their eyes poked out and noses broken; some were knocked unconscious by the thrashing.

Parts of the hazing were bizarre. In one exercise, called "drinking beer," recruits would stand on one leg and put one arm under the other leg and their finger in their mouth. "Maintain position for ten minutes," the order would come. In another exercise, they were forced to roll around on the ground as fast as they could for several minutes, after which their squad commander would yell, "Run!" and they would spurt off vertiginously in all directions, banging into each other. In another exercise, a commander would tell a group of sixty recruits to fetch a stick he threw in the middle of the pitch. "The first to get it doesn't get beaten!"

If you couldn't keep up with the strict regimen, you were punished. After committing a minor infraction, Kizito was told to step in front of his fellow recruits and dig a small hole in the pitch. "'This is your vagina,' the commander said. 'Take out your dick and fuck it!'" Kizito told me, blushing and looking down. In front of all of his fellow recruits, he was forced to hump the hole until he ejaculated. "In front of all those people, it was almost impossible," he muttered. At sixteen, he was still a virgin.

He once made the mistake of reporting sick. At the health center, he told the medic he had a headache, joining a long line of sullen soldiers with various ailments. The medic nodded and turned to a soldier, who then ran at them, beating them over the head with his cane. The medic laughed as they scattered into the bushes. "You aren't sick! See—you can still run!"

~:~

After the three-day induction course, Afande Robert addressed his recruits on the pitch. He was wearing a sweatsuit and sneakers and was holding a cane. Over a thousand soldiers stood in silent formation in front of him. "*Bakurutu*, the army is your family now. The army can be good, but you need to know that you can die at any moment. Have you ever seen people die? No?" He waved at one of his officers. "How many prisoners do we have in jail? Bring me six."

The officers brought out six weak and dirty prisoners. They were recruits like the rest of them who had been captured trying to desert the camp. Robert ordered his men to blindfold one and tie him to a eucalyptus tree on the edge of the clearing. They lined up in a "firing squad"—Kizito struggled with the English word he had obviously heard more than once in the army—and riddled the prisoner with bullets.

"Good!" Robert barked. "Now I will show you precision marksmanship!"

They brought out the next blindfolded prisoner and tied him to the same tree. Suku, a Rwandan officer known for being an expert shot, stepped forward and counted twenty-five paces from the tree. He pulled a modern-looking pistol from his holster, took aim, and shot the prisoner between his eyes.

"Good!" Robert then gave orders for four officers to pin the next prisoner down by his hands and legs. Another officer took out a hunting knife, pinned his chest to the ground with his knee, and slit his throat—"like a goat," Kizito remembered. The officer completely severed the head from the body, then brought it to the recruits, who were told to pass the bloody object around. "When I held the head, I could still feel his muscles twitching," Kizito said.

"Who is a good *kurutu* and thinks he can kill, too?" Robert cried out. A few brave soldiers put their hands up, eager to please. He called them forward and gave them knives. They slit the throats of the last three prisoners as their peers watched. The induction was over. From now on, Robert announced, they would be called soldiers, not *kurutu*.

⁓

The training settled into a kind of exhausting normalcy. Kizito spent four months at Kidote, although he says it felt like a whole year. Every morning, they would rise at 4 o'clock and go jogging for about six miles, singing songs as they went. At 6 o'clock, they would begin the military drills back at the camp. They would practice deploying in offensive formations, laying ambushes and crawling up hills. "Our commander would mount a machine gun in the ground behind us and shoot over our heads as we snaked up the hills. If you raised your head a bit, you were dead."

At 11 o'clock, the soldiers would come back to camp and eat their one meal of the day before heading back into the hills for more military drills. At 4 o'clock, they returned to learn how to take apart and reassemble guns, as well as to learn military tactics. In the evening, the officers gave them time to socialize and tried to teach them about the history and goals of their struggle—they called this *utamaduni*, or culture. At around 9 o'clock, most of the soldiers retired to their tents, exhausted, to sleep. In their newly learned military slang, this was *kuvunja mbavu*, "breaking your ribs." At night, Kizito would hear kids in other tents sobbing or reading the Bible in whispers.

The AFDL made an effort to instill their revolutionary doctrine in the recruits. The Rwandan and Ugandan officers who led the rebellion all started off as members of leftist insurgencies in East Africa. Knowledge of Marx, Mao, and Fanon had been de rigueur for their leaders, and these teachings filtered down to the lowest level. Kizito remembered them asking questions the recruits didn't understand: "'Who are you?' 'What do you believe in?' 'Why does a soldier fight?' It was the first time we had thought about such things." The teachers explained to them how Mobutu had ruined the country, how he had made people corrupt and tribalist. Higher-ranking officers and political cadres received more nuanced lectures, often in Kigali or Goma, about dialectical materialism and planned economies.

All recruits received a copy of Kabila's Marxist-inspired pamphlet, *Seven Mistakes of the Revolution*, which explained why the 1964 rebellion had failed. The pamphlet was more or less unchanged from its original 1967 version.

> **First mistake**—During the first revolution, we did not have precise political education. . . .

> **Third mistake**—We waged a war without goal or sense, without knowing why we were fighting and who our real enemy was. We rushed to seize large towns and forgot to first take small villages and to work with peasants and workers. . . .

> **Fifth mistake**—Due to lack of discipline and collaboration, we fought over ranks and fame. . . . Also everybody wanted to be in charge and to get positions for himself and his relatives.

Given the nature of the AFDL, some of the points seemed out of place. The second mistake was: "We relied too much on external support and advice." To the recruits, who were being trained by foreigners, the pamphlet was more of a diagnosis of the current rebellion's faults than a critique of the past. "It was Rwandans teaching us how to be patriotic, telling us to sacrifice ourselves for our country," Kizito reflected, shaking his head. "It was weird."

Twelve years later, Kizito seemed to have remembered little of the ideological training. The reason for their struggle was apparent for him and all other recruits: Mobutu needed to go.

Despite the misery, the training did produce camaraderie. Some of the recruits had not even reached puberty, and for many of them the army did indeed become their family. Back in Bukavu, we gathered one evening at Kizito's uncle's house, along with another former child soldier who had been at Kidote after Kizito. Both of them shook their heads and sucked their teeth when they remembered the extreme brutality and pain of boot camp. However, when I asked them to sing AFDL songs for me, smiles began to warm their faces, and they tentatively started to clap.

Jua limechomoka, wajeshi weee	The sun is coming out, oh soldiers
Kimbia muchaka	Go and run
Askari eee vita ni yeye	A soldier's work is war
Anasonga corporal, sergeant, platoon commander	He moves from corporal, to sergeant, then platoon commander
Anavaa kombati, boti, kibuyu ya maji	He wears a uniform, boots, and a water flask

Their favorite one appeared to be:

Kibonge	They are strong
Vijana walihamia msituni	The youths have moved into the jungle
Watatu wakufe	Even if three die
Wanne wa pone, waliobaki watajenga nchi	Four will remain to build our country
Kibonge!	Strong!

~∷~

After four months of training, a column of trucks pulled into camp, each marked with the name of a different town. Afande Robert called the soldiers together for one last assembly, then told them they were going to fight the enemy. The soldiers lined up in front of the trucks, where each was given an AK-47. They were told to load the gun, fire in the air, and jump into the truck. Kizito climbed in a vehicle with "Bukavu" written on the side. All he had was his gun and an extra clip of ammunition. It was March 1997; Kisangani, the third largest city in the country, had just fallen to the rebellion.

In town, the soldiers arrived in time for the inauguration of the new governor in the courtyard of the large Jesuit school, Alfajiri College. They paraded in front of the crowd. "It was like coming back from another planet," Kizito said, remembering seeing many of his friends and relatives again for the first time in four months. After the ceremony, they feasted on pots of beef stew, rice, and potatoes. It was the first time they had had meat in months. Before he gave them leave for the weekend, Kabila gave another speech, telling the soldiers that they were about to taste the fruits of their long training, that they would now be able to help liberate their country. Finally, he told them to shoot in the air three times before they entered their houses to scare away evil spirits. "The old man had funny ideas sometimes," Kizito remembered. "He was superstitious—'Don't wear flip-flops at roadblocks.''Don't ride a bicycle if you have a gun.'" That night, people in Bukavu thought another war had broken out. An hour after the soldiers left the schoolyard, shooting broke out all through town as the recruits chased away evil spirits.

~:~

Kizito's description of induction was grisly but confirmed much of what other AFDL recruits reported of their experiences in Kidote and other training camps. The rebellion needed recruits fast. The harsh basic training was intended to instill discipline and weed out those physically too weak for the upcoming war. It was as though the Rwandan officers wanted to beat out the corruption, idleness, and selfishness that had become, in Mobutu's own words, *le mal zairois*. Like Kizito, many of the recruits who went through this training were under eighteen years old—children according to international conventions. Diplomats estimated that 10,000 child soldiers (*kadogo* in Swahili) participated in the AFDL rebellion.[3] The rationale for child recruitment was simple: Many commanders consider that children make better, more loyal, and fearless soldiers. One commander of a local Mai-Mai militia told me: "You never know who you can trust. At least with the *kadogo*, you know they will never betray you."[4] Given the lack of discipline, the amount of infighting, and the regular infiltrations by their enemies, it was understandable that commanders wanted to have an inner security buffer of people they could trust.

For the most part, the kind of combat that soldiers engaged in was guerrilla warfare, involving risky ambushes and close-quarter fighting with the enemy. Soldiers did not have protective gear, and artillery was in scant supply. If you wanted to hit the enemy, you needed to be close enough to be effective with an AK-47—within two hundred meters of the target. Children were often the only soldiers who had the guts to engage in many of the operations, who actually obeyed orders, and whose sense of danger was not as well developed as that of older soldiers. The use of children as vanguard special forces meant also that they made up a disproportionate number of fatalities on the battlefield. A Mobutu commander who had organized the defense of the town of Kindu told me: "The first time I saw the AFDL troops, I thought we were fighting against an army of children! Through my binoculars I saw hundreds of kids in uniforms racing through bush, some carrying grenade launchers bigger than them."[5]

According to Kizito and other *kadogo* I interviewed, they often formed the first line of defense or offense. One such interviewee told me that in the battle for Kenge, in the west of the country, he had looked around to see dozens of his fellow *kadogo*, small children in oversized uniforms, sprawled dead on the battlefield.[6] No one has conducted a survey of battlefield casualties during the war, but it is safe to assume that thousands of child soldiers died during the Congo wars.

A WOUNDED LEOPARD

After me will come the deluge.
—MOBUTU SESE SEKO

KINSHASA, ZAIRE, DECEMBER 1996

The war caught Mobutu wrong-footed, off guard. When news of fighting in the eastern Congo broke, the Enlightened Helmsman—one of the many titles he had coined for himself—was convalescing in a hospital in Switzerland.

Initially, it was news of their leader's illness that preoccupied most Zairians more than war in the faraway Kivus. The first rumors appeared to have been influenced by the official press: Mobutu had been the victim of a savage toothache, an abscess perhaps. Conspiratorially, the CIA wrote to headquarters that he was suffering from AIDS.[1] It was the foreign press that managed to get the real story from the hospital: He had been operated on for prostate cancer. Again the rumors boiled up in Kinshasa, relegating the fighting in the east to the back pages of the newspapers. He had fallen into a coma along with his wife, they said. The voice on the radio, saying he would soon return, was really that of an actor, impersonating the Old Leopard quite admirably.

Initially, Mobutu was not worried about the fighting. "Kabila? I know Kabila," he told his French lawyer. "He's nothing. He's a petty smuggler who lives in the hills above Goma."

"Maréchal," the lawyer responded, "I think we need to be aware of the danger. I don't know Kabila, but he's at the head of organized, determined battalions. Behind him are the Rwandans, the Ugandans, and I think the Americans!"[2]

~:~

Even his bitterest enemies had a hard time believing that the all-seeing Guide was fatally sick. Over thirty-one years he had fashioned himself as the spiritual, political, and customary chief of the country. Two thirds of Zairians had known no other ruler. His face was on every banknote and countless T-shirts, table-cloths, and album covers. Schoolchildren sang his praises every morning before class: *One country, one father, one ruler, Mobutu, Mobutu, Mobutu!* The evening news on state television began with Mobutu's head descending from the heavens through the clouds.

With his silver-tipped black cane and leopard-skin hat, he was the modern version of a traditional king; no one could defy or even supplement his authority. "Does anybody know of a village with two chiefs?" he liked to ask.

His chieftaincy was not just symbolic. In 1980, during his fiftieth birthday celebrations, he was named King of the Bangala during an opulent coronation ceremony.[3] "Only God is above you," the officiator announced. He was hailed as Mobutu Moyi, or Mobutu Sun King.[4] That was not his only similarity with King Louis XIV of France. Through the 1974 constitution, he became head of all branches of government and could legislate by decree and change the consti-tution at his discretion. In some years he personally disposed of 20 percent of the budget. He was truly the father of the nation: He often presided over cere-monies where he cut ribbons on road projects or brought medicine to a hospital, magnanimous gifts from the father to his children. Visitors to Mobutu's palace—even foreign diplomats—could often expect to walk away with thou-sands of dollars in "presents."[5]

His health became a national concern on the street corners in Kinshasa, where people gathered around the newspaper stands and self-made pundits de-bated the impact of cancer treatment on the sixty-six-year-old. He had been castrated, some said. No, his penis had now swollen to twice its original size, enhancing his notorious sexual prowess.

In reality, the aging autocrat had fallen victim to his own bizarre beliefs. Long an acolyte of traditional healing and magic, he had allowed himself to be treated with natural herbs and tonics until the cancer spread through his body and forced him to seek help abroad.

Finally, on December 17, 1996, his presidential jet arrived at Njili airport. The political uncertainty and fear of a civil war (and probably cash handouts) drove tens of thousands to the airport and the street leading into the city. It was a taste of the good old days: Marching bands played; a phalanx of women danced, their dresses emblazoned with Mobutu's face; and people waved thousands of tiny Zairian flags. "Father has come! Zaire is saved!" they shouted.

Despite the widespread disdain for Mobutu and his rule, the uncertainty of what the rebels would bring fueled genuine acclamation for the despot's return. The clergy, the army, and even some opposition figures hailed his return to defend the nation against the "Tutsi conspiracy to create a Hima empire," as some newspapers put it.[6]

Mobutu ensconced himself in his residence at the center of the capital's largest military camp and tried to resuscitate his regime. He fired the head of the army and replaced him with a more competent officer. He arranged for several hundred French mercenaries to come to his aid, along with Serbian and South African soldiers of fortune. His generals met with Rwandan ex-FAR commanders, who were trying to regroup their soldiers who had been dispersed when the refugee camps broke up.

The Old Leopard, however, no longer had the power he used to. Since he had lifted the ban on political parties in 1990, he had slowly been relegated to a more symbolic role in politics. He spent most of his time in his jungle palace in Gbadolite, five hundred miles from the capital, and left the day-to-day running of the country to his prime minister. For years, Mobutu had carefully pitted Zaire's leading business and political leaders against each other to prevent them from challenging him. In the end, however, Mobutu's divide-and-rule tactics had left him with a splintered, ineffective shell of a government.

This mess was most apparent in the security forces, where competing militias vied for power and control of economic spoils. A firefight broke out at the Matadi port when a shipment of arms from North Korea came in. Troops loyal to General Nzimbi Ngbale, Mobutu's presidential guard commander and cousin, and those under General Mahele exchanged gunfire. The former wanted to sell the weapons for profit, while the latter wanted to use them to fight the rebels.

Mobutu's health began to fail him again. Within a month, he was back in Europe for further treatment. The vicious tongues in the capital began to wag with new rumors of his ill health. When the Central Bank issued yet another new banknote to keep track of rising inflation, it was quickly dubbed "the Prostate." Just like the president's gland, it was inflating daily. Just like the illness, these banknotes could seriously damage your health.

When Mobutu returned to Kinshasa the next time, in March 1997, only a fraction of the people turned out to welcome him. They waited in vain at the airport after the airplane arrived and didn't open its doors. Inside, a sickly Mobutu was struggling to stand up, his muscles having seized up during the ride. Masseuses rubbed his body as his staff shooed away the spectators and press from the airport. Hours later, leaning heavily on the arm of his wife, Mobutu exited the plane and headed home through the deserted streets.

~:~

Mobutu liked to watch television. He used to wake early in the morning, around 6 o'clock, to have a massage and watch the news on satellite television. He suffered from insomnia, which had been aggravated by his cancer medication.

The news was not good. Kabila's conquest of the country had become a media favorite, and dozens of news organizations flocked to the east of the country, streaming live feed of captured towns, with villagers celebrating their "liberation," around the world. Kabila's forces had captured Kisangani just days after Mobutu returned to Zaire in March 1997. Television cameras showed people lining the streets as the rebels marched into town, throwing down palm fronds, colorful cloths, and mattresses for them to walk on. In Washington, the White House spokesman announced: "Mobutism is about to become a creature of history."[7] With his back against the wall, Mobutu began thinking about negotiating. He fired his prime minister and handed power over to his long-standing rival, Etienne Tshisekedi, who promptly named a new cabinet, reserving some of the most important ministries for his "brother" Kabila. The Old Leopard sent his national security advisor to South Africa to see whether Kabila was open for negotiations.

Mobutu's pride, however, still shone through. He said he would meet with the rebel leader—but on his own terms and only if he asked politely. "Politely means, 'Mr. President of Zaire, my intention is to meet you.' That's polite," Mobutu said in a rare session with the media in April.

Mobutu spent his days in his residence, surrounded by his closest family— his wife, her sister, his son Nzanga, and his grandchildren. He took hot baths in the early morning and evening and drank infusions of lemongrass and ginger. In the evenings, when rainstorms had cleared the thick humidity from the air, he would sit on his balcony, overlooking rapids on the Congo River. Cocker spaniels and a family of peacocks played on the neatly trimmed lawns. Just outside the gates to his property, he could see a sign proclaiming, "Welcome Home, Field Marshal Mobutu."

The rest of the view was less pleasing. His swimming pool was overflowing and covered with algae, and the military camp was clogged with wrecks of military vehicles, many of which had been cannibalized for spare parts to sell on the black market. In the surrounding military camp, soldiers' undergarments hung from washing lines; garbage piled up in the ditches.

He unsuccessfully tried to reassert his power, even in the intimacy of his bedroom. His legendary sexual appetite had led him to marry three times and maintain dozens of mistresses. Even after several operations on his prostate, he reportedly continued sleeping with his wife and her twin sister, prompting profuse bleeding.[8] Moderation, never his strong suit, was not about to grace him in his old age.

The scenes played out in Kinshasa were both tragic and comic, dramatic and banal. Plump generals in alligator skin shoes held tea parties in their gardens as soldiers set fire to their barracks. Street children in rags and white gloves pretended to guide traffic while army bosses sold tanks for scrap metal on the black market. Kinshasa seemed to have fallen down a rabbit hole.

Then there was Mobutu's preoccupation with corpses. Two in particular bothered him. One was that of his first wife, Marie-Antoinette, who was buried in a crypt in Gbadolite. He worried endlessly that the rebels, who were within a few weeks' march of his hometown, would defile her tomb along with those of his sons, buried next to her. On the tenth anniversary of her death, ten years earlier, he had ordered her tomb to be hermetically sealed, but one could never be too sure. He radioed to Gbadolite to ask them to check her tomb, to make sure it could not be opened. His aides traded worried looks. He had long been rumored to be worried about her ghost haunting him. Some suggested that was the reason he had married twins—to protect him from her spirit. With one on each side of him, they would ward her off.

The second corpse had not yet been buried. It was that of Juvénal Habyarimana, the former president of Rwanda, whose body had been recovered after his plane had been shot down on April 6, 1994, over Kigali. The cadaver's journey is shrouded in mystery, but I have heard people in Bukavu, Gbadolite, and Kinshasa who insist they touched it, saw it, smelled its decomposing mass. Most likely, it was hurried out through Bukavu (my housekeeper there swore that her father, a commander in Mobutu's army, had kept it in their basement for two nights) and then made its way to Gbadolite, where it was kept embalmed and in cool storage.

Mobutu had been close friends with Habyarimana and was still hosting his widow, Agathe, who spent months in his jungle palace before fleeing to France. Mobutu promised that her husband would receive a hero's burial in Rwanda, presumably after he chased the RPF from power. When it became clear that this would not be the case, and the RPF was closing on Gbadolite, Mobutu had the body brought to Kinshasa. Fearing that the RPF troops would get their hands on the body, he ordered his friend to be cremated.

Cremation is not practiced in central Africa, and no one seemed to know how to go about it. Do you put him in an oven or on a pyre? Wouldn't the church disapprove? The body was kept embalmed in the hold of a cargo aircraft at the airport for three days as officials tried to figure out how to organize the ceremony. As Kabila's rebel army closed in on the capital, the military officer in charge of the body panicked and began calling around for advice. If he abandoned the body, he would be guilty of treason; if the RPF caught him with it, he was surely a dead man. He told a journalist: "If it were up to me, I would have dumped it into the river. But for Mobutu, it is like one of his own children. And even if it is one of his own last acts, he insisted on this being done correctly."[9]

Finally, an Indian Hindu priest was found to officiate. Even though Habyarimana had been a devout Catholic, Mobutu told them just to get on with it. On May 15, 1997, Habyarimana's body went up in flames in Kinshasa, over three years after his death. No one seems to know where his ashes are.

~:~

At the end of April, Mobutu was visited by a delegation from Washington led by Bill Richardson, President Clinton's special envoy to the region. The U.S. government was worried about a bloodbath in Kinshasa when the rebels arrived, and wanted to get the autocrat to step down. They discovered a hobbled man who needed help to stand and sit. He seemed divorced from reality; they informed him that his army's last stand at Kenge, 125 miles to the east of the capital, had failed. Richardson handed him a letter from Clinton asking that he step down with honor and dignity. The ambassador recalled: "He was being told:

'You'll be dragged through the streets. These things could happen to you and we are not going to stop them.'"[10]

Mobutu felt betrayed. The United States had supported him since the 1950s; he had visited the White House numerous times and met Presidents Kennedy, Nixon, Reagan, and Bush. He wrote a letter to French president Jacques Chirac: "Today, the US and Great Britain through their proxies South Africa, Uganda, Rwanda and Angola are using the ringleader Laurent Kabila to stab me in the back, taking advantage of my illness."[11]

Despite his fury, Mobutu was left with little choice. His ministers were beginning to hire boats to take their furniture and suitcases across the river to the neighboring Republic of Congo. His phone calls were beginning to go unanswered.

He agreed to meet with Kabila on May 4, 1997. The meeting place itself was the subject of long negotiations. Kabila refused to meet in Gabon or the Republic of Congo, fearing a French-backed assassination plot in its former colonies. Mobutu could not travel to South Africa because of his health. Finally, both parties agreed on a meeting on the South African navy ship *Outenika*, anchored just off the coast. South African president Nelson Mandela would mediate. Since Mobutu was unable to walk the thirty-one steps onto the boat, the hosts had to cobble together a plank strong enough for Mobutu's limousine to be driven on board.

For once, Mobutu was outshone in superstition. Laurent Kabila refused to look into his eyes during the meeting and instead stared at the ceiling; according to the prevailing rumor, he was afraid that the Old Leopard still had enough magical power left to curse him with his stare and prevent him from reaching his prize, now so close. It was the only time that the two rivals met; after fighting him for thirty-two years, the rebel leader had little to say to his foe. Hand over power, and step down without any conditions, he told him. Mobutu, insulted by the treatment, limped off the boat, refusing to strike a deal. Mandela, seventy-eight himself, had to prop him up as he walked to his car.

During the last days of the rainy season in Kinshasa, thunderous downpours pounded down on the rooftops and inundated whole neighborhoods. It didn't dampen the youths' anticipation, however. Graffiti began appearing on walls. One downtown said: "Mobutu = Problème, Kabila = Solution." Elsewhere, vandals painted over the "Zaire" on administrative buildings, scrawling "Congo," the name Kabila had adopted for the country, above. An enterprising young man climbed up a sixty-foot-high billboard, painted a mustache on Mobutu's face, and blackened out a tooth.

~:~

It is telling that the closest thing to a hero this period could muster was a traitor. General Donat Mahele was a lanky, tall man from the Equateur region, but not from the same tribe as Mobutu. He had been trained at France's elite Saint-Cyr military academy, held command positions in the Shaba wars of 1977 and 1978, and led Mobutu's troops sent to help Habyarimana beat back the RPF in 1990. He was a devout Jehovah's Witness and enjoyed a good reputation among foreign military advisors; when the army pillaged Kinshasa in 1991, he had the guts to order his soldiers to shoot their looting comrades, which helped bring the chaos under control.

Mahele was named to lead the Zairean army in December 1996. By the following April, after countless standoffs with other army commanders, he realized that it was a lost cause. Kabila controlled two-thirds of the country, including its diamond and copper mines. "At some point he realized that the morally right thing to do was to surrender before more lives were lost," José Endundo, the general's friend and a prominent businessman, remembered.

Everyone was worried that the AFDL's arrival in Kinshasa would prompt a bloodbath, with running gun battles in downtown streets, revenge killings, and indiscriminate shelling of civilian neighborhoods. At the very least, the thousands of demoralized soldiers would thoroughly loot the city before taking to their heels.

It was the Americans who provided General Mahele with the means to get in touch with Laurent Kabila. Ambassador Daniel Simpson, who had met with Kabila on a visit to Lubumbashi, arranged for a phone call to take place on May 14 at his residence. Mahele and Kabila spoke for half an hour and then again a few days later. They arranged for Mahele to read a speech on the radio, telling the troops to stand down when the rebels walked into town. He would also fly to the Zambian capital, Lusaka, to meet with Kabila and officially recognize him.[12]

First, however, Mobutu had to leave. If he was still in Kinshasa when the rebels arrived, some units loyal to him might try to put up a fight.

On May 15, Mobutu had just come back from another trip to the South African ship *Outenika*—Kabila hadn't even bothered turning up this time—to be met by his most powerful generals at his residence. General Likulia, who had taken over the prime minister's office in the final days, was adamant that they could still defend the capital. "I ordered attack helicopters with ample ammunition [in South Africa]. I even paid a sizeable down payment to make sure the equipment arrives."[13]

Likulia looked to the others to back him up. Mahele, however, had had enough. "*Voila, Maréchal*, I am no longer able to ensure your safety here."

Mobutu looked at him in amazement. "What are you talking about? I wasn't aware of this!" According to other, probably more dramatic witnesses, he looked at Mahele and said, "*Et tu, Brute?*"

Bobi Ladawa, the first lady, chimed in, "You betrayed your father! After everything he has done for you!"

Likulia looked to Mobutu's nephew, General Nzimbi, the commander of the presidential guard. "Nzimbi, you said you have 15,000 troops here in the city. What have you done to prepare our defense?" The general stared back in embarrassed silence.[14]

"I see," Mobutu said softly. "It is decided then. We shall leave tomorrow."

The gossip mill began churning as each person involved in the meeting began propagating his own version of what had happened. By the following morning, the news had gone out among the officer corps: Mahele had betrayed the nation.

~:~

The next day, Mobutu drove to the airport at dawn, opting for a small, less conspicuous vehicle, accompanied by ten cars stuffed with suitcases. Other objects had preceded them and had been packed onto a 747 jet that was waiting for Mobutu and his entourage. He had so much luggage that he had to leave part of it at the airport in the vehicles. Abandoned expensive vehicles were becoming a common sight in Kinshasa, especially at the various ports where Mobutu officials were fleeing across the river to Brazzaville in canoes, speedboats, and ferries.

Mahele spent the rest of the day preparing for Kabila's arrival in town. He was particularly worried about the presidential guards, the elite forces who had benefited most from Mobutu's largesse and who were recruited largely from his home region of Equateur. In the evening, he received a phone call from Prime Minister Likulia, who told him that riots had broken out in Camp Tshatshi, where the presidential guard was based.

Mahele decided to go there himself, accompanied only by a few other officers. "That was typical Mahele," a former colleague and friend told me. "Even in the 1991 Kinshasa riots, he patrolled town on foot with soldiers. That was too low! That's not the role of a general!"

At the gates of Camp Tshatshi, they found a gang of presidential guards shooting in the air, high on adrenaline. They stopped the group of officers and made them get out of their jeeps. Mahele entered the camp and tried to reason with them, but they shouted him down: "You have sold us out! You betrayed us, and now you will cross over to Brazzaville! What about us and our families!"

They began talking to each other in Ngbandi, Mobutu's mother tongue, saying that they should kill the traitor. Mahele was from the Mbuza tribe, but he got the message and began backtracking to the cars they had left outside the gate. His bodyguard Kazembe was waiting for him and forced open the gate, provoking the outrage of the soldiers, who shot him.

A commotion ensued—Mahele jumped in the car, while his other bodyguards jumped into the bushes on the side of the road. The presidential guard opened fire on the jeep, but when they looked inside, Mahele was nowhere to be seen.

"Sorcerer!" they cried out, looking under the seats. Finally, they found the general, hiding underneath the car. "I'm here, you fools. Do with me what you want!"

They took him back into the camp and tore off his general's stripes and red beret. A fight broke out between the Ngbandi and the Mbuza within the presidential guard about what should be done with him, but the scuffle was cut short when someone—some say Kongolo, Mobutu's notorious son—drew a pistol and shot Mahele in the back of his head.

Camp Tshatshi collapsed as the soldiers, leaderless and divided, fought over the remaining spoils.[15]

+ 12 +

THE KING IS DEAD;
LONG LIVE THE KING

A cat goes to a monastery, but she still remains a cat.
—CONGOLESE SAYING

KINSHASA, CONGO, MAY 1997

President Laurent Kabila spent his first few weeks in Kinshasa in May 1997 shell-shocked. It was understandable; he had not been in the capital since the early 1960s. In his mind, Kinshasa had become a mythical construct, a Babylon of excess and corruption, from where his archenemy had ruled for three decades.

The capital, called Leopoldville when Kabila had left, with its functioning administration and expansive infrastructure, had deteriorated into the riotous commotion of modern-day Kinshasa. In the early sixties, the city had been sculpted around a tidy, wealthy nucleus of white businessmen surrounded by the burgeoning Congolese elite and flanked by neighborhoods of blue-collar workers in relatively neat housing settlements built by the Belgians. By 1997, the population had grown from half a million to over five million. The city had burst at the seams, as villagers streamed into the ever-expanding shantytowns fanning south and eastward, away from downtown.

Kinshasa had become the third largest city in Africa and among the top twenty in the world, but it seemed like an oversized village. There was no functioning postal service or public transit system, and despite an overabundance of rainfall, over two million city dwellers did not have direct access to a water supply. Ninety-five percent of the population worked in the informal sector: lugging bags of cassava, shining shoes, hawking everything from aphrodisiacs to cigarettes and nail polish along the bustling streets. Tens of thousands of civil servants still showed up for work in old suits and ties—but were rarely paid. Garbage accumulated in the open sewers and on impromptu heaps by the side of the road, where it rotted and was eventually burned, filling the air with acrid smoke. Half of the population lived on one meal a day, scrounging together stacks of Nouveau Zaire banknotes to buy cassava flour and leaves for their evening meal; a quarter lived on a meal every two days.[1] *Kin la Belle* had become *Kin la Poubelle*—Kinshasa the Garbage Can.

The architecture of the city had changed accordingly. The statue at the train station of King Leopold, the Belgian monarch who had founded the country and owned it as his private property for twenty-three years, was gone. The various exclusive social clubs, where white privilege was carefully groomed, had also disappeared as the foreign population fled the city, first after the social upheaval around independence and then during the pillage of the early 1990s. Mobutu had tried to reorganize the city, constructing wide boulevards to the Chinese-built parliament and a new 80,000-seat stadium, the second largest in Africa. But city planning had failed: The shanties grew organically and anarchically, appropriating empty spaces as sewage and lighting systems broke down. The rich reacted by building higher walls around the few pockets of whitewashed privilege left in the Ngaliema and Gombe communes. The few public parks were taken over by hawkers and evangelists during the day and by the homeless at night.

The presidential gardens, which had housed Mobutu's zoo, were now overgrown with weeds. The zoo, once a model for others in Africa, was little more than a collection of rusty, dirty cages tended by unpaid keepers who looked after starving animals. Two of the lions had recently starved to death, and a group of expatriates had taken to collecting leftover food from upscale hotels to feed the remaining monkeys, chimpanzees, antelopes, and snakes. The abandoned zoo workers had tried raising chickens and fish on the land, but they had little hope for the animals.

~:~

Soon after Kabila arrived in Kinshasa, his advisors briefed him on the country's economy. It wasn't a pretty picture. The country's income had shrunk to a third of what it had been at independence in 1960. Inflation was at 750 percent. Between 1988 and 1996, copper production had plummeted from 506,000 to 38,000 tons, while industrial diamond production dropped from 10 million to 6.5 million carats. Coffee, palm oil, and tea production followed the same trend. Only 5 percent of the population had salaried jobs; many of those worked for the state on salaries as low as five dollars a month. There were 120,000 soldiers and 600,000 civil servants to pay and only 2,000 miles of paved roads in the twelfth largest country in the world.

To top it off, the government was broke. When Kabila's forces arrived in Kinshasa, one of their first stops naturally had been the Central Bank. The future vice governor of the bank had the honor of opening the vaults, only to find the huge cement chambers empty. A lonely fifty French franc note was left in one of the drawers, "as an insult."[2] In the ministries, most of the files had been burned or stolen, along with phones, fax machines, air conditioners, paper clips, and door handles.

~:~

Kabila, who spoke broken Lingala—the language of the capital—and knew almost no one in town, was daunted by Kinshasa. He slipped into the city under cover of night on May 20, depriving residents of a first glimpse of their new ruler. A silent motorcade rushed him to the *palais du marbre*, a marble palace ensconced in the leafy Ngaliema neighborhood. Mobutu had had several homes in the capital; Kabila would content himself with just one. His wife, Sifa, his concubines, and some of his eighteen children were staying elsewhere in town; he didn't want to mix business and pleasure. He didn't change his style or his personal habits. He continued to wear sandals and his drab, monochrome safari suits. His closet was full of identical suits in army green, navy blue, and brown, prompting his friends to joke that his tailor had an easy job. His diet remained inspired by his days in the bush: large quantities of venison, *ugali*—the thick maize meal preferred by Katangans—and simple vegetables stewed in palm oil.

Sometimes he ordered Chinese and Indian food, or he would go to the kitchen and ask his cooks to make him whatever they were eating themselves; he had kept a taste for manioc, squash, and potato leaves. Contrary to rumor, he didn't drink alcohol—he had high blood pressure and was diabetic—but consumed large quantities of strong, milky tea.[3]

His daily schedule also remained largely unchanged. He had problems sleeping—according to some because of his weight—and would wake before dawn and listen to the BBC Swahili and English broadcasts on shortwave radio on his balcony. He had a habit of waking up his advisors in the middle of the night to continue a discussion they had had the previous day. "I had to sleep with my phone next to the bed," Didier Mumengi, his information minister and protégé, told me. "He would call us at all hours and continue conversations where we had left off days previously." During these phone calls and everywhere else he went, Mzee—the respectful Swahili term for elder—carried a small, pocket-sized notebook in which he would jot notes incessantly.

In the few hours of leisure time Kabila allowed himself at the end of the day, he read history books. He was intrigued by the Russian and French revolutions, as well as by the New Deal—he thought he could draw on these historical lessons to transform the Congo. Biographies of de Gaulle, Mao, and Napoleon lined his study. On occasion, some ministers would stay on after a meeting and debate philosophy. "He was a well-read man with some strange ideas," one of his ministers told me. "I remember in one cabinet meeting, he asked us out of the blue whether we thought Sartre would have agreed with some policy we were discussing!"[4]

The image his former advisors paint of the new president is one of a man inflated by his new power but also confused and stifled by loneliness. Several times, he scared his bodyguards by disappearing from his presidential compound at night and driving his car into town, where he would drive around alone, trying to catch the city—which he barely knew—off guard. His soldiers would scramble into pickup trucks and chase after him, only to see their president get out of his car and order them to get back to his palace. A former minister remembered being asked to supervise a dredging project on one of the city's canals. "A few days after we began work, Mzee showed up at night, all alone in a battered Mercedes, to see how work was progressing. He gave us all a fright. Not that I was there to see him—it was 1 o'clock in the morning!"[5]

~:~

On May 29, twelve days after the rebels seized Kinshasa, the country got its first good look at its leader. Laurent Kabila was sworn into office, the nation's first new president in thirty-two years. The ceremony took place in front of 40,000 people in the Kamanyola stadium. The mood was festive. The war was over, Mobutu was finally gone, and a new chapter of Congolese history was beginning. In the baking midday sun, the Supreme Court's twenty-two justices stood up in thick red robes lined with leopard skin to swear in the head of state. Behind them on the podium sat the people who had made this moment possible: the presidents of Rwanda, Uganda, Angola, and Zambia. One by one, they filed passed the podium and embraced Kabila.

The celebration was momentarily interrupted by a group of around five hundred opposition activists in the crowd who chanted: "Where is Tshisekedi?" referring to the indefatigable opposition leader many wanted to have a role in the new government. They were soon drowned out by the marching band and Kabila supporters who answered with "Go to Togo!"—the small western African country where Mobutu had first fled after leaving Kinshasa.

The incident was a reminder that the new government was not a child of the democracy movement, that it had taken power by force. In the week before Kabila's speech, state television had broadcast several decrees that gave an idea about the orientation of the new leaders. The first, signed on May 17, announced that all activities of political parties would be suspended until further notice. The next, signed a day before the inauguration, declared that the president would rule by decree until a constitutive assembly adopted a new constitution. Kabila was granted plenipotentiary powers: He would legislate as well as name judges and all high-ranking administrative and military officials. To the opposition, it was a page out of Mobutu's playbook.

Many were willing to cut the new leaders some slack. After all, there were over three hundred political parties in Kinshasa when Kabila arrived, many of them so-called *partis alimentaires*, political guppies whose sole function was to "be fed" by the Mobutist system. There was little culture of democratic debate, and the one-party elections under Mobutu had hinged on cults of personality, ethnic politics, and the corruption of key opinion makers. An immediate opening to multiparty democracy and elections in this context could have led to a rebound by the Mobutists. Even Nelson Mandela, the dean of African democracy, deemed it "suicidal" for Kabila to allow free party activities before he had a firm grip on the government.[6] A group of visiting U.S. congresspeople accepted Kabila's measures, saying that the country needed stability first, even if it meant suppressing political protests in the short term.[7]

Kabila himself addressed these matters with typical flair during his inauguration speech: "You see, that's very nice all that. However, these gentlemen [who demand elections] were co-responsible for the misdeeds of the dictatorship in this country. During three decades they never organized elections, nor did they care for human rights. They now want for the AFDL to organize in haste and without delay elections, as if democracy was not something that belongs to our people but only to them."[8]

Kabila promised that these measures would be temporary and that after a transitional period of two years, political parties would be able to operate again and elections would be held. In the meantime, he named a constitutional commission—all close allies and members of the AFDL—to draft a new constitution.

~:~

Kabila's honeymoon was brief. When the ban on political activity was challenged by the vibrant local elite, Kabila lashed out.

On November 25, Arthur Zahidi Ngoma, a former UNESCO official who had recently entered Congolese politics, tried to hold a press conference at his residence. A special police unit broke into the house, filled the air with tear gas and bullets, and arrested everyone present, including several journalists. Around twenty people were taken to police headquarters, made to lie down on the cement floor, kicked in the stomach, neck, and head, and then beaten severely with sticks. Zahidi himself was awarded fifty-one lashes, one for each year of his age.[9]

Dozens of other politicians who defied the ban on party activities were rounded up and given similar treatment. The most illustrious was Etienne Tshisekedi. When Kabila first arrived in Kinshasa, Tshisekedi reached out, saying that he wanted to work with the new leadership. However, Tshisekedi quickly withdrew to a typically hardheaded position, demanding that the government be dissolved and that he be appointed prime minister, a position that had been given to him by the National Sovereign Conference in 1992. Kabila threw Tshisekedi into prison several times, but he proved impossible to shut up.

Finally, in February 1997, Kabila lost his patience and had him deported to his remote home village of Kabeya-Kamwanga "with a tractor and some soy seeds so he can put his leadership skills to the service of our agricultural sector."[10]

For human rights organizations, which had spent the previous decade taking Mobutu to task for his repressive regime, there was little respite. Within the first few months of Kabila's regime, at least twelve human rights advocates from across the country were arrested and interrogated for criticizing the government or inquiring into the detention of Mobutists; many were beaten. Nongovernmental organizations had flourished in some parts of the country during the latter years of Mobutu's dictatorship, offering a much needed counterbalance to the heavy-handed state. When they began to criticize Kabila's government, some of their leaders were arrested and told they had overstepped their limits. In the eastern gold-mining town of Kamituga, three members of a human rights group were detained after they published reports accusing the local prosecutor of corruption. They were subjected to daily beatings of a hundred to two hundred lashes until they accepted the supreme authority of the government.[11]

In October 1997, the minister of information, Raphael Ghenda, proposed outlawing direct foreign funding to nongovernmental organizations, saying that there should be a government intermediary set up for managing these funds.[12] Several months later, the government went a step further, accusing all human rights groups en bloc of "destabilizing the government and contributing to the decrease in foreign aid by disseminating false reports and lies." The government then began creating and sponsoring their own civil society groups, charged with reporting on human rights violations but also with informing the government of "foreign manipulations."[13] Soon, the government also began to pay "transport fees" for journalists attending press conferences, and in some cases the ministry of information made direct donations to impoverished newspaper editors. At the same time, they banned commercials on private radio stations, depriving them of all legitimate revenue. Security agents began regularly visiting the offices of radio stations and newspapers, asking editors what they had slated for the upcoming show or publication. Several senior editors were arrested and taken in for questioning when they published stories that embarrassed the government. The tactics came straight out of Mobutu's bag of tricks—a mixture of coercion and co-optation—and were effective. The newspapers critical of the government, *Le Phare, Le Potentiel,* and *La Référence Plus,* began to water down their denunciations.

This repression led to a renowned diplomatic incident that helped seal Kabila's fate as a pariah of the west. In December 1997, Secretary of State Madeleine Albright visited Kinshasa to meet with Kabila. Relations between the senior U.S. diplomat and the Congolese head of state were not good. Several months before her visit, during the height of the refugee crisis, Albright had called Kabila, threatening serious consequences if he didn't allow investigators into the country to find out what had happened with the missing Rwandan refugees. Kabila had hung up on Albright mid-sentence, muttering, "Imperialist!"[14]

Nevertheless, the meeting went fairly well. Albright argued that it would be in Kabila's own interest to open up political space to his critics, that it would make him look stronger, not weaker. As often, he was eloquent and affable, expressing himself in fluent English. When they walked into the rotunda of the presidential palace, where a press conference had been organized, he went first, rattling off a series of fairly uncontroversial statements. Then, an American journalist asked Kabila about the recent arrest of Zahidi Ngoma, pointing out that this had been interpreted as a crackdown on his opponents. Suddenly, Kabila became agitated and began berating the reporter. "This gentleman [Zahidi Ngoma] is not a politician," Kabila said, jabbing a finger in the air. "He's not a political leader. Do you call a political leader those who come on the street to incite people to kill each other . . . who manufacture political pamphlets with the intent of dividing people? Do you call people like that political leaders? Do you let people like that out on the street?"[15]

Then Kabila put his fingers up in a *V* for victory and said, "Viva democracy!"[16] The Americans were not amused.

~:~

In retrospect, Kabila's heavy-handedness does not make much sense. The public had been relatively favorable toward him at the beginning, and what little opposition there was against him was disorganized and weak. Why did he squander the initial goodwill with such squabbles?

Many have dismissed Kabila's hostility to domestic and foreign critics as evidence of his authoritarian nature. While it was clearly a factor, more was behind his reaction than just a despotic personality. As much as anything else, his allergic reaction to challenges to his regime stemmed from the profoundly weak position he was in. Pressed into a corner and feeling vulnerable, he reacted by lashing out.

Kabila came to power on the wings of a rebellion sponsored and, to a large degree, fought by other armies. He had tried to gain independence by surrounding himself with businessmen and intellectuals from the diaspora whom he barely knew. The people who surrounded him day and night—his personal assistant, the commander of his bodyguard, his secretary and protocol officer—were all Rwandan or Congolese Tutsi. His army was a jigsaw of foreign troops, *kadogo* (child soldiers), Katangan Tigers, and former Mobutu troops. Kabila felt like the majordomo in a house owned and lived in by others.

Some of Kabila's former associates ascribe this lack of political cohesion to the unexpectedly quick success of the rebellion. Colonel Patrick Karegeya, who had helped manage the rebellion from Kigali, told me: "We reached Kinshasa in six months. Even basic training for a soldier takes nine months! We were not prepared." Ugandans, in particular, were dismayed at the speed of their advance. Museveni drew on his own experience fighting a guerrilla war. His insurrection lasted five years, from 1981 to 1986, and received little help from other countries. This helped eliminate opportunists who were there to make a quick fortune and fostered cohesion and self-reliance among the remaining officers. The AFDL's brushfire advance across the country, coupled with the foreign domination of the rebellion, produced a weak and fractured government.

From this position of weakness, Kabila saw critics as threats. After all, most newspapers were not able to sell enough advertising or copies to cover even their overhead and sought funding from politicians. The only way entrepreneurs in Kinshasa could get ahead under Mobutu was to seek political patronage; most businesses had links to the system Kabila had just toppled. And all the main civil society groups received funding from Europe or the United States, countries that were deeply critical of him because of the massacres of Rwandan refugees.

If Kabila had given way to demands for multiparty democracy and elections immediately, he would have most likely lost power. Indeed, an independent opinion poll in June 1997 indicated that 62 percent of the capital's population supported opposition leader Etienne Tshisekedi, while only 14 percent favored Kabila.[17]

⌒⁚⌒

Moreover, the new leaders were mostly inexperienced. Following Mobutu's demise, hundreds of top officials in government agencies and ministries were sacked or fled into exile. "It was like what the Americans did with the Baath

Party in Iraq," one official in the Ministry of Mines told me. "From one day to the next, everybody was gone."[18]

The government did not have the time or the means to conduct a serious job search for all the new officials it needed. This led to ad hoc, hasty decisions. When Jean-Claude Masangu, the director of Citibank in Kinshasa, visited the new minister of finance to introduce himself, the minister sized him up: "Aren't you Congolese? Are you looking for a job? We need people like you!" Several weeks later, Masangu was appointed governor of the Central Bank (it didn't hurt that his father had been a childhood friend of Kabila's).[19]

To Kabila's credit, the first ministerial cabinet included several respected members of the opposition: Justine Kasavubu, a former Tshisekedi activist and daughter of the country's first president, became the head of civil service. Two prominent doctors and Mobutu opponents, Jean Kinkela and Jean-Baptiste Sondji, were named as ministers of telecommunications and health, respectively.

The most important portfolios, however, went to unseasoned members of the diaspora. Mwenze Kongolo, a bail officer from Philadelphia, became interior minister, and Mawapanga Mwana Nanga, an agronomist from the University of Kentucky, was named minister of finance. A few appointees didn't even know Kinshasa and had to hire drivers or guides to show them around the capital, as they had just returned from decades of exile.

Two of the new ministers had had run-ins with the law abroad. Thomas Kanza, who was in charge of regional cooperation and aid, was unable to deal with the U.S. government because he was wanted in Tennessee for fleeing a $300,000 fine for fraud. Celestin Lwangy's nomination for justice minister elicited some chuckles in the Belgian press, as he had served eight months in prison in Belgium for illegally hooking up his electricity supply to the power grid.

It was no surprise that this motley group had trouble carrying out the necessary reforms. Nonetheless, with the arrival of the AFDL, the Congolese did get their first taste of democracy. In towns across the country, mayors and governors were initially elected by popular vote. Kabila, never one for lengthy proceedings, made short shrift of ballots and simply told people to gather together in the town square or marketplace. He would then parade a number of candidates in front of the crowd and ask them to raise their hands if they were in favor. The man—almost no women stood for election—for whom the highest number of hands were raised was immediately proclaimed winner. Despite its improvised nature, this process produced some decent results. Several well-respected university lecturers were elected by popular acclamation. This experiment, however, was brought to a hasty end when Kabila realized that many of the leaders that the population wanted to elect, especially in the center and the west of the country, belonged to Tshisekedi's party.

Other initiatives were also aborted when Kabila feared that opponents of the regime could hijack them. Soon after the AFDL took power, the new minister for reconstruction announced that national and provincial conferences on reconstruction would be held so local leaders could propose development priorities. The participants, however, saw this as an opportunity to talk about much more than just development. They began condemning their new government for "misguided behavior" and "cooperation agreements with foreign armies," and they demanded the opening of political space.[20] Kabila soon suspended the whole initiative and adopted a more top-down approach toward development.

"During that first year we started a dozen projects and finished almost none," Didier Mumengi, the former information minister, told me. "Kabila was surrounded by people with no experience. We didn't have any money. And the Rwandans were still there, looking over his shoulder." Mumengi shook his head. "Kabila was a man who needed to be helped. But he wasn't." On one occasion, the president decided he wanted to create a "canteen for the people," where the poor could come and eat. Mumengi said he tried to dissuade him, saying that it would not be feasible, but the president insisted. "The people are hungry! They have a right to eat," he told them.[21] "The amount of money we wasted on bags of corn and beans!" Mumengi remembered. "That was misguided socialism."

⌁∶∽

Lastly, we have to understand the time warp that Kabila was in. For decades, he had set his compass to the cold war divide, preaching against the neocolonial domination of Africa by the United States. To people who met him in the early days of his presidency, it was as if the fall of the Berlin Wall and the collapse of the Soviet Union had passed him by; he gave the impression of a revolutionary fossilized in the 1960s. He had come of age during the anti-western socialist rebellions that swept through Africa just after independence. The writings of Kwame Nkrumah, Mao Tsetung, Walter Rodney, and Frantz Fanon lined his bookshelf; after he took power he continued to call his associates "comrade" (although, apparently none of them was allowed to reciprocate).[22]

To make matters worse, Kabila was saddled with questions about the massacre of Rwandan refugees. According to his advisors, he initially thought this, too, was an American conspiracy to smear his revolutionary government. Only later did he come to realize that RPF troops had carried out systematic killings.[23]

In all his early interactions with western diplomats as head of state, the refugee crisis dominated discussions. Immediately after he was sworn in, all contacts with the Congo's traditional donors—Belgium, the United States, the United Kingdom, and France—focused on the alleged massacres. The day of his inauguration, the UN Security Council issued a statement calling for "an immediate end to the violence against refugees in the country" and demanded full access for the UN human rights teams.[24] President Bill Clinton dispatched UN Ambassador Bill Richardson to meet with Kabila several days later. He obtained yet another promise to allow the UN investigators into the country, but Kabila turned around several days later and dismissed the initiative as a "French-inspired smear campaign."[25]

The first UN report on the massacres was published in January 1997 in the midst of the rebellion and prompted Kabila to block any further investigations. Kabila eventually accepted the deployment of another team, but this time demanded that they be accompanied by Congolese officials, whose trip expenses would be $1.7 million per day, higher than the working costs of any government ministry.[26] When the team finally deployed to the field in early 1998, they were met on several occasions by "spontaneous" mobs of locals armed with machetes and spears. The United Nations finally abandoned its efforts in April 1998.

The refugee question helped snuff out any chance for rebuilding the country. Donors didn't want to give the new government the wrong message and made funds conditional upon a serious investigation. This attitude contributed to a vicious circle. Kabila defaulted on his promises of human rights and governance, prompting aid to be cut, which led to a further radicalization of the regime. When the World Bank convened a donors' meeting in Brussels in December 1997, Kabila asked for $575 million to help rebuild the country but received a mere $32 million. Eritrean president Isaias Afeworki visited Washington around the same time and urged the United States not to give up on Kabila, warning that it could be disastrous, that Kabila needed to be helped. "Kabila stinks," he told U.S. officials, "but you have to just hold your nose and engage."[27] They didn't.

To add insult to injury, the World Bank informed the new government that they owed $14 billion in debts that Mobutu had accumulated over the years, debts on which interest would have to be paid each year. For the new government, it was the height of hypocrisy that they would have to pay back money that had served largely to enrich Mobutu's cronies and destroy the country.

Kabila, feeling let down, lambasted the "embargo" western countries had imposed on the Congo. With little money in his coffers and a collapsed economy, Kabila had to rely on donations from his allies, including $10 million a month from Zimbabwe, and on the strength of diamond exports, the main source of Congo's foreign currency.[28]

⁓∶⁓

Like a car driven by a learner not yet used to a clutch, the government lurched clumsily from one policy initiative to another. One thing was sure, however. For a man who was initially perceived as a puppet of foreign interests, Kabila left no doubt that he was in charge. During his first year in power, he had no fewer than seven ministers arrested, as well as the self-styled commander in chief of the army, two directors of his intelligence agency, and the governor and vice governor of the Central Bank. He used justice as a tool of disciplining his associates at his discretion, not as a means of enforcing the law. There were rarely any trials or verdicts, and the arrests were usually short-lived. It is possible that the accusations against the accused were well-founded, as reports of embezzlement plagued Kabila's various administrations. He himself was known to say that the AFDL was a "conglomerate of crooks." In the end, however, he realized that loyalty was more important than integrity, and he used the arrests as a means of reminding his subordinates of his power, not to impose accountability.

Kabila's idiosyncratic style extended to his personalized management of state funds. He was known to keep large stashes of money at his residence, where he would dole out stacks of bills to visitors. In early 1998, when the government tried to contract a Swedish company to print the Congolese franc as the new currency, the minister of finance complained they didn't have the funds. Kabila told him not to worry—he would get the money at home. When he came back, he brought more than $1 million in cash with him to cover the expenses.[29] Similarly, when his assistants brought to his attention that Congolese students in the diaspora were running out of stipends to pay their tuition, he took $1 million out of his safe to foot the bill. "He didn't keep records and didn't ask for invoices or receipts," remembered Moise Nyarugabo, his personal assistant at the time. "It was a disaster."

Kabila had a disdain for institutions intended to oversee the executive and hold him in check. For over two years after he took power, there was no Parliament or official budget, no means by which to hold the government accountable for its actions. "The means by which money left the Central Bank and went to pay for state projects or for salaries was an utter mystery to us," remembered Mabi Mulumba, the auditor general.[30] According to some former AFDL officials, up to half of the country's funds were managed directly by Kabila.[31]

Perhaps the funniest, albeit not most reliable, story about Kabila's personal banking system comes from Deo Bugera, the head of his political party who defected to join a new rebellion against Kabila in 1998. Like so many of the apocryphal stories surrounding Kabila, it is worth retelling, in part because it could well be true, but also because it was part of the constantly growing and increasingly surreal mythology about the new regime.

According to Bugera, a delegation of military officials from various southern African countries was visiting Kinshasa to see how the formation of the new army was proceeding. Many countries had invested in this project by sending officers to help train the new recruits and integrate Congo's fractured militias. During a long meeting with Kabila, a Tanzanian commander excused himself, saying he had to use the toilet. Kabila looked around sheepishly and finally ordered a bodyguard to find the key for the toilet. The bodyguard ran about, but was unable to come up with the key. Finally, the Tanzanian was taken to a toilet in another building much further away. After their meeting was finished, Kabila reprimanded his bodyguard with a laugh, fishing a key out of his pocket: "You idiot! I had the key the whole time! All my money is stored in that toilet—I couldn't let him in there!"

∻

After six months in power, by the end of 1997, Kabila was becoming increasingly worried for his life. Nothing seemed to be working—his quixotic plans for the

country were stymied by disorganization around him and his own erratic behavior. The coffers of the state were empty, and donors were reluctant to give
money to the regime. At the same time, the Rwandan military had permeated
the security services in Kinshasa. A Rwandan, Captain David, was Kabila's main
bodyguard and accompanied him everywhere—he held his glasses, his notebook, and his pen for him. He stood in front of his door when Mzee slept. He
rode in the front seat of the presidential car. Another Rwandan, Captain Francis
Gakwerere, was the commander of the presidential guard. Rumors of coup attempts filtered through to Kabila regularly, fueling his paranoia.

The population was also becoming increasingly discontent with the Rwandan
presence in the city. Kabila's AFDL soldiers, most of whom were from conser-
vative, rural backgrounds, cracked down on what they saw as lewd and disrespectful behavior, arresting women for wearing tight dresses and pulling people
out of taxis if they exceeded the legal passenger limit. Everywhere child soldiers
could be seen caning people splayed out on the asphalt for minor violations. It
was as if they were trying to beat propriety into Kinshasa's inhabitants.

The situation was volatile; Kabila's paranoia became a self-fulfilling prophecy.
By early 1998, diplomats and government officials in Luanda, Kinshasa, Kigali,
and Kampala were already fueling rumors about Kabila's imminent demise and
wondering who would replace him. Tired of his whimsies and monopolization
of power, former allies began plotting against him.

Moise Nyarugabo, a Tutsi from South Kivu who had been his personal assistant, was one of many Tutsi to fall out with Mzee soon after they arrived in
Kinshasa. One morning shortly after his inauguration, Kabila called Nyarugabo
into his office, where he was preparing a list of people for his first cabinet. According to him, Kabila told him without preamble:

"Look, I can't make you minister, as that would be two Tutsi in my cabinet.
I'm very sorry. You can leave now." Two weeks later, Nyarugabo found out
through friends that he had been named as the deputy director of a government
body charged with expropriating state goods that had been stolen by Mobutists.

"We had been together the whole day and he hadn't had the guts to tell me!
That day, I decided to fight him."

Nyarugabo stormed into Kabila's office. "Look, Excellency, if I bother you because I am Tutsi, I can leave you—it's not a problem. But why did you name all

of these people to your cabinet who were not with us when we were being attacked? I hid with you under tables when Mobutu was bombing us! I was loyal
to you!"

By November 1997, just six months after Kabila took power, Nyarugabo and
other Tutsi were reaching out to Mobutu's ousted generals and former ministers
in Brazzaville and Europe. It wasn't difficult to find people opposed to Kabila
and willing to fund a new uprising. In the end, Laurent Kabila would only pre-
side over a peaceful country for fifteen months, from May 1997 to August 1998,
before another war would break out in the east of the country.

"It was obvious by then that Kabila had to go," Nyarugabo said. "I talked to
several people, including Bugera. The easiest option would have been a coup d'é-
tat. But—believe it or not—at that point Rwanda didn't want to do that. It
would have been easy! But for some reason, they didn't want to go that far. Not
yet."[32]

PART III

THE SECOND WAR

ONE WAR TOO MANY

No matter how hard you throw a dead fish in the water,
it still won't swim.

—CONGOLESE SAYING

RUHENGERI, RWANDA, AND KINSHASA, CONGO, AUGUST 1998

The war to topple Mobutu had created serious security problems back in Rwanda. The Rwandan army's attack on the refugee camps caused hundreds of thousands of refugees to stream back into their country. The authorities there knew that this influx would create trouble, as their enemies would seize the opportunity to infiltrate. "We had a discussion about what to do with them," Vice President Kagame explained. "We think that it is better for them to come and we fight them here, [where] we can contain them. And you don't get problems with the international community for fighting them outside your country."[1] Between 10,000 and 15,000 enemy soldiers entered into northwestern Rwanda in the months following the invasion.[2]

These insurgents sparked the worst fighting the country had seen since the genocide. By the end of 1997, the northwest region was in upheaval, suffering dozens of insurgent attacks each month against government installations. The insurgents also targeted government officials and sympathizers in an effort to intimidate the population into supporting them.

The infiltrators, however, were militarily weak and didn't try to engage in conventional battles with the government. Instead, they adopted terror tactics, killing hundreds of Tutsi, especially Congolese refugees who were easy targets in makeshift refugee camps close to the Congolese border. Between January 1997 and August 1998, thousands of civilians were killed by both the Rwandan army and the insurgents as the tactics of insurgency and counterinsurgency became increasingly bloody.

General Paul Rwarakabije himself had infiltrated across the Rwandan border in July 1997 and become the operational commander of the insurgency, based around the town of Nyamutera. "Our headquarters was mobile," he explained. "We never spent too long in one place, but moved around, sleeping in the huts of local sympathizers."[3] The insurgents held meetings in local schools at night and brought their office along, transporting official letterhead, stamps, and maps with them. They avoided using walkie-talkies for fear of being detected or overheard. Instead, Rwarakabije and his comrades relied heavily on locals, sending letters with operational orders via local farmers or market women, who then passed them on to other sympathizers.

The insurgents were initially popular among some locals in northwestern Rwanda. This was the heartland of President Habyarimana's regime, from where he and many in his government came. The insurgents sometimes referred to themselves as *les fils du vieux*—the sons of the old man (Habyarimana). Many of the villagers there were returnees from the camps in Zaire and still harbored deep resentment against the RPF for overthrowing "their" government and for the massacres carried out in the refugee camps. They articulated their grievances in messianic terms—evangelism had found fertile ground in the camps, and preachers had been touting their people's return to the promised land. The commanders gave two of their operational sectors the code names "Nazareth" and "Bethlehem."[4]

Thus the Rwandan civil war started up again, after a hiatus of three years. The same commanders faced off again on the battlefield, only this time Kagame's troops were in power in Kigali, and Habyarimana's former army was hiding in banana groves and eucalyptus woods. The Tutsi-led Rwandan government, intimately familiar with the dangers of such an insurgency, having come to power on the back of one themselves, responded with overwhelming force. They deployed thousands of troops to the region and began ruthless counterinsurgency operations. Their first priority was to convince the population that they would suffer more if they collaborated with their enemy than if they didn't. According to human rights reports, they cordoned off areas, rounded up peasants suspected to be in connivance with the rebels, and then beat and shot many of them. Some of their victims were probably working with the rebels; many others were not.[5]

In early 1998, Rwarakabije noticed a strange development. Soldiers in his ranks were quietly defecting and going to a Congolese army training camp in Rumangabo, just across the border from where he was operating. At the same time, Congolese officers based in the eastern Congo were baffled by instructions that were coming from Kabila's army headquarters in Kinshasa. "The Rwandan commanders who were based with us were busy day and night fighting the ex-FAR and Interahamwe," a senior Congolese intelligence officer recalled, "but at the same time, Kabila sent a delegation in June 1998 to instruct us to send all the ex-FAR prisoners we had to a military base in the south of the country. We heard from our friends there that these ex-FAR were being freed and trained in the Congolese army. We were floored!"[6]

President Kabila had made his move. In his mind, if he waited too long, the Rwandans and Congolese Tutsi would remove him from power. In the early months of 1998, Kabila's army was a loose pastiche of *kadogo*, Katangan Tigers, and new recruits. The Angolans, Ugandans, and Rwandans, who had been the backbone of his rebellion, had mostly returned to their countries. He needed his own force, and in desperation he drew on the largest, most determined mercenary troops available in the region: the ex-FAR, Habyarimana's former army, which his AFDL rebellion had sought to defeat. It was a deal with the devil, one that precipitated Rwanda's new invasion.

~:~

Malik Kijege, the highest-ranking Congolese Tutsi in the Kinshasa garrison, was in a foul mood. In July 1998, Laurent Kabila sacked Colonel James Kabarebe, the Rwandan officer who had been commander of the Congolese army, and asked all Rwandan troops to leave the country. The departure of the Rwandans left the army without a real leader at a moment when hostility against Tutsi in Kinshasa was mounting and tensions between Kinshasa and Kigali were escalating. General Celestin Kifwa, the new commander, was over sixty years old and incompetent. They called him a *fetisheur*, a witch doctor, as it was rumored that he believed in magic potions and in consulting the ancestors to make decisions. When he arrived to take over his office from his Rwandan predecessor, he allegedly brought a goat with him that he proceeded to slaughter so as to chase away the evil spirits. He had hardly been seen in public since his nomination. For Malik Kijege, this was probably a good thing. One of Kifwa's bodyguards had shot a Tutsi soldier dead the day before during an argument. The less he got to see of Kifwa, the better.

Anti-Tutsi sentiment was quickly spreading through Kinshasa, whipped up by Kabila's politicians but also fed by the beatings and humiliations that residents of the capital had endured at the hands of the Rwandans. Congolese police and soldiers evicted dozens of Rwandan soldiers from apartments in downtown Kinshasa, took them to the airport, and put them on planes for Kigali. The enthusiasm of these Congolese security forces quickly boiled over; they began harassing and attacking Tutsi civilians and Congolese soldiers, prompting the justice minister to appear on national television, instructing soldiers not to bother Tutsi civilians.

Malik Kijege was well acquainted with the kind of mob violence that anti-Tutsi sentiment could provoke. During a similar frenzy in 1996, soldiers had shot and killed his aunt in the street in Bukavu. "Every time there is trouble, you can expect the crazies to take it out on us," he recalled.[7] At home, he still kept a copy of a tape distributed by ex-FAR demagogues in the refugee camps, exhorting Bantu people to rise up and chase the Tutsi down the Nile River back to Ethiopia, where they claimed the Tutsi came from.

Malik began to reach out to other Tutsi soldiers, who were dispersed throughout Kinshasa's various military camps. In case of trouble, he thought, it would be smart for them to assemble in one place to find safety in numbers. "When the Rwandans left, we stayed behind," he said. "We thought we were Congolese, not Rwandan. We had fought the war so as to defend our citizenship. We weren't about to be forced onto a plane to go to Kigali."

One evening shortly after the departure of Rwandan troops, General Yav Nawej, the newly appointed commander of Kinshasa, telephoned after he heard that Kijege was assembling Tutsi soldiers. "Malik! Where are you?" He barked at him.

"I'm at home."

"Get your weapons. I am coming to disarm you to take to you to Makala [the central prison]. Don't ask me why—that's an order!"

"General, I came here with my weapon, and I am going to leave with it."

"That's a mutiny!"

"I have a right to self-defense, General."

"Get ready then. I am coming."[8]

Shortly afterwards, Malik received another phone call from General Jean-Claude Mabila, another commander leading military operations in the capital. He threatened that he would come and disarm Malik with a tank. That made Malik laugh: "How do you disarm a couple of soldiers with a tank?"

Malik was worried that the lack of a clear chain of command would allow soldiers to take the law into their own hands and begin attacking Tutsi soldiers in the capital. Congolese troops had chafed under the command of Rwandans, who together with Congolese Tutsi had formed an elite clique within the AFDL. They were itching for a chance to get back at the Tutsi.

According to Malik, he called Joseph Kabila, the president's son, who was in China undergoing military training. The young army officer, just twenty-seven at the time, reassured Malik that he knew there were problems in the government. He sounded worried. "I'll be back in three days," he promised him.

"Three days is too long," Malik answered.

By August 2, Malik had been able to assemble 586 Tutsi soldiers in an improvised battalion at Camp Tshatshi, a large military camp in Kinshasa. "I knew exactly how many they were; I counted them." His foul mood began to lift. In front of him, on the parade grounds, he inspected the troops. They stood at attention in lines of twenty, their hands flat by their sides. Some didn't have boots; others didn't have whole uniforms. They were mostly young Tutsi recruits who had joined in 1996: students, peasants, and cowherds who had joined to fight for their community and to find adventure. Most of them had ended up walking across the country, fighting Mobutu's troops, ex-FAR, and Serbian mercenaries from town to town.

"They were inexperienced, but the morale was high," Malik remembered. "We had a key advantage: We were united; we were fighting for our survival. The others were just bandits."

That night the fighting started, heralding the beginning of the second congo war.

~:~

Didier Mumengi was awakened at 4 o'clock in the morning on August 3 by heavy shooting.[9] He lay awake for a while with a sinking feeling in his stomach as he listened to the call-and-response of a booming mortar and staccato machine gun fire. It was only a year since he had returned to the country after several decades living in Brussels, where he had spent most of his life studying, writing, and moving in the circles of the Congolese political opposition. A month before, the thirty-six-year-old had been appointed information minister by Laurent Kabila.

At 4:30 his clunky Telecel phone rang. The Congo was one of the first countries in Africa to have a mobile phone network, as a result of the absence of working landlines. Anybody of importance in the capital had a Telecel phone, a device the size of a milk carton with a rubber antenna attached to it. There were so few numbers that their owners could write all the important ones on the back of an envelope or memorize them. "Didier!" Kabila's baritone rang out.

"Yes, Excellency."

"We are under attack. You have to go to the Voice of the People [the national radio station] and talk to the country. It's important to calm people down. Tell them we have the situation under control."

"Yes, Excellency. Who is attacking us?"

The president paused. "Just tell them *inciviques*—bandits."

Mumengi quickly got dressed and jumped in his official car. On his way to the radio station, he had to double back several times and take side roads to avoid cannon fire. His mind was racing as he tried to think of what he would tell the country; he had no idea what was going on. Who exactly was attacking? Was this linked to the president's eviction of the Rwandan contingent several days before?

At 5:30 he finally reached the radio station, a nineteen-story, decrepit building surrounded by an asphalt network of major thoroughfares. He raced in the back door and up the stairs to the radio studio. All the soldiers who had been posted there had fled, knowing that the building was a prime target for any mutineers. (The first move in a military putsch is usually to seize the radio and television stations in order to control popular sentiment and encourage desertions.) The place was deserted. The usual smell of sewage wafted up through the cement stairwell, lit by flickering neon lights. He heard a noise from the broadcasting room: The journalists on night shift had barricaded themselves in there when the fighting had started. A man with shaky hands opened the door when Mumengi told them who he was. One of the journalists had died of heart failure; the others were visibly distressed.

Mumengi told them to hold on as he rushed down the stairs again and across the street to the Kokolo military camp, the largest barracks in Kinshasa. The sun was just coming up, and other than a few dogs and some laundry flapping in the breeze, there was no movement among the rows of cement houses. Mumengi finally found one desolate old man, who didn't recognize him and wasn't able to tell him who was in charge. "The place had completely fallen apart!" Mumengi remembered. "Most soldiers had moved out and rented their houses to civilians, who were cowering under their beds! Part of the parade grounds had been turned into cassava fields!"

Finally, Mumengi reached by phone a cousin who was a general in the army. He promised to come as soon as possible with reinforcements. Mumengi rushed back to the radio studio to address the nation. For Mumengi, who was known for his flowery speeches, it was one of his less inspired performances: "Citizens, patriots. Do not leave your houses, and stay calm. *Inciviques* are troubling public order. I assure you that the army has full control of the situation and will reestablish order soon." Then he had the technicians play some mellow music.

He had lied. The army didn't control anything. As Mumengi left the radio building with his cousin and hurried to the presidential palace, they saw the streets were deserted. Mortar and machine gun fire was passing overhead without any obvious target. His cousin, the army general, shook his head: "It's a mess. A complete mess."

~:~

Kabila received Mumengi at the heliport behind his presidential palace. He was wearing a dark safari suit and flip-flops and holding a walkie-talkie. Grinning, he sat Mumengi down in the middle of the concrete landing pad.

"Didier," he said, "first, don't worry. We'll survive. We will live through this." Instead of comforting him, the president's words had the opposite effect. He thought his boss had lost it. The presidential palace was only several hundred yards from the Tshatshi military camp where Malik had dug himself in. The heavy artillery fire was deafening. As they spoke, Mumengi could hear bullets whistle overhead.

Given the circumstances, Kabila was curiously jovial. "Look, my son," he started. Mumengi's father had been involved in the rebellion of the 1960s and had known Laurent Kabila. Over the past few months, Mumengi had grown close to the president, who would often call him to discuss policy. To people around Kabila, he was known as *l'enfant cheri* of Mzee. "Our Rwandan friends have always dominated us. It was like this under Mobutu—they pushed him to undergo Zairianization, which they benefited from! They asked him to sign a decree that made all immigrants into citizens. Is that normal? The Tutsi in the east had everything, while the Congolese were stuck with nothing."

The firefight crescendoed around them. Mumengi suggested they go inside the thick cement walls of his residence, but Kabila refused, saying that his presence outside would reassure his soldiers, the dozens of young men manning the parapets of his palace in green fatigues. He took his walkie-talkie and called one of his commanders, "General Mabila! Why are you firing the cannon? It's not with artillery that you will get them! Attack on foot!"

He looked back at Mumengi, who was shaken by the fighting surrounding them. "You know, Japan dominated China. That is normal. But I will not let our great country be dominated by its tiny neighbor. Can a toad swallow an elephant? No!"

Kabila instructed Mumengi to go back to the radio and speak to the people, to motivate them. "We will survive with the force of the people—you have to rally them behind us. We don't have an army, so we will need them. In the meantime, I will go look for allies." He called one of his bodyguards and asked for his pistol. "Do you have a gun?" Mumengi had never used a gun before. "Here. You must use this. From today on, you will be the minister of war!"

~:~

Meanwhile, the Rwandans had taken control of much of the eastern Congo in a matter of hours. While Colonel Kabarebe had been commander of the Congolese army, he had prepositioned units loyal to him with stockpiles of weapons in the eastern Congo. When he was sacked, he gave orders to these units to rebel against Kabila. With support of Rwandan troops who crossed the border, they took control of Goma and Bukavu and began advancing on Kisangani.

Hubris can breed fantastic courage. After taking the border towns, Colonel Kabarebe decided to go straight for the jugular by leapfrogging Kabila's ramshackle army and attacking the capital, 1,000 miles away. It was one of the most daring operations in the region's military history.

The "Kitona airlift" is still talked about by foreign military attachés and Congolese army commanders alike. A U.S. officer based in the region later wrote in a military journal: "This was an operation that exemplified audacity and courage, and its aftermath became an odyssey fit for a Hollywood script."[10]

Kabarebe commandeered a Boeing 707 at the Goma airport and loaded one hundred and eighty Rwandan, Ugandan, and Congolese soldiers on board with weapons and ammunition. "Everybody wanted to get a piece of the action," remembered a senior Congolese military officer who participated. "Mobutu's former soldiers were outraged at their humiliation by Kabila, and the Tutsi wanted to get back at the government for the treatment of their relatives in Kinshasa."[11] Soldiers deserted from their units around Goma and showed up at the airport once they got word of the operation. Kabarebe put a brash Rwandan commander called Butera in charge of the first plane to leave.

It could have indeed been a scene from a movie: With Butera brandishing his pistol behind him, the distraught pilot flew 1,000 miles across the country, over the capital to the Kitona military base, 250 miles west of Kinshasa on the mouth of the Congo River.[12] Most of the soldiers on the flight had no idea that the commander of the Kitona base had secretly defected to the Rwandan side— they expected to land in a hail of bullets. A hundred and eighty soldiers nervously gripped their AK-47s and looked warily at the flight safety cards in their seat pockets. In the back of the aisle, stacked to the roof, were dozens of wooden crates of ammunition. The soldiers spoke Luganda, Swahili, Kinyarwanda, English, and French with each other. Outside the window, they broke through the thick cloud cover to see the rolling hills of Bas-Congo province and the Congo River snaking placidly toward the Atlantic ocean. After a three-hour flight, the long landing strip of Kitona airbase came into view.

Despite the pistol-waving Rwandan behind him, the pilot began to complain that they would be killed if they landed at the heavily fortified airbase. "Don't worry," Butera said. "We have our people at the airport." Using the pilot's high-frequency radio, he programmed a frequency he said belonged to their commander on the ground. A surprisingly clear voice responded to his call in calm English: "All clear, *afande*. You can land." What the pilot did not know was that the radio Butera was calling actually belonged to his deputy commander, who was lounging in a seat at the back of the plane.[13]

When Kabarebe had been chief of staff of the Congolese army, he had studied old Belgian military maps of the region closely. Kitona was an obvious choice for several reasons. Kinshasa was connected to the Atlantic Ocean by a narrow land corridor. Almost all cargo going to Kinshasa had to pass through this umbilical cord, at the head of which sat Kitona. The military base also had a long airstrip that could accommodate aircraft weighing up to fifty-four tons. Its barracks now housed thousands of former Mobutu soldiers who had been sent there for reeducation. Their living conditions were terrible—hundreds had died from cholera and malnutrition—and, despite their notorious disciplinary problems, they would need little convincing to join in the fight against Kabila. Lastly, Kitona was close to the Inga Dam, the largest hydroelectric dam in central Africa, which supplied the capital with most of its electricity.

As the plane touched down, a few Kabila loyalists managed to shoot its nose tire out, but the commander of the airport battalion quickly defected to the Rwandan side as planned and brought his men under control, allowing the troops to disembark.

The airport was taken with barely any casualties. Back in Kinshasa, Kabila fumed as he heard about the airlift. "What kind of country is this?" he asked his advisors, imagining the airplane flying overhead. "We don't even have an air force?" The advisors called their commander in Kitona to order him to stop the landing in Kitona, but the seditious officer only responded with insults.[14]

It was a huge victory for the Rwandans, who could now send reinforcements to take Kinshasa. Overjoyed, Butera set up his satellite phone on the tarmac and called back to Kigali.

Sometimes even the Rwandans foul things up: Butera had forgotten to take down the pin code for the satellite phone, without which it was useless. In Kigali, his commanding officers waited in vain for word from the young soldier, while he tried frantically to punch in different six-digit combinations. No luck. (The correct code was apparently 123456.) The pilot also failed to reach Kigali on his ham radio.[15]

Butera had to find the closest means of communication: an oil rig in the nearby town of Banana. Finally, after hours of searching, he found an oil engineer with a satellite phone who, with a bit of coaxing, allowed him to call home. Sheepishly, he told his bosses he had made it.

∼:∼

Who had made the first move in sparking the war? From interviews with Rwandans and Congolese involved in planning the war, it is not clear whether Kabila began recruiting ex-FAR before Kabarebe began deploying his boys to the east.

What is clear is that, after only a few months of Kabila being in power, both sides realized that their relationship was going sour, driven by Kabila's paranoia and Rwanda's obsession with control. Didier Mumengi remembered, "The Rwandans in Kinshasa were a time bomb. It was clear that they were a problem, but at the same time they helped us keep the country together. It was going to be hard to get rid of them and still maintain a grip on the army and intelligence services."

For Kigali, at a time when the northwest of Rwanda was consumed by the resumption of a bitter civil war, Kabila's recruitment of its enemy constituted a strategic threat as well as a personal betrayal. Its reaction, however, was a prime example of the hubris that had come to characterize the regime. Instead of creating a buffer zone in the east of the country and using multilateral pressure to deal with Kabila, Kigali decided to single-handedly remove him from power, presumably to install a new, friendlier proxy in his place.

It is surprising that Rwanda apparently did not confer with Angola, which had played a major role in toppling Mobutu, before launching an operation just miles from its border. According to President Dos Santos, President Museveni informed him of his government's plans several days *after* the Kitona operation. Although the Rwandan government insists that it did have the green light, other Angolan officials and foreign diplomats agree that, at the very most, Kigali had informed Angola but had not tried to obtain their approval or collaboration.[16] When Kabarebe landed several thousand Rwandan soldiers within earshot of Angolan territory, the reaction in Luanda was, according to the U.S. ambassador there at the time, "What the hell are these Rwandans doing? That's our backyard."[17] Some Angolan commanders had been rubbed the wrong way by the Rwandans after helping bring Kabila to power a year earlier. "It had been everybody's victory, not just Rwanda's," commented an Angolan officer who wanted to remain anonymous. "But they acted like they were in charge in Kinshasa."[18]

❦

With a mutiny festering in the slums of Kinshasa, and rebels advancing rapidly from the west, Kabila knew that he would not be able to hold out without the support of the region. A regional summit of the South African Development Community was quickly called, and Rwanda, Uganda, Congo, Angola, and Zimbabwe glowered at each other across a table without coming to a conclusion.

It was a decisive moment in the war. In 1996, almost the whole region had jumped on the bandwagon against Mobutu, while world powers looked the other way. It had been a continental war, inspired by security interests but also by ideology. In 1998, the odds were stacked differently. The region split down the middle, with Rwanda, Uganda, and Burundi on one side and Angola, Namibia, Chad, and Zimbabwe on the other.

This time, the motives for deployed troops were less noble. Zimbabwe's president, Robert Mugabe, for example, was of the same generation as Laurent Kabila and had provided arms and money for the first war effort; Kabila still owed him somewhere between $40 and $200 million dollars for this first engagement.[19] More importantly, his own besieged government was fraying at the edges after eighteen years in power. A mixture of corruption, poor economic management, and the expropriation of 1,500 white farms had prompted food riots, a fiscal crisis, and international opprobrium. As expensive as the military adventure in the Congo was, it also offered many much-needed business opportunities for Mugabe's inner cabal. Shortly after toppling Mobutu, his state ammunition factory obtained a $500,000 contract from Kabila's government, a Zimbabwean businessman extended a loan for $45 million, and businessmen close to Mugabe began negotiating potentially lucrative transport, food, and mining deals with the Congolese.[20] When Rwanda attempted anew to overthrow the regime in Kinshasa, this time without rallying a regional alliance around them, Mugabe saw his investments in jeopardy.

Angola's interests were much more related to its twenty-three-year-old civil war with UNITA. For decades, the rebels had maintained rear bases in Kinshasa, where Savimbi had frequently met with Mobutu and CIA operatives and had sold tens of millions of dollars of diamonds. In May 1998, Jonas Savimbi's rebels had scuppered a peace process that they saw as increasingly biased toward the government. They launched attacks throughout northern Angola, close to the border with the Congo. In addition, another Angolan rebel movement, the Front for the Liberation of the Enclave of Cabinda (FLEC), appeared to be making inroads in Cabinda, a tiny Angolan enclave just north of the Kitona airbase, where around 60 percent of Angola's oil is drilled, providing it with about half of all national revenues. According to French government officials, FLEC had been in touch with the Rwandan government before the Kitona airlift.[21]

The diplomatic tug-of-war continued for several days, with South African president Nelson Mandela attempting to mediate between the two sides to pre-

vent a continent-wide war breaking out. His attempt earned him the scorn of
Mugabe, who told him to shut up if he didn't want to help defend the Congo.
Kabila's office was equally blunt, suggesting that "age had taken its toll" on the
venerable African leader.[22]

∻

At Malik Kijege's makeshift headquarters at the Tshatshi military camp, he
began receiving distress calls from Tutsis hiding in Kinshasa. According to the
reports he received, Kinshasa was quickly succumbing to the throes of anti-Tutsi
frenzy. Once again, leaders had resorted to ethnic diatribe to rally the population
behind them.

Kabila addressed a march in downtown Kinshasa, where he whipped up the
crowd against the Tutsi invaders. The demonstration was full of histrionics.
"They want to create a Tutsi empire," the president announced, dressed in military fatigues. His information minister, Didier Mumengi, also dressed in a green
uniform, told the crowd that the Tutsi rebels had "embarked on the extermination
of the Congolese people of Bukavu." Tshala Mwana, a famous singer and allegedly
the president's mistress, led the parade dressed in white, tugging two goats on a
leash with signs identifying them as Deo Bugera and Bizima Karaha, the two
most famous Tutsi in Kabila's government who had defected to join the rebellion. Some of the marchers brandished signs: "We will make Rwanda the twelfth
province of the Congo," and "No to Tutsi expansion in the DRC and Africa." As
the cheering crowd looked on, the famous, brawny wrestler Edingwe—he could
often be seen jogging and singing with his followers along the Kinshasa streets
at dawn—stepped up and slit the animals' throats.[23]

Kabila promised that he would distribute guns to the population so that it
could defend itself against the aggressors. Soon, thousands of youths, including
many street children and delinquents, were streaming into recruitment centers
in Kinshasa. Every day, several hundred young men filed into the Martyrs' Stadium, learned how to use a gun, and sang songs. One of the standards was: "You
Rwandans, God has not chosen you. If you want dialogue, we'll have dialogue.
If you want war, we'll have war."

The line between the Rwandan government and the Tutsi people as a whole
was quickly blurring. Demagogues in Kinshasa bore a heavy responsibility in
whipping up ethnic animosities in the capital. But they didn't have to work too
hard. Rwandan troops had humiliated and angered residents in the capital during

their year-long stay. Kinois—as the inhabitants of the capital were known—had been working for years against Mobutu's dictatorship. They had marched in the tens of thousands and had seen their brothers and sisters tortured and killed, only to see their victory snatched away by a bunch of foreigners. As Kinois often quip: "We put Mobutu in the ambulance. All Kabila did was drive the corpse to the cemetery." Then the new rulers, who didn't speak their language and didn't look like them, began beating them and telling the women they dressed like prostitutes. They felt emasculated and abandoned to hunger and poverty.

Kabila gave orders for soldiers to shoot any Tutsi found with a weapon. Among the people, there was little distinction between a Tutsi civilian and a Tutsi soldier. "When the fighting starts, they all pull guns out from under their beds," Congolese would often tell me. "The Tutsi in school with me yesterday are in the streets today in uniform." Congolese soldiers stormed a U.S. embassy compound in Kinshasa, where American families were waiting for evacuation. They harassed several African Americans they suspected of being Tutsi in disguise, stole some money, and left. Another gang raided the upscale Memling Hotel in downtown Kinshasa, where many wealthy families had sought refuge, and went from room to room looking for high cheekbones and hooked noses.

After several days, the government organized a systematic round up of all remaining Tutsi, ostensibly for their own protection, and created a camp for them next to a military barracks in town. Hundreds of Tutsi were crammed into squalid quarters with little food, water, or medical supplies.

~:~

Back at the Tshatshi military camp, Malik Kijege fielded calls from Tutsi soldiers around the country. Congolese Tutsi had been left in military bases around the country after the Rwandans left. As soon as the rebels announced their insurgency against Kabila, these Tutsi were seen as Rwanda's fifth column and were attacked. In Kisangani and Kalemie, dozens were killed. Over a hundred Tutsi officers in a training camp in Kamina, in the southern Katanga Province, were rounded up and executed. It was as if the mobs believed treason was genetically encoded in Tutsi identity.

Other messages were coming in to Malik's command post from Tutsi stranded in various Kinshasa neighborhoods: five trapped in a garage in Kintambo, an elderly woman who couldn't walk hidden with a non-Tutsi family in

Bandal. He formed small squads to venture out into Kinshasa on foot and try to rescue them. They still had their government-issued walkie-talkies and were on the same frequencies as Kabila's soldiers. The rival sides insulted each other over the static crackle.

"War is weird," Malik later told me with a laugh. "In order to prevent them from understanding us, we resorted to a pig Latin we used when we were kids. "We said words backwards: 'Teem su ta eht sag noitats'—meet us at the gas station. Or added syllables:'Meetzee atzee gaszee stationzee.'" Congolese Tutsi babbled their way through the treacherous downtown streets at night, sometimes walking twenty miles in a single expedition, raiding banks and pharmacies for money and medical supplies. Finally, they succeeded in shepherding dozens of Tutsi civilians to the embassies of France, Belgium, and the Republic of Congo. From there, convoys were organized to bring the Tutsi in speedboats across the river to neighboring Brazzaville.

~:~

After his incendiary speech, Kabila had retreated to Lubumbashi, 1,000 miles from Kinshasa and near the border with Zambia. It looked to be a good place from which to flee the Congo—if he had to, which seemed ever more likely. From there he continued his diplomatic offensive to bring in Angolan, Namibian, and Zimbabwean troops. He left a confused war council behind in Kinshasa: a bunch of his ministers, mostly civilians dressed in military garb, who appeared on national television and tried to calm the population."Our army had disintegrated," Didier Mumengi remembered. "Our best units had gone westwards to stop the advance of the rebels. We were left with a bunch of policemen." Mumengi himself was seen almost daily at press conferences, looking out of place in his green fatigues.

It seemed impossible to stop the Rwandan advance. They were moving twenty miles a day, capturing army stockpiles and sending government soldiers scattering. Commander David, who had been in charge of President Kabila's bodyguard, was part of the rebel advance. He had kept an address book with telephone numbers of Kabila's ministers and advisors. As the rebels advanced, David would make taunting phone calls to Kinshasa.

"Mumengi, you better pack your bags—we will be in Kinshasa tomorrow night," he told the information minister when they were still two hundred miles away. He rang other ministers to give them updates on how far they had reached and to ridicule the Congolese army's feeble efforts.

Kabila ordered his entire cabinet to Lubumbashi. Senior members of government, especially those from Katanga, heeded his call, packing their families into SUVs. At the airport, luxury vehicles crammed the tarmac, unloading mattresses, suitcases, and entire wardrobes to send to Lubumbashi. Didier Mumengi, who didn't know anyone in Lubumbashi, decided to stay, against the pleas of his wife, who implored him to flee. He resorted to giving his distressed family sleeping pills so they could sleep through the night.

Then, without warning, the lights went out throughout the city. The Rwandan offensive had captured the Inga Dam, the huge hydroelectric power plant on the Congo River a hundred and fifty miles west of Kinshasa. The city of five million people went dark, with only a few hotels and office buildings lit by backup generators. Even those generators were soon winding down, as the rebels also cut the pipeline bringing fuel to the city. People were stuck in elevators, food rotted in freezers, doctors in some hospital emergency rooms had to operate with flashlights, and water pumps stopped working. When the energy minister, Babi Mbayi, gave a phone interview to a foreign journalist, saying that they had some technical problems with the electricity supply, Commander David called him from his satellite phone and said, "Babi, you think this is a technical problem? Wait till we reach Kinshasa."

Rwanda's decision to cut electricity to the capital sticks in the memory of Kinois to this day. That the rebels would jeopardize the lives of sick hospital patients and hamstring water and fuel supply was the last straw for many and only further justified their violent hatred of the Tutsi.

The city's fate was looking increasingly sealed. The ministers who had stayed behind in Kinshasa held an emergency meeting at the ministry of planning. As a sign of how dire the situation had become, the army commander sent soldiers to provide security for the ministers, but they showed up without guns, loafing about sheepishly. One of the army generals took the floor and solemnly told his colleagues that they wouldn't be able to defend the city. The finance minister then cleared his throat and, somewhat embarrassed, announced that he had made the decision to empty the state's coffers. "I have tallied the money left in the Central Bank," he told the stunned room. "There is $22,000 for each of us. I have put it in sacks in a truck outside. Use it well."

~:~

Finally, just as the city had lost hope, the tide turned. On August 18, seeking international legitimacy for intervening, President Mugabe of Zimbabwe convened a meeting of the Southern African Development Community (SADC) security committee, an organ over which he presided. They hastily approved a military intervention to support Kabila against "foreign aggression," although they did not have the quorum or the mandate to do so. The decision also deepened a row between Mugabe and President Nelson Mandela, who advocated a diplomatic approach.[24] Mugabe, with typical gusto, told Mandela, "Those who want to keep out, fine, let them keep out. But let them keep [their] silence about those who want to help."[25]

By the morning of the following day, four hundred Zimbabwean troops were digging trenches around Kinshasa's Njili airport, and several attack helicopters patrolled the skies. Two days later, Angolan president Dos Santos, who had been sitting on the fence, made up his mind that it was better to have the devil you know ruling Kinshasa than a political unknown.[26] Thousands of Angolan troops began streaming across the border with tanks and armored personnel carriers to recapture the Kitona military base from the Rwandans. The Angolan military, which brought with it attack helicopters and MiG 23 fighter bombers, began raining bombs and artillery fire down on the Rwandan-led troops. Malik Kijege remembered the Angolan air force hitting an oil pipeline, sending a plume of fire into the night, illuminating the scattering rebel forces.

As the Angolans moved in from the west, cutting off the Rwandans' rear base and supply chain, Zimbabwean and Congolese forces squeezed them from Kinshasa. "It looks like there will be a Banyamulenge sandwich," a western diplomat commented, lumping all of the invading troops—Rwandans, Ugandans, Congolese—into one generic term.[27]

Within days, the tide had turned. With no escape route, the rebels made a desperate run for Kinshasa, hoping they would be able to fulfill their mission with the ammunition and food they had left. At night, rebel troops in civilian dress began infiltrating the densely populated Masina and Njili neighborhoods on the northwestern outskirts of town, close to the airport. Bolstered by Zimbabwean and Angolan troops, Laurent Kabila returned to Kinshasa and announced that victory was theirs. Exhorting people to take up sticks and spears to defend the city, he declared that, "The people must be completely mobilized and armed to crush the aggressors."[28] His cigar-smoking chief of staff was less subtle. "The rebels are vermin, microbes which must be methodically eradicated," he said on state radio.[29]

The population heeded the call. They pounced on a dozen people they suspected were rebels, looped tires around their necks, doused them in gasoline, and made them into human torches. Charred bodies lined one of the main streets in the popular Masina neighborhood. A foreign television crew captured on film two Congolese soldiers throwing a man off a bridge and shooting him dead as he tried, with his legs broken, to crawl out of the water to safety. The images went around the world and were later memorialized on the Internet. It isn't clear, however, whether these final casualties were Tutsi. The Rwandans had recruited many of Mobutu's former soldiers. Eyewitnesses suggest that it was these recruits, mostly youths from the western Congo, who were sent as spies into Kinshasa, as they knew their way around and could blend into the local population.[30] The last part of the battle for Kinshasa featured a group of several hundred of these soldiers stripping off their uniforms before being cornered in a field of eucalyptus trees outside Kinshasa. Kabila's chief of staff laughed as he told the story at a press conference, cigar in mouth: "The rebels are like monkeys, swinging in the trees with no clothes."[31]

～:～

As with many episodes of the war, the battle for Kinshasa was not without its share of surreal moments. A group of around seventy Tutsi was stuck in the Burundian embassy for several weeks, unable to move because of the fighting. They had congregated there from throughout Kinshasa in the hope that the Tutsi-led government of Burundi would provide them protection. The nearby Swiss embassy sent packages of food and water to keep them afloat, but the living conditions were deteriorating by the day. The embassy was housed in a small building, and a dozen people slept in each room. Ambassador Martin Sindabizera, himself a Tutsi, paced back and forth through the corridors, speaking with Burundian president Buyoya about possible evacuation plans. His phone rang nonstop with requests from Tutsi throughout Kinshasa—and even several Hutu who also felt targeted—to come and get them. "I wasn't able to do anything for most of them. It was soul-wrenching to hear their pleas hour after hour and feel so helpless."[32]

When he received word that there was an influential Rwandan family trapped not far from the embassy, Sindabizera decided to go himself. On the street in front of their hideout, several policemen stopped his car and told him to get out. As he stepped out, one of them yelled: "*Betaye masasi!*" After a year in Kinshasa, the ambassador knew enough Lingala to understand what that meant: Shoot him! The policeman loaded his gun, but an older soldier stopped him. "He has diplomatic license plates," he pointed out calmly. "You can't shoot him just like that. We have rules in this country." Giving way to this reasoning, the soldiers took him in for interrogation. In a small cell at the nearby police station, the ambassador found a bizarre group of people, all of whom were alleged to be guilty of plotting against the state: two of his own advisors, whom he had sent ahead to evacuate the Rwandan family; a group of five mixed-race women in tight jeans and makeup, accused of having been mistresses of Tutsi politicians in Kinshasa; and a dozen cowed street children and soldiers who may have been involved in the rebellion or were just victims of a shakedown. "It was generalized paranoia," the ambassador remembered. "They pulled in people to make money, for the shape of their noses, for anything at all." After four hours of interrogation, the ambassador was set free. "Don't talk to the BBC!" they ordered.

Back at the embassy, the situation was getting worse by the day. Several of the people seeking refuge had medical conditions, and he didn't think they would be able to hold out much longer. The sewage system was breaking down, and the water pumps only worked intermittently. Finally, Burundian president Pierre Buyoya decided on a risky evacuation. He sent a jet from Bujumbura with several trusted soldiers, while the ambassador sent a trusted Indian businessman with several thousand dollars down the fifteen-mile road to the airport to dole out bribes to all of the roadblock commanders. He kept the biggest sum for the commander of the airport. They would make a run for it.

The ambassador laughed when he remembered the operation. "The pilot thought he was flying to Brazzaville. Only a fool would have accepted to fly a Burundian aircraft into Kinshasa airport during that mess." Since the Brazzaville airport was just several miles across the river from the Kinshasa landing strip, it was easy to pull off. Several minutes before landing, the Burundian army officer on board pulled out a pistol in the cockpit. "Change of plans," he told the terrified pilot. "We are landing in Kinshasa."

The Burundian convoy, crammed to capacity with children, women, and diplomats, hurtled through the deserted streets as the bribed policemen and soldiers pulled away the roadblocks they had set up. At the airport, the passengers rushed onto the plane. At the last moment, just as the plane was beginning to taxi onto the runway, several pickups full of soldiers sped in front of it, blocking its path. The ambassador called the airport commander, alarmed, asking him what had happened with their arrangement.

"I can't do anything, sir," he responded. "It's the presidential guard." The ambassador sighed, looking down the rows of the airplane, full of anxious faces and crying children. "I thought the game was over," he remembered. "I was sure that Kabila must have pulled the plug on our operation." Having seen what had happened to other Tutsi in Kinshasa, they expected the worst. The ambassador told the pilot to lower the boarding ramp so he could talk to the Congolese commander. The few Burundian officers on the plane loaded their pistols and waited anxiously.

The passengers gawked through the windows as they saw Kabila's soldiers, the same ones who had been rounding up their friends and relatives, help a Tutsi woman in expensive clothes out of a black SUV with tinted windows. Soldiers grabbed her suitcases and designer bags and made for the Burundian airplane. Not a word was exchanged between the Congolese and Burundian soldiers. The woman brushed past the dumbfounded ambassador in a cloud of perfume, only to be greeted by irate shrieks from the rest of the passengers. Several Banyamulenge women got up and began attacking the newcomer, cursing, spitting, and pulling at her clothes. "Traitor!" "Bitch!" The Burundian soldiers, pistols in the air, had to intervene to break up the melee.

"I didn't know whether to laugh or to cry," the ambassador remembered. "This was Kabila's mistress! My other passengers had recognized her. The president obviously didn't think it was a good thing for her to stay on."

The pilot, perplexed and nervous, came on the intercom, ordering everybody to sit down as he taxied the plane to the runway.

✦ 14 ✦

THE REBEL PROFESSOR

Ernest Wamba dia Wamba was an unlikely candidate to lead a movement to overthrow Laurent Kabila. A quiet, unassuming man with a professorial demeanor, he had spent most of his life in academic institutions in the United States and Tanzania, far more familiar with the intricacies of existentialist philosophy than with revolutionary politics. When he became the president of the new Rwandan-backed Congolese Rally for Democracy (RCD) rebellion on August 16, 1998, it came as a surprise even to his family. His story illustrates the tragic state of Congolese leadership: Even when a man with pristine political and ethical credentials tries to effect change, the results are poor.[1]

Wamba had been fascinated by politics since he was a boarding student at a Swedish missionary school in western Bas-Congo Province, close to the Atlantic Ocean, in the 1950s. It was a turbulent time for the region. Wamba was born not far from the birthplace of Simon Kimbangu, a local Christian prophet and anticolonial activist who rejected the white clergy's monopoly on religion. Wamba was from the Kongo ethnic community, which had made up one of Central Africa's oldest and largest kingdoms and was at the forefront of the Congolese independence movement. While still a teenager, he was swept up by the weekly rallies and protest marches that embroiled the region. Even at Wamba's high school, when the Swedish missionaries were out of earshot, the Congolese teachers would encourage them to chant: "What do we want? Independence!"

Wamba was a precocious student. He mined the school library for books on contemporary philosophy. "He wasn't content with village life, with the state his country was in," Mahmood Mamdani, a fellow political scientist and a close friend, remembered. Studying continental philosophy was a means of emancipating himself, of feeling part of something larger. Engrossed by Jean-Paul Sartre's writings, he sent the famous philosopher a letter when he was in his early teens. To his surprise, Sartre wrote back, and the two had a brief correspondence.

After graduating with high marks, he was one of three students from his school to receive a scholarship to study in the United States. He went to Western Michigan University in Kalamazoo, about as far from his tropical homeland as he could imagine, where he wrote his senior thesis on French philosophers Maurice Merleau-Ponty and Jean-Paul Sartre and was admitted for graduate study at Claremont University in California.

As with many Africans in the diaspora, distance from his homeland catalyzed his interest in its politics. "I was not radicalized about Africa until I came to the United States," he later reflected. "It is strange, but I became much more aware of what was going on in Congo in the United States than I had ever been in Congo."[2] He followed developments in his home country closely and became a strident critic of Mobutu's dictatorship. He married an African American woman and became active in the American civil rights movement through the Student Nonviolent Coordinating Committee. In academic circles, he was known as a pan-Africanist; he advocated a version of democracy more in tune with traditional African forms of government.

In 1980, Wamba returned to the continent with his family to take up a position at the University of Dar es Salaam, which President Julius Nyerere was promoting as a center of African learning, attracting academics and political activists from around the region. A year later, Wamba was arrested during a visit to Kinshasa, an incident that drew the attention of Nyerere, who helped get him out of prison. Nyerere then called on him for advice on Great Lakes politics, in particular the Burundian peace process.

When the war in the Congo started, the former Tanzanian president had been retired after several decades as head of state but remained closely involved in regional politics. Ugandan president Museveni had asked Nyerere to endorse Kabila, but the former president was skeptical. Nonetheless, Kabila was well connected, which was crucial: His right-hand man was married to the daughter of Nyerere's former vice prime minister.[3] Nyerere finally met Kabila in his rural hometown, and the Congolese rebel leader spoke passionately about self-determination and his vision for the Congo. Nyerere asked Wamba for advice. The professor was critical of Kabila, given his reputation as a smuggler and thug, but Nyerere was swayed by other leaders in the region. He authorized Tanzanian intelligence officers, trainers, and artillery to support the AFDL—and to keep an eye on Kabila. He even lent the rebel leader one of his personal bodyguards.

Kabila visited Dar es Salaam several more times, and each time Nyerere made sure that Wamba was on hand. The more he saw of Kabila, however, the more doubts he had. Kabila seemed aloof and stubborn, always friendly and charismatic in their private meetings, but unwilling to implement suggestions the Tanzanians made. On one occasion Nyerere organized a meeting between Kabila and several of his close friends, including Wamba, to help develop a coherent political ideology; the rebel leader stood them up. Wamba remembered Nyerere shaking his head. "He can't even show up to meetings on time," he told Wamba. "His deputy [Kisase Ngandu] was assassinated in mysterious circumstances. This is not looking good." To top it off, Nyerere's intelligence officers based in the field reported confusion and infighting within the rebel alliance.

When the AFDL took power in Kinshasa, Kabila invited Nyerere to visit. The elder statesman was deeply disappointed. Traveling in a presidential convoy from the airport, he sighed impatiently as he saw Kabila's security detail chase other cars off the road and bring traffic to a halt. "That's not how a president is supposed to behave," he muttered to Wamba, who was accompanying him. Together they toured the capital, Bas-Congo, and a military base in the south, where Tanzanian officers were training the new army. There his men told him that the new recruits increasingly only came from Kabila's own Lubakat tribe. In a private meeting, he warned Kabila, "Our support was not for you; it was for the Congolese people. If you don't watch out, the same thing will happen to you as happened to Mobutu."[4] Before he left, Nyerere gave a press conference at his hotel, where he told journalists: "I came to the Congo and saw its leaders. But I didn't see a single new road, hospital or school."[5]

☙ ☙

The Congo war spun its leaders like a centrifuge; the more ruthless, politically adept ones managed to stay at the center and reinvent themselves through new business deals or political alliances. The lightweights, however, were flung to the fringes of political life. Dozens of these figures are scattered through Kinshasa's suburbs, living off money they had set aside or real estate they manage. The revolution devoured many of its children, spitting them out when it had sucked what it needed out of them. Wamba was one of these pieces of flotsam: After the end of the war, he had obtained a position as a senator in Parliament, but soon he was unemployed. He had preferred to stay in his country, enveloped by memories of past achievements and friends, than return to the anonymous surroundings of Dar es Salaam. In 2007, during a research trip to Kinshasa, I managed to track him down. He appeared to have given up any political ambitions. When I told his former rebel colleagues that I was going to see him, they were all surprised that he was still in town.

"I would be happy to meet," he told me over the phone, "but I live a bit outside of downtown, and my car has broken down. Could you come to my place?"

I hadn't realized what Wamba meant by "a bit outside of downtown." I drove about twenty miles through grimy suburbs, until the pavement gave way to sandy side streets lined by broken-down houses with fading paint and rusty, corrugated iron roofing. Wamba had given me a street address, but there were no numbers on the houses. I asked around, but nobody seemed to know a Professor Wamba dia Wamba. Finally, a matronly woman selling sugar and manioc flour on a piece of gunnysack recognized the name—"Ah! That old politician!" I had passed his house several times. In the courtyard, a scrawny dog barked at me. A polite lady showed me into the living room and asked me to wait—Professor Wamba was having a bath.

The living room was simple. A glossy, generic picture of a waterfall hung on one wall. The other had a picture of Wamba in a suit signing the 2002 peace deal in Pretoria, South Africa. The sofa was decorated with circular doilies crocheted in neon yellow and purple yarn. I leafed through several magazines on the table; there was a three-month-old issue of *Jeune Afrique* and the newsletter of Mbongi a Nsi, a Kongo cultural organization he headed. When I used the bathroom, there was no light or running water.

Several minutes later, Wamba welcomed me into his study, a small room lined with books and magazines. On the wall next to his desk was a series of A4-size laminated photographs of people. There was his son Philippe, who had died in a car accident in 2002; Rashid Kawawa, the former Tanzanian vice prime minister; as well as Che Guevara, Patrice Lumumba, and a row of fading pictures from the 1950s of Wamba's family. As he began to speak, I mentally went over all the things I had heard about him from people who had known him in Dar es Salaam or during the rebellion, trying to reconcile the image of a misguided rebel leader, dressed in army fatigues and with a nine-millimeter pistol at his side, with this avuncular, soft-spoken man. How could someone invested for so many years in promoting democracy and civil rights have become derailed?

~:~

In early 1998, as the Rwandans began falling out with Kabila, Kigali began piecing together a new rebellion. Vice President Paul Kagame sent emissaries throughout the region and contacted others by phone in Brussels and the United States. When Wamba arrived in Kigali in early August 1998, most of the other future leaders of the RCD were already there.

Wamba was baffled when he arrived at the small guesthouse in Kabuga, in the suburbs of the Rwandan capital, where the prospective leaders had gathered. Former Mobutist ministers sat next to former AFDL rebels who had fought against Mobutu. Opposition politicians who had been imprisoned and tortured by Kabila sat next to Rwandan security officers who had been in charge of Kabila's army. It was an alliance of malcontents; the only thing they had in common was their disdain for Kabila. How could they ever work together?

Despite the disparate backgrounds, many of them, like Wamba, had solid credentials. For example, there was Zahidi Ngoma, a former high-ranking official for UNESCO, based in Paris. Zahidi had been a long-standing opponent of both Mobutu and Kabila and had been arrested in Kinshasa shortly after the AFDL's victory, beaten, and nearly starved to death in prison. Also present was Joseph Mudumbi, a human rights lawyer from South Kivu who had reported on abuses in the Rwandan refugee camps in the face of harassment and death threats. He had been awarded a prestigious prize by Human Rights Watch in 1995. Other members included Jacques Depelchin, a Stanford-trained historian who, together with Wamba dia Wamba, had drafted the African Declaration Against Genocide, and Etienne Ngangura, the head of the philosophy department at the University of Kinshasa. To western diplomats, they seemed genuinely bent on bringing about a responsible and functional government. Surely the idealism of these scholars and activists would help this rebellion to succeed where the previous one had failed?

And yet it was clear from the beginning that their independence would be severely limited by Rwanda's influence. After all, it was Kigali that had brought them together and provided them with soldiers, phones, and houses. Indeed, by the time the besuited politicians met in Kigali, the armed insurrection on the ground was already two weeks old, had taken control of the border cities of Bukavu and Goma, and was advancing on Kinshasa. The political leadership of the RCD was attached as an afterthought, an appendix to the military machine. "We thought we would take Kinshasa within a month at the most," Colonel Patrick Karegeya, one of the masterminds of the Rwandan offensive, told me. "We didn't pay that much attention to the political wing."[6]

Wamba could not claim that he didn't know what he was getting into. Like the others, he, too, had been contacted by the Rwandan government. A few days after his arrival in Kigali, it was Paul Kagame who, in a closed-door meeting with the aspiring rebels, suggested that Wamba become president of the movement. Wamba had a good international reputation, the Rwandan leader argued, and had not participated in the previous rebellion, which could make him appear a neutral arbiter among the various other tendencies represented. Crucially, Wamba was close to former Tanzanian president Nyerere and, by virtue of his membership in the pan-Africanist movement, could also sway other African leaders such as Mandela, Museveni, and Graça Machel, the former first lady of Mozambique. "Any objections?" Kagame asked. Of course, there were none.

~:~

Wamba had his reasons for advocating a military rebellion. He had been a front-seat observer to the various resistance movements against Mobutu's dictatorship. Over twenty-five years, he had watched the autocrat, with the help of the United States, France, and Belgium, skillfully crush and co-opt any opposition to his rule. At the end of the cold war, persistent protests forced Mobutu to accept multiparty democracy, and he called for a National Sovereign Conference, in which Wamba participated, to decide the future of the government. When the conference elected Etienne Tshisekedi as its leader, Mobutu simply ignored the verdict and imposed his own prime minister. Wamba didn't see much hope for pacifist opposition to a regime that locked up and tortured its opponents.

The genocide in Rwanda finally ripped Wamba out of academic complacency: "[It] was the turning point, my road to Damascus. Here you are, a social scientist who has been theorizing about social movements, trying to understand how African societies work, how they might be changed for the better. Then you see that genocide is taking place right in front of your face, and you find yourself powerless to do anything."[7] When he received the phone call telling him that he could take the lead in a new rebellion and, without the hardships and improbabilities of grassroots organizing, play a decisive role in shaping a new, albeit armed, opposition, he didn't hesitate.

In a speech to African philosophers, he obliquely justified his position: "Congolese academics talk of the Congolese population as being ignorant and President J. Kabila as knowing nothing. They are happy doing their routine theoretical work and not caring much about the fact that they are sitting in a sinking boat. I find this attitude deplorable. . . . Development can only be consciously pursued and not left to chance or to others."[8]

Many others with similarly high ideals made the same deal with the devil as Wamba. After all, being a leader takes vision and charisma, but it also requires propitious circumstances. Hadn't Che Guevara tried and failed, limping away malnourished and dejected? Hadn't Tshisekedi, who had marched with tens of thousands against Mobutu in 1992, also been reduced to a marginal figure, with only a handful of diehard supporters heeding calls for protest marches? They had failed because the circumstances had not been ripe for them, whereas Wamba and his new comrades now did have the right circumstances: a formidable, time-tested military machine that could undoubtedly take them to the summit of the state. Change and power were being offered on a silver platter.

~:~

A total of twenty-six dissidents were ferried out to a small hotel in Kabuga, on the outskirts of Kigali, and spent several days debating the structure and composition of their new rebellion. As they debated, Rwandan army officers milled about outside in gumboots, toting machine guns.

"It was a strange bunch," Wamba remembered. He had a tendency to close his eyes for minutes on end and stroke his forehead when we spoke. "You had capitalists and socialists. You had Mobutists and those who had thrown them out of power. You had academics and people who apparently had never read a book."

This amalgam produced tense moments, as at the beginning, when Kalala Shambuyi, a radical from the Belgian diaspora, stood up and pointed at Lunda Bululu, who had been prime minister under Mobutu. "I will not be associated with Mobutists after all they did to my country!" He walked out, but was later calmed down and brought back in. On another occasion, the Rwandans showed the draft of a press statement to Zahidi Ngoma, the rebellion's first spokesperson, who exploded, protesting, "I am not in primary school! I can draft my own press statements!"

For most of those assembled, their differences of opinion didn't matter much, as they believed they would be in Kinshasa in a matter of weeks or, at the most, months. Wamba found himself alone arguing for a "democratizing rebellion." Military pressure for him was just a means to begin negotiations with Kabila. "Most of the people in that room hadn't thought about strategy, how they would use their power to bring about social change. They just wanted military victory." Some RCD leaders already began discussing which positions they would get when they got to Kinshasa. In the meantime, Wamba held forth in long speeches about Congolese history and their responsibilities toward the Congolese people.

Many in the group saw Wamba as out of touch with reality. "He was an old professor in sandals," one remembered. "He knew a lot about Marxist theory and African history. But what did he know about governing? About leading a rebellion?"[9] A Ugandan commander who was in charge of Ugandan troops told a leading member of the RCD: "Let the old man write his books, we'll get to work."[10]

A Rwandan military escort took the group to its new headquarters in Goma, Mobutu's former palace on Lake Kivu, where chandeliers and marble floors recalled the good old days before the pillaging and destruction. The Rwandans, in an effort to build team spirit, made the RCD leaders sleep together in the same house. This sparked indignation from some.

Rwandan influence was initially subtle. In the meetings of the RCD assembly, delegates sent from Kigali were often in attendance, but the Congolese debated freely and fiercely over the direction the movement should take. Tito Rutaremara, an old Left Bank Parisian intellectual who was an influential RPF ideologue, gave presentations on how to develop revolutionary ideology. But no one could impose cohesion and a sense of purpose. "It was like herding cats," Wamba remembered. "Most of the people in the movement were not sincerely interested in democracy." They had learned from the Mobutu and Kabila school of governance: They thought power was developed through intrigue. Each leader developed his personal contact in Kigali. Diplomats became used to seeing the RCD leaders at the luxury Umumbano Hotel in Kigali each week, sitting at the same corner table on the terrace, meeting with Rwandan officials. All of the main leaders of the RCD had houses in Kigali, just a three-hour car ride from Goma.

"It was difficult to say who was in charge," Wamba said. "Our executive council met once every two weeks and took decisions. But then I found out others were sending conflicting reports to Kampala and Kigali." It was a typical case of *traffic d'influence*—using personal contacts as leverage behind the scenes to get what you wanted.

The cacophony became so bad that Vice President Kagame had to intervene on several occasions. Once he convened the leadership in Kigali and told them an anecdote about a king. "The monarch had a wonderful advisor who saved him many times," he told his audience. "As a reward, one day he told his advisor that he could make one wish that he would grant him without condition. The advisor told him: 'I have but one simple request. When I want to tell you something, can I whisper it in your ear?' The king, baffled by the request, granted it immediately. From then on, whenever there was an important decision to take, the advisor would go up to the king and whisper banalities in his ear—he talked about the weather or what the cook would make for dinner—and the king would nod. The advisor would then go and tell the court that the king had agreed with his recommendations regarding national policy." Kagame then thundered, wagging his finger. "Some of you fools come and see me here in Kigali, just to say hello and ask about my family! Then you go and tell the rest that Kagame agrees with your decision on this or that matter." He banged his fist on the table. "I will have none of this!"[11]

But the Rwandans were not just innocuous bystanders. Approval for all major expenditures from the RCD budget had to come from Kigali. Both RCD finance minister Emmanuel Kamanzi and chief of staff General Jean-Pierre Ondekane spent most of their time in Kigali, making decisions without conferring with the rest of the RCD leadership. Major leadership changes were imposed by Kigali, and all military operations were led by Rwandan commanders in the field. The more the RCD's disorganization became apparent, the more Kigali began to intervene. "Were we dominated by Rwanda, or were we just very weak?" a former RCD leader asked rhetorically. "It wasn't clear."[12]

∼:∼

It quickly became obvious that Wamba was ill-suited as president of the RCD. He tired of Rwandan interference and the gluttony of his colleagues. From the first days of the rebellion, as their soldiers were blazing across the country, he called for a cease-fire and negotiations with Kabila, causing Rwandan commanders to grind their teeth in frustration. Finally, the height of impudence, he called for a financial audit of the rebellion and made its leaders declare their income and belongings. The results were embarrassing to the RCD: While their coffers were almost empty, many leaders were buying houses in South Africa. Jean-Pierre Ondekane, the military chief of staff who had a taste for diamond rings and used skin-lightening cream, had bought a sports car that he imported to Kigali. "How would he ever drive that thing on Goma's terrible roads?" Wamba wondered.

"After just four months, things were so bad between us we wouldn't talk much together," Wamba remembered. The last straw came on New Year's Eve 1998, when Wamba was scheduled to give a seasonal radio address. His colleagues were with family or friends, enjoying the holiday, when they heard him on the radio: "There is zero oversight of the leaders of the rebellion. This is why even the most notorious incompetence does not elicit the slightest reprimand. The professional relationships have been transformed into a nepotistic politicking: Scratch my back and I will scratch yours."[13] Zahidi Ngoma, who was enjoying a glass of wine at home, rushed to the phone and called the radio station. "Cut him off!" he ordered.

Predictably, the RCD leaders were called to Kigali to explain their supreme disarray. Both Rwanda's president, Pasteur Bizimungu, and its vice president, Paul Kagame, attended the meeting. Wamba complained that any initiative he undertook was blocked by others, in particular the Mobutists. Some Tutsi raised their voices to say that Wamba was excluding them based on their ethnicity. Then Wamba interjected, "I wasn't even given a Christmas dinner! What kind of rebellion is this?"

The other members sighed, and an old Mobutist complained, "This debate has sunk too low. Christmas dinner!"

Bizimungu responded, "No! What the president is saying is important! How can you feed fifty million people if you can't even feed your president?"

Kagame took the floor. "Your problem is that you don't love your country. You need to suffer; you are living the good life. When we were in our rebellion, we were so poor that we didn't have plates to eat out of. We took banana leaves and put them in a hole in the ground to eat our meals."

The debate turned acrimonious, with Zahidi accusing the finance minister of signing contracts in his bathrobe at home and not even informing them, while Wamba was lambasted for having his head in the clouds. The Rwandans intervened to calm the group down, but it was clear that the rift would be difficult to mend. In early 1999, Wamba was toppled as the president of the RCD.

~:~

The rebellion was militarily successful. By the beginning of 1999, the RCD had seized over a quarter of the country, including the third largest city, Kisangani, and were headed toward the mining hubs of Lubumbashi and Mbuji-Mayi. Under the strict guidance of the Rwandan army, the Congolese battalions performed relatively well, although they became well-known for pillage and abuse. Faced with aerial bombardments and artillery barrages from the well-equipped Zimbabwean and Chadian armies (the Angolans chose mostly to stay behind and guard Kinshasa and Bas-Congo), the RCD fought well on a shoestring, using guerrilla tactics to their advantage.

Politically and socially, however, the RCD was a disaster. Outside of the Hutu and Tutsi population of North Kivu, the movement was never able to convince the population that it wasn't a Rwandan proxy. Spontaneously, local militias—focused on ethnic self-defense—were formed, claiming to be protecting Congolese against foreign aggression. The RCD responded with a brutal counterinsurgency, targeting civilians in response to attacks. Within the first four months, several massacres took place, in which over 1,000 civilians were killed. "At first I didn't believe the reports," Wamba said when I asked him about these massacres. "But then I started using my own, parallel channels of information and discovered it was true. But I had no control over the military, and by the time I had found out, I had already fallen out with the others."

I pressed him on one massacre in particular, at Kasika, which happened just weeks after he took the helm of the RCD, on August 24, 1998. According to

UN investigators, as well as witnesses I interviewed, at least five hundred civilians were butchered by Rwandan and RCD troops there.

Wamba looked at me in shock. "Five hundred? No, impossible." I told him that I had been there myself to interview eyewitnesses. "No, no. That isn't possible," he insisted, shaking his head.

In his office in Goma, Wamba was isolated from the suffering of the population. The leadership created the semblance of a functioning administration, with an executive council and legislative assembly playing the role of executive and Parliament. Laws were passed, press conferences called, and budgets discussed, but all this was a sideshow to the military operations. "Sometimes it felt like the only thing we did was sit in meetings all day," José Endundo, an RCD finance commissioner, remembered. "Meetings that went nowhere and had no impact."

The organization lacked not only ideological vision, but also the means with which to implement it. One of Wamba's largest frustrations was his inability to carry out any sort of social or humanitarian project for the population. According to one leader, 80 percent of the RCD's $2.5 million revenues each month went to feeding soldiers and buying supplies for military operations.[14] "We had health and transport departments but no money to build roads or schools," Wamba said. They had over 15,000 soldiers who were deployed in an area the size of France. They had to feed the troops and provide for everything from credit for the satellite phones to fuel for the vehicles and bullets for their guns. The RCD was a predator that sucked resources out of the population and provided next to nothing in return.

~:~

According to many of his former rebel colleagues, Wamba was never in it for personal gain. Even when I visited him, the collar of his shirt was threadbare; he complained that he had been threatened with eviction on several occasions after he was unable to pay the rent. When I asked him about a friend of his, he tried calling him, but realized sheepishly that he had run out of phone credits.

Anyone who has spent much time in the Congo can understand Wamba's desire to bring about radical change through armed rebellion, given the lack of viable options. But his gravest sin was to have remained in the rebellion for so long despite its glaring flaws. A former colleague of his quoted a Swahili proverb to me: "Don't get into a ship with a hole in the bottom; it will eventually sink."

He said of Wamba, "I don't think he raped or killed or stole, but he was part of a machine that did. He is guilty of that at least."

Perhaps the only good decision Wamba could have made was to leave the movement. Instead, he stayed on and made increasingly bizarre choices. In July 1999, Wamba made a desperate effort to raise funds for infrastructure projects— he wanted to open up the hinterlands' economy by rebuilding three hundred and fifty miles of road from Kisangani to Bunia, close to the Ugandan border. He signed a deal with the African Union Reserve System, a previously unknown company, to set up a central bank with a new currency, "for the advancement and economic development for the Congo." The company would be financed by Congolese gold and diamonds and would remit 35 percent of profits to Wamba's treasury, with a $16 million loan up front. The company's owner was Van Arthur Brink, who presented himself as the ambassador of the Dominion of Melchisedek, a fanciful spiritual order that sold banking licenses in the name of a virtual state. Unsurprisingly, it was a swindle. The crook's real name was Allen Ziegler, who was on the run from the U.S. Securities and Exchange Commission for fraud worth $400,000, and who had set up shop on the small Caribbean island of Grenada. The rebels, of course, never saw a cent of the promised money.

Suliman Baldo, the senior Human Rights Watch researcher for the Congo at the time, shook his head when I asked him about Wamba. He had been in touch with Wamba for years during the rebellion. The professor would call him frequently from his rebel base on his satellite phone to tell his side of the story. "Wamba became a farce," he told me. "I would meet him in the bush surrounded by child soldiers, and he would tell me he is an advocate of children's rights."[15] When dissent broke out within Wamba's group, his soldiers repressed it harshly, beating alleged conspirators to death.[16]

Wamba's theories had clashed with the brutal realities of Congolese politics. One period during the war epitomizes this. In August 1999, Wamba was cooped up in Hotel Wagenia, a run-down, colonial-era hotel in the middle of Kisangani, as the town descended into a bloody street battle between Ugandan and Rwandan troops. His Ugandan minders had told him that the Rwandans wanted to kill him, so he spent much of his time in his room, on a satellite phone or writing. His surroundings were not conducive to creative thinking. Not only were there the sporadic bursts of machine gun fire, but the hotel had suffered the same dilapidation as the rest of the city—the water, when it ran, was rusty; the electricity was unreliable; and humidity filled the walls, floorboards, and mattresses with a dank, fetid smell. The heat was unbearable, and the extreme humidity was only leached out of the air during the late afternoon thunderstorms.

Nonetheless, Wamba was prolific. Visitors to the hotel were sometimes turned away by the guards, who said, "The president is writing." The professor's essays often seemed to have little bearing on the tumult around him. As the Kalashnikovs crackled outside, Wamba wrote an open letter to the Belgians, exhorting them to examine their rule in the Congo and to follow the visionary teachings of former colonial governor Pierre Ryckmans and Prime Minister Patrice Lumumba. Other open letters followed, including one to the people of the United States and others to the population of Kinshasa and to the Congolese diaspora. Another letter from the time was—somewhat ironically given the context—a Maoist-inspired reflection on the relation between theory and practice within the rebel movement: "[The founding statutes of the RCD] should affirm that the individual submit himself to the organization, the minority to the majority, the subaltern level to the upper level, the whole organization to the political council."[17]

༈

A Congolese friend once described the curse of Congolese politics as "the reverse Midas effect." "Anything touched by politics in the Congo turns to shit," he told me. "It doesn't matter if the Holy Father himself decides to run for president, he will inevitably come out corrupt, power-hungry, and guilty of breaking all ten of the holy commandments."

His view was extreme, but there is no doubt that there is little trace of responsibility in recent Congolese politics. Wamba is not the only civil rights activist or university professor who joined the various Congolese rebellions. Dozens of others with solid human rights credentials joined and were soon plunged into the dirty world of Congolese insurgent politics. Wamba comes out relatively unscathed in comparison. As misguided as he may have seemed, at least he didn't become involved out of self-interest.

Expatriate workers in the Congo are often heard to say, "You know how it is—they don't have any ideology. The Congolese like fun and dancing. They can never stand up for themselves." "They would sell their sister for a Gucci suit and sunglasses; you can buy anybody here." "They are like children; you need to teach them, kindly but firmly."

This sort of patronizing attitude is common among expatriates—be they Indian, European, Arab, or American—in the Congo. Rarely do they ponder why these alleged traits have developed. The lack of responsible politics, is not due to some genetic defect in Congolese DNA, a missing "virtue gene," or even something about Congolese culture. Instead, it is deeply rooted in the country's political history.

Since the seventeenth and eighteenth century, when European and Arab slave traders penetrated deep into the country and captured hundreds of thousands of slaves, often in complicity with local chiefs, hastening the disintegration of the great kingdoms of the savannah that ruled from the Atlantic seaboard throughout the center and south of the country, the Congo has suffered a social and political dissolution. It was the victim of one of the most brutal episodes of colonial rule, when it was turned into the private business empire of King Leopold; under his reign and the subsequent rule by the republican Belgian government, the Congo's remaining customary chiefs were fought, co-opted, or sent into exile. Religious leaders who defied the orthodoxy of the European-run churches faced the same fate: The prophet Simon Kimbangu died after thirty years in prison for his anticolonial rhetoric.

Under Mobutu, the price of resistance was so great that few ever dared to stand up and be counted for fear of being chopped down. Resistance to dictatorship in other countries has been most successful when it can call on strong, well-organized structures of like-minded supporters, such as labor unions, churches, or student groups. In the Congo, where in any case only 4 percent of the working-age population had jobs in the formal sector, there were few labor unions to speak of. In the early 1990s, fewer than 100,000 students in higher education were dispersed among dozens of universities and training centers across the country. Mobutu had tamed these institutions, consolidating all labor and student unions and forcefully integrating them into his ruling party. The country's biggest institute of higher learning, Lovanium University, previously run by the Catholic Church, was nationalized along with several Protestant universities. Mobutu even forced the Catholic Church to accept the establishment of cells of his political party within religious seminaries.

Some Congolese leaders have courageously stood up in protest: Lumumba before independence, Tshisekedi during Mobutu's reign, and the countless journalists, priests, doctors, and human rights defenders who opposed oppression and injustice. Once these individuals become members of government, they are confronted with two problems: the lack of a popular base and the abject weakness of the state. Unable to implement policy and attacked on all sides by rivals, they have been either co-opted, killed, or forced to quit.

If the fiercest ideology or ethics that can be found in the country is ethnic, that is because no other institution has been strong enough for the people to rally around. Unfortunately, ethnic mobilization is usually exclusive in nature and does not form an equitable or truly democratic basis for the distribution of state resources; also, given the manipulation of customary chiefs, even this vessel has been corrupted. It will take generations to rebuild institutions or social organizations that can challenge the current predatory state without resorting to ethnicity.

Wamba came to power alone and isolated. He didn't have a political power base and had few allies in the rebellion he had joined. Most importantly, the organization was fractured into different interest groups and dominated by Rwandan interference. For a political scientist, Wamba had grossly underestimated the necessity of having a strong organization to implement the lofty reforms he dreamt of. Instead of leaving, however, Wamba retreated into the cocoon of his ideas and theories, writing letters and giving interviews to leftist American and African journals. He became a victim of his own idealism, reduced to irrelevance.

THE REBEL START-UP

The fact is that a man who wants to act virtuously in every way necessarily comes to grief among so many who are not virtuous.

—NICCOLO MACHIAVELLI

GBADOLITE, CONGO, JULY 1999

When the Rwandans launched their war against Laurent Kabila in August 1998, Jean-Pierre Bemba, a six-foot-two, two-hundred-and-seventy-pound, millionaire-turned-rebel leader started his own rebellion in the north of the country, the Movement for the Liberation of the Congo (MLC). Although he received backing from the Ugandan army and from an assortment of former Mobutists, for the most part, his rebellion was about Jean-Pierre Bemba.

In July 1999 Bemba captured Mobutu's hometown of Gbadolite. Over thirty years, Mobutu had turned the sleepy jungle town, which counted only 1,700 souls at independence in 1960, into a monument to his corruption and profligacy. He built three separate, sprawling palaces for himself and his visitors. One of the palaces was a replica of a Chinese pagoda, complete with gilded dragon figurines, jade roofs, and carp-filled ponds. Ceramic tiles were flown in from Europe, pure-bred sheep from Argentina, and birthday cakes from Paris' best patisseries. The village—one of the most remote corners of the country, five hundred miles from Kinshasa, ensconced in thick rain forest—featured luxuries most Congolese towns could only dream of: a hydroelectric power plant; a four-mile-long airport, one of the longest in Africa, which could accommodate Concorde jets; and a nuclear bunker that could shelter five hundred people. Satellite dishes provided crisp color television and a phone network. At the height of his reign, Mobutu lavished $15 million a month on the maintenance of this dreamland. It was a surreal African Shangri-la.

By the time Jean-Pierre Bemba arrived in Gbadolite, the town had been ransacked by successions of different armed groups—first Rwandans and the AFDL, then Chadian troops flown in to help Kabila fight Bemba. The crystal chandeliers and silverware had been stolen and the walls of the palaces stripped bare of anything that could be looted. Large avant-garde paintings had been replaced by graffiti—"Fuck Mobutu," read one—and glass from broken windows crunched underfoot. The fleet of Mercedes had been gutted; the carp were long since belly-up, and Mobutu's pet leopard was rumored to be stalking the overgrown palace gardens. The wardrobes in town were full of thousands of white gloves, aprons, and suits belonging to the hundreds of the dictator's former domestic staff, now out of work.

Amid the ruins, Jean-Pierre Bemba set up his headquarters. Bemba was the son of one of Mobutu's closest business associates and had himself been a protégé of the late president. When he had walked into Gbadolite, the streets had filled with thousands of supporters wearing Mobutu T-shirts and cheering him on. His family came from the region, and most of his top army commanders had made their career in the Zairian army. Even in style and personality, he spoke with similar bombast and condescension as the late, great *Maréchal*.

Bemba was a spectacle. Dressed alternately in a smart business suit or in army fatigues, he would receive his visitors in his father's house in Gbadolite, surrounded by his equipment: several satellite phones, a high-frequency radio, and a wide-screen television. From this central command post he would stay in touch with diplomats, his commanders in the field, and friends and family in Europe. On the coffee table in front of him was a stack of society rags: *Paris Match*, *L'Express*, *Vanity Fair*, all rarely more than three months old. He spent hours watching CNN and French news, staying abreast of world events. For journalists who had just flown over hours of impenetrable rain forest without seeing a paved road, the rebel leader seemed lost in another world, far from the thousands of square miles of jungles that his army controlled. One reporter who visited him tells the story of watching CNN as news broke of John F. Kennedy Jr.'s death in a plane crash off Martha's Vineyard. Bemba was apparently crestfallen, obviously identifying with the dead scion of the Kennedy family. "Why did he choose to fly at night, in those conditions? Why?" he lamented, slapping his knee and shaking his head.[1] As for Congolese caricaturists, they were fond of depicting him as an overgrown, spoiled baby in diapers, crying because someone had taken his rattle away.

As always in the Congo, the myth reveals a bit of the man, but not much. Bemba is certainly endowed with a bloated ego and an overly keen business acumen. But he also managed to do something that no other rebel leader in the Congo had done: He built a rebel movement that was able to control a large part of the country while maintaining popular support, all without excessive outside interference.

∼:∼

"This book is the history of a struggle," Bemba writes in the afterword of his autobiography. "Struggle against dictatorship. A struggle for freedom. A struggle of so many men and women fallen on the field of honour so that an ideal can triumph."[2] Grand words, but hardly the reality. Over the years, Bemba developed into a politician with an articulated ideology, but for most of his life he was a businessman interested, above all, in personal success.

Jean-Pierre grew up with a silver spoon in his mouth. His father, Saolona, the son of a Portuguese trader and a Congolese woman from Equateur Province, had worked his way up from a small-time coffee grower to be head of one of the largest business empires in Zaire. Based for much of his early career in the coffee growing region of Equateur, Saolona made a fortune when the coffee price peaked following the Brazilian coffee frosts of the 1970s. He grew close to Mobutu and benefited from the nationalization of foreign companies in 1973, expanding his coffee business and diversifying into manufacturing and transportation. By the 1980s, he ran a conglomerate with 40,000 employees. He was one of the richest men in Zaire, elected numerous times as head of the Congolese Business Federation.

Jean-Pierre's mother died when he was only eight, leaving a hole in his upbringing. His father married again and had affairs with several other women, providing Jean-Pierre with over two dozen half-brothers and sisters. Not long afterwards, he was sent to boarding school in Brussels and would only see his father when he visited while on business trips or when Jean-Pierre returned home for vacation. "His mother's death affected him deeply," José Endundo, another affluent entrepreneur who joined his rebellion, remembered. "From then on, he always seemed to be alone."

The distance and loneliness fueled Bemba's desire to succeed and led him to further idolize his father. "Jean-Pierre was the first child, the oldest," Michel Losembe, the director of Citibank in Kinshasa and a childhood friend, recalled. "He was being groomed to succeed." During his high school vacations, he would return home to work in the coffee fields and to help manage the ever-growing network of family businesses.

Meanwhile, he led a discreet life in Brussels. "He was never his daddy's boy, never arrogant, never throwing his wealth around," Losembe remembered. He lived in a three-thousand-square-meter villa in a wealthy suburb of Brussels, but he almost never invited his friends to his home. He liked to socialize, but even when he went out on the town, he would always split the bill and even ask to have the wine deducted from his share if he didn't drink. He got a reputation among the Congolese in Belgium for having *maboko makasi*—tight fists. Wary of Congolese who sought to ingratiate themselves, he preferred hanging out with Belgian aristocrats' children just as wealthy as he was. They would go on hunting trips to the Ardennes during their vacations and test-drive each others' new sports cars.

Looking at pictures of Bemba at that time, one finds it hard to believe that it's the same man. In his high school snapshots, he is a tall, thin boy who seems to be smiling despite himself. He was obsessed with excelling in everything he did—tennis, squash, studies. When he flunked out of his first year of university in Brussels, he was so disappointed that he spent the whole summer cramming to pass a state exam so he could get into the prestigious Catholic Institute of Higher Commercial Studies (ICHEC) business school. He succeeded. "He wasn't super intelligent or quick," a Belgian classmate remembered, "but he was incredibly determined and rigorous."

During this time, and contrary to later statements, Bemba did not show any interest in politics. Like most people at ICHEC, he focused on the world of profits and losses, economies of scale and price elasticities. He was wary of criticizing Mobutu, as his father's business increasingly depended on his relations with the government. On his trips home, he, too, would rub shoulders with the

Kinshasa elites, as his father began delegating much of his work to him. By the time he graduated from university in 1986, at the age of twenty-four, Bemba was managing most of his father's foreign business interests and bank accounts.

With this promotion, Bemba's character changed. He moved to Kinshasa, and his father made him the manager of one of his largest companies, Scibe Airlift. In a country the size of western Europe, where the national road network had collapsed, there was a lot of money to be made in air transport. By that time, Scibe had become the unofficial government carrier, ferrying goods and people around the country. Jean-Pierre ran the company with an iron fist, waking up every morning at 4:30 to go the airport. With his employees and business partners, he mimicked his father's aggressive management style. He yelled at workers, insulted air traffic officials, and fired people who didn't perform. "The difference between Jean-Pierre and his father," one of his friends remembered, "was that with Saolona, at 7 o'clock, after work, that aggressive mask fell, and he became a nice, relaxed guy. With Jean-Pierre, the mask stuck."

Throughout this time, Jean-Pierre had become close to Mobutu. His father brought him along on his trips to Gbadolite, where the dictator was spending more and more time, and Mobutu took a liking to the enterprising young man. Mobutu's own children had mostly disappointed him—several had joined the military or intelligence services, where they were known for their crude brutality, womanizing, and crooked deals. The most promising one, his favorite son, Niwa, passed away in the 1980s, probably of AIDS. Over the years all of his other sons from his first marriage would die as well. Mobutu began to treat Jean-Pierre like a member of his own family. When the young entrepreneur visited Europe, he would fly back with gifts for Mobutu. On one occasion, he sent a massive birthday cake back on one of his Scibe airplanes.

Meanwhile, Jean-Pierre was longing to start his own business, to emerge from his father's shadow. The privatization of telecommunications in the early 1990s provided the opportunity. Like the rest of the state's infrastructure, the phone grid had collapsed, prompting investors to experiment with new cellular phone technology that was too expensive for widespread use in the developed world. A Congolese Tutsi businessman, Miko Rwayitare, convinced Mobutu in 1986 to set up Telecel, one of the first mobile phone companies in Africa. He distributed hundreds of clunky, brick-sized phones to ministers, and the service proved to be both incredibly successful and expensive. With charges as much as $16 per minute, Mobutu complained to his advisors about the millions of dollars in telephone bills, as well as Rwayitare's ties to his political rivals. Jean-Pierre saw a business opportunity and stepped in: He told the president he would start a new company, Comcell, and offer cheaper rates. Mobutu was delighted. So was Saolona Bemba, who followed his son's business exploits with great pride.

Comcell prompted Jean-Pierre's first foray into politics. As the young entrepreneur set up transmission towers across Kinshasa, he met with sharp resistance from the political heavyweights surrounding Miko. They tried to undermine his nascent company and prevent customers from signing up with Comcell. In response, Jean-Pierre mounted his first military operation, using a gang of presidential guards to sabotage a Telecel antenna in Kinshasa. "To be in business back then, you had to have muscle to protect you," recalled José Endundo, who at the time was as influential as the Bemba family. Jean-Pierre Bemba got used to driving around Kinshasa behind tinted windows, escorted by two vehicles with bodyguards. A friend of his remembers getting into the passenger seat of his car around that time, only to find a grenade at his feet.

As the Zairian economy capsized, economic opportunities became scarcer, and political patronage more important. When the poorly paid army went on a rampage in Kinshasa in 1991 and 1993, pillaging thousands of stores and houses, the Bembas lost millions of dollars. Increasingly, Jean-Pierre used his ties to Mobutu to defend his businesses. He obtained procurement deals from the army for the supply of fuel, uniforms, and boots and even carried out confidential diplomatic missions for Mobutu in the region. He made friends with top generals, who controlled much of the government's spending, and when Mobutu fell sick with prostate cancer, Jean-Pierre visited him on his sick bed in France.

~:~

By the time the AFDL arrived in Kinshasa, Jean-Pierre had fled to Europe; by that time he owned several sumptuous villas in Portugal and Belgium. His father, however, stayed, in order to look after the family business and properties. Not surprisingly, when Laurent Kabila arrived in Kinshasa, Saolona Bemba became one of the first people he locked up. "When you talked about Mobutu's business elite, Saolona was foremost," Henri Mova, Kabila's transport minister at the time, recalled. "We had to arrest him."

When Jean-Pierre heard about his father's arrest, he was terrified what might happen to him. He contacted several Mobutu officers who had fled across the Congo River to Brazzaville and tried to organize a prison break for his father. At the last minute, when preparations were already at an advanced stage, Saolona himself told his son to stand down. It was too risky, he said. This is just about money. He was right: After paying half a million dollars, he was released.

Jean-Pierre's investments—a dozen planes, warehouses full of goods, coffee plantations, a mobile phone network—were all sunk costs, based in the Congo. While many other entrepreneurs had been able to make the transition between Mobutu and Kabila, Bemba's intimacy with Mobutu was too well-known. He was also too proud to come begging Kabila to forgive him for past alliances.

Bemba was an avid pilot and liked talking in aviation jargon. When asked why he had doggedly pursued his dream of rebellion, he once responded: "In an aircraft at take-off, you reach decision speed, after which, no matter what happens, you have to continue accelerating and take-off or else you risk crashing the plane. I had reached decision speed."[3]

⌒⋮⌒

Some sociologists have put down insurgencies to "blocked political aspirations."[4] If this is true, many others from Mobutu's entourage would have had better reason to start an insurgency than Jean-Pierre Bemba. Following Mobutu's demise, the complacency of his lieutenants and strongmen was astounding: All of his ministers, the heads of his powerful security services, and his personal advisors contented themselves with comfortable exiles in Europe and South Africa. Instead, it was a political neophyte who took up the struggle against Kabila.

Once Jean-Pierre Bemba had decided on starting a rebellion, he had various choices. He had naturally been in touch with Mobutu's former generals in exile but was skeptical about their abilities given their recent ineptitude. They were also divided into different, competing networks, the result of decades of divide-and-conquer manipulations by Mobutu. Bemba also wanted to avoid direct association with Mobutu's regime.

Then there was the new Rwandan-backed rebellion that had begun gestating in the early months of 1998. Bemba had met Ugandan president Yoweri Museveni during one of his business trips before the war and had kept in touch since.[5] Museveni was worried about the way Laurent Kabila's regime was shaping up, and he was eager to identify new, more reliable figures in the Congolese diaspora. He recommended Bemba to General Paul Kagame, who was busy cobbling together the RCD rebellion. In Kigali, however, Bemba didn't like the look of what he saw. "Militarily, the choice of this movement to lean exclusively on its Rwandan ally to the detriment of developing a Congolese capacity, makes me think that this method cannot lead to the creation of a credible popular movement," he wrote after a two-hour meeting with Kagame.[6] He was also worried by the phalanx of Congolese political and economic heavyweights already assembled in Kigali. It was clear that if he joined, he would not be the leader of the new movement, but milling around in mid-level bureaucracy. Back in Kampala, he explained his reservations to Museveni and pushed for a second option, "a real alternative force to Kinshasa's dictatorial regime."

Museveni himself was beginning to have his doubts about Rwanda's approach, which seemed too top-down and controlling. "We had a different strategy," Colonel Shaban Bantariza, the army spokesman, told me. "For us, the Congolese were supposed to learn how to manage and rule themselves." The Ugandan army was inspired by its own experience as rebels, fighting for six years in the bush with little external support, relying on the local population. Bemba fit the Ugandan model. "He was convincing," Bantariza said. "You could spend two hours with him, and he would give you a clear, structured vision of what he wanted to do with his country."[7] The Ugandans agreed to back Bemba and enrolled him in accelerated military training.

Shortly after the beginning of the second war in August 1998, they agreed with the Rwandans to split operational sectors, with the Ugandans taking the area north of Kisangani and the Rwandans staying to the south. Kisangani itself would remain under joint command.

To start their own rebellion, the Ugandans recruited 154 Congolese in Kisangani in September 1998 and began training them along with Bemba. That number would later take on mythical proportions for Bemba, who claimed that he conquered the area north of Kisangani with a mere 154 soldiers. That was, at least initially, not true. As Bemba sweated away in the training camp with his soldiers—he was made to goose-step, snake around on his considerable belly, and take apart an AK-47 in thirty seconds—RCD troops with Ugandan support were advancing to the north, fighting pitched battles with Kabila's troops.

The key moment for Bemba came when Uganda seized the strategic town of Lisala, the birthplace of Mobutu, in Equateur Province, and the Ugandan commander, General James Kazini, assembled the RCD troops and told them to turn in their walkie-talkies "for reprogramming." General Kazini sat down with the Congolese officers and gave them a choice—you can return to Kisangani and work with the Rwandans, or stay here with us and help us build a new rebellion. Most chose the latter.

It was in the midst of this Kigali-Kampala catfight that the Movement for the Liberation of the Congo (MLC) was born. Bemba, who had been working for several months with friends from the Congolese diaspora on drafting statutes and a political program, quickly called the BBC radio service to announce his new rebellion.

~:~

The MLC's beginnings were shaky. Applying himself to the rebellion with the same tenacity as he did to his business empire, Bemba managed to recruit a hodge-podge of young men and women from the business and political class of Kisangani. Of the founding members of the MLC, there was a journalist for the state radio station, the local manager of Bemba's phone company, a territorial administrator, two former Mobutu officers, and several businessmen. None of them was over forty years old. For the most part, they were political unknowns.

Slowly, Bemba began to take over control of the military wing of the MLC from the Ugandans. He leveraged his contacts among Mobutu's former officers to rally some of the most capable around him, making sure to stay away from the most infamous and corrupt. It had not been for lack of experience and knowledge that Mobutu's army had lost the war, and hundreds of officers, marginalized or in exile, were eager to get back into the fray. Bemba handed the military command over to Colonel Dieudonné Amuli, the former commander of Mobutu's personal guard and a graduate of several international military academies. Other officers' résumés included stints at Fort Bragg and Fort Benning (United States), Sandhurst (United Kingdom), Nanjing (China), Kenitra (Morocco), and academies in Egypt and Belgium. Although the Ugandans continued to provide military support, in particular through artillery, training, and logistics, by early 1999 the Congolese were largely the masters of their own rebellion, expanding their rebel force from 150 to around 10,000 troops within two years.

Slowly, on the back of the MLC's growing reputation, a second wave of political figures began to board flights from Europe to join up. Their pedigree was as impressive as those of the military officers. This time it was the well-heeled diaspora, the members of the Kinshasa elite, educated in Europe and the United States. There were the young and westernized, like Olivier Kamitatu, the son of a founding father of the Congo who had been Bemba's inseparable friend in business school in Brussels. Then there were the Mobutists-turned-opposition-activists, including former prime minister Lunda Bululu and two other former ministers, and the businessmen, such as the erstwhile heads of the Congolese business federation and the Congo-Belgian chamber of commerce. In groups of two or three, they arrived on Ugandan military planes in Gbadolite, which by mid-1999 had become command central of the rebellion. They walked around the pillaged town dumbstruck.

~:~

Then came the luck, and with it the birth of the Bemba myth. From the early days of rebellion onwards, the portly MLC leader, who had had less than a month of formal military training in his life, was present along the front lines and insisted on participating in military operations. When the Chadians and Kabila's troops tried to attack the MLC base in Lisala, Bemba flew into town under gunfire and drove around in a pickup truck, rounding up and regrouping his scattered soldiers. "If you have to believe in miracles, that wasn't the only one," he later wrote.[8] A day later, a rocket-propelled grenade whistled by him, missing him only by several feet. The day after that, amid a shower of gunfire, a Ugandan transport plane landed, unloaded, and took off again without major damage. "It was incredible," a friend, who had been in touch with Bemba on a monthly basis by satellite phone, recalled. "It was as if he was blessed with special powers."[9]

The MLC leaders began constructing a myth around Bemba's exploits, a panegyric that fit well into the Congolese tradition of praise singing. The youths called him "Baimoto," a dazzling diamond that blinds the enemy. Radio Liberté, the MLC radio station, began transmitting programs infused with Bemba's legend. It was supposed to provide the glue to keep the disparate elements of the MLC together: Bemba the soldier, Bemba the liberator, always on the front line, always with the troops. "It did the trick," a former MLC commander told me and then laughed: "The problem was he began to believe it himself."[10]

Bemba adopted the title of Chairman of the MLC, in part reference to his business upbringing, in part a wink to Chairman Mao's cult of personality. Progressively, his ego became more and more bloated, even as he himself put on more weight. "Bemba was the MLC," said José Endundo, the MLC's former secretary for the economy. "He was an incredible egomaniac."[11] His commissioners and counselors couldn't just go and visit him in his house in Gbadolite; they would have to wait to be called. At the entrance to his house, soldiers would frisk the MLC leaders, even the frail professor Lunda Bululu, Zaire's former prime minister, who was in his sixties. Inside, officials sprawled on Bemba's leather couches, but even there, they were obliged to call him Mr. President or Chairman. For some of the leaders, who had boozed and danced with Bemba in high school or had known him when he was still in diapers, this treatment grated.

Bemba's massive ego initially had a positive impact on the organization. According to many of his former colleagues who later left the rebellion, he ruled strictly but fairly. "He respected us," Endundo remembered. "And he was a good manager." But for most of Bemba's lieutenants, the goal was clear: to sit tight and wait for negotiations with Kabila's government. If they had to endure Bemba's narcissism until then, they would.

As opposed to most other rebel movements in the Congo, which spent much of their life spans embroiled in internecine squabbles, Bemba was the unquestioned leader of the MLC, politically as well as militarily. From command central on his couch, he micromanaged the organization, one hand on the remote control of his television, another on his satellite phone or ham radio.

While he promoted debate about internal policy and strategy, he was the only one to maintain contacts with foreign leaders. He almost never invited other MLC leaders along when he visited President Museveni, his biggest ally. The same went for other contacts. "He had a fabulous address book," Endundo recalled. "He would speak to [Gabonese] President Omar Bongo, [Libyan leader] Muammar Ghadaffi, [Republic of Congo] President Sassou Nguesso." Likewise, none of the other political leaders in the MLC had much to say about military operations. Bemba sat together with the commander of the Ugandan troops and

Colonel Amuli and discussed military strategy. In several cases, he went so far as to overrule his Ugandan counterparts.[12]

⋰⋱

Bemba did not have a hard time being popular in Equateur Province. The MLC arrived on the heels of two years of occupation, pillage, and abuse by Rwandan, Congolese, and Chadian troops. Each group had accused the local population of supporting Mobutu and blamed them for hosting such luxurious, wasteful projects as the Chinese pagodas and the hydroelectric dams. When Bemba arrived, he was treated as a *mwana mboka*, a son of the soil, a hometown hero. People lined the streets when Bemba arrived in a town, waving flags of Zaire and chanting Bemba's name.

More than one former MLC official I interviewed compared Bemba's management style to that of a private entrepreneur: "He ran his army like a company," or "the MLC for him was an IPO, an initial public offering." Nonetheless, even those who fell out with him concede that it was better organized and more successful than other rebellions. Its leaders were members of the Kinshasa elite, and tribalism, which was a problem for other rebel movements, was not an issue here. There was no interference from Kampala in political matters, and the group of decision makers was small and relatively united. Most MLC leaders were not motivated by immediate financial gain—many of them were independently wealthy—but rather by a return to power in Kinshasa.

In any case, there was little profit to be gleaned from Equateur. It was a relatively poor province, especially since its coffee, rice, and palm oil plantations had fallen into disrepair. After taking all the money they had found in the coffers of the banks—UN investigators tallied around $1.5 million "liberated" from three banks at the beginning of the rebellion—there was little money to be made. According to François Mwamba, the head of their finances, they rarely got more than $50,000 a month. "Once, I had to spend ten hours on the back of a motorcycle, hanging on to a kid with an AK-47 strapped on his back, just to collect $2,000 from a bank in the jungle town of Banalia," Mwamba told me. "Do you think I would be doing that if we were flush with cash?"[13]

Given their financial limitations, the MLC had little to offer the local population in terms of services. They organized communal labor to rebuild some roads and bridges, but even they admitted it was rudimentary.[14] Most of their money went to buying food and medicine for the army and paying for air transport. What the rebels could provide, however, was the most sought-after commodity in the region: security. A poll carried out in 2002 in the province concluded that 70 percent of locals felt protected against crime. The same number indicated that they would vote for Bemba and the MLC if elections were held then.[15] Indeed, when elections were eventually held in 2006, Equateur was the only province where the population voted massively in favor of the armed group that had ruled them during the war, casting 64 percent of their ballots for Bemba in the first round and 98 percent in the second. Almost everywhere else in the country, the population clearly rejected its rulers.[16]

≈⋮≈

The problems arose when the MLC began expanding its military operations outside of Equateur in 2001. The northeastern region of Ituri, which borders Uganda to the east and Sudan to the north, was quickly turning into a quagmire for the Ugandan army. There, as opposed to Equateur, there was an abundance of natural resources, ranging from gold to timber, on top of the lucrative customs offices at the Congo-Uganda border, which collected millions of dollars of revenues a month. The district shared no front line with Kabila's forces; nonetheless, Uganda had deployed a large military contingent there, ostensibly to protect their border. In addition, Ituri had a history of ethnic rivalries, especially between the pastoralist Hema people and the Lendu farmers. Ugandan army commanders quickly became involved in semiprivate business ventures, with different commanders backing various local ethnic militias in order to corner lucrative parts of the market. In January 2001, President Yoweri Museveni, who approved of Bemba's management of Equateur Province, asked Bemba to move eastward to take the leadership of a new coalition of rebel movements, including several Ituri-based factions and the MLC. Bemba accepted, attracted by the greater status it would provide him, as well as by the substantial revenues to be garnered.

The alliance, dubbed the Front for the Liberation of the Congo, was a disaster. After some early successes in calming ethnic rancor, Bemba was quickly embroiled in a struggle with the other armed groups for control of the region's resources. Instead of trying to find a negotiated solution, Bemba retaliated with force, launching the ominously named "Clean the Blackboard" operation intended to wipe out his rivals. The attack quickly degenerated into a messy counterinsurgency operation, as 3,000 MLC troops collaborated with a Hema militia to loot, abuse, and massacre locals they accused of collaborating with their enemies. A local witness described the brutality to human rights investigators:

> The Hema and the "Effaceurs" [MLC] came into town and started killing people. We hid in our house. I opened the window and saw what happened from there. A group of more than ten with spears, guns and machetes killed two men in Cité Suni, in the center of Mongbwalu. I saw them pull the two men from their house and kill them. They took Kasore, a Lendu man in his thirties, from his family and attacked him with knives and hammers. They killed him and his son (aged about 20) with knives. They cut his son's throat and tore open his chest. They cut the tendons on his heels, smashed his head and took out his intestines. The father was slaughtered and burnt.[17]

The shine had come off Bemba's reputation. The rebel coalition fell apart, and Bemba retreated to Equateur Province. "He was getting reckless," an MLC official confided. "We were broke and had engaged in a massive recruitment drive in the expectation of joining a national army, so we needed money to feed our soldiers."

This money was supposed to come from another military adventure, this time on foreign soil. In October 2002, following a coup attempt, the president of the Central African Republic, Ange Felix Patassé, asked Bemba to come to his aid. Bangui, the capital of the strife-torn country, was just across the river from one of Bemba's bases. It was a purely mercenary affair, with Patassé paying Bemba cash in return for sending 1,000 troops to help ward off the attack. Once again, Bemba's troops committed atrocities, pillaging villages and raping dozens of women. Bemba, who himself visited his troops deployed there and followed the operations closely, suffered another dent to his reputation. This time, the consequences would be more serious. Five years later, he would be arrested and forced to stand trial for his soldiers' abuses in front of the International Criminal Court.

~:~

In the meantime, life in Gbadolite for the rest of the MLC leaders was bucolic and slow. After all, their headquarters was 1,000 kilometers from Kinshasa. You could not reach a major town without boarding an aircraft and flying over a thick expanse of forest. The leaders would wake up late in their air-conditioned houses in Gbadolite and spend the day in meetings or on the phone with friends and diplomats. At times, they worked hard, sometimes late into the night. There were letters to write to the African Union and United Nations, a draft constitution to put together, and political strategy to hatch. Other times, there was nothing to do but find new ways to ward off boredom. Some would listen to classical music, while others would walk through Mobutu's abandoned gardens, listening to parrots, hornbills, and mousebirds or hunting for Mobutu heirlooms that previous pillagers had missed. They inspected Mobutu's private chapel, containing the tomb to his first beloved wife, Marie-Antoinette, which in better times used to elevate once a year on her birthday via a solar-powered device. In the evenings, when there was no work to be done, some would watch satellite TV with Bemba, although "that could get a little boring after a while," one MLC leader admitted.

For the former Mobutists, who had been living in exile in their villas in Europe, life in Gbadolite wasn't easy. "Gone were the days of champagne drinking, parties with two hundred servants, and people flown in on Concordes," Endundo remembered. He was particularly bitter about having to run his various businesses from the isolation of the jungle town. He ran up satellite phone bills of up to $40,000 a month. Thambwe Mwamba, a former minister of public works for Mobutu, arrived in mid-2000, asking his new colleagues whether there was somewhere to get a manicure in town. Some MLC officials took to riding bicycles, a skill that some had to relearn, as there were only a few vehicles in town, all belonging to Jean-Pierre Bemba. "We got into a fight with him one time," a former MLC commander remembered, "because he didn't want to loan us a pickup to drop us off at our house. It was a pickup we had captured from the Chadians! Not his personal vehicle!"[18]

When asked about how much they earned during the war, all MLC officials respond with the same guffaw. In the early days, when the MLC just controlled a handful of mid-sized towns in northern Equateur, the tax revenues weren't enough to pay salaries. High-ranking cadres received a daily food allowance of around $4; less important officials had half as much. Their diet was a tedious repetition of fish, rice, and various manioc, pumpkin, and bean leaves stewed in palm oil. "Once, after much complaining," said Thomas Luhaka, the MLC defense commissioner, "the commander gave me $40. I thought that was a lot!"

But boredom was perhaps the biggest challenge. The hydroelectric plant on the Ubangui River was still working and supplied the town with electricity day and night. The wives of the leaders, themselves ensconced in their houses in Europe, would send them care packages via Kampala with all the luxuries they needed: cheese, ketchup, chocolate, smoked ham, and even condoms. The latter item didn't go to waste: There was still a coterie of beautiful women in Gbadolite, educated at the local Jesuit school, one of the best in the country under Mobutu, who had worked at the Enlightened Guide's court. For some of his time in Gbadolite, Bemba lived with one of these women, the beautiful and tall Mayimuna, with whom he ended up having several children, much to the dismay of his wife, who had stayed in Portugal.

≺∶≻

I met with Jean-Pierre Bemba once after he had left the rebellion, in 2005, by which time he was vice president in the transitional government. He greeted me at his desk, wearing a suit and tie. In front of him was a laptop on which "I can see all the revenues and expenditures of the government budget in real time," he said—his portfolio included economy and finance. Just before I had arrived, he had been perusing a book that lay next to the laptop on the table: *The 48 Rules of Power* by Robert Greene. It was a good indication of his philosophy. He was more Machiavelli—the inspiration behind the book—than Mao or Marx. As with Machiavelli, who wrote during a time of upheaval and infighting among Italy's various city states, idealism wouldn't get you very far in the world of Congolese politics, and it had never been part of Bemba's arsenal. Most of his own autobiography, *The Choice of Freedom*, was ghostwritten by his own ideologues: Olivier Kamitatu and Thambwe Mwamba. As an MLC friend once put it, "you can't teach people with twenty years of experience in politics new tricks. Jean-Pierre Bemba was no Che Guevara."[19]

Congolese rebel politics since the 1960s has been either an elite or an ethnic affair, or—most often—a mixture of both. There has rarely been a successful experiment in building an insurgency from the ground up without outside help. Almost every single Congolese rebel group was helped on its way by an outside patron: Rwanda, Uganda, DR Congo, Angola, and Zimbabwe. The semi-exceptions are the various ethnic self-defense forces, usually called Mai-Mai, that operate in the eastern Congo and that sprang up in response to outside aggression. Many of these groups, while initially autonomous, only became powerful when they were co-opted by Kinshasa to wage a proxy war against Rwanda and Uganda. And almost all remained confined by the limits of their ethnicity. As Che Guevara himself had concluded at the end of his sojourn in the country in 1965, the rebels were "devoid of coherent political education . . . revolutionary awareness or any forward-looking perspective beyond the traditional horizon of their tribal territory."[20]

It was therefore no wonder that the MLC would break up after the war. One by one, most of the heavyweights in the party had been thrown out of the movement, which was now battered and broken. Tired of Bemba's ego, and broke after years of unpaid labor, many gladly accepted offers from Kabila to join his party, while others struck out on their own. Even Olivier Kamitatu, the well-spoken secretary-general of the party, who had been inseparable from Bemba since their school days, had bailed on him, taking a job as minister of planning for Kabila. Rumors abounded that Olivier's new house had been financed by Kabila, and he was often seen driving around in a new, shiny Hummer. Those who had remained in the party were consumed by incessant squabbling. The transformation from a rebel group into a political party had failed: The authoritarianism that Bemba had used to keep people in line in the jungle was now ill-placed. Opportunism, once a centripetal force in the MLC, had now burst the seams of the movement, flinging members in all directions.

Nonetheless, during its heyday, the MLC was as good as it gets for a Congolese rebel movement. Although supported by Uganda, it was run by Congolese under a more or less unified command, supported by the local population, and relatively disciplined. But the MLC also shows us the limitations of rebellion in the Congo. Like most rebellions, it was run by an educated elite, while all of its foot soldiers were local peasants. There was little ideology that took hold at the grassroots level other than opposition to the enemy and tribal loyalty.

16

CAIN AND ABEL

KISANGANI, CONGO, MAY 1999

In May 1999, the city of Kisangani, later dubbed the City of Martyrs, fell victim to the worst bout of urban warfare the Congolese war had ever seen. The battle had dramatic consequences: It spelled the end of the Rwandan-Ugandan alliance and brought to the fore the plunder of the country's riches.

The city's reputation had not always been so bleak. The town of a million people was located in the middle of the country at a bend in the Congo River. In the 1960s, it had been an attractive city laid out along grand avenues lined with jacaranda and mango trees. It is clear that the Belgians had had big plans for the jungle city: Italianate turrets and futuristic, Art Deco architecture; streets named after Chopin, Beethoven, and Belgian royalty; and a city divided by the great river into "Rive Droite" and "Rive Gauche," reminiscent of Paris.

Kisangani formed a trade hub with the eastern provinces by road and with Kinshasa by river. Roads branched out into the jungles to the north, where there were large ranches and coffee plantations, and merchants brought huge bags of rich palm oil down the river in dugout canoes. However, Mobutu's kleptocracy had reversed the flow of time in the town, as buildings crumbled and the jungle reclaimed land. The novelist V. S. Naipaul portrayed the demoralizing aura of the city in his 1979 book, *A Bend in the River*:

> The big lawns and gardens had returned to bush; the streets had disap-
> peared; vine and creepers had grown over broken, bleached walls of concrete

or hollow clay brick. . . . But the civilization wasn't dead. It was the civilization I existed in and worked towards. And that could make for an odd feeling: to be among the ruins was to have your time sense unsettled. You felt like a ghost, not from the past, but from the future. You felt that your life and ambition had already been lived out for you and you were looking at the relics of that life.[1]

The country had only further decayed since Naipaul had visited it. Throughout my travels in the eastern Congo, I would come across overgrown train tracks, phone poles devoured by termites and moss. In remote valleys, entire villas complete with horse stables and swimming pools had been reclaimed by nature.

The war had further sapped the life out of Kisangani. The whitewash had faded from the Art Deco facades, the pavement was cracked and overgrown with grass, and most shops were boarded up and empty. River traffic had all but ceased, as no boats were allowed up the river from Kinshasa into rebel-held territory. With no fuel or spare parts available, the only motorized traffic on the streets were a few dozen vehicles belonging to humanitarian organizations. The only means of leaving the town—unless you wanted to trek on foot for a week through the forest—was by plane, so all luxury goods had the cost of an air ticket slapped on their price tag.

The isolation had its impact on the locals. Almost 10 percent of children were severely malnourished, retarding their physical and mental development and making them prone to disease.[2] The inhabitants now had to rely on the tens of thousands of *toleka* ("let's go" in Lingala), the bicycle taxis with cushions bolted onto their baggage racks for passengers. Except for the parish and several hotels, which had diesel-run generators that sometimes worked, the city was left in the dark after sunset. Kerosene lamps and candles flickered in bars at the roadside. The beer factory was one of the only businesses to stay open during the war, churning out a watered-down, overpriced product.

~:~

Kisangani became the graveyard of Rwandan and Ugandan reputations, where the two countries' lofty rhetoric gave way to another, more tawdry reality. Since the beginning of the first Congo war in 1996, the two countries had been able to maintain the pretense that they were involved in the Congo out of domestic security concerns. Even when this illusion became difficult to maintain—Why were their troops stationed three hundred miles from their borders? Why did they have to overthrow the government they themselves had put in place in Kinshasa to protect themselves?—they continued to benefit from staunch support from the international community, in particular the United States and the United Kingdom.

Then, in 1999 and 2000, the alliance between Rwanda and Uganda fell apart, as the two countries fought three battles in the streets of Kisangani. Thousands of Congolese died as the two countries sought to settle their differences on foreign soil. With this internecine violence, their pretext of self-defense crumbled.

But what was their real motive in fighting over the City on the River? To many, the battle in one of the region's main hubs of the diamond trade was the final proof that the two countries were really just seeking self-enrichment. The reality was, as always, more complex. Yes, access to resources was increasingly supplanting ideology and self-defense as a motive in the conflict, but the root of the fighting was just as tightly linked to personality and regional politics.

~:~

The root of discord between Rwanda and Uganda can be traced back to the anti-Tutsi pogroms in Rwanda around independence in 1962. Hundreds of thousands of Tutsi fled to Uganda around this time, where they grew up in refugee camps as second-class citizens, not allowed to work and discriminated against by the Ugandan government. Within the squalid confines of the camps, they looked backwards to a more glorious past and forward to their children's future, sending them to school on UN scholarships.

In the early 1980s, Ugandan youth gangs and paramilitary groups began harassing and abusing the Rwandan immigrants, accusing them of taking their land. Unwilling to return to Rwanda, where the Hutu-dominated government limited opportunities for Tutsi, and facing discrimination in Uganda, hundreds of these young Tutsi had joined Yoweri Museveni's rebellion in the late 1970s. "These Rwandans were better educated than many of us," a Ugandan army spokesman told me. "Many of them were put into military intelligence; that was where we could use them best."[3] Paul Kagame was one.

When Museveni came to power in 1986, Kagame became the head of military intelligence. Other Rwandans became defense minister, head of military medical services, and chief of military police. The relationships between Ugandans and Rwandans were deeply personal. The best man at Kagame's wedding would become the chief of staff of the Ugandan army. Later, when Kagame launched his own rebellion in Rwanda, he and his fighters would cross into Uganda and eat and sleep at the house of President Museveni's military advisor.[4] A senior Ugandan intelligence official told me, "they had uncles, cousins, and brothers-in-law in our army."[5]

The heavy Rwandan presence in the security services stirred resentment among Ugandans, and land conflicts involving the 200,000 Tutsi refugees living in southern Uganda were becoming a nuisance for President Museveni. Under pressure from his domestic constituencies, he was forced to backpedal on promises of resettlement and citizenship for these refugees, and many Rwandans in the army were demobilized. This rejection was tantamount to betrayal for Tutsi officers who had risked their lives liberating Uganda, only to be dismissed as foreigners. As one officer put it: "You stake your life and at the end of the day you recognize that no amount of contribution can make you what you are not. You can't buy it, not even with blood."[6]

The Rwandans were disappointed but were focused on other matters. Helping Museveni take power in Uganda had only been a stepping stone to overthrowing the government in Rwanda. Just one year after their victory in Kampala, the Rwandan Patriotic Front was formed. Museveni provided them with weapons, medicine, and a rear base from which to operate. For many Ugandans, their debt to their Rwandan allies had been repaid.

~:~

The Congo wars saw the Rwandans usurp the role of regional power from Uganda. From the beginning, they seemed eager to show their former mentors that they could do better.

The first, bloody shock came within several months of the initial invasion in 1996. Among the four Congolese leaders of the rebellion, the veteran rebel Kisase Ngandu was closest to Kampala. He had been supported by Museveni against Mobutu for years and slept, ate, and drank at a government safe house when he was in Kampala. Once in the Congo, however, Kisase had railed against "Tutsi colonialism" and had shown himself to be fiercely independent of Laurent Kabila, who as spokesperson was the leader of the group. In January 1997, Kisase Ngandu and his bodyguard were found dead by the road outside of Goma.

"The Rwandans killed Kisase. They didn't want any competition," a senior Museveni advisor told me.[7] The Ugandans considered pulling out, but they hesitated, knowing that if they did so all the work they had put into the rebellion would have gone to waste. So they gritted their teeth and soldiered on, providing artillery support and mechanized units that the Rwandans, largely still a guerrilla-style infantry army, didn't have. Nonetheless, the wars were led and executed mostly by Rwanda, which gave them a much stronger influence with the Congolese and gave Rwandan entrepreneurs preferential access to business deals.

The result of this complex history was a feeling of resentment from the Ugandans, who felt sidelined in Kinshasa when Laurent Kabila came to power. Above all, they accused Kigali of political immaturity in dealing with the Congolese rebellions. "I was worried about the direct involvement of the Rwandese troops in the combat role," Museveni reflected later. Museveni preferred to let the Congolese develop their own rebellion: "Let them understand why they are fighting."[8]

For the Rwandans, Museveni's attitude smacked of hypocrisy. After all, they had helped him come to power and as recompense were told to leave the country. They liked to invoke a Swahili saying: *Shukrani ya punda ni teke* (The gratitude of a donkey is a kick). Even in the Congo, the Rwandans felt like the Ugandans were overbearing and constantly trying to teach them how to go about their business. "It was jealousy," one of Kagame's advisors told me. "Museveni couldn't deal with the fact that we were now stronger and more successful than him. He forgot that we were no longer refugees in his country. He couldn't order us around!"[9]

～:～

Wamba dia Wamba arrived in Kisangani on a Ugandan C-130 cargo plane in May 1999. He had fled Goma with a Ugandan military escort after his RCD colleagues had threatened to kill him. He had then met with President Museveni, who apologized to him for his clash with the Rwandans: "Wamba, you will die because of my mistake. I never thought our Rwandan friends could become our enemies!"[10] Nonetheless, Wamba and Museveni decided he should return to Kisangani to try to launch a new rebellion, this time without meddlesome interference from Kigali. The elderly professor insisted on a slow, democratizing rebellion that would develop grassroots support and a firm ideological commitment. In the meantime, fighting should be kept to a minimum. "Unconditional negotiations with Kinshasa!" was Wamba's slogan.

When Wamba arrived in the city, he found it divided into a Rwandan and a Ugandan zone, each with Congolese rebel allies. The two opposing commanders were taunting each other. The city streets in the center of the town were almost deserted. Pickups with anti-aircraft guns and heavy machine guns mounted on the back patrolled the town. It was a game of chicken, with each side ratcheting up the pressure to see if the other would blink. Rwandan soldiers hauled a Congolese man out of a Ugandan pickup by force, claiming he had defected from the RCD. In retaliation, Ugandan soldiers kidnapped the bodyguard of a top RCD commander while he was being lathered up in a barber shop.

General James Kazini, the Ugandan commander, was holed up in a timber factory on the edge of town, where he would spend his afternoons drinking Ugandan gin, chain-smoking, and commanding his units over a walkie-talkie on a table in front of him. He was a colorful character with a pug nose and a reddish shine to his cheeks where skin-lightening cream had burned him. To Ugandan journalists who visited him he complained about his twenty-seven-year-old Rwandan counterpart, Colonel Patrick Nyavumba, based just a mile away, "Patrick? Patrick is just a boy. I am a brigadier. Who is he to discuss anything with me?" He told them the Rwandans were behaving like a colonial power in the Congo and pointed to Wamba's defection from the RCD as proof that Kigali was trying to manipulate its Congolese allies by remote control. When the journalists pressed him on why Uganda was there, he explained, "Uganda is here as a midwife to Congolese liberation. The Rwandans want to have the baby themselves!"[11]

Even though the two armed forces were supposed to maintain a joint command in the city, Kazini soon began to make decisions on his own. He arrested the pilots of Rwandan aircraft arriving in Kisangani with supplies, accusing them of not notifying him of their arrival. One night, he ordered Ugandan tanks to parade through the Rwandan part of town for three hours after midnight, thundering an artillery barrage into the surrounding forests, "Just to show them that they were a professional army with tanks and the Rwandans were a bunch of bush fighters," as one Ugandan journalist with him at the time put it.[12] The Rwandan commander retorted, telling the reporters who visited him, "[Kazini and I] went to the same university, but now he thinks because I live in *manyatta* [straw huts], I am no good! Tell him that he is an *afande* [respected commander] but that I don't respect his methods."[13]

Almost as an afterthought, the same journalists visited Wamba, who had become a minor player in the standoff. "The answer for the problems of the Congo does not lie with the military, but in the enlightenment of the people," he told them, sounding ever more like Candide.[14]

~:~

Then there were the diamonds. In dozens of riverbeds around Kisangani, locals pan for the gems, spending days knee-deep in water. As in much of central and western Africa, Lebanese traders had cornered the diamond trade, taking advantage of transnational family networks that reach from Africa to the Middle East and Belgium. While many other shops in Kisangani closed, the main streets were still lined with dozens of small diamond stores with huge, painted diamonds decorating their walls. Their names voiced the traders' eclectic backgrounds and dreams of a better future: Oasis, Top Correction, Force Tranquille, and Jihad.

Only traders with close connections to the military commanders felt safe enough to keep their safes flush with hundred dollar bills to buy the rough stones from diggers. Between 1997 and 1999, official Ugandan exports of diamonds grew tenfold, from $198,000 to $1.8 million. Rwanda's official exports leaped from $16,000 to $1.7 million between 1998 and 2000, even though neither country has diamonds of its own.[15] The real value of exports is likely to have been much higher, as the gems were easy to smuggle in pockets and suitcases. One of the thirty-four diamond shop owners in Kisangani reported that over six months in 1998 alone, he paid $124,000 to various Ugandan commanders, and industry insiders suggested that both countries together bought up to $20 million in uncut stones a month.[16]

The trade proved to be divisive, as each side brought in their own traders, lugging suitcases full of money counters, microscopes, satellite phones, and precision scales. For the Ugandans, it was the experienced Belgian trader Philippe Surowicke, who had spent years dealing diamonds with rebels in Angola.[17] The Rwandans flew in a bevy of Lebanese traders. Each were protected by a phalanx of Ugandan or Rwandan soldiers, respectively. Not surprisingly, a standoff developed.

~:~

Wamba's arrival put a match to this powder keg. Much to the chagrin of the Rwandans, who had just ousted him from the RCD leadership, he began holding rallies in downtown Kisangani to large crowds riveted by his demand for an immediate end to hostilities and talks with Kinshasa. He created a rebellion,

dubbed RCD–Movement of Liberation, which would be free of Rwanda's meddlesome interference. He was ferried around town in a Toyota 4x4 with tinted
windows, followed by a pickup bristling with Ugandan soldiers. Thousands of
people flocked to his rallies, and the *toleka* bicycle taxis accompanied him, ringing their bells, as he paraded through town. "He was a poor speaker," one Kisangani resident told me of Wamba. "He sounded like a university lecturer. But he
had denounced the Rwandans! For us, that was very brave."[18]

Both the original RCD and Wamba's new dissidents had set up radio stations that they used for trading insults and threatening each other. "Why do
the Rwandans want to colonize the Congo? The population doesn't want you—
recognize it!"[19] taunted Radio Liberté, Wamba's station. Its rival station responded by accusing the professor of recruiting ex-FAR *génocidaires* into his
army, the ultimate insult for the Rwandans. "The Ugandans can't even deal with
a bunch of rebels in Uganda. How are you going to deal with the Rwandan
army?"[20] Day and night the population of Kisangani had to endure these insults
being flung back and forth over the airwaves, raising tensions to a fever pitch.[21]

The fighting broke out following Wamba's return from a two-week stay in
Uganda on August 7, 1999. His radio announced a rally in front of his hotel,
while the rival station warned people to stay off the streets. Ugandan and Rwandan troops deployed in force to the city center and soon heavy machine gun and
mortar fire broke out as both sides fought from house to house in an effort to
seize key strategic locations: the Central Bank, Wamba's hotel, the two airports,
and the Ugandan and Rwandan headquarters. The two sides traded insults over
a shared walkie-talkie frequency. General Kazini taunted his Rwandan counterpart: "Just wait. I'll send just one company of men for you—they will bring
me back your balls on a plate."[22]

The fighting began in seriousness on Sunday afternoon around 2:30. Thousands of soldiers filled the broad avenues, taking cover in people's living rooms,
in sewage ditches, and in schools. Over six hundred people, mostly women and
children, were stuck in the International Community of Women Apostles of
God evangelical church for three days without food or water. A soccer team,
dressed in cleats and jerseys and on its way to play its rivals across town, was
forced to seek refuge in sewage ditches as bullets whistled overhead. Seven bar-
bers and their clients were stuck in the Salon Maitre Celestin barbershop next
to Hotel Wagenia in a room just twelve feet by twelve large. They spent three
days without eating or drinking, forced to use a corner of the room as a toilet.

~:~

Pastor Philippe is a minister in a local Kisangani church and a carpenter. He is a small man with large, rough hands, a wispy grey beard, and a wooden crucifix around his neck. I visited him in his workshop, not far from the river, surrounded by hardwood shavings that gave off a rich aroma. He peered at me through huge, horn-rimmed glasses. He lost three children in the fighting, he told me, his voice barely changing in tone, his fingers interlocked.

When the war started, he had been at home, having just come back from church. He was listening to some church tapes on his stereo when he heard the first mortar hit the ground; the cups on the coffee table shook, and a picture of his wife on the wall fell down and shattered. Immediately the rat-a-tat cracks of the AK-47s started, whistling through the leaves of the mango trees outside. He and his nine children raced to lie face down on the floor of the corridor. They had experience in war, like many Congolese. They knew that AK-47s had enough power to go through a brick wall and still kill: "You really need two brick walls to protect yourself."[23]

They lay in the corridor for the rest of the day, listening to the church tape wind down the batteries as the mortars fell around them. Their Tshopo commune was one of the worst hit: It was on the front lines between the two forces. Through the windows they saw soldiers moving house to house, crouching behind trees and in doorways for cover. They were in a Rwandan-occupied area, and the Tutsi officers frightened them. In 1997, the minister had worked in a small village south of Kisangani when the Rwandan army had passed through, chasing the fleeing Hutu refugees and militias. He saw them slit the throats of four Hutu soldiers and throw them into the river. "You have to understand, the Tutsi are like a wounded leopard; it's like they're brain-damaged after what happened to them," he said. "They lash out at anything."

Finally, after a full day of lying on the floor in the heat, the fighting stopped for several minutes. The only sound was of babies crying in a neighbor's house. Through the window, they could see the bodies of several soldiers sprawled in the dust; blast craters had changed the look of their street and sprayed dirt onto the surrounding houses.

Two of his children—Sophie, sixteen, and Claude, twenty-two—decided to see if they could go out and try to find some water; the tap in their house was running dry, and they were all feeling faint for lack of water. There was a communal tap across the street, and they could see a woman filling a plastic jerry can. The minister watched his two children step out of the house just as a mortar hit the street in front of them. When Philippe picked himself up off the floor, he found Sophie's body twisted in front of his house, her face a bloody pulp and her neck almost severed. Claude was moaning and grabbing his leg, which had been hit by shrapnel. Blood had completely soaked his pants and was oozing onto the street. The minister tied a tourniquet around his thigh, grabbed a wheelbarrow from the backyard, put him in it, and raced down the street to the health center run by the Red Cross. The fighting had started up again, and bullets were whizzing through the air, but he knew that Claude would die if he didn't get him help.

At the health center, the nurses were lying on the cement floor, surrounded by patients with bandages soaked in Mercurochrome and blood, also lying on the floor. They helped Claude onto the ground and worked on stemming the blood loss from his ruptured artery. But they didn't have surgical equipment or blood to help him; all they had left was some Novocain a dentist had brought. The hospital was a mile away.

The minister unclasped his hands and looked at me. "I saw him bleed to death in front of me. I buried him in my compound, right next to Sophie." He paused for a long time, but his voice was steady. "There was no time for a proper funeral. Actually, you can find hundreds of bodies buried in people's gardens around the city for the same reason. We are living on top of our dead."

~:~

Wamba himself was pinned down on the floor of Hotel Wagenia for three days. The Rwandan troops were more experienced in guerrilla tactics. Bolstered by the arrival of hundreds of additional troops in the early days of the fighting, they eventually gained the upper hand by cutting the Ugandan troops in town off from their headquarters outside of town. In a panic, the Ugandan officers stationed with Wamba evacuated him, carrying him piggy-back into an armored vehicle that, surrounded by special forces firing continuously in all directions, broke through Rwandan lines and reached the embankments of the Congo River. Wamba, hugging his leather briefcase with his documents and books in it, was rushed into a dugout canoe and paddled across the river to a textile factory, where the Ugandan army had dug in.

The scene at the factory complex was one of terror. The Indian-born director was holed up in his office, where he hid under his desk, while women and children lay on the floor in the bathrooms. Several mortar shells hit the building, blowing holes in the corrugated roofing and sending shrapnel flying. The Ugandans barricaded Wamba into a room lined with sandbags and told him to stay down; he almost collapsed from stress and dehydration.

Hrvoje Hranjski, a Croatian reporter for the Associated Press in Kigali, was embedded with the Rwandan army during the battle. He flew in on one of their flights and stayed in a small house behind their commander's residence. He was friends with some of the Rwandan officers and spent the evenings drinking *waragi* gin, smoking, and talking with them. Most were well-educated and curious about international affairs; they discussed the similarities and differences between wars in the Balkans and those in Central Africa.

It was clear to Hrvoje that the Rwandans were better organized than their enemies. "They were motivated and followed orders. The Ugandans didn't seem to know why they were fighting." The Rwandans were cut off from their base at the airport but quickly organized an air bridge with helicopters and infiltrated their soldiers through the jungle. The Rwandans, used to years of guerrilla warfare, fought their way from house to house with their AK-47s, dodging bullets. After battles, the Rwandans would always make sure to gather their dead and bury them, whereas the Ugandans often left their soldiers on the streets, leaving the impression that hundreds of Ugandans had died and almost no Rwandans. The Ugandans, for the most part, stayed in their trenches and in their armored personnel carriers. "The Rwandans won the battle with guts," Hrvoje said.

Hrvoje had good reason to admire them. Early on in the battle, he was hit by a Ugandan sniper while coming out of the Rwandan commander's house. The bullet pierced his shoulder, went through his lung, and lodged next to his spinal cord. As the Rwandans did not have medics, they staunched the bleeding and waited until the fighting had died down before rushing him to a plane for Kigali. "They saved my life, those guys."

The siege lasted three days, after which the Rwandans controlled much of the city, although they had not been able to get to Wamba or conquer the textile factory. By the time the fighting was over, the air in the city had begun to fill with the stench of rotting flesh in the tropical heat.

Kisangani, round one, went to the Rwandans. Red Cross volunteers patrolled the town in their white uniforms, daubing the corpses with lime until they could get a truck to pick them up. They shook their heads: On the bodies of mostly young Ugandans, some had pictures of their mothers, others of their young wives.

~:~

Other than finger-wagging by diplomats, there were few consequences for the occupying forces. A joint investigation by the Rwandan and Ugandan army commanders arrived in town and agreed on taking steps to prevent further fighting, but little was done. The Ugandans moved their positions to the north of town but continued to beef up their arsenals. The RCD and Rwandans could not refrain from gloating, showing the bodies of Ugandans on Congolese television and warning spectators that this was the consequence of challenging them. They banned *toleka* riders—around 2,000 in the whole town—from working, accusing them of complicity with Wamba and the Ugandans. They even dismantled the famous scaffolding set up by the Wagenia fishermen in the Congo River; they said the fishermen had helped guide the Ugandans to safety during the fighting. The scaffolding, imposing thirty-foot-tall pieces of timber lashed together and anchored in the rapids, had been a tourist attraction in Kisangani since the first Belgian colonial postcards were made. The Rwandans certainly did not know how to make themselves loved.

The feuding had all the characteristics of typical sibling rivalry; camaraderie was never far from one-upmanship. At night, in the Gentry Dancing Club—a dingy, dark bar decorated with Christmas lights and cigarette advertisements—Ugandans and Rwandans mingled, sometimes even dancing together and paying for each others' drinks. The bar was a study in stereotypes: the Rwandans were dressed in spotless camouflage fatigues and were reserved, clustering in small groups. The Ugandans were boisterous in their plain green uniforms and Wellington boots, mingling with the sex workers and singing along with the music. Their respective Congolese rebel allies were on the high end of the frivolity scale, sometimes even wearing makeup and nail polish.

The festivities could quickly turn sour, however. An altercation over a woman led to recriminations over who had won the last round of fighting. "We can't figure whether you Ugandans are real soldiers or just Boy Scouts," one Rwandan teased. "Have you seen our T-55s?" the Ugandans retorted, referring to their

Soviet tanks. "Maybe we should show you." To make matters worse, the Rwandans sometimes paraded about town in captured Ugandan uniforms, boasting about the vehicles they had captured during the fighting.

Other factors added to the tension. After five years in power, the RPF's authoritarianism was beginning to grate, resulting in high-level defections from the Rwandan government. Of course, given their historical ties to Uganda and the current frosty relations, it was only natural for these defectors to flee to Kampala. The speaker of Rwanda's parliament and the former prime minister both fled across the border toward the north. A group of Tutsi university students followed after they were harassed by security officials.[24] They were all welcomed with open arms in Kampala. Irked, General Paul Kagame accused his Ugandan counterpart of arming ex-FAR and Interahamwe to fight against him.

The accusations made little military sense. At the same time as their feuding in Kisangani was tying down thousands of troops, both countries were engaged in a push on Kinshasa through Equateur and Katanga, respectively, yet the vitriol reached a level never expressed toward Kabila. The strong friendship between Rwanda and Uganda had soured into a toxic brew. Museveni belittled his former allies as "those boys," while Rwanda's government spokesman fired back: "For a man surrounded by marijuana addicts and drunkards, Museveni has chosen the wrong analogy."[25]

Finally, on June 5, 2000, the inevitable happened. Ugandan General James Kazini, who had been itching for months to get back at the Rwandans, launched a new offensive. This time, the Ugandans unleashed a far heavier artillery barrage on Kisangani, in complete disregard for the hundreds of thousands of civilians cowering in their homes. UN observers estimated that 6,000 artillery shells fell on the city over the following six days, accompanied by heavy machine gun fire and rocket-propelled grenades. At the same time, residents in the Tshopo neighborhood, located along the river on the front line of the conflict, saw Ugandans and Rwandans storming their streets, digging trenches in their gardens, and breaking into their houses to fire through the windows. As the fighting began during the morning, thousands of schoolchildren were once again pinned down by the fighting, sometimes between the feet of soldiers, whose spent cartridges rained down on their heads.

The result was devastating. At least 760 civilians were killed during the six days of fighting, and 1,700 were wounded. According to UN investigators, 4,083 houses were damaged, of which 418 were completely destroyed, and forty-nine schools were badly damaged or destroyed. Water and electricity were cut off in the whole town, and doctors at the main hospital had to operate with flimsy flashlights in the dark, using muddy river water to wash their hands.

Pastor Philippe was not spared by the second round of violent exchange, which once again engulfed his Tshopo neighborhood. After losing two children the previous year, he had tried to school his children in how to act if the war broke out, but there was only so much he could do. People had to go on working, studying, and playing.

The fighting found him at home with most of his family. However, his son Jean-Marie had gone out to the market to buy rice and vegetables; for two days, they didn't know where he was. Finally, a neighbor came to tell the minister that he had seen his son on Seventeenth Avenue and that he thought the youth had made it to the forest, where many had fled.

When the conflict finally ended, however, there was no sign of Jean-Marie. The minister went to Seventeenth Avenue to ask around for him. Finally, a Red Cross worker showed him a bunch of clothes and bags they had found alongside some bodies in a house. His son's school satchel, caked in blood, was there. According to the Red Cross worker, the residents of the house where the bag had been found had gotten into an argument with a Rwandan soldier outside. What it had been about was anyone's guess. The soldier had leaned into the house and sprayed the room with bullets. By the time the fighting had stopped, the bodies had decomposed so much that the Red Cross had to bury them immediately.

"I was sad I couldn't bury my son next to his siblings," Philippe said in a calm voice. "But we still remember his birthday every year. We eat fried catfish, his favorite." He paused again for a long time. "I was also angered by the arrogance of these two countries. Coming to settle their differences 300 miles from home, killing innocent civilians. What did we ever do to them?"

I asked him whom he blamed for their deaths. He shrugged. "There are too many people to blame. Mobutu for ruining our country. Rwanda and Uganda for invading it. Ourselves for letting them do so. None of that will help bring my children back."

✦ 17 ✦

SORCERERS' APPRENTICES

Death does not sound a trumpet.
—CONGOLESE SAYING

EASTERN CONGO, JUNE 2000

In June 2000, a nonprofit charity published a mortality study that estimated that 1.7 million people had died as a result of the conflict between August 1998 and May 2000. This study, conducted by the epidemiologist Les Roberts for the International Rescue Committee, shocked the world. Further studies, published in respected medical journals and confirmed by other epidemiologists, were conducted in subsequent years; in 2004, the charity estimated that 3.8 million had died because of the war since 1998.[1]

Roberts was rigorous in his methods: He sent out teams to six separate sites throughout the eastern Congo where, using a random GPS selection of households within a grid on a map, the researchers approached huts and asked whether anyone had died during the past year. After interviewing 2,000 people, the researchers obtained an average mortality rate for the area. They subtracted from this rate of deaths from before the war and obtained an "excess death rate"—in other words how many more people died than was normal.[2]

The number of deaths is so immense that it becomes incomprehensible and anonymous, and yet the dying was not spectacular. Violence only directly caused

2 percent of the reported deaths. Most often, it was easily treatable diseases, such as malaria, typhoid fever, and diarrhea, that killed. There was, however, a strong correlation between conflict areas and high mortality rates. As fighting broke out, people were displaced to areas where they had no shelter, clean water, or access to health care and succumbed easily to disease. Health staff shuttered up their hospitals and clinics to flee the violence, leaving the sick to fend for themselves.

Almost half of the victims were children—the most vulnerable to disease and malnutrition. A full 60 percent of all children died before their fifth birthday. Step out of a car in many areas of the eastern Congo during the war, and you were often confronted with children suffering from *kwashikor*, or clinical malnutrition. It was a bizarre sight to see such listless children surrounded by lush hills. Congo is not Niger or Somalia, where famine and malnutrition are closely linked to drought. Here, the rainy season lasts nine months a year in most parts, and the soil is fertile. But the harvests were often stolen by hungry militias, and farmers were unable to access their fields because of the violence.

⁓

So how did Congolese experience the violence? Many Congolese never did; they only heard about it and suffered the economic and political consequences. But for millions of people in the east of the country, an area roughly the size of Texas, daily life was punctuated by confrontations with armed men.

By 2001, fighting along the front line in the middle of the country had come to a standstill as a result of several peace deals. The east of the country, however, had seen an escalation of violence, as local Mai-Mai militias formed in protest of Rwandan occupation. This insurgency was fueled by rampant social grievances and by Laurent Kabila, who supported them with weapons and money. The Mai-Mai were too weak to threaten Rwanda's control of main towns and roads, but they were able to prompt a violent counterinsurgency campaign that cost Rwanda whatever remaining legitimacy it once had.

It was this proxy war fought between Kigali and Kinshasa's allies that caused the most suffering for civilians. Without providing any training, Kinshasa dropped tons of weapons and ammunition at various airports in the jungles of the eastern Congo for the Hutu militia as well as for Mai-Mai groups. The countryside became militarized, as discontented and unemployed youth joined militias and set up roadblocks to "tax" the local population. Family and land disputes, which had previously been settled in traditional courts, were now sometimes solved through violence, and communal feuds between rival clans or tribes resulted in skirmishes and targeted killings.

The RCD rebels, Rwanda's main allies in the east, responded in kind. In both South Kivu and North Kivu, governors created local militias, so-called Local Defense Forces, to impose rebel control at the local level. By 2000, at least half a dozen such forces had been created by various RCD leaders. But instead of improving security, these ramshackle, untrained local militias for the most part just exacerbated the suffering by taxing, abusing, and raping the local population. Local traditional chiefs, who were the de facto administrators in much of the hinterlands, either were forced to collaborate or had to flee. In South Kivu, half of the dozen most important customary chiefs were killed or fled. In some areas, new customary chiefs were created or named by the RCD, usurping positions that had been held for centuries by other families.

The Rwandan, Ugandan, and Congolese proxies eventually ran amok, wreaking havoc. These fractious movements had not been formed organically, did not have to answer to a popular base—after all, they had been given their weapons by an outside power—and often had little interest other than surviving and accumulating resources. The dynamic bore a resemblance to Goethe's sorcerer's apprentice: As with the young magician's broom, the rebel groups split into ever more factions as rebel leaders broke off and created their own fiefdoms, always seeking allegiances with regional powers to undergird their authority. According to one count, by the time belligerents came together to form a transitional government in 2002, Rwanda, Uganda, and the Congo had over a dozen rebel proxies or allies battling each other.[3]

~:~

The massacre in Kasika, a small jungle village a hundred miles west of the Rwandan border, was a prime example of these tactics.[4] Kasika has attained mythical status in the Congo. Politicians have invoked its name in countless speeches when they want to drum up populist support against Rwanda. Children in Kinshasa, who had never been close to the province of South Kivu, are taught about Kasika in classes intended to instill patriotism; Kabila's government cited it prominently in a case it brought against Rwanda in the International Court of

Justice. It was here that the RCD took its first plunge into mass violence just days after its creation in August 1998, massacring over a thousand villagers in reprisal for an attack by a local militia.

Kasika is nothing more than clusters of mud huts built around a Catholic parish on a hill overlooking a valley. It was the headquarters of the customary chief of the Nyindu ethnic community, whose house and office sat on a hill opposite the parish, a series of large, red-brick structures with cracked ceramic shingles as roofing, laced with vines.

When I visited, the only place to spend the night was at the parish guesthouse, which the church had recently equipped with several beds so that visiting priests could spend the night before saying Mass. Just above the house, on a small hill, was the church itself, a larger structure covered with green corrugated iron roofing and with rows of small holes in its sides for ventilation. The hall inside echoed when we opened the wide doors; it was bare except for some rickety wooden benches, and a large cross hung above a dais.

"This is where it all happened," explained the groundskeeper, who was showing me around.

"They were killed in here?"

He nodded. "Twenty-three. Including three nuns, the priest, and a catechist."

The hall didn't show any sign of violence. "Where are they buried?" I asked.

"You just walked over their graves," he said, smiling.

Outside, in front of the church was the tomb of an Italian missionary, Father Mario Ricca, set neatly in cement and slate with the date "23.6.1973" chiseled into a stone plaque. He had founded the parish many decades ago and had stayed there until his death. Next to his tomb, overgrown with grass, were five other, barely visible graves. My guide pointed to what looked like a vegetable garden next to the tomb, where several wooden crosses had been stuck amid squash vines and weeds.

"We never had the time to give them a proper burial," he said regretfully. "We have nothing to remember them by. It is a shame."

It was a disturbing image for a culture that reveres its ancestors. I later walked through town with my guide to visit other graves. He pointed vaguely at piles of dirt, long overgrown with shrubs and vines, by the side of the road. He had no idea who was buried where. "There are hundreds buried like this," he said. There were no crosses, and no one had taken the time to rebury the bodies in a cemetery or even just weed the mounds they were currently buried under. Nowhere in town was there a monument to the dead. It was as if the town was still in a daze from the massacre and, a full decade later, hadn't had the time to collect its wits enough to commemorate its victims.

~:~

The massacre followed what would become the standard mold for RCD abuses. Days after the rebellion began, a battalion of RCD and Rwandan soldiers marched through Kasika. The road was strategic, as it led to several lucrative gold mines. They had been sent to join up with rebel troops that had been stuck in Kindu, a major trade town on the Congo River two hundred miles to the west. Those marooned troops were led by Commander Moise, a legendary fighter and the second-highest ranking Munyamulenge commander among the rebels.

When the RCD rebels passed through Kasika on their way to Kindu, they stopped to meet with the traditional chief, François Naluindi, a young thirty-five-year-old who was extremely popular among his Nyindu tribe. He had launched several local farming cooperatives, through which he was trying to develop and educate the largely peasant community. He had recently married, and his wife was seven months pregnant.

Naluindi met with the Rwandan officers and slaughtered several goats for them to eat. The atmosphere was cordial, but the chief was nervous. In the backlands of his territory, a young upstart chief called Nyakiliba had been causing trouble. He had begun arming some youths with spears and old machine guns, saying that he would defend his country against the Tutsi aggressors. Like many other local militias, he called his group Mai-Mai ("water-water"), claiming that he had magic that would turn his enemy's bullets into water. Nyakiliba's real goal, Naluindi was told by his advisors, was much more mundane: He wanted to claim rights to a traditional territory much larger than his own and was trying to inflate his importance. He was a small-time thug but could stir up trouble nonetheless.

Just before the Rwandans arrived, Naluindi had held an emergency security meeting with Nyakiliba, warning him not to do anything brash. "You think you will be a hero, but you will have me and the population killed," a village elder who attended the meeting remembered him saying. "I hear you have seven guns. They have hundreds. How will you win?"[5]

Before the RCD rebels pulled out of town on the way to Kindu, their commander asked Chief Naluindi how the security situation was. Damned if I tell him, damned if I don't, he thought, and he reassured the officer that everything was peaceful. The Mai-Mai, however, hadn't listened to the chief, and a few miles outside of town they took a couple of potshots at the troops before running into the bush. The village held its breath, but there were no casualties, and the rebels continued on their way.

The troops picked up Commander Moise, exhausted from his week-long trek through the jungle, and made their way back toward the Rwandan border. On the morning of Sunday, August 23, 1998, a column of several hundred RCD soldiers passed back through Kasika. The population recalled their typical appearance: wearing gum boots and carrying their belongings and ammunition boxes on their head. A truck full of soldiers brought up the rear of the column, along with a white pickup carrying the officers.

It was the dry season, so the road was in decent condition, but the pickup had some mechanical problems and was lagging behind. As it came around a bend close to Chief Naluindi's house, the Mai-Mai launched another attack on the RCD convoy, opening fire from a hut overlooking the road and riddling the pickup with bullets. Commander Moise died on the spot, along with two other officers. The remaining RCD soldiers fired back, but by then Nyakiliba and his boys had already fled into the bushes.

The commotion prevented the villagers from going to church. They watched in dismay through their windows as Rwandan troops came back to the site of the killing, bundled the bodies up, and transported them back to Bukavu. Troops milled about Kasika that day, searching for Mai-Mai, but the situation was otherwise calm. Nyakiliba and his Mai-Mai had fled to his home village in the mountains, thirty miles away. In the evening, an RCD officer visited the parish and asked to use the high-frequency radio there to contact their headquarters in Bukavu. According to the catechists who overheard his conversation over the crackly radio, the officer received instructions, but they couldn't make out exactly what was said.

~:~

It was not difficult for me to find a witness to the massacre. The groundskeeper at the church showed me to a small mud hut built on the slope beneath the road.

This was where Patrice,[6] a local handyman and a catechist at the church, lived. It was a typical hut for the region: a low structure built on a frame of bamboo sticks, with mud packed onto the sides to keep out the cold at night. Patrice, a deferential man wearing an untucked, stained shirt, told me to sit on a bench in the corner. The shack was barely big enough for both of us, but people attracted by the presence of a foreigner quickly gathered by the window to listen to our conversation. On the wall there was a faded picture of Jesus in a wooden frame with a saying in Swahili: "A drunken wife arouses anger. Her shame cannot be hidden." Arranged on a crossbeam overhead were Patrice's few belongings: a machete, a row of Chinese-made AA batteries held together by a rubber band that served as a power source for his transistor radio, and a broken storm lantern.

"There was a thick mist in town that morning," he began. "There had not been a Mass on Sunday due to the commotion, so the priest rang the bell to call the village to Mass that Monday morning. It must have been around 6:30. We saw some soldiers on the way to Mass, but didn't think anything of it."[7]

I had been awakened just that morning by a similar Mass. A catechist had struck the old rim of a car tire before slow choral singing in Swahili began to the beating of drums. When I peered through the air ducts in the side of the church, I had seen several rows of women and men swaying gently and clapping their hands. It was the same air ducts, according to Patrice, through which they saw the Rwandan soldiers gathering outside. They had machine guns and small hatchets slung across their shoulders.

"The priest had just begun blessing the host," Patrice remembered, "when they entered the church. The priest was alarmed, but didn't interrupt the consecration, motioning discreetly with one hand to the sacristy behind him, at the back of the church. I was sitting at the front of the church and made a run for it with six others. We hid in the thick bushes by the back door before the soldiers blocked off the exit."

At this point, the crowd outside Patrice's window began groaning and sucking their teeth. They knew what came next.

Patrice spoke calmly, making sure he didn't forget any details. "The Tutsi tied up the people in the church, hands behind their backs, and then took the priest and the three nuns outside. I could hear the nuns screaming, screaming: 'Don't kill our father—please don't kill him. Take us instead!' Father Stanislas, the priest, told them to calm down, that the Lord would provide. The soldiers separated them, taking the nuns to the convent next door and the priest to the parish, where they forced him to give them money and his radio. My friend the plumber was hiding in the ceiling and heard all of this. Then they told the priest to kneel down and pray. And shot him in the back of his head."

The crowd outside the hut where we were sitting erupted into lamentations: "They killed them all!" "They killed our Father!" "He was such a good man!" "His poor father went crazy afterwards—he was all he had!" "Animals!" Patrice looked down at his hands and shook his head. The name of the priest, he told me, was Stanislas Wabulakombe. In their language, it meant "What God wants, he does."

~:~

The gunshots at the parish house triggered the massacre in the church. The soldiers began by using their hatchets to bludgeon the worshippers to death—so as not to alert the village, some of the villagers I interviewed said. Others said it was to save bullets. When Patrice emerged from the bushes the next day, he found most of the victims with crushed skulls. The three nuns were lying in the convent with their underwear around their ankles; he suspected they had been raped. One of them was still breathing when he found her, but she died before they could get her to the local health center. In the parish, he found the priest dead, face down on the floor in his white robes. As he walked around, he heard the voice of the plumber from his hiding place in the ceiling: "I'm up here! They shot me in my buttocks, but I'm still alive!"

Another group of soldiers had gone to the chief's residence. They were furious, the villagers said, that he had lied to them about the security situation and that they had been ambushed twice. They also thought that the Mai-Mai, who recruited along ethnic lines, were inherently linked to the customary chief. Chief Naluindi's whole extended family had sought refuge in his house, thinking that they would be safe there. "In our tradition, the *mwami* [chief] is sacred," the chorus outside Patrice's house lamented. "You don't kill the *mwami* during the war. Killing him is like killing all of us."

At least fourteen people were in the chief's house when the soldiers arrived. The rebels killed all of them. Villagers who had run into the bushes came back the next morning and found the chief's pregnant wife eviscerated, her dead fetus on the ground next to her. The infants of the chief's younger brother had been beaten to death against the brick walls of the house.

The way the victims were killed said as much as the number of dead; they displayed a macabre fascination with human anatomy. The survivors said the chief's heart had been cut out and his wife's genitals were gone. The soldiers had taken them. It wasn't enough to kill their victims; they disfigured and played with the bodies. They disemboweled one woman by cutting her open between her anus and vagina, then propped up the dead body on all fours and left her with her buttocks facing upwards. Another corpse was given two slits on either side of his belly, where his hands were inserted. "*Anavaa koti*—they made him look like he was wearing a suit," the villagers told me. Another man had his mouth slit open to his ears, was put in a chair and had a cigarette dangling from his lips when he was found. The killers wanted to show the villagers that this would be the consequence of any resistance. There were no limits to their revenge—they would kill the priests, rape the nuns, rip babies from their mothers' wombs, and twist the corpses into origami figures.

"We had seen people killed before," Patrice told me. "But this was worse than killing. It was like they killed them, and then killed them again. And again."

~:~

Around twenty miles further north on the road to Bukavu lay the town of Kilungutwe. It was situated on the banks of one of the many tributaries that flow into the Congo River far to the west and was known as the gateway to the jungle from the highlands to the northeast. On the day of Nyakiliba's ambush in Kasika, several dozen traders from Bukavu arrived at Kilungutwe for the large market that was held there every Monday. Michel,[8] a thirty-nine-year-old trader from Bukavu, was on a truck that had dropped them off a few miles before the market. There had been an accident, he was told by the Congolese soldiers there. No trucks were allowed down the road. Anxious to get to the market to sell the salt, sugar, soap, and clothes he had brought, Michel took off on foot down the road, along with around sixty other traders.

When they arrived in Kilungutwe, they noticed something strange. The streets were almost deserted, and a large number of Rwandan soldiers were milling about. A bunch of Congolese soldiers passing in a truck waved at them furtively to go back in the direction they had come from, but they didn't understand. "We thought it had just been an accident," Michel remembered.[9] As they passed over a large bridge made out of tree trunks, a group of four Tutsi soldiers hissed at them.

"Hey! You! Put down those bags!" The soldiers were tall and lanky and had long knives in their belts. They separated the locals from the Bukavu traders. To the group of around ten locals they said, "Ah! So it is your children who have been killing us!" The locals protested that they didn't know what they were talking about, but the soldiers began beating them anyway.

It was only later that Michel found out that the rebels who had been ambushed in Kasika had radioed ahead and told their advance party to stop wherever they were and to "clean up." The soldiers herded the traders and the locals into a small house below the road, a sturdy cement structure about twenty feet by forty feet, with blue wooden doors and windows and a corrugated iron roof. The sixty people stood packed like sardines in the small house. The sun went down, leaving the room in darkness except for some cracks in the window, through which they could see a fire that the soldiers had lit outside. It was hot and humid, and the air was filled with the sound of muttering and breathing. Several people prayed out loud. A baby's cry turned into a persistent wail, until finally her mother began sobbing and said that her baby was about to suffocate.

"We called the soldiers outside and asked them to have pity on the newborn," Michel told me.

Without asking any questions and as if on cue, the soldiers let the woman out. Suddenly, the prisoners heard screams coming from outside, first from both mother and child, then just from the child, then silence. Michel was not near a window, but someone who was whispered, his voice wavering. "Knives. They are using knives," he said. "They grabbed her hands and feet and slit her throat," another said. All of a sudden, the room was full of people crying and praying to God in French, Swahili, and whatever other language came to their lips.

Michel was in the back of the room, where he was crushed against a wall as the others tried to get as far as possible from the door, through which the soldiers came and grabbed people one by one. "This is for our brothers that you killed," they heard the soldiers tell their victims outside. The screams were silenced as the throats were slit and the next person was dragged out of the house. It took what seemed to Michel to be an eternity to empty the room. As the people thinned out, he was able to get a better look at his surroundings in the half-light. He saw that one of the thin ceiling boards was loose. He hastily climbed up and bumped into several other people lying in the small space between the ceiling and the roof. It was even hotter and danker here, and he could feel the bodies of his neighbors trembling with fear. He was close to fainting and felt like vomiting.

After a while, the screams faded below them and they could hear soldiers shuffling around and the sound of bodies being moved outside. Someone was counting, then a voice in Kinyarwanda said:

"How many did we put in the house? Did you count?"

"Yes, there were at least sixty."

"Are you sure? Where did the rest of them go?"

"I'll check again."

Feet began to scrape the floor below them and then someone poked the ceiling boards.

"*We!* You up there! How many are there?" Michel's neighbors' trembling increased until he was afraid they would begin to rattle the ceiling boards. "I can hear you up there! How many are you?"

After poking for a while, the soldier went outside. They hear the men muttering with each other, and then several came back into the room. Suddenly, an iron spear tip burst through a ceiling board not far from where Michel was lying. The boards were made out of flimsy plywood and the spear pierced it easily. The next jab hit Michel's neighbor in the leg, who cried out.

"Come down now, or we will get our guns! Just tell us how many you are, and then come down!"

Several more spear jabs came through the roof. Three of Michel's fellow prisoners climbed down from the hideout. Michel turned to a woman who was lying next to him.

"We must pray now," he told her. "We are going to die." She started crying.

∾∶∽

I met Michel many years later in Bukavu through a minister in his church. Michel—he wanted me to use a fake name to protect his identity—fidgeted while he sat in my living room in Bukavu and spoke in bursts. When I asked him how he had survived, he said I would not believe him and was then silent for several minutes, twisting his boney hands and looking at the ceiling.

"When I looked to my side, I saw a woman in white lying next to me," he finally said. "I hadn't seen her before, and I thought it was strange that she was wearing all white. I turned to the woman lying on my other side, who was sobbing, and asked her, 'Do you see her? The woman in white?' It was very strange to see a woman dressed all in white. It was very dusty then; it was the dry season. White clothes were maybe things you wear to church or to a baptism. And she seemed—she seemed to be *glowing*. My neighbor shook her head and continued sobbing. Then the woman in white said—her voice didn't seem to be coming from her mouth, but from inside my head—she said, 'Stand up! Stand up now!' And I gathered my strength and just stood up. The roof was very low—you couldn't even kneel there—but as I stood up, a sheet of roofing came undone from its bolts, and I could see the night sky. There was no moon that night, I remember. I stood up and slid down the roof. 'Someone's getting away!' one of the soldiers cried out, and they opened fire. I could hear the bullets whistling by me and going into the ceiling where I had been lying with the others. But I wasn't hurt. I jumped down from the roof and began running into the bush that surrounded the house. My legs were moving on their own." Michel looked at me. "That angel saved me. God saved me."

He told me that he ran through the palm trees and the cassava fields that surrounded the village as shots rang out behind him. He kept on running until he found the hut of a relative of his on a hill several miles away. Together, they watched the village burn in the valley below them.

The next morning, they watched the columns of soldiers departing toward Bukavu. When they were gone, Michel and his relatives went down into town, where ashes and smoke still filled the air. They found a mound of bodies smoldering next to the house where he had been held prisoner. The corpses had been doused in gasoline and set on fire. They had been reduced to a tarry mess of charred skin, bones, glasses, and belt buckles. They found dozens of other bodies strewn across town, in houses, on the street, and in ditches beside the road. In some cases, the corpses had been stuffed down pit latrines. They found the charred remains of one body in an oil drum used to brew palm oil.

Over the next several days, the survivors buried hundreds of bodies. The better known among them—the chief, the priest, the nuns, an evangelical minister, a local administrator—were given their own grave. Others were dumped in anonymous mass graves by the roadside, where the soil was soft and deep. Still others were left to decompose in the latrines, water tanks, and septic pits where their killers had thrown them. Neighbors buried their neighbors, mothers and fathers buried their children, and ministers buried their church members. They were in a rush; they didn't know when the rebels would be back through town. They had to bury their dead and then leave. People I spoke with said they had counted 704 people they had buried themselves; a United Nations investigation conducted years later concluded that there had been over 1,000 victims.[10]

~:~

Mass violence does not just affect the families of the dead. It tears at the fabric of society and lodges in the minds of the witnesses and perpetrators alike. A decade after the violence, it seemed that the villagers were still living in its aftershocks. They had all fled after the massacre; no one wanted to stay in town. They fled deep into the jungles, where they crossed the strong currents of the Luindi River. It was only on the other side that they felt safe. They lived in clearings, where they built grass huts. There was no place to start farming, and no one had the energy to cut down the brush and trees to start planting cassava and beans, so they ate what they could find: wild yams, caterpillars, forest mushrooms, and even monkeys when they could catch them. Exposed to the cold at night and deprived of adequate nutrition, many newborns and old people died. A scabies infestation ravaged their makeshift camps, and they couldn't even find the most rudimentary medicine for their various afflictions. They would sometimes visit their homes along the main road, but they would do so like burglars, at night and quickly, for fear of detection.

Some of them had radios, and they gave the nickname "Kosovo" to their hometown of Kasika after they heard of the war and massacres in the Balkans. The main difference, of course, was that the press was giving the small Balkan region, barely a sixth the size of South Kivu Province, nonstop coverage, while no foreign journalist visited Kasika for a decade.

Social life was deeply affected as well. The death of their traditional chief, along with the only priest, left the community without any leaders. "They killed our father and our mother," one villager told me. The church closed down, and the chief's family was embroiled in a succession battle that the RCD finally put an end to by imposing someone of their choice, much to the chagrin of many community members. Again and again, the villagers told me how the chief's death had affected them much more than anything else. The well-being of the community was vested in the chief; he presided over harvest ceremonies, gave out land, and blessed weddings. Who would call for *salongo*, the weekly communal labor, to be performed? Who would reconcile feuding families and solve land conflicts?

The community felt orphaned in other ways too. After the massacre, not a single national politician came to visit them and hear their grievances. While Kasika featured in thousands of speeches that lambasted Rwanda and the RCD, no investigation was ever launched, and no compensation was ever offered for any of the victims. The lack of justice had allowed the villagers to stew in their resentment and had made their anger fester into more hatred.

"I hate the Tutsi," Patrice told me. "If I see a Tutsi face, I feel fear."

I ask them if they could ever forgive the soldiers for what they did.

"Forgive whom? We don't even know who did it," someone outside Patrice's house said.

∾∾

In Kilungutwe, I met with some local elders at an open-air bar on the main street, not far from where Michel had hidden on the night of the massacre. The meeting turned into a popular assembly, as people heard what we were talking about and gathered around.

"We are still living through the massacre," one elder who had lost his wife and two children told me. "There has been no justice, not even a sign on a tree, or a monument in the honor of those who died that day."[11]

"We all lived in the forests like animals for five years," said a man in a plaid shirt and a baseball cap. "Our children are all illiterate because of this. Go to primary school here, and you will find fifteen-year-olds sitting on the benches."

The conversation turned toward Nyakiliba, the Mai-Mai militia commander who had commanded the fateful attack on the rebel convoy that had sparked the massacre. After the violence, many youths joined the Mai-Mai.

"What else were they supposed to do?" an elder said. "They wanted to avenge their families."

"Avenge?" another man retorted. "They were unemployed and hungry—a weapon made them a man. Don't think they were any better than the Tutsi!"

A chorus erupted from behind the men. "Yes, they were just as bad!" After the massacre, the RCD rebels had fought running battles with the ramshackle militia. When the population fled into RCD territory, they were accused of being Mai-Mai, while in Mai-Mai territory they were accused of being RCD spies.

"It was all nonsense," several people said at once. "They just wanted to rob us, all of us."

"For years, you couldn't find a single chicken, goat, or guinea pig in our homes. That was the Mai-Mai's food," a woman piped up from the back. A group of young men loitered about at the back of the crowd muttering among each other. This was the Mai-Mai demographic: young, unemployed, and disaffected.

I had heard from many men, but the longer we talked the more women also gathered around on their way back from the fields, balancing hoes on their heads, faded cloths wrapped around their waists. Given the preponderance of sexual violence in the region, I wanted to give them a chance to speak but didn't want to embarrass them in front of the men.

"I just want to give the women a chance to speak, as they are often the ones who suffer the most," I started cautiously. "Does any woman want to talk about her problems?"

I had barely finished when a woman at the back cried out: "*Baba!* All of us, all of us here have been raped! Every single one of us!"

A dozen other women raised their voices in angry agreement as the men looked at their feet, shaking their heads.

A woman in a green headscarf and pink sweater pushed her way to the front. "I have a child from rape. My husband doesn't like me anymore because of it. And the men who did it to me are around still in this village! They are our own children who joined the Mai-Mai!"

According to United Nations reports, over 200,000 women have been raped in the eastern Congo since 1998. Demographic surveys suggest that up to 39 percent of women have experienced sexual violence, at the hands of civilians or military personnel, at some point in their lives.[12] Given the nature of sexual violence, it is difficult to know how pervasive the phenomenon really is and what exactly is at the root of this epidemic, but there is no doubt that the situation is extremely dire.

~:~

Back in Kinshasa several months later, I brought up the Kasika massacre with Benjamin Serukiza, the former Munyamulenge vice governor of South Kivu. He had been friends with the slain Commander Moise and was personally accused of having ordered the revenge killings. He was driving me home in his battered Mercedes. On his dashboard, there was a sticker proclaiming "I ☐ Jesus Christ"—he was a devout, evangelical Christian, he told me, like many Banyamulenge.

Of course, he denied any personal involvement in the massacre, so I changed tactics and asked him whether in retrospect the war had been good for the Banyamulenge. He seemed tired—shortly afterward he would be diagnosed with a brain tumor and was hospitalized in South Africa—and was obviously unhappy with the question.

"You act like we had a choice. We didn't. We had to save ourselves," he said as he navigated the potholes in the road. After a long pause, he added, "The war was good and bad for us." Measuring his words carefully, he said, "But so many of us died. If you go to the high plateau, you won't see a cemetery. But every family there has lost at least one child, if not more, to the war. Our dead are buried across the Congo. We have nowhere to go and mourn for them."[13] He estimated that up to a quarter of all youths joined the war. Very few of them had returned to the high plateau.

The first to join and those who rose the highest in the rebellion were from the small number of educated youths who had left their homes in the high plateau to study in high schools and seminaries in the region. They were almost all under thirty-five: The RPF wanted young, dynamic blood that would be loyal to them. They experienced a double sense of estrangement: from their families and their traditional way of life and from their fellow students, who made fun of them precisely because they were backward and Tutsi. This alienation attracted them to the ideals and promises of the RPF. This elite, with the help and at the prompting of the Rwandan government, then returned at the beginning of the war to rally to the cause their cousins, brothers, and friends in the high plateau.

As always, these youths had many motivations. There were the ones they talked about incessantly: the longing to be accepted as Congolese citizens, to obtain land rights, and to be represented in local and provincial administration. Of course, many of the youths also wanted to succeed, to obtain power and fame. As with Serukiza, the careers of many ambitious Banyamulenge had been blocked by the discrimination and favoritism fostered by Mobutu.

But had this war been successful for them? The young class of Banyamulenge was extraordinarily successful in the short run. The difference between 1994, when there had barely been a single Munyamulenge in public office, and 1998 was dramatic. During the RCD, hundreds of Banyamulenge obtained high-ranking positions in the intelligence services, army, provincial administration, and police. Azarias Ruberwa, who had studied in Kalemie and become a lawyer in Lubumbashi, was the president of the RCD; Bizima Karaha, who had studied medicine in South Africa, became the powerful minister of interior and security chief; Moise Nyarugabo, who had also studied law in Lubumbashi, became the minister of justice. For a short period, they had succeeded in controlling the odious state apparatus that had been their bane for decades.

Their ascendance, however, only further soured relations with other communities. It was as if the RCD wanted to coerce the population into reconciliation. When confronted with resistance from local militias and civil society, which opposed what they perceived as Rwandan aggression, the RCD responded with repression. This merely fueled local resistance, and the region descended into vicious, cyclical violence.

In South Kivu, where this violence was perhaps the worst, it was often Banyamulenge who were in charge of intelligence offices, army brigades, and the police. The worst stereotype of the Congolese was confirmed: that of the treacherous and brutal Banyamulenge, nestled next to the cockroach, snake, and vermin in their bestiary. Commenting on the similar conundrum of military rule by the Tutsi minority in neighboring Burundi, former Tanzanian president Julius Nyerere observed, "The biggest obstacle is that those who are in power, the minority ..., they are like one riding on the back of a tiger. And they really want almost a water-tight assurance before they get off the back of the tiger because they feel if they get off the back of the tiger, it will eat them."[14]

~:~

There will be long-term repercussions of the Banyamulenge's participation in the two rebellions. In 2002, a opinion poll asked people whether they thought Banyamulenge were Congolese. Only 26 percent thought so.[15] In 2004, when a Munyamulenge commander led a mutiny against the Congolese army in the eastern border town of Bukavu, the population there reacted by launching a vicious witch hunt against Tutsi in town. The United Nations had to evacuate the entire Tutsi population, around 3,000 women, men, and children with mattresses and bags piled high on UN cars, from town. In 2007, when rumors spread in the southern town of Moba that a convoy of Banyamulenge refugees might be returning home from Zambia, local politicians provoked riots, protesting the "return of foreigners to our country." These resentments are in part bred by opportunist demagogues but are also grounded in the brutal rule by the AFDL and RCD in the eastern Congo between 1996 and 2003.

As I was about to get out of the car, I pressed Serukiza again whether he thought the war had been worthwhile.

He sighed. "I'm sure we didn't have a choice. For some, it was self-defense. We couldn't sit around and not do anything. But people hate us almost more today than before; it is just that they are tired of fighting. So no, it was a failure."

THE ASSASSINATION
OF MZEE

KINSHASA, CONGO, JANUARY 16, 2001

On January 16, 2001, Laurent Kabila's military advisor Colonel Edy Kapend was sitting on the lawn outside of Kabila's office at the official residence.[1] They had made it into a new year, he thought to himself, which was an achievement in itself. The Rwandan army had almost taken their mining capital, Lubumbashi, but had been stopped at the last moment. Now the president was trying to transform himself politically by forcing a Burundian Hutu rebellion, which had been supported by Kabila against the Tutsi military junta in their country, to go to the peace table with the Burundian government, which would improve Kabila's international reputation. Later that day, he would fly to Cameroon to announce those talks; then he would fly to Washington to try to rebuild bridges with George W. Bush's incoming administration. Things were looking up—at a New Year's gathering, the president had even given some of his closest staff presents of 100,000 Congolese francs, which, even though the rising inflation meant that the gift was only worth around $500, was a highly unusual gesture for tight-fisted Kabila.

As Kapend waited outside, Kabila was speaking with his economic affairs adviser, Emile Mota, about his upcoming trip. The president was wearing his habitual safari suit—off-white this time—and was in a good mood. Across town, a large peace rally was being held at the national stadium, and the gloom of the past year seemed to have lifted from the capital. The French doors were open to the terrace—Kabila did not like air conditioning—so that a breeze from the Congo River could blow through. Rashidi Kasereka, one of Kabila's body-guards, clicked his heels together at the door to ask for permission to enter. It was lunchtime, and security was lax, as some bodyguards had gone to eat.

Like most of the president's bodyguards, Rashidi was a former child soldier—*kadogo*—from the Kivus, who had been with Kabila for years. Kabila was used to Rashidi approaching him, so he wasn't taken aback when the young man bent down to whisper something in his ear. As Rashidi stepped up, he pulled out a pistol and fired three times, hitting the president in the neck, abdomen, and shoulder. Another bullet lodged in the sofa next to where Emile Mota was sit-ting, terrified.

Briefly stunned in shock outside, Colonel Kapend grabbed the gun of one of the presidential guards and ran around the building, to the patio outside the president's office, only to find another bodyguard standing over Rashidi's dead body. Furious, Kapend shot another round of bullets into the corpse.

Inside, Kabila's secretary, Anny, ran through the corridors, screaming that *le chef* had been shot. The president lay sprawled on the floor in a pool of blood, still clutching some documents in his hand. Within several minutes, the presi-dent's Cuban doctor and the minister of health had arrived, ripped open his shirt, and tried to resuscitate him. He had clenched his tongue between his teeth, and Kapend thought he could hear him moaning still.

Finally, a helicopter pilot was located to fly the president to the Ngaliema medical clinic nearby. The doctors and soldiers tore down the long velvet cur-tains from the windows to transport him. "He was so heavy that even four of us had a hard time lifting him," an aide remembered.[2]

Immediately, the president's closest associates called an emergency meeting, together with the military representatives of the Angolan and Zimbabwean armies.[3] They had no idea who was behind the assassination, but they worried that dissidents within the army would take advantage of the power vacuum. They decided to keep the assassination a secret until they could decide what to do.

They bundled Kabila's corpse, together with all the nurses, doctors, and cleaning staff from the clinic, into a presidential airplane and flew them to Zim-babwe. Colonel Edy Kapend went on television that afternoon ordering the army high command to stay calm and maintain discipline. He did not say a word about the coup that many in the capital assumed must be under way. The next day the government put out a clipped statement, saying that the president had been injured in an assassination attempt and was in Harare for treatment. In the streets, Angolan and Zimbabwean soldiers patrolled and manned key roadblocks.

When he was finally pronounced dead several days later, the news stunned the capital. Mzee, as most Kinois refer to him, had been the overwhelming figure of Congolese politics since his arrival in Kinshasa, no matter what one thought of him. Congolese had become used to his weekly television and radio appearances, his long, verbose, and often funny harangues about domestic and international politics. Within his own cabinet, it was Mzee's metronome that kept the beat and made sure that all the disparate interest groups stayed in line and were prevented from infighting. It was as if the conductor had died in the middle of a symphony and now the horns, strings, and percussion were vying for primacy.

～:～

No one had been a more insistent augur of Kabila's death than the man himself. "He spoke about it all the time," Information Minister Didier Mumengi remembered.[4] The president had thought that it would be a western conspiracy, that he had prevented foreign corporations from getting at Congo's resources, and that they would eliminate him. He saw himself as Patrice Lumumba, the independence hero who was gunned down in a Belgian-American plot almost exactly forty years to the day before Kabila's own assassination.

Kabila was paranoid but not necessarily wrong. There was good reason for western corporate interests to be angered. Kabila had reneged on several mining contracts, most notably with Banro, a Canadian company, and with Anglo American, a London-based mining giant.

But Kabila was an obstacle to more than just corporate interests. Three years after he had taken power, his war machine was failing, Congo's economy was in tatters, and he had failed to carry out any meaningful reforms. At the beginning of the 1998 war, the social misery had been made bearable thanks to the upsurge in patriotism that the Rwandan aggression had provoked. Just after the Rwandan attack on Kinshasa in August 1998, 88 percent of people polled in Kinshasa said they had a favorable impression of their president, a leap of 50 percent from a year before.[5] For a brief period, the capital forgot about its misery and hunger and channeled its energies into supporting the government. When asked about the reasons for the war, a full half of Kinois answered that they thought it was "a conspiracy of western powers," while 19 percent thought it was due to "Tutsi hegemony in central Africa."[6] Few cared about the incompetence of their own government.

The euphoria had been short-lived, however. The war bankrupted the country and undermined Kabila's ambitious development plans. By 2000, inflation had risen to 550 percent, and civil servants were barely paid. Long lines of cars gathered in front of gas stations, waiting for fuel; the only reliable providers of gasoline were black-market hustlers—the so-called Ghadaffi, named after the oil-rich Libyan leader—who set up shop under broad-rimmed umbrellas along the streets with their jerry cans and siphons. Mutinies broke out in the capital's military barracks when poorly paid soldiers refused to go to the front line. On several occasions, Kabila's motorcade in Kinshasa was stoned in the densely populated shantytowns. As he passed by, women lifted their colorful blouses to show him their stomachs, crying that they were hungry. Several billboards with Mzee's picture, exclaiming, "It's the man we needed!" had to be taken down, as they became subject to regular pelting with rotten fruit.

~:~

Inflation, corruption, and general administrative stagnation: These were the characteristics of Laurent Kabila's regime. In retrospect, Kabila's supporters blame all of his regime's woes on the war. In reality, however, Mzee helped bring his problems on himself through a slew of incoherent and poorly executed initiatives.

The government's monetary and fiscal policies were a case in point. In order to hoard much-needed foreign currency, the government decreed that all monetary transactions would take place in Congolese francs, and it kept the currency at an artificially high value. Traders had five days to exchange their U.S. dollars and euros for Congolese francs or face sanctions. They then had to pay all of their taxes according to the official rate. Since the rate at the Central Bank was four times lower in 2000 than that on the black market, incomes of businesses and civil servants were devastated. Of course, the few government employees who were allowed to buy foreign cash at the official rate made a killing, encouraging them to keep inflation high.

"Mzee wanted solutions *now*, not two years in the future. We would go to him with elaborate plans for the economy," his information minister remembered, "but he would say 'Two years! I will be dead in two years. Bring me projects that can bring us cash in two weeks!'"[7]

The war scuttled all plans for long-term reform and prompted quick fixes that only further debilitated the state. The diamond industry was another example. With the former cash cows of the economy—the state-run copper and cobalt companies—moribund, the government was almost solely reliant on diamonds and oil, which made up 75 percent of exports.[8] However, Kabila's monetary policy prompted diamond sellers to smuggle most of their goods to neighboring countries to avoid transactions in Congolese francs. To make matters worse, in August 2000 the president granted a monopoly of all diamond sales to Dan Gertler, a young Israeli tycoon, in return for $20 million a year. The move was intended to provide the government with some much-needed cash, but as a result Kabila crippled the sector and alienated the powerful Lebanese diamond trading community in Kinshasa. Without smuggling, the entire diamond market in the Congo was estimated to be worth $600 million. Under Kabila's whimsical policies, Congolese exports shrunk to barely $175 million.[9]

~:~

In the meantime, the news from the front line was consistently bad. All Congolese belligerents and their foreign allies had signed the Lusaka Cease-fire in August 1999, but—invoking Mao Tsetung's dictum "talk/fight, talk/fight"—Kabila was determined to fight to the end. He consistently blocked the deployment of a UN peacekeeping mission, believing it would prevent his military triumph.

By August 2000, however, Kabila was alone in still believing in victory. The war had stumbled fitfully into its third year. The Ugandan-backed MLC (Movement for the Liberation of the Congo) rebels routed the government's troops in the north of the country, pushing down the Congo River toward the regional hub of Mbandaka, just several hundred miles up the river from Kinshasa itself. In the center of the country, Rwandan troops and their RCD allies had surrounded the garrison city of Ikela, cutting off Congolese and Zimbabwean troops and slowly starving them.

The government readied itself for a decisive standoff in the small fishing village of Pweto, on the southeastern border with Zambia. "For Mzee, Pweto was a symbol of resistance," a presidential advisor told me. "He wanted to defend it at all costs."[10] If Pweto fell, little would stand in the way of Rwanda from taking Lubumbashi, the country's mining capital and Kabila's hometown.

The leader of the Burundian Hutu rebels in the Congo at the time remembered Kabila calling him in August 2000. "He said: 'This time we will break their back,' and told me to get ready for a new offensive."[11] Kabila freed up $20 million for the operations and moved his army command to Pweto, entrusting the offensive to General John Numbi, an electrical engineer and former head of a Katangan youth militia.

Many officers didn't share Kabila's optimism. General Joseph Kabila, the titular head of the army since 1998 and the president's son, told the Burundian rebel commander in private he didn't believe they would succeed. Zimbabwean commanders muttered similar doubts and said their soldiers would just hold defensive positions. The Burundian rebel leader himself had been let down on several occasions, taking control of towns only to wait in vain for reinforcements that Kabila had promised him. He also shared the general skepticism regarding General Numbi's competence: "He spent his time elaborating plans on his laptop and drawing sketches that nobody paid much attention to. He wasn't a real soldier."

Like much of the state, the Congolese army was a hulking, decrepit edifice. Although the president claimed to have 120,000 soldiers, most diplomats put the real figure at around 50,000, a mix of former Mobutists, *kadogo* recruited during the first war and trained by Rwandans and Ugandans, Katangan Tigers, and new recruits. Some foreign military analysts put precombat desertion rates—those who fled even before fighting had begun—as high as 60 percent; only front line units received regular pay and food. In Kinshasa, families of soldiers on the front line were routinely evicted from their houses so new recruits could be lured by offers of free lodging. Even then, the army was hard-pressed to attract new soldiers and by 2000 had begun to enlist the young children of soldiers to send to the front.[12]

While many officers had significant expertise, much like his predecessor President Kabila valued loyalty more than competence and left many important operations in the hands of old *maquisards* (bush fighters) or inexperienced Katangans. Even where competent officers were deployed, the president often micromanaged operations himself and used parallel chains of command, confusing his own offensive.

Given this shambles of an army, Kabila had to rely on his allies. Zimbabwe had increased its deployment to the Congo to 11,000 troops, while Angola and Namibia had smaller contingents, tasked largely with defending Kinshasa. There were also 15,000 to 25,000 Burundian and Rwandan Hutus who were working for Kabila on a mercenary basis.

~:~

It was just north of Pweto, in the small village of Mutoto Moya, that, amid the long elephant grass of the savannah, one of the war's most important battles took place. Located in the middle of gently rolling plains, the village stood at the gateway to Lubumbashi, the capital of the mineral-rich province, just four days away by foot along good roads.

Around 3,000 Rwandan and Burundian troops had been held at a stalemate for months by twice as many Zimbabwean and Hutu soldiers. The two forces stared at each other across 8 miles of twin trenches, separated by a one-mile stretch of empty land.

Mutoto Moya was one of the only instances of trench warfare in the Congo. Both sides had dug man-high trenches that meandered for miles. Inside the muddy walls, one could find kitchens, card games, makeshift bars, and cots laid out for soldiers to sleep. This was one of the few instances when Africa's Great War resembled its European counterpart eighty years earlier.

For the Rwandan and Burundian soldiers, many of whom had grown up in cooler climates, the conditions were poor. It was hot and humid, and huge, foot-long earthworms and dung beetles shared the space with the soldiers. When it rained, the soldiers could find themselves standing knee-deep in muddy rainwater for hours, developing sores as their skin chafed inside their rubber galoshes.

Many came down with malaria and a strange skin rash they thought was caused by the local water supply. Termites from the towering mounds nearby ate into the wooden ammunition boxes, and jiggers lay eggs under soldiers' skin. Luckily for the Rwandan staff officers, every couple of months they could go for much-needed R&R on a nearby colonial ranch, where there were dairy cows, electricity, and a good supply of beer.

It was telling that the most important front of the Congo war was being fought almost entirely by foreign troops on both sides. "The Rwandans didn't

trust the RCD with such an important task," remembered Colonel Maurice
Gateretse, the commander of regular Burundian army troops. "They had behaved
so badly that we radioed back to their headquarters, saying they should be removed. They would use up a whole clip in thirty minutes and come and ask for
more. These guys were more interested in pillaging the villages than fighting."[13]

A cease-fire negotiated between the two sides held until October 2000, when
Laurent Kabila unilaterally launched his offensive. In an effort to prevail by sheer
numbers, the Congolese cobbled together a force of over 10,000 soldiers, including many Rwandan and Burundian Hutu soldiers. With the support of armored
cars and Hawker fighter aircraft from the Zimbabwean army, the Congolese
forces overran the enemy trenches and pushed their rivals back to Pepa, a ranching town in the hills some thirty miles away. There, Laurent Kabila's troops took
control of the strategic heights overlooking the town. Zimbabwean bombers
pursued and bombed the retreating troops, forcing them to hide during the day
and march at night.

Back in Kigali, President Kagame was furious. He radioed his commander
on the ground, an officer nicknamed Commander Zero Zero, who was known
for his brutality and his love of cane alcohol. Kagame told him that if he failed
to retake Pepa, "don't even try to come back to Rwanda." The Burundian commander, Colonel Gateretse, received a similar warning from his commander back
home, who told him he would have to walk back to Burundi—three hundred
seventy miles through the bush—if he lost.

In order to retake Pepa, they would have to scale a hill with almost no cover
and with thick buttresses prickling with heavy machine guns and mortars at the
top. "It was like those movies I saw of the Americans at Iwo Jima," the Burundian
commander commented. "We would have to hide behind every hummock and
bush we could find." They received reinforcements over the lake from Burundi:
An additional 6,000 Rwandan and Burundian troops arrived on barges for the
onslaught.

They launched their challenge early in the morning. Thousands of young soldiers clambered up the steep slopes toward the fortifications above. There was
little brush for cover; this was cattle country, and all the trees had been chopped
down for pasture. "It was a massacre," Colonel Gateretse remembered. Kabila's
army "sat at the top with their heavy machine guns and just mowed the kids
down. You would hear the mortars thunder, the rat-tat-tat of the machine guns

and screams as our boys fell." One by one, the walkie-talkies of their officers try-ing to scale the hill went dead.

After two days and hundreds of casualties, the Rwandans and Burundians sat together to rethink. They decided to send a light, mobile battalion around Kabila's position to attack from the rear, while the bulk of the troops continued their frontal offensive to distract their adversaries. The flanking maneuver, how-ever, was risky, as the terrain was difficult and the Congolese had patrols throughout the surrounding areas. The soldiers would have to cover forty miles by foot in one night to catch them by surprise, a tough feat even by their stan-dards. They forced some unlucky locals at gunpoint to serve as guides for them and set out at nightfall at a light trot with little equipment other than their AK-47s, several clips of ammunition, and a few rocket-propelled grenade launchers.

It worked. After a morning of catfights up the mountain, incurring even more casualties, suddenly the machine guns at the top of the hill went silent, then turned around, and began firing the other way. The flanking expedition had bro-ken through Kabila's rear guard, sandwiching the remaining troops. In a des-perate surrender attempt, Kabila's soldiers put up any white material they could find over their sandbags: tank tops, tarps, underwear. It didn't make much dif-ference. "We didn't take many prisoners, we were too angry, and, anyway, where would we have put them?" Colonel Gateretse remembered. It was their turn to mow down the enemy.

Most of Kabila's forces, however, escaped, and began running back toward Pweto, toward their army's forward operating base. Much of the Congolese top brass had assembled there, including General Joseph Kabila.

What followed was a three-week-long road battle as the Congolese, Hutu, and Zimbabwean forces retreated under constant fire. The road wound through the bucolic cattle country, lined with eucalyptus trees planted by Belgians de-cades before. The Rwandans had the tactical advantage: They were highly mo-bile, carried only the essentials, and ambushed the Congolese at every turn in the road. The Congolese were encumbered by their artillery, tanks, and armored vehicles; they sought refuge on the high ground to the sides of the road, using bunkers and foxholes they had dug there. But inevitably, the Rwandans would outpace them and cut off individual units.

A *Washington Post* journalist who visited the road later reported: "The road south toward Pweto remained speckled not only with green and white butterflies, but with corpses—here the body of young man cut down clutching an AK-47, here a splayed green poncho topped by a skull."[14]

In the meantime, panic was breaking out in Pweto. The government's coalition had made the fatal mistake of bringing the bulk of its armory across the Luvua River. Only one ferry, however, was available for transport, and there wasn't enough time to evacuate their equipment before the Rwandans arrived. Worse still, under duress, Congolese logistics broke down. "President Kabila told me that they had run out of ammunition," one of his commanders remembered. "It was very suspicious. All of a sudden, we ran out of everything—fuel, ammunition, money."[15]

With the Rwandans just a few miles away, the army high command, including General Joseph Kabila, tried to board a helicopter to flee back to Lubumbashi, only to find that there was no fuel for that either. "It was like Mobutu all over again," a presidential aide told me. "Someone had sold all the helicopter fuel to make a profit. We were the victims of our own ineptitude."[16]

The group of generals had to scramble to the ferry—aptly named *Alliance*, a dirty-pink, rusty contraption—along with their Zimbabwean colleagues and flee across the Zambian border. When the ferry got back to the Congolese side, soldiers tried frantically to load a forty-ton Soviet T-62 tank on board. They misjudged the balance, and the ferry sunk in the harbor along with its precious cargo.

It was a fitting end to the rout of Congolese forces. When the Rwandans arrived in the fishing town hours later, they found a neat line of thirty-three tanks, armored personnel carriers, trucks, and one ambulance lined up in front of the ferry and charred a crispy black. The fleeing soldiers had doused the equipment with diesel and set it alight. Unopened syringes from the medical kits cracked underfoot. Amid the jettisoned equipment, they found a note left by a fleeing officer that read: "*Attaque*."[17]

⁕

President Laurent Kabila, who had been following the fighting from Lubumbashi, two hundred miles away, was devastated. For twenty-four hours he had no news from his son Joseph, whom he considered the closest member of his confused, sprawling family network. When he heard that his son and the rest of the army command had fled to Zambia, he had them all arrested, including Joseph, and brought back to the Congo.

Kabila urgently flew to Zimbabwe to obtain assurance that they would prevent Lubumbashi from falling, but President Mugabe was visibly upset. One Zimbabwean official commented: "[Kabila] is like a man who starts six fires when he's only got one fire extinguisher.... The fire fighters are the Zimbabwean Army."[18] The war in the Congo was costing Mugabe $27 million a month and a consistent battering by Harare's newspapers, which complained about the costly war in the Congo while at home there were food riots. Shortly before the Pweto debacle, Mugabe lost a key referendum to amend the constitution, while the opposition made huge gains in parliamentary elections. "Enough," he told Kabila. "Negotiate with your enemies."

Desperate, Kabila flew to Angola, where he met with President Edouardo Dos Santos. There, the message was even more severe. By the end of 2000, the Angolan army, which had never sent many troops to the front line, had badly thrashed Jonas Savimbi's UNITA rebels in the north of the country and was no longer so dependent on Kabila's military collaboration. One of Kabila's aides recalled: "Dos Santos told him to liberalize the diamond trade, float the exchange rate, and meet with his opponents."[19] In other words: Everything you have tried has failed. The stick hasn't worked; you have to try with some carrots now.

In order to ram the message home, the Angolan president confided that western intelligence services were conspiring to get rid of Kabila and that several of his generals had been contacted. But then he smiled and patted his counterpart on the back: "I told them not to do anything—better a scoundrel we know than one we don't."

Kabila was deeply affected by this conversation. "He talked about it for days after he got back to Kinshasa," his aide said.[20] The president knew that he didn't have the finances or the military domestically to prop up his dysfunctional government and that without the backing of Angola and Zimbabwe his days were numbered. Kabila asked his staff to draw up a list of opponents he could negotiate with, but nobody had faith in dealing with him anymore. He sunk into an insomniac depression, canceled all his meetings, and withdrew to his presidential palace. Stubble began appearing on his usually clean-shaven face, and he told his aides, "If Lubumbashi falls, I will kill myself."[21]

⌒:∼

So who ordered the killing of Mzee? Congolese imagination is knotted around Kabila's death, entangled in multiple narratives and histories that compete to explain why the scrawny bodyguard shot the president. Part of the problem is that there were too many people who had a reason, who stood to benefit from his death. As the *Economist* quipped, fifty million people—the country's entire population—had a motive. By the time of his death, Kabila had managed to offend or alienate not only his enemies but also most of his allies.

There are two main theories about his death. The first, the one supported by the Congolese government, lays the blame squarely at Rwanda's doorstep, saying that Rwanda had acted through a gang of discontented former child soldiers from the Kivus close to Anselme Masasu. When Edy Kapend had informed Joseph Kabila of his father's death, the twenty-nine-year-old reportedly teared up on the phone, and before Kapend could fully explain what had happened, he blurted out, "Those people from the Kivus killed my father."[22]

Anselme Masasu—known as "Toto" to his friends, for his youthful appearance (*mtoto* means "child" in Swahili)—had grown up along the border between Rwanda and the Congo, the son of a father from the ethnic Shi community and a Tutsi mother. He had many Tutsi friends, and when they left school to join the RPF rebellion in the early 1990s, Masasu, eager for adventure, joined up as well. He was twenty and rose to the rank of sergeant in the Rwandan army. His charisma and keen wit brought him to the attention of his superiors, and he was chosen as the fourth member of the AFDL leadership in 1996. The Rwandan army hoped that he would be able to encourage non-Tutsi youth in the eastern Congo to join what they feared might be perceived as an exclusively Tutsi affair. Even before the AFDL invasion, Masasu infiltrated and began enlisting children and young men to the cause. He was considered the commander of the *kadogo*, always present on the front line, eating beans and corn with his "children." Years later, many former *kadogo* I spoke to still referred to him with respect and love— he had been their father after they had left home.

Masasu remained close to Colonel James Kabarebe, even after the Rwandans had been kicked out of the Congo. As one of the original founders of the AFDL, Masasu often exaggerated his position, calling himself commander in chief of the army and granting himself the rank of general. "He rose from sergeant to general in nine months," recalled former Rwandan intelligence chief Patrick Karegeya. "I think it went to his head." In the ethnically fuelled politics of Kinshasa, Masasu represented the Kivutian wing of the army and was seen as a threat by Katangans close to Kabila.

In November 1997, President Kabila had Masasu arrested and put out a press statement, accusing him of "fraternizing with enemies of the state" and clarifying that he was not a general. He was sentenced to twenty years in prison, of which he served fifteen months, some of it in solitary confinement in a cell one square yard in size. When *kadogo* protested and signs of a possible mutiny appeared, Kabila allowed him to go free.

Nevertheless, as soon as Masasu was set free, he began criticizing Kabila again in the foreign press, claiming that he had been unjustly imprisoned. In Kinshasa, the security services became convinced that he was recruiting former *kadogo* to attempt to overthrow the president. They accused him of holding meetings with 1,200 *kadogo* as part of an effort to start a new insurgency. A witch hunt for *kadogo* from the Kivus was launched in Kinshasa. Security services stripped detainees bare and searched for ritual scarification on their chests and backs, claiming that Masasu was anointing his adepts with traditional medicine to make them invincible to bullets. Unfortunately, many soldiers from the east carried such scars from when traditional healers had treated them for pneumonia or bronchitis as infants.

Masasu was arrested along with over fifty other soldiers. Several weeks later, on November 27, 2000, he was executed on the front line at Pweto.

~:~

Young recruits from the Kivus constituted up to a third of Kabila's army of 50,000. Since the early days of his rebellion, Kabila had surrounded himself with child soldiers, much to the chagrin of visiting diplomats and dignitaries, who were often accosted by the youths asking for a couple of dollars or some cigarettes. When one visiting foreign businessman, a friend of the president, warned him against using these *kadogo*, Kabila replied, "Oh no, they could never hurt me. They've been with me since the beginning. They are my children."[23] In another frequently described incident, the *kadogo* prevented Kabila's wife from leaving the residence, protesting that they hadn't been paid and were hungry. In order to shut them up, she opened up the chicken coop behind the residence and allowed them to help themselves to the hens and eggs.[24]

Masasu's execution prompted riots in military camps in Kinshasa, and hundreds of *kadogo* were arrested or fled across the river to Brazzaville. Although details are murky, at least several dozen were executed by firing squad in the capital.[25] It was then, according to interviews of *kadogo* carried out by a French journalist, that a fateful meeting was held among the young Kivutians who had remained in the president's bodyguard.[26] "I will kill him," Rashidi Kasereka is reported to have said, furious over the killing of his friends, to a group of twenty other presidential guards, who cheered their approval.

After the assassination, a group of *kadogo* fled across the river to neighboring Brazzaville. According to the Congolese authorities, they had been part of the plot to assassinate Kabila. The president of the neighboring Republic of Congo, Denis Sassou Nguesso, who didn't want to appear to be sheltering coup plotters, promptly arrested them and had them brought back to Kinshasa. Several of them had been close to Masasu—they included his former chief of staff and military advisor. According to Kabila's security services, when they interrogated these prisoners, they admitted to being part of a plan to kill Kabila. The *kadogo* said they had received money to organize the coup from Lebanese businessmen; the security services had already suspected their involvement and had executed eleven Lebanese. The businessmen had allegedly been incensed by Kabila's grant of the quasi-monopoly of diamond sales to the Israeli trader. "It was strange, though," remarked Kabila's national security advisor, who had followed the interrogations. "They were very calm during our questioning. They said that they knew they would soon escape."[27] Sure enough, shortly afterwards, the leaders of the Masasu group engineered a break from the Makala prison through an inside job.

The *Le Monde* journalists, who spoke with several of the fugitives, concluded that the assassination had been the work of a bunch of bitter former child soldiers who were seeking revenge. This is possible. However, the whole affair—the lax security at the presidency, the escape from prison, the murder of the Lebanese—seems to be too well choreographed, too slickly greased to have been the doing of a few renegade bodyguards. There are several indications that Rwanda was directly involved. First, according to the Congolese security services, before fleeing, the Masasu crew admitted to being in cahoots with Kigali. Second, when they did flee, along with several affluent Lebanese businessmen, they made their way directly to Rwanda, where some were eventually given influential political and business positions by the government. Last, a former Rwandan security official told me that he had seen Colonel James Kabarebe on the day of the assassination. Kabarebe, who was still running Congo operations for the Rwandan army and would soon be promoted to become head of the army, reportedly slapped him on the shoulder and said, "Good news from Kinshasa. Our boys did it."[28]

~:~

Others, however, dismiss the Rwandan conspiracy theory. If the Rwandans had wanted to get rid of Kabila, the argument goes, they would have launched an offensive, either in Kinshasa or along the front line, to accompany their coup. Instead nothing happened. In fact, the assassination ended up working against Rwandan interests, as the dead president's successor was able to reestablish support for his country among diplomats, reinvigorate the peace process, and emasculate Rwanda's Congolese ally, the RCD.

Skeptics of the Rwandan conspiracy theory, including the French political scientist Gérard Prunier, usually point their finger at Angola, President Kabila's erstwhile ally. In 2000, the Angolan army had come close to crushing UNITA, its rebel adversary of twenty-five years. Nonetheless, according to UN investigators, UNITA continued to rake in revenues of $200 million a year through diamond deals, and it appeared that Kabila, in a desperate bid for cash, had begun to allow UNITA to deal through Lebanese gem traders in Kinshasa. The Angolan rebels would mask the true origin of the diamonds, and Kabila would get hefty kickbacks in return. According to French and British insider periodicals, by the end of 2000 UNITA operatives were once again active in Kinshasa. President Dos Santos, who had supported the initial rebellion against Mobutu precisely to root out UNITA bases in Zaire, was livid.[29]

This hypothesis is supported by the curious behavior of General Yav Nawej, the commander of Kinshasa who had close ties to Angola, along with Edy Kapend, the president's military advisor. The day before the assassination, General Yav, as he was known, ordered the disarmament of select northern Katangan units in Kinshasa's garrison, who were the most loyal to Kabila. Then, within hours of the assassination, General Yav ordered the execution of eleven Lebanese, including six minors, belonging to a diamond trading family. In the meantime, Kapend had gone on the radio and *ordered* the commanders of the army, navy, and air force to maintain discipline and calm, rankling these officers, who thought such commands to be far above his pay grade.

According to this scenario, the Angolans did not instigate the assassination but found out about it ahead of time and then told their men in Kinshasa—Yav and Kapend—not to intervene. Indeed, it is difficult to imagine the *kadogo* acting on behest of Angola, as they had few links to Luanda and were much closer to Rwanda. It is, however, equally difficult to believe that only the pro-Angolan officers within the presidency would have discovered the coup plot, given the porous information networks in Kinshasa. This theory is also challenged by the subsequent arrest of both Kapend and Yav, the former for having allegedly orchestrated the assassination, the latter for his extrajudicial execution of the Lebanese citizens. One would imagine that if Angola had wanted to get rid of any leaks of information, they would have eliminated both altogether—prisons in the Congo are notoriously porous themselves. It also isn't clear why Joseph Kabila, who is known for his deep attachment to his father and may have had a good idea of who killed him, would have so easily assumed the presidency surrounded by people who had been involved in the plot.

~:~

Any number of narrative strands could have ended in Laurent Kabila's death. Other theories include one that he died of a natural death: He had apparently fallen sick with malaria the day of his death, and according to a human rights organization, the doctor at the clinic where he was treated did not notice any bullet wounds on his body. Another conjecture is that he had been shot by a group of his own generals whom he had sacked for their shoddy performance in Pweto. A year later, Kabila's deputy director of protocol appeared in exile in Brussels, suggesting that the Zimbabwean army was behind the murder but providing little evidence or rationale for his claim.[30]

As so often in the Congo, the truth may never be known. Observers of Congolese politics should steel themselves with a deep skepticism of simple truths in general. Information, in particular regarding matters of state, is often rooted in hearsay and rumor. Indeed, politicians have become adept at using rumors as a tactical weapon, spreading them on purpose to distract from the truth or to smear their opponents.

Sometimes it seems that by crossing the border into the Congo one abandons any sort of Archimedean perspective on truth and becomes caught up in a web of rumors and allegations, as if the country itself were the stuff of some postmodern fiction. This is, in part, due to a structural deficit; institutions that could dig deep and scrutinize information—such as a free press, an independent judiciary, and an inquisitive parliament—do not exist. But it has also become a matter of cultural pride. People weave rumors and myths together over drinks or while waiting for taxis to help give meaning to their lives. It may, for example, be easier to believe that Joseph Kabila's real name is Hippolyte Kanambé and that he is a Rwandan, acting in the interests of Paul Kagame, or to believe that the conflict in the Congo was all an American corporate conspiracy to extract minerals from the country. Either might be easier to swallow than the complex, tangled reality. Doesn't it give more meaning to the Congolese's grim everyday existence?

A military tribunal in Kinshasa held a nine-month-long trial at the central prison of 135 people arrested in conjunction with Kabila's assassination. Day after day, prisoners, soldiers, family members, and people in search of entertainment filed into the court, ushered to their seats by prisoners in blue-and-yellow uniforms. The judges sat in front of a mural that had been painted by a prisoner with an artistic bent: a rustic picnic next to a pond, garnished with wine, grapes, a violin, and a bouquet of roses. As the defendants stood and gave their testimony, the audience jeered or clapped. They were particularly noisy during the speeches of Colonel Charles Alamba, the chief prosecutor, who distinguished himself by long, irrelevant digressions. At one point, he castigated Edy Kapend for having had children with more than one woman. "We practice monogamy here—we don't recognize polygamy!"[31] The audience groaned in dismay.

The court did not provide the accused with decent defense lawyers and barred independent observers from the courtroom for much of the trial. The prosecutors were military officers and as such answered to their superiors, a fact that undermined their independence. Many had little or no legal training. They arrested and put on trial wives of some of the soldiers, including Rashidi's, without any evidence to indicate they were involved. Emile Mota, the economic affairs advisor who had been present during the assassination, was arrested while he was on the witness stand because he allegedly had contradicted himself. At no point did anybody provide convincing evidence that any of the accused was guilty, nor did the reasons behind Kabila's death become any clearer.

The judge eventually sentenced thirty people to death, ten of whom had been tried in absentia.

~:~

By the time of his death, Kabila had become the central figure in the country. Everything about him was big, from his figure to his bombastic language to his acts. In many ways, he was heir to the man he had spent most of his life trying to overthrow: Mobutu Sese Seko. Laurent Kabila, too, was a strong, often autocratic ruler who governed by decree and repressed all opposition. "*Kabila, c'était un vrai chef,*" Congolese often remember fondly. He was in charge, a fact he reminded most of his associates of by arresting them for short periods and then releasing them again; almost no one escaped this treatment. But there were no monumental relics of his rule: Kabila was not given to the same kind of Louis XIV extravagances as his predecessor. He lived a relatively modest life and had little tolerance for most kinds of corruption. If there is one thing the Congolese will remember Mzee for, it is the war. It consumed both Kabila and his government and pushed them into a frenzy of patriotism and, at times, xenophobia. He became obsessed with winning. After all, he had grown up a rebel and felt much more at ease in trying to win a war than to rule a country. But when he became a martyr to his most dear cause, the country heaved a sigh of relief.

⊹ 19 ⊹

PAYING FOR THE WAR

GOMA, ZAIRE, NOVEMBER 1996

"Illegal, illegal! What the hell does 'illegal' mean?" Mwenze Kongolo responded when I asked what he thought about the "illegal exploitation" of Congolese resources by foreign companies and states. Mwenze had been the powerful interior minister under Laurent Kabila, and he was himself a shareholder in several mining deals. "We needed money to finance the war. We used our mines and resources to stave off foreign aggression. Is that illegal?"[1]

Many have come to criticize the deals struck between Kabila's government and states in the region to finance the war. Others have condemned Rwandan and Ugandan profiteering during their occupation of the eastern Congo between 1998 and 2002. As usual, a coarse brush was used to paint these different forms of involvement with the same broad strokes, sacrificing nuance for caricature. For all the states involved, economic interests played a role but were woven into a complex web of domestic and regional, political and corporate considerations. In some cases, politicians did exploit natural resources for personal profit; in others, they did so to finance the war and government operations, although often by very dubious means. Foreign governments and companies were involved, but again, in a wide variety of forms, ranging from direct complicity to more tangential responsibility.

~:~

The first invasion of the Congo in September 1996 had everything to do with security and geopolitical concerns and only little to do with business. It was

Mobutu's support of Angolan, Ugandan, and Rwandan rebels that provoked the incursion, not his neighbors' greed for the Congo's minerals. As the rebellion advanced, however, money soon became a decisive factor.

As parts of the country became independent of control from Kinshasa, they slashed import and export taxes by 70 percent. Goma became a hotbed of entrepreneurship, as investors from all over the world were attracted to the region. Doing business with the rebels at that time was a risky proposition. No large corporations threw their weight behind Laurent Kabila, afraid that Mobutu could make a comeback and they would be perceived as turncoats. This opened the door for risk-seeking entrepreneurs not confined by the strictures of large, publicly owned corporations.

Jean-Raymond Boulle fit this profile. He was one of the first prominent entrepreneurs to get in touch with the AFDL rebellion in the early months of 1997, when the rebellion controlled no more than a thin sliver of the eastern border region. Boulle had a typical profile for investors in the Congo: erudite, adventurous, and risk-seeking. A soft-spoken forty-seven-year-old from Mauritius, Boulle had been educated in South Africa and the United Kingdom. He drove a Bentley and had settled in a mansion in Monaco, but he was no stranger to the rough-and-tumble of African mining. He had become involved in the business at an early age, following his mother, who had been an experienced diamond dealer; he had gone to work for the South African diamond giant De Beers in Zaire and Sierra Leone in the 1970s. Frustrated by the company's bureaucracy, he left to start his own company in 1981. In 1994, he had his big break, when one of his geologists stumbled by accident on the world's largest nickel deposit in Voisey Bay, Canada, while he was prospecting for diamonds. After stiff bargaining, Boulle sold the concession, walking away with $400 million, which he promptly invested in a new company, American Mineral Fields, a joint venture with a land surveyor from Hope, Arkansas, the hometown of President Clinton. Boulle was never too shy to remind potential partners where his company was based and to mention that he had met Clinton on several occasions, including at his inauguration celebration at the White House.[2]

When the war broke out, no major investor had been actively mining in the Congo in years. At the same time, however, the Belgian and Congolese state had already invested billions over the years in prospecting and conducting feasibility studies. This considerably reduced the risk for private capital. Companies could

buy known quantities of copper and cobalt, anticipating roughly how much surface rock needed to be removed, water needed to be dredged, and infrastructure
needed to be renovated or installed. In some cases, foreign businessmen colluded
with officials from Gécamines, the state-owned mining corporation, to obtain
their technical evaluations and feasibility studies. "They rewrote them, put their
letterhead on top, and then simply said that they had done a technical study," a
former Gécamines official, who—like most mining officials—refused to be
named for this book, told me.[3]

Boulle had already attempted to get involved in mining under Mobutu, obtaining two mining concessions that contained an estimated $20 billion in cop-
per and cobalt.[4] But Mobutu had canceled the contracts, handing one of them
to Anglo American, the continent's largest mining conglomerate. Rankled by
the dictator, Boulle, who worked in tandem with several brothers, reached out
to Mobutu's opponents. When Kisangani, the country's third biggest city, fell
in March 1997, Boulle made his move, shutting down his office in Kinshasa and
opening a diamond trading house in an area controlled by the AFDL. "Do you
wait until everybody gets here and be last or do you get in early?" his brother
Max Boulle told the press at the time. "We've made a conscious decision to get
in early."[5]

Since the AFDL had shut down all other diamond dealers in town, Boulle
was able to turn a handsome profit. In return, he reportedly paid the rebels $1
million in "advance taxes" on the diamonds.[6] Diamond traders were so desperate
to sell their diamonds that they literally broke down the door of Boulle's office.
The Mauritian also allowed the rebellion to continue using his corporate Lear
jet, although he later claimed that it had been commandeered. In April 1997,
after the AFDL had seized control of Lubumbashi, the country's mining capital,
they awarded Boulle with the mining deals that Mobutu had recently called into
question. In return, the Mauritian mining magnate was supposed to dole out
an $80 million down payment, a quarter of which he reportedly advanced to the
AFDL.[7]

Other mining executives soon followed Boulle's lead. The Swedish venture
capitalist Alfred Lundin, who, like Boulle, had already been in negotiations with
Mobutu's government, began talks with the AFDL over the country's greatest
mining prize, the Tenke Fungurume mine, in March 1997. Tenke was widely ac-
claimed as the largest copper mine in the world, with an estimated $26 billion

in copper reserves. Lundin gave the rebels $50 million up front as a down payment, which was supposed to go to the state mining company.[8] "There are moments in the history of mining when you can make deals like this under excellent terms," Lundin said at the time.[9] Indeed, the terms were not bad: In return for $250 million paid to the Congolese state and a $1.5 billion investment in making the mine functional, Lundin would be able to operate tax-free and retain a 55 percent share in the mine.[10]

Were these deals illegal? Possibly. After World War II various war crime tribunals found German and Japanese companies guilty of crimes of pillage, either through the direct seizing of assets or by buying goods that had been stolen by others. In one case, for example, the U.S. military tribunal at Nuremberg found the manager of a German mining company guilty for having carried out excavation in a coal mine in Poland that he had been granted by the Nazi government.[11] In the Congo, Boulle and Lundin also signed deals with rebels, not with the legitimate government. Moreover, the cash down payments—amounting to perhaps $70 million—came at a crucial time for the rebellion, two months before it reached the capital, covering the cost of the final push.

～:～

The Congo is often referred to as a geological scandal. This is not an exaggeration. In the late 1980s, it was the world's largest producer of cobalt, third largest producer of industrial diamonds, and fifth largest producer of copper. It has significant uranium reserves—infamous for having contributed to the Hiroshima bombs—as well as large gold, zinc, tungsten, and tin deposits.

Like so many of the country's problems, the mismanagement of these assets dates back to colonial times. In 1906 already, the Belgian government gave the Société générale de Belgique, a powerful trust affiliated to the state, a mining tract of 13,000 square miles in Katanga, the size of Belgium.[12] Under the exceedingly favorable terms of the deal, the company would get a ninety-nine-year monopoly over any mineral deposits it could identify in the next six years. It was also granted the management of the state railroad line that would help export the copper and cobalt ore, for which the colonial state would provide local labor. Société générale set about creating the three most powerful companies in the Belgian Congo: the Upper Katanga Mining Union, the Bas-Congo to Katanga Railroad Company, and the International Forest and Mining Company.

Mineral and agricultural exports from the Congo fueled the creation of some of the biggest Belgian conglomerates and personal fortunes, developing the Antwerp port and creating a copper smelting industry.

Mobutu nationalized the Upper Katanga Mining Union in 1967 and rebranded it Gécamines, while other mining companies in the Kivus and Katanga were also converted into state-owned enterprises. The government proceeded to use the mining company as a cash cow, systematically milking it for money to fund Mobutu's patronage network instead of reinvesting earnings in infrastructure and development. In order to carry out this scheme, the autocrat forced all mineral exports to be sold through a state mineral board, which would then hand over its revenues to the state treasury. Nonetheless, thanks to rising world copper prices, Gécamines remained the country's largest source of employment and income, providing over 37,000 jobs at its peak, running thirteen hospitals and clinics, and contributing to between 20 and 30 percent of state revenues.

A confluence of factors brought about Gécamines' demise in the 1990s. Copper prices plunged as low-cost producers such as Chile stepped up production and world demand dipped. The army pillages of 1991 and 1993, along with the ethnic purging of Kasaians from Katanga in 1993, drove much of the experienced expatriate staff out of Gécamines and contributed to the cutting of foreign development aid that had helped prop up the ailing mining sector. Finally, the years of mismanagement took their toll. In 1990, the huge underground Kamoto mine collapsed, leading to an abrupt drop in production of 23 percent. Exports declined from a high of 465,000 tons in 1988 to 38,000 tons just before the war, while cobalt production slipped from 10,000 to 4,000 tons in the same period. Similar trends affected all other mineral exports, leading to a vertiginous contraction of the country's GDP by 40 percent between 1990 and 1994.

Pressured by donors to relinquish the state's grip on the economy and desperate for revenues, Mobutu allowed his prime minister, Kengo wa Dondo, to begin gradually privatizing the mining sector in 1995. Most of the contracts that were later negotiated with the AFDL, including the American Mineral Fields and Lundin agreements, were amendments to and confirmations of deals that had already been struck with Mobutu's government in 1996. The notion that the war was fueled by international mining capital eager to get its hands on the Congo's wealth does not hold water; the war slowed down privatization of the sector by a decade, as insecurity and administrative chaos prevented large corporations from investing. It was not until 2005 that major new contracts in Katanga were approved and investors began to invest significant funds.

∾:∾

Kabila's antipathy toward free-market capitalism shone through in other ways. The rebellion applied its half-Marxist, half-liberal approach to mining, adopting a slipshod policy that imposed harsh conditions on large foreign companies while favoring shadowy investors who often lacked the resources and expertise necessary to develop mining concessions. Kabila was not happy with the huge copper and cobalt deposits that had been doled out—according to the government, the president had never actually put pen to paper on the deal—to American Mineral Fields, and he suspended the negotiations. His minister of mining accused two of the biggest mining companies, De Beers and Anglo American, of "monopolism" and "lack of social responsibility" and stripped them of some of their Congolese assets.[13] The government began demanding that any foreign investor provide 15 percent of the planned investments as a nonrefundable cash payment up front and that they keep the involvement of expatriate staff to a strict minimum. It put the largest existing mine, the collapsed Kamoto polygon, up to an open tender but then forced the six companies that applied to work together as a consortium to develop the asset. Not surprisingly, the deal collapsed. "C'était un désastre," a Gécamines official told me, holding his head in his hands. "Laurent Kabila? Mon Dieu."

Soon, however, this approach had exhausted itself. Together with his Rwandan partners, Kabila revived an idea he had from his days as a *maquisard* in the 1970s and created a parastatal company called the Mixed Import-Export Company (COMIEX). Before arriving in Kinshasa in May 1997, Kabila had funneled a total of at least $31 million in private and state capital into COMIEX accounts at two Rwandan banks in Kigali.[14] The funds included the $25 million down payment from Lundin, $3.5 million from the state mining company, and several hundred thousand dollars from a state coffee plantation in North Kivu.

The idea of creating a large holding company to manage the ruling elite's interests in the economy was not a new idea. In Rwanda, the RPF ruling party had a wide-ranging network of investments in banking, real estate, and industry through companies such as Tristar and Prime Holdings. In Ethiopia, the government would pursue a similar model. This allowed the government to dominate and benefit from the private sector without having to subject its activities and financial transactions to the public scrutiny required of state-owned companies. COMIEX initially functioned as the rebels' bank, but Kabila did not fuse the company with the Central Bank when he came to power in Kinshasa. "COMIEX was never registered as a parastatal and put under the official control of the state," Mabi Mulumba, the auditor general at the time, remembered. "It was a private trust run by people close to President Kabila, but entirely created with state assets."[15]

One of Kabila's lawyers remembers having warned the president against funding a private company with state resources. The president laughed and told him, "But this law you are talking about, it is man who made it, no?"[16]

∾∶∾

When the second Congo war broke out on August 2, 1998, President Laurent Kabila knew that he didn't have the resources or the army to beat back the Rwandan troops who were rapidly approaching the capital. Their indigence was underscored when Kabila sent an urgent delegation to Luanda to plead for military assistance to repel the Rwandan offensive. "First pay us the debt that you owe us," the Angolan foreign minister told the envoys, referring to a $6 million debt Kabila owed for military support during the first war.[17] The Congolese government also owed the Zimbabwean government over $5 million for deliveries of weapons and equipment, and it was clear that neither country would be willing to spend the resources needed without something in return.

Like an entrepreneur trying to fend off bankruptcy, Kabila started putting up his country's most valuable assets as collateral to secure further loans. He transformed COMIEX into a sprawling conglomerate that struck up partnerships with the Zimbabwean and Angolan state in massive timber, petroleum, mining, banking, and agricultural projects. In Harare, President Mugabe copied his comrade's business plan, setting up his own privately registered, state-run hybrid called, somewhat ironically, Operation Sovereign Legitimacy (OSLEG), through which he intended to funnel investments and any eventual profits.

The assets involved were enormous: OSLEG went in fifty-fifty with COMIEX in a timber business that received 3,800 square miles from the Congolese state to log, as well as in Sengamines, one of the country's most lucrative diamond concessions. Several banks were set up to manage the cash flows to and from these various projects, and shares in the front companies were reserved for parliamentarians and ministers in both governments.[18] The management of Mugabe's corporation OSLEG included the commander of the Zimbabwean Defense Forces, General Vitalis Zvinavashe, as well as the minister of defense, along with top officials in the state mining company and minerals marketing board.[19]

This kind of business climate favored enterprising, rough-mannered, and unscrupulous businessmen. Billy Rautenbach fit this mold. A former race car driver and the son of a wealthy Zimbabwean trucking magnate, Rautenbach took over the family business when his older brother died in an accident, and he set up lucrative car dealerships throughout southern Africa. He was known for his sharp temper. "He used to run the company by yelling at people. All day he would yell at people," a former business associate told me.[20] Over the years, he accumulated charges in South African courts ranging from customs fraud to theft to involvement in the murder of a former business rival. The murder charges were later dropped and Rautenbach eventually settled for the fraud charges, paying $5.8 million in fines.[21]

In September 1998, Laurent Kabila's government handed the entire Central Mining Group over to Rautenbach to manage as part of a deal with its Zimbabwean allies. Gécamines officials lamented Rautenbach's bad temper and the fact that he cherry-picked the best ore, instead of systematically excavating the rock, which damaged the long-term profitability of his Kakanda mine. "He brought in these new machines that weren't appropriate for the job," one Gécamines official who was there at the time complained, "and picked holes throughout the concessions. It looked like a half-exploded minefield!"[22] Mining analysts were particularly outraged with the immense size of the concession that Rautenbach had obtained. There was no way that he would be able to work on more than a small part of the concession. In the meantime, some of the most lucrative copper and cobalt deposits in Africa lay fallow.

President Kabila was initially happy with Rautenbach's performance, as he was one of the few people who seemed to be able to squeeze any profit out of the various moribund state-run companies, and just months later made him the director of Gécamines. "Kabila would be on the phone every week with Rautenbach, asking him for more money for the war," one Gécamines employee remembered.

Rautenbach did not perform poorly at first. By one estimate, he made $20 million from the Kababankola processing facility alone over eighteen months, while in Likasi he was processing 150 tons of cobalt a month, worth $6 million.[23] "He kicked ass, got people to work, and cranked out production," another mining executive remembered.[24] However, Rautenbach was out to make quick cash, as was the government, and did not reinvest much of his earnings into the upkeep of infrastructures. By the end of 1999, Gécamines' mineral production had fallen, and creditors were seizing shipments in order to pay back debts. Moreover, Rautenbach had made powerful enemies by laying off 11,000 state workers and canceling all previous marketing agreements for cobalt, transferring them to one London-based company. In March 2000, Kabila replaced the Zimbabwean with a local businessman.

Similar deals proliferated, usually featuring dubious businessmen and get-rich-quick schemes. In 2000, John Bredenkamp, a Zimbabwean arms dealer who has been involved in busting sanctions on Zimbabwe, obtained six concessions with estimated mineral reserves of $1 billion. He gave a down payment of $400,000 and promised 68 percent of net profits to the Congolese and Zimbabwean governments. The same year, another South African entrepreneur with a criminal record, Niko Shefer, met with President Kabila and obtained a deal to trade diamonds through Thorntree Industries, a joint venture with the Zimbabwean army. Shefer's rap sheet included setting up a pyramid scheme with an evangelical church in Florida and a five-year prison sentence for fraud in South Africa. This time, Shefer was intent on taking advantage of a discrepancy between the official and the black-market exchange rates in the Congo to profit from diamond trading. A South African intelligence report details a conversation between Shefer and a potential business partner:

> The official exchange rate is currently $1 = CF [Congolese Francs] 4.5. The unofficial (referred to as "parallel") rate is $1 = CF 28. Most foreign imports come in at the parallel rate. KABILA has agreed that Thorntree can buy Congolese Francs at $1 = CF 16 whilst diamond and gold purchasing will be conducted at the official rate. This mechanism will create huge margins that will give Thorntree a distinct advantage over its competitors. KABILA agreed to this proposal because he will personally receive 30 per cent of Thorntree's discount. SHEFER estimates that CF 40 to 60 million a month will be needed to cover the requirements of initial buying operations. . . .

The potential margin is very attractive. For example, at the end of November [1999], I saw a package of 3000 carats, 80% gemstones, bound for
the Oman-backed company. The parcel was worth $2.5 million; they paid
the CF equivalent of $200,000.[25]

It is difficult to know exactly how much money the various actors involved
made. According to UN estimates, between 1998 and 2001 the Congolese government took roughly a third of Gécamines' profit to fund the war effort, sending tens of millions of dollars to the Zimbabwean government to cover its
military expenses.[26] The International Monetary Fund, working from incomplete budgetary data that probably excluded some revenue, concluded that at
the height of the war in 2000, the Congolese government was spending 70 percent of its expenditures on "sovereign and security items," a budget line that was
managed entirely by the presidency and dedicated mostly to the war.[27] That
amounted to over $130 million for that year alone. Some money also went di-
rectly to paying the Zimbabwean army—both Rautenbach and Bredenkamp
gave money directly to Zimbabwean army commanders to pay for their bonuses,
as well as for food and medicine for the soldiers.[28]

Other money transfers circumvented the Congolese state and went straight
to Harare. According to one account, Rautenbach sent between $1.5 and $2 million a month to government officials back home.[29] According to several high-
ranking Zimbabwean officials, when Rautenbach was removed from the
leadership of Gécamines in March 2000, he threatened to reveal exactly how
much President Mugabe and Justice Minister Mnangagwa had made during his
tenure at the Congolese parastatal.[30]

In the end, like everything in the Congo at the time, the Zimbabwean profiteering degenerated into a piecemeal approach, as Zimbabwean government officials took advantage of their military links to conduct private business. In
October 1998, state-owned Zimbabwean Defense Industries obtained a $53
million contract to supply the Congolese government with food and equipment,
much of which would be transported by General Zvinavashe's private transport
company.[31] The head of the state weapons manufacturer, Colonel Tshinga Dube,
also took advantage of his contact in the Congo to set up his eponymous diamond mining company, Dube Associates—apparently not too concerned with
hiding his conflict of interest—in the Kasai province, although without much
success.[32]

By the time of the second Congo war, Mugabe was beleaguered by trade union strikes, food riots, and mounting inflation. He had also just embarked on a move that would come to dominate the next decade of Zimbabwean politics and bring him enemies from all corners of domestic and international politics: the expropriation of 45 percent of the country's commercial farmland from its mostly white owners. After eighteen years in power, some of his former allies had begun to openly question his leadership. Dzikamayi Mavhaire, a powerful parliamentarian, moved to amend the constitution, arguing that Mugabe should be limited to two five-year terms. "The president must go," he told an open session of Parliament. The government *Herald* newspaper also began running surprisingly critical editorials, fustigating the land redistribution policy.[33]

In this context Mugabe was eager to maintain the loyalty of key allies, particularly in the security services. As the economy at home shrunk, so did opportunities for domestic patronage. The Congo war provided the opportunity he needed to keep his collaborators happy and busy elsewhere. This explains the urgency with which the Congolese and Zimbabweans set up their joint ventures and how easily Zimbabwean officials gave up on getting their debts reimbursed through the mining ventures.

∽:∼

At the end of the day, and despite the considerable profits that some Zimbabwean businessmen and officers made, Operation Sovereign Legitimacy did not get a good return on its investments in the Congo. Lured by the promise of vast mineral deposits, the Zimbabwean generals did not realize that rich veins of turquoise copper and blue cobalt were locked up in layers of granite and slate. Unable to finance the billions of dollars of infrastructure rehabilitation and investment needed, Zimbabwe had to content itself with smaller deals—slag heaps, artisanal diamond production, and small-scale mining. Many loans given to the Congolese government were never paid back, and Rautenbach, like other clever businessmen, preempted much of his profits going to Harare through some accounting technicalities. He would sell the ore to one of his offshore holding companies at production price, reducing any profits that could have been taxed by the Congolese state or shared with his Zimbabwean backers to almost zero.[34] "Zimbabwe ended up with the dirty end of the stick," Professor Kampata, an official in the Congolese ministry of mines, told me. "The Congo, at least, got what it wanted: military assistance."[35]

The Zimbabweans did not want to invest the billions of dollars needed to get the various diamond mines, copper processors, and timber mills up and working again. In the Senga Senga diamond mine, the Zimbabwean-appointed managers tried to run the elaborate mining equipment on diesel, which they imported over thousands of kilometers, instead of investing in repairing the nearby hydroelectric plant. At the Kababankola mine, Bredenkamp's managers contented themselves with carting off and processing the tailings and slag heaps that were left over from previous mining operations; any further excavation was deemed too expensive. The Zimbabwean Electricity Supply Authority thought it could make money through hydroelectric power production on the Congo River, but here again they would have had to invest billions in refurbishing turbines and setting up power lines.[36] As for the enormous logging concession in northern Katanga, the Zimbabwean managers could not attract the investors they needed to buy trucks and, above all, fix the hundreds of miles of roads that were needed to export the timber.

The promised mining El Dorado failed to materialize.

~:~

As Kinshasa leveraged its copper, cobalt, and diamond mines to obtain Zimbabwean support, the Rwandans and their RCD allies funded their military operations in the Congo largely by trading in Congo's gold, coltan (used for capacitors in cell phones and video game consoles), tin, and diamonds. The key difference is that a racket run largely by Rwandans and their allies, not by Kinshasa, was perceived as foreign exploitation, a strange distinction given that Laurent Kabila had been brought to power by the Rwandans and had not been confirmed by elections.

To understand mining in the eastern Congo, airports are a good place to start. Given the collapse of roads and railways in the country, planes were often the only way to get from one place to another.

Pierre Olivier was an institution in Goma.[37] The son of a local chief who had worked for the Belgian colonial administration, he has chestnut-colored eyes and big, muscular features that make his limbs seem oversized, almost bloated. I got to know him over several years; he could often be found on local soccer fields on the weekend, protecting the goal line and chatting with friends. He had been taught to fly by his father, who had had a passion for hunting. In the late 1970s, when the hinterlands of the Kivus only hosted a quarter of its current population, they would take a small Cessna to overgrown airstrips in the jungles of Walikale and Maniema to camp out in the wilderness and hunt for antelope and hippopotamus. In some places, pygmy trackers with bows and poison arrows would accompany them; once, he remembered, a local chief with a feathery headdress came to meet them, borne on a palanquin.

By age fourteen, Pierre had learned to fly and shoot a double-barreled shotgun. When he was sixteen, he and his father founded their own airplane company, flying merchandise into jungle towns to the west of Goma and taking bags of minerals and palm oil out. They would land on roads and on bumpy, dirt airstrips overgrown with elephant grass. "Back then, our only problem was paying off Mobutu's thugs," he said, laughing. "That was problem enough."[38]

∽:∾

As soon as the second war started in August 1998, it was clear that there had been a shift in motivation. "Business," Olivier said emphatically. "The first war had been about getting rid of the refugee camps and overthrowing Mobutu. The second was about business."

The security imperative was still present for Rwanda. The northwest of their country was engulfed in a brutal insurgency, led by Rwarakabije's Hutu rebels. But the second war was a much more costly exercise, involving up to 35,000 Rwandan soldiers who became bogged down in trench and counterinsurgency warfare hundreds of miles into the Congolese jungle. In addition, some Rwandan businessmen, together with leading RPF politicians, had become aware that there were hefty profits to be made in the Congo, particularly in the minerals trade.

Rwanda's shifting priorities became clear to Pierre in his flights. He flew their troops into mining areas, where Rwandan commanders would be in charge of loading tons of tin and coltan into airplanes. Pierre proceeded to count towns off on his thick fingers: "Lulingu, Punia, Kalima, Kindu, Walikale—we emptied the minerals stockpiled there at the beginning of the second war. There was so much ore, it took us weeks."[39]

This first phase of profiteering targeted the low-hanging fruit, assets that were easily converted into cash. Between November 1998 and April 1999, the Rwandan army and its RCD allies removed between 2,000 and 3,000 tons of tin ore and up to 1,500 tons of coltan from the warehouses of SOMINKI, a state-run mining company active in the Kivus, worth between $10 and $20 million, depending on the grade of the ore.[40] The Congolese commander of the RCD troops, Jean-Pierre Ondekane, brazenly entered the Central Bank offices in Kisangani and seized between $1 million and $8 million in Congolese francs, which he then dispatched to Kigali.[41] Similar looting was carried out in the area controlled by the Ugandan army.

For the most part, this initial pillage targeted state companies and large businessmen. In many towns the Rwandan troops were relatively disciplined and even arrested or executed soldiers who stole. The occupying army, however, had a difficult time maintaining logistics chains into the deep Congolese forest, and they often granted advancing columns the right to sustain themselves through pillage. A Belgian missionary based in Kongolo, northern Katanga, described the arrival of Rwandan troops there:

> Going from house to house, they first stole everything they could find for food, including goats and chickens. For firewood, they took furniture that they found in the houses, even the cradles! Afterwards, as they were installing themselves for a long period, they stole beds, mattresses and sheets. They also got their hands on generators and heavy material, sending these home to Rwanda by road and air. . . . They took more than five hundred gallons of fuel and two vehicles belonging to the medical service, not to mention the beating and injury of the parish priest and the theft of his belongings.[42]

The occupying forces then set up structures through which they could extract new resources. In the area occupied by the Rwandans, this was done systematically, by controlling all stages of mineral production, from the digging to air transport to the export company in Kigali. The Rwandan army sent hundreds of prisoners—mostly Hutu who had been accused of taking part in the genocide—from jails in western Rwanda to work in coltan, gold, and tin mining pits. "You should have seen the look on the faces of those people," Pierre said, recalling the ones he transported. "They were sad, exhausted, depressed." Elsewhere, the diggers came voluntarily and were paid for their work, but were often supervised by soldiers. At the landing strips, it was always Rwandan soldiers or their RCD allies who accompanied the shipments of coltan and cassiterite (un-refined tin ore).

According to Pierre, only several businessmen close to Kigali were allowed to ship minerals out from the Rwandan-controlled mines. "They monopolized the mines," he insisted. Benjamin Serukiza, the former RCD vice governor of South Kivu, confirmed this: "I had to mediate between local businessmen and the Rwandan brigade commander here. He only wanted to allow one Rwandan trader, who was close to the Rwandan government, to have access to the mine. He said it was for security reasons, but we knew it wasn't."[43]

~:~

The initial profits, however, were nothing compared to what was to come. "Everything changed in 2000, when the coltan price soared," Pierre Olivier re-membered. It was a fluke. That year, the information technology bubble coin-cided with heightened demand for cell phones and the Christmas release of a Sony PlayStation console. Demand for tantalum, the processed form of coltan, had been rising steadily for years, but now the markets got caught up in a buying frenzy. Within months, the local market price of tantalum shot up from $10 to $380 per kilo, depending on the percentage of ore content, while the world price peaked at $600 per kilo of refined tantalum.[44] Dozens of *comptoirs*—mineral trading houses—opened up in Bukavu and Goma to take advantage of the coltan rush.

That rush injected millions into the local economy. Exports from the eastern Congo and Rwanda soared to somewhere between $150 and $240 million in 2000 alone, and profit margins were high.[45] Cities in the region were flush with cash, and wild rumors circulated of small-time traders becoming millionaires within months. As most Congolese do not have domestic bank accounts, their investments went overseas or were put into local real estate, fueling a construc-tion boom. Everywhere you looked there was scaffolding made out of eucalyptus saplings, especially along the popular lakefront properties. The nightclubs were full, and patrons paying in hundred-dollar bills were not uncommon.

Olivier had his own stories of opulence. In 2000, in the middle of the coltan boom, he flew to Kigali, where a sullen man in a cheap suit boarded the plane with a jeep-load of battered cardboard boxes, sealed with cheap tape. It was evening, and the man insisted on sleeping onboard the airplane, along with several of his

bodyguards, before flying to Bukavu the following day. It was only when his cus-
tomer was disembarking that the strange man approached him with an impish
smile and confided to him: He had been sleeping on $15 million in Congolese
and U.S. bills, he cackled, and hurried off. "Cash flow," Olivier said, shaking his
head, "was always a huge problem. The banks didn't work, so people had to travel
with tens of thousands of dollars on them."

~:~

The coltan price stayed high between June 2000 and July 2001, producing record
profits for the RCD, the Rwandan government, and their business associates.
Some researchers estimate that net profits made by Rwandan companies could
have been as high as $150 million for this period for coltan alone, while other
researchers calculate total profits made off the minerals trade at $250 million
per annum throughout their occupation.[46] For Rwanda, whose entire annual
budget was $380 million at the time, this income made its expensive involvement
in the Congo possible. President Kagame himself described their involvement
in the Congo as "self-sustaining."[47] He was more than right. Rwanda's official
military budget was $55 million in 2001, almost a third of total spending, but
the London-based International Institute for Security Studies put the real
amount at $135 million.[48]

But was it just about sordid greed? Were the vampires sucking blood just to
quench their grisly thirst, or was there a more nuanced explanation? Individual
Rwandan commanders did get rich—it was difficult not to notice the influx of
luxury SUVs and the construction of elegant houses in Kigali during the war.
Nevertheless, for the most part, the profits facilitated the war. The Rwandan
government had an army of 60,000 soldiers to pay and supply. At the same time,
the regime was facing its own political challenges. Its first two prime ministers
had defected, along with dozens of high court judges, ministers, diplomats, army
officers, and even soccer players. They all protested widespread abuses by the
security services, a repressive political climate, and a general authoritarian drift.
Like many one-party regimes that faced stiff opposition, the Rwandan Patriotic
Front increasingly resorted to patronage and repression to deal with dissent.

"It would be a mistake to see this just as personal greed," the former high-
ranking RCD officer told me. "They were very organized; they provided military
escorts to mineral shipments so that we couldn't stop them at the border; they

decided which businessmen could do business. But I also saw Rwandan officers jailed and beaten for having stolen money!"[49] Indeed, according to one human rights report, despite the profits coming out of the Congo, civil servants in Rwanda were asked to give up to one month's salary per annum as contribution to the war effort.[50] For many Rwandans, from the presidency down to the school teacher, the war in the Congo was an ideological project, not just an opportunity to plunder.

The government set up a Congo Desk within the external intelligence office that dealt with all aspects of Congo operations. Anyone interested in doing business in the Congo would have to pass through the Congo Desk, which would help them with security and to obtain tax exemptions. "There were many Rwandan businessmen who came to the Congo to do business—this is true," Patrick Karegeya, who as intelligence chief played a key role in providing protection, told me. "But it was all legal business, there was nothing illegal about it."[51]

Nonetheless, many of these companies had close family or financial ties to the Rwandan government, employing army officers as directors or allotting substantial shares to the party. Rwanda Metals, a company that the ruling party controlled, was the main buyer of minerals from the eastern Congo, and the managing director was appointed directly by the presidency. There was also a host of smaller companies, such as Great Lakes General Trade, which was co-managed by Major Dan Munyuza, an influential RPA officer who worked for the external intelligence office. The chief of security for Rwanda in the Congo, Major Jean Bosco Kazura, was a partner in another Kigali-based company that imported coffee and diamonds from the Congo. According to UN investigators, General James Kabarebe himself would sometimes coordinate the purchase and transport of coltan, tin, and gold through Rwanda.[52]

∾:∾

"I was just doing business," Pierre responded when I asked him if he had any regrets about working with the rebels and mining companies during the war. That is the usual refrain echoed by businessmen throughout the war zone. "In any case," the burly pilot continued, "all the flights for the rebels we did were pretty much at gunpoint."

It was difficult not to believe the good-natured pilot. He laughed. The subtext read: Of course you had to cut corners, bribe people, deal with dubious clientele.

But this is the Congo—if we didn't get our hands dirty once in a while, we would be out of business.

He had a point. According to a World Bank study, if you paid all of your taxes in the Congo—a full thirty-two different payments—you would be dishing out 230 percent of your profits.[53] In other words, you can only survive by cutting corners. The tax system had lost its overall coherence, as revenue-collecting agencies had proliferated over the years, each using exorbitant tax rates as blackmail to obtain bribes. The tax code was never intended to be followed; the state had created regulations that begged to be broken and had dreamt up its own subversion, pushing a large part of the economy into the informal sector so that individuals could profit.

The individuals who profited were, obviously, those in charge. During rebel rule in the eastern Congo, the businessmen who prospered were, for the most part, those who curried favor with the political and military leaders. "We all had our friends in the rebel high command we could call up when we had problems," Pierre Olivier said. "They needed us because we flew for them. We needed them because they were the bosses." Did he feel uncomfortable about this symbiosis? "That's the way things work. Did I have a choice?"

Business in the Congo required a healthy dose of pragmatism. For many, cut-and-dry morality was out of place here. This conundrum became clear to international charities, as well, which set up their bases in Goma to provide food and health care to victims of the violence. Many rented the houses of businessmen close to the rebels, as they, of course, had the nicest compounds with sumptuous gardens, often overlooking the lake. Humanitarian groups also used trucking companies and shopped for groceries in stores linked to the military enterprise. It was almost impossible to avoid.

～:～

Similar moral dilemmas affect affluent western consumers, as well. It wasn't just Congolese and Rwandans who made a fortune. The minerals were transported, processed, and consumed by companies and consumers elsewhere, especially in Europe, Asia, and the United States. In some cases, these companies had close relationships with rebel groups. For example, the Belgium-based company Cogecom bought tin and coltan directly from the RCD monopoly, sending money into RCD coffers. Another joint venture by American and Dutch businessmen, Eagle Wings Resources, engaged Paul Kagame's brother-in-law as its local representative, which gave it easier and cheaper access to the Congolese minerals. These companies then sold their minerals on to large processing companies, including U.S.-based Cabot Corporation, Chinese Ningxia, and German H. C. Starck. The transport was assured by multinational logistics companies such as the state airline of Belgium, Sabena, while financing was supplied by large regional banks and, in one case, by Citibank.[54]

This supply chain was unearthed by UN investigators and other analysts, triggering an immediate reaction from international business circles. Some denied allegations outright; others protested that there was nothing illegal about buying or transporting minerals from the eastern Congo. This is partly true. International law does little to regulate human rights abuses associated with trade. The Organization for Economic Co-operation and Development (OECD) put forward Guidelines for Multinational Enterprises, but these are voluntary, and violations have few consequences. Some countries, like the United States, have domestic laws that can be used to hold companies based there responsible for their conduct overseas. A wave of lawsuits, for example, was filed in U.S. courts in the 1990s and 2000s based on the Alien Torts Statute, but plaintiffs have to prove that companies had not only knowledge of abuse but also intent, which is difficult to prove even about companies directly involved with rebels, let alone those four steps removed along the supply chain. Some international lawyers argue that companies can be held liable under international law for buying misappropriated goods, much the way one can be charged in domestic courts for purchasing stolen goods, but this logic has not gained much traction outside of UN tribunals.[55]

In other words, consumers are not held responsible for the conditions under which minerals are produced. In the Congo, despite the occasional hue and cry raised by the media, corporate responsibility has been largely ignored—the supply chain is more convoluted, passing through traders, brokers, smelters, and processing companies. The tin and coltan that come from the Congo are mixed with those from Brazil, Russia, and China before they make it into our cell phones and laptops. There is a burgeoning consensus in international law that we should care about the conditions under which the products we consume—sweatpants, sneakers, and even timber—are produced. If we can hold companies accountable for their business practices, we will give an incentive to the Congolese government to clean up the mining sector. The "conflict minerals" legislation signed into law by President Obama in July 2010 is a step, albeit a small one, in the right direction.

PART IV

NEITHER WAR
NOR PEACE

⊹ 20 ⊹

THE BEARER OF EGGS

KINSHASA, CONGO, JANUARY 2001

There are several versions of the story of how Joseph Kabila was chosen to succeed his father. A popular one goes as follows: The day after Laurent Kabila's assassination, the inner cabal of the presidency meets to decide who would become president. Around a table are the Who's Who of Congolese power politics: Katangan strongmen, the high brass of the army, and the regime's economic kingpins.

A cacophony ensues as the group argues over who is best suited for the job. Gaetan was Kabila's favorite, one claims; Victor has the best ties to Angola and Zimbabwe, another suggests.[1] Finally, as the tensions reach a climax and the country teeters on the brink of civil war, General Sylvestre Lwetcha, the old, frail commander of the armed forces and a renowned witch doctor, bangs his fist on the table.

"Silence!" The general, who had fought side-by-side with Laurent Kabila during the bush rebellion, pulls out his side arm, a Magnum nine-millimeter pistol, cocks it to his temple, and shoots himself six times. Smoke billows up around his head, filling the room, as his colleagues cough and wave their hands in disbelief.

When the smoke clears, the bulletproof general slams his pistol down on the table, slowly clears his throat, and says, "I have decided that General Joseph Kabila will become president of the Democratic Republic of the Congo!" He looks around the table slowly and asks calmly, "Are there any questions?"

~::~

Of course, this is not what really happened. The truth is buried under hundreds of competing rumors and may never be entirely uncovered. But according to various people who took part in the meetings, the following is as accurate as we might get.

On the morning following Mzee's death, his closest associates met at the City of the African Union, a sprawling complex of government buildings overlooking the Congo river. Edy Kapend, Laurent Kabila's powerful military advisor, presided over the meeting.[2] The president's taciturn son Joseph had flown in the previous night from Lubumbashi, still in shock.

Kapend began by reminding everybody of an oral will that the deceased president had given his close associates several years earlier, when he was suffering from a severe illness. "He told us that in case he died, his son Joseph was supposed to take power," Kapend reminded the small group. Several people nodded. Others contested the will, claiming that Joseph was only supposed to take command of the military, while the political leadership should be handed to someone else. Let's set up a special committee to study the matter, someone else suggested.

A debate ensued in the air-conditioned rooms, which Kapend cut short by pulling down a military map of the eastern Congo. Bold, red arrows marked where the Rwandan offensive was threatening Lubumbashi and Mbuji-Mayi. "We can debate this all night if you like, but if we are weak and divided, our enemies will take advantage. We need to decide now."

After some squabbling, everyone in the room realized there was little choice. They needed someone who could command the respect of the army and their allies alike. If they chose anyone else besides Joseph, the government was at risk of collapsing into internecine fighting. Joseph was young, shy, and practically unknown on the political scene, but this could be a good thing. "The logic was: The weaker the person we chose, the less he was likely to be contested, as they thought they could influence him," one of the people who attended the meeting told me.[3]

The ayatollahs of the Congolese government were in for a surprise. The weak, introverted successor turned out to be much smarter and more independent than anybody had suspected. Within a year of his nomination, Joseph would rid himself of almost everybody who had put him in power. He also launched a peace process, setting the gears in motion to bring an end to the war and paving the way for elections.

⌒∶∾

It would have been difficult to find someone more different from his father than Joseph Kabila. Where his father was authoritarian and confrontational, Joseph was shy and reclusive. In his first speech to the nation on January 26, 2001, he stumbled through his prewritten text in halting, uninspired French. He was not very fluent, as he had grown up mostly in Tanzania and was more comfortable in Swahili and English. Several days later, he asked an advisor to help him through his first meeting with the diplomatic corps. "You do the talking," he said uneasily.[4]

For the Congolese public, the contrast was jolting. "He doesn't smoke, doesn't drink, doesn't like going out to dinner, doesn't have a large wardrobe, doesn't have a lot of good friends, and doesn't speak the languages of the people he's going to govern," an American reporter observed.[5] In an early television interview in the United States—he avoided the press in his home country until he had a better command of French—his expression was wooden, his hands folded in front of him, barely moving when he answered questions.

So who was Joseph Kabila? From the first day of his presidency, the Congolese rumor mill began churning. As usual, most of the talk was not about government affairs, but about his ethnicity and origins. He wasn't the real son of his father, some said. He is really Tanzanian, others tattled—he can't speak French. Or even: He killed his own father to take power!

⌒∶∾

Joseph Kabila and his twin sister, Janet, were born in Mpiki, South Kivu, on June 4, 1971, in the grass-thatched rebel headquarters of his father. Overlooking the camp was the so-called Mlima ya damu, the Mountain of Blood, named for the battles that had taken place there against Mobutu's army.

Most agree that Joseph is the son of Laurent Kabila. The deep attachment between the two attests to this: Mzee doted on Joseph while in office and elevated him from a simple soldier to the commander of his army. However, short of DNA testing, the mystery of Joseph and Janet's biological mother will be more difficult to solve.

The official mother, Sifa Mahanya, married the rebel leader in 1970 and would remain his wife until he died, albeit alongside a gaggle of mistresses. She was responsible for the women's wing of the rebellion and a member of the revolutionary courts. It was Mama Sifa, as she is known today, whom most of Mzee's former comrades recognize as the mother of the current president.[6]

A second, plausible version is provided by members of Joseph Kabila's entourage. They say that Joseph's mother was a Rwandan Tutsi called Marcelline Mukambuguje, who was one of the many Rwandans who joined Kabila in his *maquis* in the hope of using Zaire as a rear base to overthrow the Hutu-dominated dictatorship in Rwanda. Mukambuguje was allegedly kept from public sight when Laurent Kabila was president in order to prevent the public from discovering Joseph's real mother. A Tutsi mother would obviously not do in a country at war with Rwanda.

As soon as he became president, his alleged mother was bundled away to the United States to live. This is not just Internet apocrypha—although the blogosphere does abound with these rumors—but allegations relayed by people close to the president, including a close former advisor, a bodyguard, and members of his family.[7] Every once in a while, rumors make the rounds among diplomats and the elite in Kinshasa that a mysterious elderly woman was seen in the presidential chambers or gardens. Of course, this version of his parentage is lapped up by the opposition and many Kinois, who think Kabila never stopped working for the Rwandan government, a sort of Tutsi Manchurian candidate.

~:~

Shortly after Joseph's birth, Kabila's troops kidnapped a group of American students from a Tanzanian chimpanzee research project, earning them international infamy. While the rebels did manage to obtain a hefty ransom, Mobutu's army launched a new offensive against Kabila, pushing his soldiers out of their highland redoubt into inhospitable jungles to the west. Given the danger and poor living conditions, Laurent Kabila decided it was best for his family to move to Tanzania, where he had good connections inside the security services.

In Dar es Salaam, Joseph and Janet enrolled in the French school under fake names, pretending to be from a western Tanzanian tribe in order to escape the attention of Zairian intelligence agents active there—Laurent Kabila's deputy was scooped up by such spies and taken to Kinshasa, after which he wasn't heard from again.

According to one of Joseph's classmates, he was intelligent, proficient in English, and an admirer of martial arts and sports cars. Nonetheless, even then he was a silent loner. When he did speak about politics, he liked to discuss the exploits of the heroes of his father's generation—Che Guevara, Thomas Sankara, and Yoweri Museveni.[8]

"The small boy already had the personality of a leader, he dreamed of being a soldier, of leading an army," recalled his mother, Sifa Mahanya, who, according to Tanzanian security sources, was with Joseph during his whole childhood. He used to play with small model cars and trucks in their house, lining them up into military convoys.[9]

Joseph underwent a brief military training in southern Tanzania but spent most of his youth helping his father with his businesses, which for a while included transporting large shipments of fish along Lake Tanganyika. The young man drove trucks for thousands of miles, from Zambia through Tanzania to Uganda.[10]

When Laurent Kabila got in touch with the Rwandan army in 1995 to prepare for the invasion of Zaire, Joseph accompanied him to the meetings. Once the war started, the twenty-five-year-old was entrusted to Colonel James Kabarebe, the Rwandan field commander of operations. The two lived under the same roof and traveled together to the front lines to inspect the troops. Officers remember seeing Joseph Kabila, known as Afande Kabange[11] by his soldiers, everywhere along the front lines, but he rarely spoke. The image that remains for most from that time is of a young man, his military cap pulled low over his sunken eyes, a silent fixture in the room. The war had a serious impact on his psyche. "The worst thing that I have ever seen is the sight of a village after a massacre; you can never erase that from your memory."[12]

After the AFDL's victory, Joseph kept a low profile in Kinshasa. He lived in the same house as several Rwandan commanders and began to explore the capital. He visited the famous bars and nightclubs of Bandal and Matonge, where *ambianceurs* (lovers of the nightlife) and *sapeurs* (dandies) strutted the latest fashion and ate grilled goat washed down with bottles of Primus or Skol beer. Until today, scurrilous Kinois still claim to have drunk beer with Joseph or have seen him trying out a dance move. ("He used to love the women!" some claim. "No! He was too timid, he couldn't even dance." "Alligator skin shoes, that's what he liked. My little brother sold him his first pair!")

In early 1998, his father sent him on a military training course to China; his father had himself once visited the Nanjing military academy decades earlier.

This training, however, was short-lived, as he was called back home when the second war began. Despite his brief military career—at that point, he had served a grand total of three years in military uniform, including a year of basic training in Tanzania—he was promoted to the rank of general and named acting chief of staff of the army.

It was an abrupt change for him; he had had little experience in military operations.[13] Now he commanded tens of thousands of Congolese troops against the very Rwandans who had trained him. As soon as he got off the plane from China, he rushed to defend the capital from his former mentor and friend, James Kabarebe.

Few remember much of Joseph Kabila during the next few years. He rarely met with foreign military advisors, and even in meetings with his own staff he spent most of the time listening. In any case, it is not clear how much power the young general had; his father made many important military decisions, like, for example, the battle for Pweto in 2000, and Zimbabwean and Angolan generals also had strong influence.

The Congolese officer corps was an amalgam of former Mobutu officers, Katangan Tigers trained in Angola, Mai-Mai from the Kivus, and newly recruited child soldiers. Without much experience, the president's son showed he was adept at navigating the tensions between these different groups, making friends and listening to their advice. He established a small coterie of young army officers, some of whom had also gone for training in China—not the most experienced officers, but fiercely loyal to him.

~:~

As much as Joseph admired his father, he also realized that his views were outdated. In his first address to the nation, just days after he had laid his father to rest, Joseph announced a sea change in foreign policy. George W. Bush had just been elected in the United States, and Kabila's message was directed at him: "Without beating around the bush, I recognize there has been mutual misunderstanding with the former administration. The DRC intends to normalize bilateral relations with the new administration."[14] At the same time, he promised to liberalize the diamond trade and float the currency, promote a new mining code, and—most importantly—immediately try to resuscitate the peace process. Several months later, he allowed political parties to operate again. Where his father had governed by ideology, Joseph was a pragmatist.

To underscore his point and to bolster his position, Joseph immediately embarked on a diplomatic offensive. As one political analyst of the region remarked, "Devoid of any national constituency, he had decided to treat the international community as his powerbase."[15] The American ambassador in Kinshasa, William Swing, invited him to take up an invitation to the National Prayer Breakfast in Washington that had been extended to his father. He traveled first to Paris, where he met with President Jacques Chirac, and then on to Washington, where he met with Secretary of State Colin Powell and later, privately, with President Kagame, with whom he discussed the possibility of a peace deal. He finished off his tour with an address to the UN Security Council in New York, all within a few months of becoming president.

His presidency marked an abrupt U-turn in government policy. His father had insisted that the war would be *longue et populaire.* It had been the former, but certainly not the latter. His son immediately abandoned this purely military approach.

After his speech at the UN, diplomats lined up to shake Joseph Kabila's hand and applauded his desire to restart the peace process. His eagerness to comply with the demands of the United Nations put Rwanda on the defensive for the first time since the beginning of the war. Other factors also played in his favor. The American representative to the UN remarked, "We do not believe that Rwanda can secure its long-term security interests via a policy of military opposition to the government of Congo." The British UN ambassador asked President Kagame to bring an end to the plunder of the eastern Congo.[16] Several months later, a UN report concluded that Rwanda and Uganda were plundering the eastern Congo for personal enrichment and in order to finance the war.

The new Kabila was no pacifist. He did not stop fighting with his enemies; he just changed tactics. He largely respected the front line cease-fire but provided weapons and supplies to fuel the Mai-Mai insurgency on his enemies' turf. It was as brilliant in its logic as it was brutal. The ramshackle Mai-Mai were little military threat to the RCD and their Rwandan allies, who had much greater firepower, but they provoked ruthless counterinsurgency operations by Rwanda and its allies, making them even more unpopular. It was typical guerrilla warfare, as practiced by Mao Tsetung and Che Guevara: Keep the enemy swinging with nine-pound sledgehammers at flies.

Suddenly, it was Rwanda and Uganda who were seen as the obstacles to peace. The RCD rebels refused to allow UN peacekeepers to deploy into their territory, seeing it as a "declaration of war," prompting demonstrations against them in Kisangani and Goma.[17] Kabila, on the other hand, urged the Security Council to increase its deployments and to relaunch the investigation into the massacres in the refugee camps that his father had so adamantly blocked.

~:~

Within his own government in Kinshasa, the new president took equally drastic steps. Three months after he came to power, he sacked almost his entire cabinet, including most of the people who had chosen him as his father's successor. The aging generals who had fought side by side with his father since the 1960s received handsome pensions and were retired. In their place, he appointed a new group of technocrats, young Congolese who had not been as tainted by corruption and warmongering. The new finance minister came from the International Monetary Fund, the new information minister was a U.S.-educated journalist. The average age of the new ministers was thirty-eight.[18]

But who was in charge during these turbulent reforms? Who allowed Joseph Kabila to take such drastic steps and reverse his father's policy?

To a certain extent, during the early days of his presidency, the government was guided by Kabila's international partners. Western ambassadors came with wish lists of people they would like to see sacked and made decisions that needed to be made to advance the peace process. Both the Angolans and the Zimbabweans were tired of the war and encouraged Kabila to bring an end to the conflict. After all, most of the population saw the various rebel factions—with the possible exception of Jean-Pierre Bemba's MLC—as foreign proxies and would not vote for them during elections. "Sign a peace deal, stand for elections, and consolidate your power" was the advice of western and African diplomats alike.

In general, Joseph Kabila seemed much less in charge than his father, who had managed state affairs with an iron fist. Joseph was not often seen on television and rarely took charge in cabinet meetings. Where almost of all his father's ministers had spent at least a few days in prison, Joseph almost never arrested any collaborators. Instead he slowly marginalized them if they fell out of favor.

Government officials often did not know where they stood with the president, a style of management that kept everyone guessing. When they went to present projects, he would nod at their comments but not say anything. Thinking that he wanted more explanations, they would expound further, only to be met by more silence or a few words. Encouraged by his polite smiles and silence, they would leave thinking they had succeeded in convincing him, only to find out weeks later that he had canceled the project.

This kind of prevarication often shone through in his contacts with international partners as well. "It used to infuriate Kagame and Museveni," a UN official who attended meetings of the heads of state told me. "Kabila would be silent throughout the meeting; then someone would come and whisper something in his ear, and he would answer."[19]

~:~

Kabila's reticence also marked his personal life. He kept out of the limelight, avoiding cocktail parties and other social events. He would wake up at around 6 o'clock in the morning, check the news and his e-mail, and work out in his exercise room, lifting weights and sweating on his stationary bike. Before he assumed the presidency, he lived in a modest townhouse with his common-law wife, Olive Lemba, a light-skinned woman he had met in the eastern Congo during the AFDL. He doted on his young daughter, Sifa, named after his mother.

Surrounded by well-groomed bureaucrats, Joseph was conscious of his modest background. He began French classes soon after he arrived in Kinshasa and enrolled in an online course in international relations at Washington International University, a small outfit based in King of Prussia, Pennsylvania, from which he obtained a bachelor's degree after completing ten courses online. His French improved considerably, as did his self-confidence.

Diplomats who met him regularly were often impressed by his knowledge of world affairs and understanding of the region. A favorite rhetorical tool he liked to use was to defend his record by comparing the Congo with western countries. "You criticize democracy here, but our elections turnout was over 80 percent— in the U.S., barely half of the voters show up," he told an American diplomat.[20] When confronted with allegations of corruption, he countered with the Enron scandal in the United States and Silvio Berlusconi's manipulation of laws to protect himself from prosecution.

He did not have many close friends. His twin sister, Janet, and his younger brother, Zoé, visited frequently, and a Tanzanian friend showed up from time to time. In the evenings, he would relax in front of the television and play video games with his brother, a habit that earned him the nickname "Nintendo" from a skeptical French ambassador.[21]

He also began to take an interest in designer watches, clothes, and sports cars. On weekends, he relaxed in his Kingakati ranch outside of Kinshasa, drove rally cars around a dirt track, and received a few select diplomats and businessmen. One had the impression of repressed energy, a man looking for a release valve. In Kinshasa, foreigners going for a morning jog along the Congo River—a secluded, leafy area with shady streets and ambassadorial residences—would sometimes be surprised by the young president whizzing by on a motorcycle, followed by a pickup full of sheepish presidential guards. Unfortunately, he could only drive his Maserati around the street outside his presidential house in Kinshasa, and then only up to half its maximum speed; there were too many potholes.

~:~

Joseph Kabila's greatest accomplishment was the peace deal with his rivals. Of course, peace was in his interest, as he was recognized as the incumbent president and controlled the bulk of economic assets and state administration, while his main military rivals were tarnished by their association with Rwanda and Uganda.

In February 2002, after several false starts, Kabila finally met with his main military and political challengers in South Africa for the Inter-Congolese Dialogue, peace talks that would result, after ten months, in a comprehensive deal that would unify the country.

The setting for the Inter-Congolese Dialogue was surreal. The South African government had leased part of the Sun City luxury resort, once an entertainment haven for apartheid South Africa elites. The inaugural ceremony took place in the Entertainment Center's Superbowl area, a stone's throw away from Jungle Casino and the Bridge of Time, gaudy buildings decorated with stone elephants and artificial waterfalls. Three hundred and thirty Congolese delegates spent their free time trolling the slot machines and racking up tabs at the bars.

After two months of talks, on the eve of the deadline fixed by the facilitators, the government and the MLC shocked the conference. Following late-night meetings in a nearby hotel, the two delegations announced that they had reached a bilateral agreement, making Joseph Kabila president and Jean-Pierre Bemba prime minister in the joint government. The talks collapsed in furor, as Kabila and Bemba went back to their respective headquarters to set up the government, while the RCD went back to the trenches.

The deal was bound to fail. Bemba refused to come to Kinshasa to take up his position, citing security concerns. In the meantime, regional fault lines began to shift. Together with their British counterparts, the American diplomats went on the offensive with Rwanda and Uganda. Washington abstained from a vote to renew the International Monetary Fund's loans to Rwanda, while London privately made clear to Kampala that it would not extend further loans if it did not withdraw its troops. In June 2002, President Kagame committed to withdrawing all Rwandan troops within three months. Museveni followed suit in November. Journalists lined up at border posts to see a total of 30,000 foreign troops march across, as crowds of Congolese celebrated.

The RCD and MLC, already destabilized by their allies' withdrawal, further weakened their positions with blunders on the battlefield. In May 2002, RCD commanders brutally put down a mutiny in Kisangani, killing over a hundred sixty civilians. Bodies that had been eviscerated and weighed down with stones floated to the surface in the Congo River in plain sight of journalists and UN investigators. To the north, the MLC launched an attack against a rival faction of the RCD while also deploying troops to support President Patassé in the neighboring Central African Republic. On both fronts, Bemba's soldiers were guilty of egregious human rights violations.

In November, the delegates trudged back to South Africa. This time President Mbeki, wary of prolonging the Sun City circus, took matters into his own hands. Instead of allowing commissions to develop their own power-sharing proposals, Mbeki presented his plan and gave delegates firm deadlines to come back with counterproposals. "Mbeki had a bash-heads-together philosophy," one of the organizers commented. "He told the delegates that if they didn't agree on a solution, he would shut down shop and tell them to go home."[22] Back home, churches and human rights activists demonstrated in streets across the country against their leaders' turpitude. In Bukavu, women marched bare-breasted through the streets in protest.

Mbeki combined strong-arming with copious incentives. While Kabila obtained the presidency as well as a vice president, the RCD and the MLC garnered vice presidential positions, as did the political opposition. Sixty-one ministries, six hundred twenty parliamentary seats, and over fifty state companies would be split up among the signatories. The former belligerents were attracted by a generous sharing of spoils; impunity and corruption were, to a certain extent, the glue holding the fragile peace together. As opposed to other transitions in Sierra Leone and Liberia, where warlords were not allowed to stand for public office, the transition in the Congo stacked the new government with the very people who had plunged the country into internecine conflict. "It was the only way out," Philip Winter, the chief of staff of the Facilitation, remarked later. "Did it compromise the future? Yes. But it was the only way out of a difficult situation."[23]

On December 16, Mbeki submitted a final proposal to the delegates in the plenary session and gave them half an hour to deliberate. An hour later, as the bewildered delegations were still squabbling over clauses and details, he invited Jean-Luc Kuye, the head of the civil society group, to the podium to sign the deal. Under almost physical pressure from their hosts, the remaining delegation heads solemnly filed up to the podium as applause, at first hesitant, began to crescendo behind them. After an all-night session, at 7:30 in the morning, Mbeki asked the delegates to rise and sing the Congolese national anthem. After five years of war and millions of deaths, the country was unified once again.

~:~

Figuring out how power works in Kinshasa is a complicated affair. Foreign businessmen arriving from Europe or China have to spend weeks to get to the right people in government. Connections are everything. *Il a un bon carnet d'adresses*— "He has a good address book"—is high praise from entrepreneurs in the capital.

This institutional weakness of the courts, whose members are appointed by the government, and political parties, who have no traditional base in Congo, has privileged the emergence of a small clique of power brokers around the president, a kitchen cabinet of roughly a dozen individuals with direct access to the president and who help him rule.

This state of affairs developed slowly, during Joseph Kabila's tenure in the army, as he traveled through the country and realized that his father's defiant militarism was going nowhere. He became friends with a group of young, sophisticated Congolese officials, all convinced that Laurent Kabila was on the wrong track, especially in regard to his dismissive attitude of the United States, South Africa, and Europe.

The most important of these Young Turks was Katumba Mwanke. He has since acquired an almost mythical status in Kinshasa court politics as the éminence grise behind the throne. As a young man, he left Zaire to study and work in South Africa as a banker for HSBC Equator Bank. When the war began, he found himself in an ideal position, given his ties with business in South Africa and his family connections. He is married to the sister of Laurent Kabila's former finance minister, and, importantly, he is also from Kabila's home province of Katanga, although not from the same tribe.

Katumba arrived on a mission for his bank in the early days of the rebellion and, because of Laurent Kabila's desperate need for competent officials, was immediately offered a position in the ministry of finance. It was difficult not to like him: He was short, unpretentious, and polite; he spoke with a slight stammer when excited. When the Lunda and Lubakat, the two main ethnic communities in Katanga—both of which claimed Laurent Kabila through his mother and father, respectively—began squabbling over leadership positions in the province in 1998, Kabila asked around for a good Katangan official who was not from either of those communities and had not been a Mobutist. Katumba Mwanke, who is from the minority Zela community, was a perfect fit.

Katumba spent the next three years as the governor of the country's richest province, endearing himself with Kabila's family and getting close to the powerful mining corporations active in the province. He was a key player in the transfer of mining concessions to Zimbabwean businessmen, putting his signature on state contracts with executives such as Billy Rautenbach.[24]

In 2000, when the Rwandan army launched its onslaught on Lubumbashi, and Laurent Kabila sent Joseph to take command of the defense of his home province, Katumba shielded Joseph from the droves of family members who all arrived in the country's mining capital wanting favors from him. At a time when problems abounded—pay for the soldiers didn't arrive on time, there was no fuel or spare parts for the vehicles, the satellite phone was out of air time—Katumba had "one great quality," a UN analyst told me. "As opposed to many others, when he promised something, he would always deliver."[25] He was both business-savvy and very reliable, a prized combination.

When Joseph became president, he brought Katumba to Kinshasa, giving him the broad title of minister of the presidency and state portfolio. Working out of a modest office in the downtown Gombe neighborhood, Katumba was officially in charge of state assets, the various national companies that included the main diamond and copper concessions, as well as steel mills, coffee plantations, and the national water and electricity company.

In practice, however, Katumba was tasked with not just running these companies but milking them for funds to supplement the presidency's discretionary budget. Bank records, for example, show that he signed orders for the state diamond company to transfer $2.3 million directly to several weapons manufacturers in eastern Europe, without passing through the Central Bank or the Ministry of Finance.[26]

Katumba was also the point man for bringing in much needed investment to the Congo. In part, this had been made possible through reforms in investment and mining codes, which the World Bank had helped create. But despite the streamlined system set up by the mining code, investors had to obtain approval from the presidency for large investments. This was Katumba's job—brokering and approving deals with international companies. According to numerous people within the mining industry, Katumba's office is an unavoidable stop on the way to securing an important contract. A UN investigation called Katumba "a key power broker in mining and diplomatic deals" and recommended him for sanctions; the *Financial Times* called him "the *primus pilus*, the Dick Cheney of the Congo."[27]

The mining sector, which had remained relatively locked up during the war for lack of interest by investors, suddenly experienced a massive privatization spree, helped along by Katumba. Between February 2004 and November 2005, the government concluded deals for 75 percent of the Congo's copper reserves.

This fire sale of assets went against all principles of best practice in international mining. Several nonprofit companies got hold of two of these contracts belonging to Dan Gertler and Belgian magnate George Forrest, which had been kept strictly confidential, and gave them to the reputed mining law firm Fasken Martineau DuMoulin for analysis. The lawyers' conclusion was that the contracts were so poorly structured that the private companies "will have been totally reimbursed in capital and interests of all loan and advances and will have derived substantial benefits from the control exercised on the operations prior to [the DRC partner] receiving any remuneration on its contributions."[28]

The World Bank's top mining expert, who had pushed long and hard for the privatization of the mining sector, cautioned in an internal memo that neither Gertler's nor Forrest's company, which now owned some of the world's largest copper concessions, had any experience in industrial mining. "There has been a complete lack of transparency with respect to the negotiation and approval of these contracts," he wrote, further worrying that the deals could deeply embarrass the Bank.[29]

The reason for these rushed and shoddy contracts, diplomats and industry experts indicated, was because of impending elections in 2006. Everybody in the industry I spoke to told me the same thing: Both Gertler and Forrest contributed considerably to Kabila's campaign coffers, although both deny this.[30] It was expensive to canvass such a vast country, set up offices in all of the 145 territories, print hundreds of thousands of T-shirts and posters, and buy the loyalty of musicians, customary chiefs, priests, and politicians.

~:~

A key word in the Congolese lexicon of corruption is *enveloppe*. If you want to buy votes in Parliament to squelch the audit of your state-run company, you pass around envelopes. When you want to obtain a lucrative contract to supply the police with beans and rice, you make sure the officials on the procurement board all get envelopes delivered to their home.

The operative verb is usually "to circulate," and typically used in the passive voice, as if the envelopes were floating around on their own accord. *On a fait circuler des enveloppes* (envelopes were circulated around). The *enveloppe* preserves the dignity of the recipient: You avoid the crude embarrassment of receiving naked cash from your benefactor. After all, who can turn down an anonymous envelope whose contents are unknown?

Katumba Mwanke was a master of the *envelopperie*. An opposition parliamentarian told me that, after being called to a meeting at the presidency to discuss an upcoming vote, Katumba thanked him for coming and gave him a small, white envelope. "It's for your transport costs," he said. Inside was $1,000 in crisp hundred-dollar bills.[31] Another friend, a lawyer who had to deal with him regularly, told me that Katumba had a Little Red Book with names written in it. Quite in contrast to Mao's synonymous booklet, this one had names accompanied by a series of arrows, checks, and asterisks. "This was the off-the-books payroll," my friend told me. The names included judges, generals, ministers, opposition parliamentarians, and journalists. Perform your job well, and Katumba could augment your salary by several thousand dollars; perform poorly, and you could find yourself broke and on the street.[32]

This mode of governance is typical of Kabila, what some in Kinshasa call the "informalization" of government. "The president prefers informal networks, parallel command structures," a veteran political analyst for the United Nations told me. "It gives him greater leeway to rule."[33] Instead of passing through his

Ministry of the Interior, for example, Kabila will call governors or military commanders directly. Instead of authorizing decent official salaries for civil servants, he allows many to scrape by on salaries of less than $100 a month, only to send them envelopes of several thousand dollars at his discretion to keep them happy. This parallel management weakens institutions but makes officials depend directly on the presidency.

~:~

Until Kabila won the 2006 elections, many observers cut him some slack. When he first came to power, the country had been divided by war, and he did an admirable job in uniting the country and marginalizing his opponents. During the transitional government, between 2003 and 2006, he had to share power in a clumsy arrangement with seven different parties. In this tangle of graft and power-sharing, it was difficult to get anything done. He was applauded for having brought an end to the war that had divided the country. For this, he won 58 percent of the national vote in 2006. People believed in his campaign motto: "Joseph Kabila—The Bearer of Eggs, He Doesn't Squabble, He Doesn't Fight." Kabila was balancing the fragile peace in his hands; he could be trusted not to start fighting again.

But three years after the elections, Kabila struggled to articulate a vision for the country. In the economic arena, there has only been little improvement in the lives of the average Congolese. In Kinshasa, where few appreciate Joseph Kabila's somber and lackluster character, people say, "Mobutu used to steal with a fork—at least some crumbs would fall between the cracks, enough to trickle down to the rest of us. But Kabila, he steals with a spoon. He scoops the plate clean, spotless. He doesn't leave anything for the poor."

Kabila's presidency has been marred, above all, by an ongoing insurgency in the eastern Congo. In 2004, during the transitional government, General Laurent Nkunda launched an insurgency against the fledgling Congolese government. A Tutsi from North Kivu, Nkunda had been a commander in the RCD and claimed that he was only trying to protect his community from the ex-FAR and Interahamwe who still lurked in the province.

There were, however, other, less noble reasons behind his rebellion, as well. The RCD was aware of its lack of popularity among Congolese and had little hope of winning in the 2006 elections. For the RCD leadership and the Rwandan government, both of whom encouraged Nkunda to go into rebellion, the new rebellion was a means of keeping their influence in the eastern Congo in the case of electoral defeat. Their fears came true: In presidential and parliamentary polls, the RCD wasn't able to garner more than 5 percent of the vote. They had gone from controlling almost a third of the Congo, including some of the most lucrative trade and mining areas, to almost nothing.[34] The fear of anti-Tutsi persecution combined potently with business and political interests to fuel a new rebellion.

Kabila tried in vain to defeat Nkunda militarily, launching four major offensives against the rebellion and sending over 20,000 troops to the Kivus. Repeatedly, during the lulls in fighting, his government tried negotiating peace deals. Finally, in 2009, Kabila struck a deal directly with the Rwandan government, allowing them to send troops into the Congo to hunt down the Democratic Forces for the Liberation of Rwanda (FDLR) in return for arresting Nkunda and integrating his troops into the Rwandan national army.

At the same time, Kabila faced challenges in Bas-Congo Province in the far west of the country, where the mystical Bundu dia Kongo sect was protesting abuses by the regime and demanding—sometimes violently—the right of self-determination. He also had to deal with the hundreds of bodyguards loyal to former vice president Jean-Pierre Bemba, who had refused to disarm and integrate into the national army after their leader was narrowly defeated in the presidential elections.

In both cases, Joseph Kabila reacted with disproportional force, eschewing negotiations and sending in hundreds of police and soldiers to put down both challenges to his power. Hundreds of unarmed civilians died in Bas-Congo, some brutally dismembered; over three hundred were killed during the battle for downtown Kinshasa. Hundreds of others were rounded up and tortured.[35] In the words of the opposition, "the Bearer of Eggs has made one huge omelet." Encumbered by weak security services, the government seems stuck between brutal repression and pallid negotiation.

~:~

But Joseph Kabila's problems go further than just weak state institutions. He is surrounded by business and political leaders with their own interests and power bases. He is an outsider who was handed the presidency on a platter, without having to climb his way up through the ranks of a party or army, earning the respect and loyalty of his fellows. He knows that he can just as easily be removed from power; the example of his father is fresh in his memory.

Reforming the state will require tackling entrenched interests and mafia-like networks that permeate the administration. In doing so, he risks offending powerful people, who could then try to unseat him. In 2004, after a botched coup attempt in downtown Kinshasa, I remember speaking with outraged security agents who told me, "We know who is behind [the coup attempt], but we can't do anything!"[36]

It is therefore perhaps not surprising that Kabila has chosen not to promote neutral, efficient state institutions, but rather to strengthen his own personal security and business networks. This attitude is perhaps most palpable in the domain of security sector reform. After the elections, Kabila had an army of 150,000 patched together from half a dozen different armed groups. Many of its officers were illiterate and had never had any formal military training. There were only a few military prosecutors for the whole province of North Kivu, where over 20,000 soldiers are based. There was no formal process of procurement, and army officers regularly commandeered civilian trucks and airplanes for transport. "We managed the army informally," a general told me. "The real power was held by people in the presidency or close to the president, not by the official chain of command."[37]

This state of affairs could be understood for the duration of the transition, when Kabila was wary of his former rivals on the battlefield pulling a fast one on him. After all, he didn't want to meet his father's fate. But he has scarcely showed more willingness for reform since the elections. Purchases of military equipment continue to be carried out by officers close to the presidency, not the logistics department, and Kabila himself has a reputation for micromanaging military operations against Nkunda, sometimes countermanding his officers and sowing confusion. He has maintained a relatively large and well-equipped presidential guard of over 10,000 troops under his direct control, but he has not been able to improve the performance of the rest of his army. As under Mobutu, this approach may prevent his own troops from overthrowing him, but it will also keep him from consolidating peace in the rest of the country.

Does Kabila want a strong state? Or does he perceive strong institutions, such as an independent judiciary and lively opposition, as a challenge to his authority? Is he condemned to negotiate with militias and other power barons around the country, or will he be able to suppress these parallel networks of power?

These are perhaps the most important questions for the country's future. The attitude of his advisors is not encouraging:

> Politics is always dirty, is always a fight. This is not Switzerland! If we liberalize the political sphere and the economy, allow for unrestrained democracy, the same self-obsessed people who drove this country into the ground under Mobutu will come to power again! You see free press and political activity—we see opponents, plotting our demise. In order to reform and promote growth, we need to curtail some civil liberties and control part of the economy. It is a lesser evil for a greater good.[38]

This language is eerily reminiscent of the Mobutu regime's earlier days. President Kabila is intent on centralizing power to the detriment of an efficient state bureaucracy and the rule of law. In 2009, he suggested that he wanted to change the constitution to prevent decentralization, extend term limits, and bring the judiciary further under his control. His government has expropriated several lucrative oil and mining concessions from multinational corporations, allegedly in order to distribute them to companies close to him. As so often in politics, what appears to be politically expedient for those in power rarely overlaps with the public interest. The lesser evils of the regime become entrenched, while the greater good is never realized.

Conclusion: The Congo, On Its Own Terms

> *Africa is never seen as possessing things and attributes properly part of "human nature." Or when it is, its things and attributes are generally of lesser value, little importance and poor quality. It is this elementariness and primitiveness that makes Africa the world par excellence of all that is incomplete, mutilated and unfinished, its history reduced to a series of setbacks of nature in its quest for humankind.*
>
> —ACHILLE MBEMBE

The Congo casts a spell on many visitors. It is difficult to explain why. The author Philip Gourevitch once wrote, "Oh Congo, what a wreck. It hurts to look and listen. It hurts to turn away."[1] The Congolese tragedy certainly has something of a car-wreck attraction to it. Nine governments battled through a country the size of western Europe, walking thousands of miles on foot through jungles and swamps. Over five million people have died, and hundreds of thousands of women have been raped.[2] If anything should be important, it is the deaths of five million people.

Or is it? The Congo war is actually rarely seen as a problem of joint humanity. Instead, it is either portrayed in western media as an abject mess—a morass of rebel groups fighting over minerals in the ruins of a failed state—or as a war of good versus evil, with the role of villain played alternatively by the Rwandan government, international mining companies, the U.S. government, or Congolese warlords. In the twenty-four-hour news cycle, in which international news is devoted largely to the war on terror and its spin-offs, there is little interest in a deeper understanding of the conflict, little appetite for numbers as unimaginably large as five million. Instead, a few shocking individual images command the headlines. Activist and *Vagina Monologues* founder Eve Ensler wrote in the *Huffington Post* that she had heard horrific stories ranging from "women being raped by fifty men in one day to women being forced to eat dead babies,"[3] while the *New York Times* reported how a woman was "kidnapped by bandits in the forest, strapped to a tree and repeatedly gang-raped. The bandits did unspeakable things, she said, like disemboweling a pregnant woman right in front of her."[4]

All of these stories are true. The conflict has seen acts of cannibalism, girls as young as five being raped with gun barrels and sticks, and women buried alive. Journalists have a responsibility to report on these atrocities, and people are often jolted awake by such horrors. In addition, millions of dollars have gone to dedicated organizations and health centers in the region that are helping survivors cope and restart their lives.

These advocacy efforts have also, however, had unintended effects. They reinforce the impression that the Congo is filled with wanton savages, crazed by power and greed. This view, by focusing on the utter horror of the violence, distracts from the politics that gave rise to the conflict and from the reasons behind the bloodshed. If all we see is black men raping and killing in the most outlandish ways imaginable, we might find it hard to believe that there is any logic to this conflict. We are returned to Joseph Conrad's notion that the Congo takes you to the heart of darkness, an inscrutable and unimprovable mess. If we want to change the political dynamics in the country, we have above all to understand the conflict on its own terms. That starts with understanding how political power is managed.

~:~

Perhaps the most nagging, persistent problem I have witnessed while researching and writing this book has been the lack of visionary, civic-minded leadership. The constant refrain from Congolese and foreigners alike is: Why do most Congolese political officeholders seem so morally bankrupt? If change can only come from Congolese themselves, how will this be possible?

On one of my trips back to the United States from the Congo, I spent time in a library reading Thomas Hobbes. The English philosopher, a founder of western political thought, was writing in the wake of the Thirty Years' War (1618–1648), which devastated much of central Europe and caused the deaths of millions of civilians. That war was the result of a complex mixture of political competition, violent localism, ideology, and greed. Hundreds of different fiefdoms battled against each other, egged on by the divide between Catholicism and Protestantism, as well as by competition for power in the Holy Roman Empire. The war was notorious for its marauding bands of mercenary soldiers, who fought for the highest bidder and who laid waste to entire regions searching for bounty. Historians often use the Latin phrase *bellum se ipsum alet* to describe the phenomenon—the war feeds itself. This is a concept many Congolese commanders would understand.

Writing three years after the end of the Thirty Years' War, Hobbes had good reason to be pessimistic about the state of nature, which he believed to be one of "war of man against man." Life in this state was "solitary, poor, nasty, brutish and short." In view of this, it was in the common interest to forfeit individual rights to the state—the Leviathan, in Hobbes's parlance—in return for protection. This was the first notion of a social contract, which justified a government's rule and made it responsible to its citizens.

But the Congo does not have a Leviathan, a state that can protect its citizens or even impose a monopoly of violence. In contrast with the Thirty Years' War, which helped produce the European system of nation-states, it is unlikely that the Congo wars will forge a strong state. As these pages have made clear, the story of the Congo wars is one of state weakness and failure, which has made possible the ceaseless proliferation of insurgent groups, still numbering around twenty-nine in late 2010. These armed groups fight brutal insurgencies and counterinsurgencies that, as the United States discovered in Vietnam and Iraq, are not so much about controlling territory as about controlling civilians, who are brutalized in order to obtain resources and as retaliation for attacks by their rivals.

Congolese state and society have not always been so weak. In the fifteenth century, large kingdoms with sophisticated governance structures began forming in the savannahs in the center and west of the country. The Kongo kingdom, based in the far west along the Atlantic coast, at one point was able to field over 20,000 infantrymen and archers in battle, funded through an elaborate system of taxes, and had diplomatic representatives at the Portuguese, Spanish, and papal courts. The Lunda and Luba kingdoms, based in the center of today's Congo, in the savannahs along the Angolan border, developed a successful model of government based on sacred kingship and local councils that spread through neighboring regions.

Since then, however, the Congo has been the victim of four hundred years of political disintegration. Starting in the sixteenth century, several million slaves were exported from the Congo by both European and Arab slave traders, sparking devastating wars between rival kingdoms over the lucrative trade as well as huge population shortages in parts of the country. Then, starting in the nineteenth century, Belgian colonial administrators dismembered what remained of most Congolese kingdoms, naming hundreds of new chiefs, severing ties between the rulers and their local councils, expropriating vast tracts of land, and allowing Belgian officials to take over many functions of the customary rulers. They created a colonial state whose purpose was to extract resources and—in its later days—provide basic services to the population, but this state was never intended to be accountable to its citizens. Unions, political parties, and other forms of mobilization were brutally suppressed by colonial authorities until the final days of their rule.

The colonial authorities then handed over government to a Congolese people almost wholly unprepared to manage their vast state. There were a handful of lawyers and university graduates in the country; under Belgian rule, no African could become an enlisted officer in the army, and all important positions in administration were held by white foreigners. At the same time, Belgian business interests and cold war politics led to the external backing of military strongmen and the repression of nationalist mobilization.

This historical legacy weighs heavily on the present. Since independence, the story of political power from Joseph Mobutu to Joseph Kabila has been about staying in power, not about creating a strong, accountable state. This is understandable. In the Congo, everything flows from political office: the best business deals, influence, and status. For those outside of power, there is scant opportunity to prosper. These rulers have treated strong public institutions as threats, eroding the capacity of the army so as to maintain tight control over key units and undermining an independent judiciary and parliament. The biggest fear of Mobutu's and Kabila's regimes has not been a foreign invasion—Mobutu was incredulous to the end that a neighboring country could oust him—but internal collapse. They feared even their own bodyguards and ministers would stab them in the back. The Congo of today is in some ways more similar to the sixteenth-century Italy of Machiavelli—and its court intrigues comparable—than to any modern twenty-first-century state.

A central reason, therefore, for the lack of visionary leadership in the Congo is because its political system rewards ruthless behavior and marginalizes scrupulous leaders. It privileges loyalty over competence, wealth and power over moral character. Well-intentioned (albeit misguided) leaders like Wamba dia Wamba are spun to the outside of this centrifuge, while the more guileful ones stay at the center. Spend some time in the Grand Hotel in Kinshasa, where politicians mingle and deals are struck, and you will realize that the welfare of the Congolese people is absent from their conversations, while court intrigues and battles for power are a matter of obsession.

This is not to say there is no ideology in the Congo. It is full of firebrand nationalists who are tired of the humiliation of being "the doormat of Central Africa, on which visiting armies clean their shoes," as one friend griped. But the political system has failed to channel this ideology into responsible leadership. The only viable means of popular mobilization remains ethnicity, although even that has been gutted of much of its moral content by generations of customary rulers co-opted and repressed by the state. These ethnicity-based organizations, whether political parties or armed groups, mobilize for greater resources for their own narrow community, not for the public good. This in turn fuels corrupt systems of patronage, whereby ethnic leaders embezzle public funds in order to reward their supporters.

~:~

In Europe, states were forged through war, trade, and technology. The rulers who could not raise enough taxes to fund large standing armies were ultimately overthrown. War required taxes, which in turn spawned large bureaucracies to gather and administer the revenues.

In the Congo, there has been little pressure on rulers to create strong armies or bureaucracies. For years, Mobutu relied on outside help to put down rebellions, calling on South African mercenaries and Moroccan, Belgian, and French soldiers, whom he could pay in cash or commodities. He had little need to create a strong administration—which could then become a breeding ground for political opposition—as he could get plenty of revenues from the copper mines and foreign donors. Joseph Kabila has largely privatized the economy and has strengthened tax collection, but he is wary about creating a strong rule of law that could tie his hands. Even the violence in the Kivus region, which continues until today, has not prompted major reforms in his army or police; he has preferred to co-opt dissent rather than to promote an impartial, disciplined security service. And instead of business elites demanding greater accountability and less corruption from the government, they are often themselves dependent on patronage from Kinshasa.

No one factor has produced the kleptocratic, venal political elite. Certainly social and educational issues also play a role. But it is clear that political elites react to incentives and that no meaningful reform will result as long as these incentives are skewed against the creation of strong institutions. Buoyed by foreign support and revenues from copper, oil, and diamonds, the government feels little need to serve its citizens and promote sustainable development. Why empower nettlesome parliaments, courts, and auditing bodies if they will just turn around and harass you?

This state of affairs should force foreign donors to think more carefully about contributing billions of dollars to development in the Congo without pondering the long-term repercussions. The donors—mainly the World Bank, the International Monetary Fund, the European Union, the United States, and the United Kingdom—usually insist that this money is politically neutral, that it does not directly benefit the political elite. This is true, as most of the money is for schools, roads, health care, and water projects. But all development is deeply political. By taking over the financing of most public services, donors take pressure off the Congolese government to respond to the needs of its citizens. Ultimately, the rule of law will be created not through a capacity-building project in the ministry of finance but through a power struggle between the government, local elites, and business circles. Donors need to figure out how to most responsibly insert themselves in this dynamic and not just pave roads, build hospitals, and reform fiscal systems.

~:~

But why should we help at all? First, because it is not just an act of joint humanity. We owe it to the Congolese. Most obviously because of the centuries of slavery, colonialism, and exploitation of rubber, copper, and diamonds, which benefited western companies and helped build Belgian cities. Those past injustices should be reason enough for feeling a moral debt toward the country, but we don't need to go so far. Most of the foreign companies operating in the Congo today are listed on stock exchanges, are incorporated in Europe or North America, or obtain their financing from banks based in those countries. Many of these companies are engaging in questionable behavior that would be proscribed in their home countries. Big mining companies have signed contracts that provide little revenue to the state and have allegedly provided large kickbacks to government officials. Smaller trading companies buy minerals from the eastern Congo without scrutinizing the origins of their shipments to make sure they are not funding armed groups. So we should do what we can to allow the Congolese to benefit from their riches, not be held back by them.

This is not to say that the war has been fueled by western governments eager to get their hands on Congolese riches. There is little evidence for that. It is certainly true that many companies, Congolese and foreign, have benefited enormously from the conflict. Nevertheless, for the most part it was small, junior outfits that made a fortune—the conflict postponed major industrial mining and investment for over a decade. Similarly, while some western diplomats flourished through their corrupt dealings in the Congo, it would be wrong to flip causality on its head and say that western businesses and diplomats caused the war. For the most part, the mining companies go where profit margins take them, and the embassies in Kinshasa do their mandated job of helping them. The problem has been one of regulatory failure; of mining cowboys allowed to get away with mass fraud, hiding behind shell companies registered in Caribbean islands and working the corrupt stratosphere of Congolese politics; and of western governments not caring about the behavior of their companies once they leave their borders.

Second, we should give Congolese an opportunity to decide on how to deal with their violent past. A key fallacy of international engagement has been the idea that justice is an impediment to peace in the region. Time and time again, diplomats have actively shied away from creating an international court to prosecute those responsible for the many atrocities committed during the war. One of the most disheartening moments in my research, repeated countless times, was hearing survivors explain that they didn't have anything to help them address their loss—the killers hadn't been brought to justice, and often they didn't even know where their loved ones were buried. The Congo is something of an outlier in this sense: Sierra Leone, Kosovo, East Timor, Rwanda, and the former Yugoslavia have all had tribunals to deal with the past. Yet in the Congo, where many of the perpetrators are still in power, the victims are left to stew in their frustration.

It is precisely because many former warlords are still in power that diplomats have been wary of launching prosecutions. This has resulted in an army and government replete with criminals who have little deterrent to keep them from resorting to violence again. At the time of this writing, in October 2010, the United Nations released a report summarizing the most egregious war crimes committed in the country between 1993 and 2003 and recommending that a special court be established. This time, donors and the Congolese government must seize the opportunity. This is not to say that we should impose an international tribunal on the Congo; it may not be the best solution. But the Congolese people should be given the chance to know some of the truth of what happened during the war and to hold accountable those responsible. Two hundred and twenty Congolese civil society organizations have written in support of the UN report and have called for a conference to decide on how best to proceed. Such an initiative would be an important signal to the elite, proving that impunity is not the glue of the political system.

⌒∶∽

In large part, however, our sins have been of omission. We simply do not care enough. Contrary to what some Congolese believe, President Obama does not wake up to a security briefing on the Congo with his morning scone. Generally, we do not care about a strange war fought by black people somewhere in the middle of Africa. This sad hypocrisy is easy to see—NATO sent 50,000 troops from some of the best armies to Kosovo in 1999, a country one-fifth the size of South Kivu. In the Congo, the UN peacekeeping mission plateaued at 20,000 troops, mostly from South Asia, ill-equipped and with little will to carry out risky military operations. In exchange, the Congo has received plentiful humanitarian aid—a short-term solution to a big problem.

This apathy has allowed simplistic notions to dominate policy toward the region. This was most evident in dealing with Uganda and Rwanda. Throughout the conflict, donor aid made up for over half of the budget of Rwanda and over a third of that of Uganda. The largest providers were the European Commission, the United Kingdom, and the United States, governments that felt understandably guilty for not having come to Rwanda's aid during the genocide.

In addition, both Central African countries had impressive records of development and poverty reduction: over a period of ten years, donor aid helped lift 13 percent of Rwandans and 20 percent of Ugandans out of poverty. Compared with other African countries, such as that of the Congo, at least here donors knew that their aid dollars and pounds were being put to good use.

The donors were, however, myopic. They clearly recognized the relatively positive developments taking place within Rwanda's borders but were generally indifferent toward the conflict next door. When Rwanda reinvaded the Congo in August 1998, Washington and London protested but did not use their mighty diplomatic and financial leverage on Congo's neighbors. "We did the right thing with Rwanda," Sue Hogwood, a former UK ambassador to Rwanda, said. "We needed to help them rebuild after the genocide. We engaged and challenged them over human rights abuses, but they also had genuine security concerns."[5]

Rwanda did have security concerns. One of Kagame's political advisors expressed a typical view to me: "When the United States was attacked on September 11, 2001, you decided to strike back against Afghanistan for harboring the people who carried out the attack. Many innocent civilians died as a result of U.S. military operations. Is that unfortunate? Of course. But how many Americans regret invading Afghanistan? Very few."[6]

This point of view does not allow for moral nuances. Once we have established that the *génocidaires* are in the Congo, any means will justify the ends of getting rid of them, even if those means are not strictly related to getting rid of the *génocidaires*. Was the destruction of Kisangani necessary to get rid of them? The killing of tens of thousands of civilians? The pillaging of millions of dollars to finance the war effort?

Policymakers in the region have often only had blunt instruments to deal with complex issues. In the case of the Rwandan refugee crisis, for example, it would have been best to send in an international military force to demilitarize the refugee camps and separate the soldiers from the civilians. That would have required hundreds of millions of dollars, and a risky intervention soon after the UN fiasco in Somalia.[7]

In the absence of such large-scale engagement, dealing with the refugee problem, especially after Rwanda had invaded, was like doing brain surgery with oven mitts. As several hundred thousand refugees fled across Zaire, the U.S. ambassador to Kigali told his bosses in Washington, "The best way we can help is to stop feeding the killers who will then run away to look for other sustenance, leaving their hostages behind. If we do not, we will be trading the children in Tingi-Tingi against the children who will be killed and orphaned in Rwanda [by the killers when they return]."[8] What he didn't mention is that the only way to stop feeding the killers was to stop feeding the civilians as well.

We cannot do peacemaking on the cheap, with few diplomats and no resources. It will not only fail but also lead to simplistic policies that can do more harm than good.

∽∶∾

The Congo war had no one cause, no clear conceptual essence that can be easily distilled in a couple of paragraphs. Like an ancient Greek epic, it is a mess of different narrative strands—some heroic, some venal, all combined in a narrative that is not straightforward but layered, shifting, and incomplete. It is not a war of great mechanical precision but of ragged human edges.

This book is an exhortation to raise the bar and try harder to understand this layered complexity. The Congo's suffering is intensely human; it has experienced trauma on a massive and prolonged scale, and the victims are our neighbors, our trading partners, our political confreres and rivals. They are not alien; they are not evil; they are not beyond our comprehension. The story of the Congo is dense and complicated. It demands that all involved think hard. This means diving into the nuts and bolts of Congolese politics and working to help the more legitimate and responsible leaders rise to the top. This means better, more aggressive, and smarter peacekeeping and conflict resolution; more foreign aid that is conditional on political reforms and not just on fiscal performance; and more responsible corporate investment and trade with the Congo.

We should not despair. If there is one thing I know after having worked on the Congo for a decade, it is the extreme resilience and energy of the Congolese people. As the eccentric singer Koffi Olomide sings, referring to his country, "This is hell's system here. The fire is raging, and yet we don't get burned." With all of their hardships, one would imagine the Congolese to be less vibrant and more cynical. Yet they are not.

There are no easy solutions for the Congo, no silver bullets to produce accountable government and peace. The ultimate fate of the country rests with the Congolese people themselves. Westerners also have a role to play, in part because of our historical debt to the country, in part because it is the right thing to do. This does not mean imposing a foreign vision on the country or simply sending food and money. It means understanding it and its politics and rhythms on their own terms, and then doing our part in providing an environment conducive to growth and stability.

Notes

INTRODUCTION

1. Julie Hollar, "Congo Is Ignored, Not Forgotten," Fairness and Accuracy in Reporting, May 2009, www.fair.org/index.php?page=3777, accessed March 8, 2010.

2. Nicholas Kristof, "Darfur and Congo," *On the Ground* (blog), *New York Times*, June 20, 2007, kristof.blogs.nytimes.com/2007/06/20/darfur-and-congo/, accessed March 8, 2010, quoted in Hollar, "Congo Is Ignored."

3. The Congolese colloquially call the Belgians *noko*, or uncles, and like to make fun of their fondness for mayonnaise on their French fries.

4. Achille Flor Ngoye, *Kin-la-joie, Kin-la-folie* (Paris: L'Harmattan, 1993), 147 (my translation).

5. The country's name was switched back to the Democratic Republic of the Congo in 1997. When discussing the period 1971 to 1997, I will refer to the country as Zaire.

6. Gauthiers de Villers and Jean-Claude Willame, *Republique democratique du Congo: Chronique politique d'un entre-deux-guerres, octobre 1996–juillet 1998*, Cahiers Africains 35 (Paris: L'Harmattan, 1998), 85.

7. His name has been changed to protect his identity.

CHAPTER I

1. A controversy still surrounds the downing of the plane. Opponents of the current regime and some academics insist that the RPF rebels shot it down, while the RPF and other regional experts maintain that it was extremists within the Habyarimana government.

2. Scott Straus, "How Many Perpetrators Were There in the Rwandan Genocide?" *Journal of Genocide Research* 6, no. 1 (2004): 85–98.

3. Kathi L. Austin, *Rearming with Impunity: International Support for the Perpetrators of the Rwandan Genocide*, Human Rights Watch, vol. 7, no. 4 (May 1995).

4. Unless otherwise indicated, information about Rwarakabije's life in this chapter is based on a series of interviews with him in Kigali between 2007 and 2009.

5. Hannah Arendt, *Eichmann in Jerusalem: A Report on the Banality of Evil* (New York: Penguin, 2006), 135.

6. This section draws on a discussion of identity formation in Rwanda in David Newbury, *Kings and Clans: Idjwi Island and the Lake Kivu Rift* (Madison: University of Wisconsin, 1991); as well as Jean-Pierre Chrétien, *The Great Lakes of Africa: Two Thousand Years of History*, trans. Scott Straus (New York: Zone Books, 2003), 171–190, 281–290; and Catherine Newbury, *The Cohesion of Oppression: Clientship and Ethnicity in Rwanda, 1860–1960* (New York: Columbia University Press, 1988), 73–150.

7. Quoted by Chrétien, *The Great Lakes of Africa*, 283.

8. Gérard Prunier, *The Rwanda Crisis: History of a Genocide* (London: Hurst, 1997), 143n27.

9. Philip Verwimp, *An Economic Profile of Peasant Perpetrators of the Genocide: Micro-level Evidence from Rwanda*, HiCN Working Paper 8, Households in Conflict Network, University of Sussex, 2003, www.hicn.org/papers/perp.pdf.

10. Straus, "How Many Perpetrators?," 94. Other authors contest this figure; the range varies from between tens of thousands to several million perpetrators.

11. Jean-Paul Kimonyo, *Un genocide populaire* (Paris: Karthala, 2008); Scott Straus, *The Order of Genocide: Race, Power, and War in Rwanda* (Ithaca, NY: Cornell University Press, 2006).

12. Prunier, *The Rwanda Crisis*, 100–102, 147, 148; Alison Des Forges, Eric Gillet, and Timothy Longman, *Leave None to Tell the Story: Genocide in Rwanda* (New York: Human Rights Watch, 1999), 506–507.

13. Austin, *Rearming with Impunity*, www.hrw.org/reports/1995/Rwanda1.htm, n25.

14. Des Forges, Gillet, and Longman, *Leave None to Tell the Story*, 506.

15. Linda Melvern, *A People Betrayed: The Role of the West in Rwanda's Genocide* (London: Zed Books, 2000), 131.

16. African Rights, *Rwanda: The Insurgency in the Northwest* (London: African Rights, 1998), 103.

17. African Rights, *Rwanda: Death, Despair, and Defiance*, rev. ed. (London: African Rights, 1995), 657, quoted by Prunier, *The Rwanda Crisis*, 314.

18. Amos Elon, "Introduction," in Arendt, *Eichmann in Jerusalem*, xiv.

CHAPTER 2

1. Gérard Prunier, *Africa's World War: Congo, the Rwandan Genocide, and the Making of a Continental Catastrophe* (Oxford: Oxford University Press, 2009), 30.

2. Quoted by Joel Boutroue, *Missed Opportunities: The Role of the International Community in the Return of the Rwandan Refugees from Eastern Zaire, July 1994–December 1996*, Rosemarie Rogers Working Paper 1, Inter-University Committee on International Migration, Massachusetts Institute of Technology, June 1998.

3. Beatrice Umutesi, *Fuir ou Mourir au Zaire* (Paris: L'Harmattan, 2000), 95.

4. Prunier, *Africa's World War*, 26, quoting UNHCR field notes.

5. Johan de Smedt, "Child Marriages in Rwandan Refugee Camps," *Africa: Journal of the International African Institute* 68, no. 2 (1998): 211–237.

6. Umutesi, *Fuir ou Mourir au Zaire*, 93, 94.

7. *Breaking the Cycle: Calls for Action in the Rwandese Refugee Camps in Tanzania and Zaire*, Doctors Without Borders, November 10, 1994, http://www.doctorswithout borders.org/publications/article.cfm?id=1465.

8. John Eriksson, "Synthesis Report" of the *International Response to Conflict and Genocide: Lessons from the Rwanda Experience*, Danish International Development Assistance, March 1996, 29, quoted by Fiona Terry, *Condemned to Repeat? The Paradox of Humanitarian Action* (Ithaca, NY: Cornell University Press, 2002), 175.

9. Umutesi, *Fuir ou Mourir au Zaire*, 88.

10. Terry, *Condemned to Repeat?* 186, 187.

11. Ibid., 204, 205.

12. Ibid., 190.

13. Author's off-the-record interview with a UN official, New York, July 2007.

14. Kurt Mills, "Refugee Return from Zaire to Rwanda: The Role of UNHCR," in *War and Peace in Zaire/Congo: Analyzing and Evaluating Intervention, 1996–1997*, ed. Howard Adelman and Govind C. Rao (Trenton, NJ: Africa World Press, 2004), 163–185; *Final Report of the United Nations Technical Mission on the Security Situation in the Rwandan Refugee Camps in Zaire*, 1994, www.grandslacs.net/doc/2745.pdf.

15. Boutroue, *Missed Opportunities*, 62–64.

16. Quoted by Boutroue, *Missed Opportunities*, 31, 32.

17. Terry, *Condemned to Repeat?* 171.

18. Boutroue, *Missed Opportunities*.

19. *Rwanda/Zaire: Rearming with Impunity*, Human Rights Watch Arms Project, May 1995.

20. The Great Lakes region of Africa consists of the countries located around lakes in the Great Rift Valley. The region is loosely defined but usually includes Uganda, Rwanda, the Democratic Republic of the Congo, Burundi, Kenya, and Tanzania.

21. Gérard Prunier, *The Rwanda Crisis: History of a Genocide* (New York: Columbia University Press, 1995), 279n139.

22. Agence France-Presse, Brussels, October 29, 1996.

23. Quoted by Simon Massey, "Operation Assurance: The Greatest Humanitarian Intervention that Never Happened," *Journal of Humanitarian Assistance*, February 15, 1998, jha.ac/1998/02/15/operation-assurance-the-greatest-intervention-that-never -happened.

24. Ibid.

CHAPTER 3

1. Stephen Kinzer, *A Thousand Hills: Rwanda's Rebirth and the Man Who Dreamed It* (Hoboken, NJ: Wiley & Sons, 2008), 254.

2. Philip Gourevitch, "After Genocide," *Transition* 72 (1996): 188.

3. Kinzer, *A Thousand Hills*, 232.

4. Gérard Prunier, *The Rwanda Crisis: A History of the Genocide* (London: Hurst & Co., 1997), 62.

5. Richard Grant, "Paul Kagame: Rwanda's Redeemer or Ruthless Dictator?" *Daily Telegraph* (London), July 22, 2010.

6. "When Kagame Turned 50," *New Times* (Kigali), October 25, 2007.

7. Author's interview with Andrew Mwenda, New Haven, Connecticut, March 2010.

8. Author's interview with former RPF soldier, Nairobi, July 2007.

9. Author's telephone interview with U.S. intelligence officer, June 2009.

10. Steve Vogel, "Student of Warfare Graduates on Battlefields of Rwanda; Rebel Leader Ran a Textbook Operation," *Washington Post*, August 25, 1994.

11. Prunier, *The Rwanda Crisis*, 62.

12. Filip Reyntjens, *La Guerre des Grands Lacs* (Paris: L'Harmattan, 1999), 52; *Report of the Joint Mission Charged with Investigating Allegations of Massacres and Other Human Rights Violations Occurring in Eastern Zaire (Now Democratic Republic of the Congo) Since September 1996*, United Nations General Assembly, A/51/942, July 2, 1997, 17, 18.

13. Quoted in the film *Afrique en morceaux* (1999), directed by Jihan El Tahran.

14. Peter Rosenblum, "Irrational Exuberance: The Clinton Administration in Africa," *Current History* (May 2002): 197.

15. The Ugandan rebels included the Lord's Resistance Army (LRA), a brutal rebel group that initially drew support from the Acholi community of northern Uganda, who had made up a large part of Milton Obote's army and had been marginalized after Museveni's arrival in power. The LRA were not yet active in Zaire, but several other Ugandan rebel groups were, with support from both Mobutu and the Khartoum government. Shortly afterwards, Sudanese intelligence operatives based out of northeastern Zaire helped create the West Nile Bank Liberation Front (WNBLF), made up of former partisans and soldiers close to former Ugandan dictator Idi Amin. In addition, Sudan lent support to several other rebel groups, including two small Ugandan Islamist organizations, the Tabliq and the Uganda Muslim Liberation Army (UMLA), both of which claimed to be outraged by the alleged massacre of Muslims at the hands of Museveni. To complicate the picture further, there was also a group of leaders from the Baganda community, the Allied Democratic Movement (ADM), who attacked Museveni for continuing to repress the kingdom of Baganda, the largest precolonial monarchy in the region, and also began to recruit soldiers. As neither ADM nor UMLA had significant grassroots support, the Sudanese put them in contact with remnants of the National Army for the Liberation of Uganda (NALU), a rebel militia based among the Konjo ethnic community in the Ruwenzori Mountains

of western Uganda, who had felt marginalized from Uganda politics since the colonial era. Together, these three groups formed the Allied Democratic Forces (ADF).

16. "Congo Rebels Were Museveni's Idea," *Monitor* (Kampala), June 1, 1999.

17. "Supplementary Report of the Monitoring Mechanism on Sanctions Against UNITA," Security Council Document S/2001/966, October 8, 2001.

18. The figure for displaced people comes from the UN consolidated appeal for Angola, January–December 1996; military expenditure information comes from the Stockholm International Peace Research Institute (SIPRI).

19. Matthew Hart, "How to Steal a Diamond," *Atlantic Monthly*, March 1999.

20. Author's interview with Rwandan intelligence official, South Africa, January 2009.

21. Author's interview with Don Steinberg, former U.S. ambassador to Angola, New York, June 2007.

22. "Kabila Shouts Down Museveni," *Monitor* (Kampala), June 2, 1999.

23. Thabo Mbeki, "Statement on Behalf of the African National Congress, on the Occasion of the Adoption by the Constitutional Assembly of 'The Republic of South Africa Constitution Bill 1996.'"

CHAPTER 4

1. Author's interview with human rights activist, Bukavu, March 2008.

2. BBC monitoring of *Voix du Zaire* newscast, October 9, 1996. His comments about six days were made off air to one of the international journalists.

3. See, for example, his submission to the Goma peace conference in 2008: "Reaction de Monsieur Lwabanji Lwasi Ngabo, Vice-Gouverneur Honoraire du Sud Kivu, à la declaration du porte parole des Banyamulenge à la conference de Goma," January 15, 2008.

4. Much of this chapter is based on the author's interview with Serukiza, Kinshasa, November 2007. He passed away not long afterwards from complications from cancer.

5. Isidore Ndaywel, *Histoire Générale du Congo: De l'héritage ancien à la République démocratique* (Paris: Duculot, 1998), 382–383 (my translation). Also see Koen Vlassenroot, "Citizenship, Identity Formation and Conflict in South Kivu: The Case of the Banyamulenge," *Review of African Political Economy* 29, nos. 93–94 (2002): 499–515.

6. I owe this insight to Mauro DeLorenzo, who studied the Banyamulenge for his doctoral dissertation at Oxford University.

7. Historians of Rwanda also record emigrations from southern Rwanda toward Congo around this time. Catherine Newbury, *The Cohesion of Oppression: Clientship and Ethnicity in Rwanda, 1860–1960* (New York: Columbia University Press, 1988), 48–49.

8. Lazare Sebitereko Rukundwa, "Justice and Righteousness in Matthean Theology and Its Relevance to the Banyamulenge Community," PhD thesis, University of Pretoria, November 2005, 317.

9. Ibid., 292.

10. Ibid., 129.

11. Quoted by Cosma Wilungula, *Le Maquis Kabila, Fizi 1967–1986* (Paris: L'Harmattan, 1997), 24 (my translation).

12. Manassé Ruhimbika, *Les Banyamulenge entre deux guerres* (Paris: L'Harmattan, 2001), 25.

13. Leslie Crawford, "Hutus See France as Their Saviour," *Financial Times* (London), June 27, 1994.

14. Anzuluni Bembe, the president of the national assembly and himself a Bembe from South Kivu, authored the decree, implying that the Banyamulenge were Rwandan immigrants who had fraudulently acquired Congolese citizenship.

15. Haut Conseil de la République, Parlement de Transition, "Resolution sur les réfugiés et population déplacés dans les regions du Nord et du Sud-Kivu," signed in Kinshasa, April 28, 1995.

16. Letter from the Commissaire de Zone d'Uvira, October 26, 1995, quoted by Ruhimbika, *Les Banyamulenge*, 32.

17. A group of Banyamulenge leaders, led by Dugu wa Mulenge, their only provincial parliamentarian, wrote to denounce this recruitment of Banyamulenge. The estimates for the number of Banyamulenge in the RPF come from Ruhimbika, *Les Banyamulenge* (300) and Serukiza (1,000).

CHAPTER 5

1. Much of this chapter is based on the author's interview with Deogratias Bugera, Johannesburg, April 2008. Thomas Nziratimana, Bugera's former chief of staff, also provided helpful information.

2. Author's interview with former AFDL member, Kinshasa, November 2007.

3. The exact size is a matter of contention. According to Brooke Grundfest Schoepf and Claude Schoepf, "Gender, Land, and Hunger in Eastern Zaire," in *African Food Systems in Crisis*, vol. 2, *Contending with Change*, ed. Rebecca Huss-Ashmore and Solomon H. Katz, Food and Nutrition in History and Anthropology, vol. 7 (New York: Gordon and Breach, 1990), King Leopold ceded 12 million hectares, or 46,000 square miles, to the National Committee for the Kivus, a state agency, but that was soon reduced to 300,000 hectares, which is a tenth of the size of Belgium.

4. Séverin Mugangu, "Les politiques legislatives congolaise et rwandaise relatives aux refugiés et émigrés rwandais," in *Exilé, réfugiés et deplacés en Afrique Centrale et orientale*, ed. André Guichaoua (Paris: Karthala, 2004), 639.

5. Paul Mathieu and Mafikiri Tsongo, "Enjeux fonciers, déplacements de population et escalades conflictuelles (1930–1995)," in *Conflits et guerres au Kivu et dans la*

région des grands lacs: Entre tensions locales et escalade régionale, ed. P. Mathieu and Jean-Claude Willame, Cahiers Africains 39 (Paris: L'Harmattan, 1999), 20–25.

6. Jean-Pierre Pabanel, "La question de la nationalité au Kivu," *Politique Africaine* (1993): 41, 43.

7. There was no effort to implement the law until 1989, when the government began to identify voters. This process provoked violence—Banyarwanda in Masisi burned down registration booths.

8. The UN Special Rapporteur on Human Rights in Zaire put the figure at 3,000, while Amnesty International suggested it could be as high as 7,000, citing humanitarian officials Roberto Garretón, UN Special Rapporteur, *Report on the Situation of Human Rights in Zaire,* December 23, 1994, paragraph 90; Amnesty International, *Zaire: Violence Against Democracy,* September 16, 1993.

9. Bugera was in touch with two leading Rwandan officers who were coordinating these operations, Major Jack Nziza and Colonel Kayumba Nyamwasa, both of whom would play major roles in the subsequent Rwandan invasion of the Congo.

10. Joel Boutroue, *Missed Opportunities: The Role of the International Community in the Return of the Rwandan Refugees from Eastern Zaire, July 1994–December 1996,* Rosemarie Rogers Working Paper 1, Inter-University Committee on International Migration, Massachusetts Institute of Technology, June 1998.

11. This was later confirmed by documents they recovered after they had captured the refugee camps.

12. Anonymous tract written by the Collective of Congolese Patriots (COPACO), dated February 10, 2000.

CHAPTER 6

1. Erik Kennes with collaboration by Munkana N'Ge, *Essai biographique sur Laurent Désiré Kabila* (Paris: L'Harmattan, 2003), 29.

2. Ibid., 29.

3. Quoted by Piero Gleijeses, *Conflicting Missions: Havana, Washington, and Africa, 1959–1976,* Envisioning Cuba (Chapel Hill: University of North Carolina Press, 2002), 72.

4. Kennes, *Essai biographique,* 72.

5. Ernesto "Che" Guevara, *The African Dream: The Diaries of the Revolutionary War in the Congo,* trans. Patrick Camiller (New York: Grove, 2000), 6.

6. Ibid., 86.

7. Ibid., 244.

8. William Galvez, *Le rêve Africain de Che* (Antwerp: EPO, 1998), 302, quoted by Kennes, *Essai biographique,* 174.

9. Wilungula Cosma, *Le Maquis Kabila, Fizi 1967–1986* (Paris: L'Harmattan, 1997), 112; Kennes, *Essai biographique,* 264.

10. Kennes, *Essai biographique,* 302.

11. Jean-Baptiste Sondji, a hospital director in Kinshasa who went on to become health minister under Laurent Kabila, met with Kahinda Otafire, one of President Museveni's point men on the Congo, in Brussels as early as 1993 to discuss regime change in his country. He spoke to Tshisekedi about Uganda's proposal, but the opposition leader didn't want to have anything to do with an armed insurrection. Patrick Karegeya confirmed this. Author's interview with Jean-Baptiste Sondji, Kinshasa, February 2008.

12. Lemera is a town in South Kivu where the first AFDL training camp would be located. Coincidentally, the neighborhood in Kigali where some of the Congolese rebels were staying was also called Lemera.

CHAPTER 7

1. This description comes from Thomas Nziratimana, chief of staff of Deo Bugera and later vice governor of South Kivu, whom I interviewed in Kinshasa, July 2006, as well as General Malik Kijege, a leading Munyamulenge commander, whom I interviewed in Kinshasa, November 2007.

2. "West 'Fooled' by Banyamulenge," *Voix du Zaire*, Bukavu, October 25, 1996.

3. Author's interview with Bembe civil society activist, Baraka, March 2008.

4. Manassé Ruhimbika, *Les Banyamulenge entre deux guerres* (Paris: L'Harmattan, 2001), 47.

5. Ibid., 49.

6. Alex's name has been changed to protect his identity.

7. See also *Report of the Mapping Exercise Documenting the Most Serious Violations of Human Rights and International Humanitarian Law Committed Within the Territory of the Democratic Republic of the Congo Between March 1993 and June 2003*, United Nations High Commissioner for Human Rights, October 2010, 74. The death toll given by UN investigators was 152 for this incident.

8. Several days later, a German journalist ventured into the squalid camp on the Rwandan side of the border, to where the Tutsi survivors had fled. Amid the blue UNHCR tents, a wizened man approached him with a black book. Musafiri Mushambaro, the president of the Uvira community there, paged through the book, counting the dead: "Sange 20, Muturure 9, in Burugera 3, Lweba 89, Kamanyola 37." He had 217 names in his book, all men. They were separated from their families, driven together, and shot, he said.

9. According to a UN report published in 2010, 101 people died that day in Abala. *Report of the Mapping Exercise*, 135.

CHAPTER 8

1. The information on Prosper Nabyolwa's experiences stems from a series of interviews by the author with General Nabyolwa in Kinshasa in July 2005, December 2007, and July 2008.

2. "Declaration of the Population of South Kivu Following the 'March of Anger, Protest and Denunciation Against the Aggression by Tutsi Rwandans of Which Zaire and Its People Have Become Victims,'" Bukavu, September 18, 1996, quoted by Olivier Lanotte, *Guerres sans frontiers: De Joseph-Désiré Mobutu a Joseph Kabila* (Brussels: GRIP, 2003), 42.

3. *Demain le Congo*, no. 244 (1997): 7, quoted by Isidore Ndaywel, *Histoire Générale du Congo: De l'héritage ancien à la République démocratique* (Paris: Duculot, 1998).

4. Author's interviews with hospital staff, Lemera, March 2008; Amnesty International, *Zaire: Violent Persecution by State and Armed Groups*, November 29, 1996, 5.

5. "A Hole in the Middle of Africa," *Economist*, July 8, 1995.

6. Library of Congress, *Country Study: Zaire*, 1994, 312.

7. Crawford Young and Thomas Turner, *The Rise and Decline of the Zairian State* (Madison: University of Wisconsin Press, 1985), 275.

8. Honoré Ngbanda Nzambo, *Ainsi sonne le glas: Les derniers jours du Maréchal Mobutu* (Paris: Editions Gideppe, 1998), 46 (my translation).

9. William Reno, "Sovereignty and Personal Rule in Zaire," *African Studies Quarterly* 1, no. 3 (1997), www.africa.ufl.edu/asq/vi/3/4.htm.

10. Author's interview with General Prosper Nabyolwa in Kinshasa, December 2007.

11. Young and Turner, *Rise and Decline*, 259.

12. Michael G. Schatzberg, *The Dialectics of Oppression in Zaire* (Bloomington: Indiana University Press, 1988), 59.

13. Library of Congress, *Zaire*, 303.

14. Author's interview with José Endundo, owner of a large aviation company, Kinshasa, December 2007.

15. Nzambo, *Ainsi sonne le glas*, 88.

16. Author's interview with Deo Bugera, Johannesburg, March 2008.

17. Author's interview with Patrick Karegeya, Dar es Salaam, January 2008.

18. "Plus jamais le Congo," *Observatoire de l'Afrique centrale* 6, no. 10, March 4, 2003, www.obsac.com.

19. Cherif Ouazani, "James Kabarebe et la mémoire de la guerre de libération de l'AFDL," *Jeune Afrique Intelligent*, April 29, 2002 (my translation).

20. When Joseph Kabila came to power in 2001, some of his closest military advisors were former Katangan Tigers.

21. Author's interview with former FAR commander, Kinshasa, July 2009.

22. Stephen Smith, "L'Armada de mercenaires au Zaïre: Commandés par un Belge, 280 'affreux' mènent la contre-offensive," *Libération*, January 24, 1997; Philippe Chapleau and Francois Misser, *Mercenaires S.A.* (Paris: Desclée de Brouwer, 1998), Chapter 6.

23. Gérard Prunier, *Africa's World War: Congo, the Rwandan Genocide, and the Making of a Continental Catastrophe* (Oxford: Oxford University Press, 2009), 129.

24. Quoted in the film *Afrique en morceaux* (1999), directed by Jihan El Tahran.

25. Gordana Igri, "Alleged 'Assassins' Were No Strangers to France," in *Balkan Crisis Report*, Institute for War and Peace Reporting, November 26, 1999.

26. James Astill's interview with General James Kabarebe, Kigali, May 2004.

27. Author's interview with Colonel Fely Bikaba, Kinshasa, July 2006.

28. Prunier, *Africa's World War*, 142.

29. "Canadian Deal Worth Millions to Zaire's Rebels: $50 Million Investment Likely to Find Its Way into Kabila's War Chest," Associated Press, May 10, 1997.

30. Mark Sherman, "McKinney Reassured About Zairian Refugees, Elections," *Atlanta Constitution*, May 14, 1997.

CHAPTER 9

1. Robert Gribbin, *In the Aftermath of Genocide*, U.S. Congress Hearing before the Subcommittee on International Operations and Human Rights, December 4, 1996, 198.

2. No one really knew exactly how many refugees remained in Zaire. At one point, the UN refugee agency suggested the number could be as high as 600,000, the UN Department of Humanitarian Affairs said 439,500, while the U.S. general Edwin Smith put the figure at 202,000 and the Canadian general Maurice Baril at 165,000. Filip Reyntjens, *The Great African War: Congo and Regional Geopolitics, 1996–2006* (Cambridge: Cambridge University Press, 2009), 85–86.

3. Quoted by Johan Pottier, *Re-imagining Rwanda: Conflict, Survival and Disinformation in the Late Twentieth Century* (Cambridge: Cambridge University Press, 2002), 175.

4. Ibid., 175.

5. Beatrice Umutesi, *Fuir ou mourir au Zaire* (Paris: L'Harmattan, 2000), 131.

6. Ibid., 147.

7. *Forced Flight: A Brutal Strategy of Elimination in Eastern Zaire*, Médecins Sans Frontières (Doctors Without Borders), May 1997, www.msf.org/msfinternational/invoke.cfm?component=report&objectid=A63A4532-BEA0-4BB1-A7AE1EEB4B D27AC7&method=full_html.

8. According to Doctors Without Borders, mortality rates were as high as 21 deaths per 10,000 people in some camps. By comparison, the mortality rate in a healthy population is around 0.6 per 10,000, a rate of 2 per 10,000 constitutes an emergency, and 4 per 10,000 is an out-of-control emergency.

9. *Forced Flight*.

10. Ibid.

11. See Kisangani Emizet, "The Massacre of Refugees in Congo: A Case of UN Peacekeeping Failure and International Law," *Journal of Modern African Studies* 33, no. 2 (2000): 173–179; Gérard Prunier, *Africa's World War: Congo, the Rwandan Genocide, and the Making of a Continental Catastrophe* (Oxford: Oxford University Press,

2009), 148. Both of these authors, however, use 1.1 million refugees as a starting point, a figure of unknown accuracy, given the lack of a census in the camps.

12. Alan L. Heil Jr., *Voice of America: A History* (New York: Columbia University Press, 2003), 264.

13. *Report of the Mapping Exercise Documenting the Most Serious Violations of Human Rights and International Humanitarian Law Committed Within the Territory of the Democratic Republic of the Congo Between March 1993 and June 2003*, United Nations High Commissioner for Human Rights, October 2010, 278.

14. Ibid., 77–116, 273–277.

15. Colin Nickerson, "Refugee Massacre Unfolds in Congo: Witnesses Tell of Slaughter of Hundreds by Kabila's Soldiers," *Boston Globe*, June 1, 1997, A1. The figure of nine hundred bodies buried comes from Andrew Maykuth, "Tutsis Slaughter Hutu Refugees," Knight-Ridder Newspapers, June 8, 1997. UN investigators, who were barred from visiting Mbandaka, suggested that between 200 and 2,000 people may have been killed there.

16. Nickerson, "Refugee Massacre Unfolds in Congo."

17. Author's interview with Beatrice Umutesi, Brussels, August 2009.

18. Thomas P. Odom, "Guerrillas from the Mist: A Defense Attaché Watches the Rwandan Patriotic Front Transform from Insurgent to Counter-Insurgent," *Small Wars Journal*, n.d., smallwarsjournal.com/documents/swjmag/v5/odom.htm#_ftn11, accessed March 20, 2009.

19. Howard French, "Kagame's Hidden War in the Congo," *New York Review of Books*, September 24, 2009.

CHAPTER 10

1. Much of the material for this chapter stems from several interviews with Kizito (whose name has been changed to protect his identity) in Bukavu in early 2008. I also interviewed six other former AFDL soldiers, all of whom had similar experiences.

2. All commanders were called *afande*, a word derived from the Swahili and Turkish *effendi*, an honorable person.

3. Watchlist on Children in Armed Conflict, *Country Report: DR Congo*, www .watchlist.org/reports/files/dr_congo.report.20060426.php?p=15, accessed July 29, 2010.

4. Author's interview with Colonel Fely Bikaba, Kinshasa, November 2007.

5. Author's interview with General Siatilo Ngizo, Kinshasa, July 2009.

6. Author's interview with "Trésor," Kinshasa, July 2009.

CHAPTER 11

1. Michela Wrong, *In the Footsteps of Mr. Kurtz: Living on the Brink of Disaster in the Congo* (London: Fourth Estate, 2000), 263.

2. Quoted in the film *Afrique en morceaux* (1999), directed by Jihan El Tahran.

3. The irony here was that the Bangala identity was largely the creation of colonial authorities out of a conglomeration of tribes, although Mobutu was trying to present himself as a precolonial authority.

4. Michael G. Schatzberg, *The Dialectics of Oppression in Zaire* (Bloomington: Indiana University Press, 1988), 72.

5. For an example of this, see the film *Mobutu, Roi du Zaire* (1999), directed by Thierry Michel.

6. Valentin Nagifi, *Les derniers jours de Mobutu a Gbadolite* (Paris: L'Harmattan, 2003), 52 (my translation).

7. Scott Straus, "Americans Meddling, Zairians Charge U.S. Unpopular with Residents Convinced It Backed First Mobutu and Now Rebel Leader," *Globe and Mail* (Toronto), April 12, 1997.

8. Nagifi, *Les derniers jours de Mobutu*, 77.

9. Howard French, "Ending a Chapter, Mobutu Cremates Rwandan Ally," *New York Times*, May 16, 1997.

10. Wrong, *In the Footsteps of Mr. Kurtz*, 272.

11. Félix Vundwawe Te Pemako, *A l'ombre du Léopard: Vérités sur le régime de Mobutu Sese Seko* (Brussels: Editions Zaïre Libre, 2000), 322 (my translation).

12. Wrong, *In the Footsteps of Mr. Kurtz*, 274–277.

13. Tshilombo Munyegayi, "La chute de Mobutu et la mort Mahele racontées par le général Likulia," *Le Potentiel*, July 10, 2005 (my translation).

14. Tshilombo Munyengayi, "La chute de Mobutu et la mort Mahele racontées par le général Likulia," *Le Potentiel*, June 25, 2005.

15. This version of the story was related to General Siatilo Ngizo and General Prosper Nabyolwa by the survivors of the incident, including General Matthieu Agolowa.

CHAPTER 12

1. Eric Tollens, "Food Security in Kinshasa: Coping with Adversity," in *Reinventing Order in Congo: How People Respond to State Failure in Kinshasa*, ed. Theodore Trefon (London: Zed Books; Kampala, Uganda: Fountain, 2004), 48.

2. Author's interview with Nestor Diambwama, Kinshasa, November 2007.

3. Information about Kabila's lifestyle came from the author's separate interviews with Didier Mumengi, Mwenze Kongolo, Jean Mbuyu, and Moise Nyarugabo in Kinshasa, October 2007, and from an interview with Deogratias Bugera in Johannesburg, April 2008.

4. Author's interview with Babi Mbayi, former minister of planning and development, Kinshasa, November 2007.

5. Ibid.

6. "Mandela, Museveni Meet Over Regional Issues," *Xinhua News Agency*, May 27, 1997.

7. Tom Cohen, "Kabila Sworn in as President, Promises Elections Within Two Years," Associated Press, May 29, 1997.

8. Gauthiers de Villers and Jean-Claude Willame, *Republique democratique du Congo: Chronique politique d'un entre-deux-guerres, octobre 1996–juillet 1998*, Cahiers Africains 35 (Paris: L'Harmattan, 1998), 76.

9. Ibid., 107; *Uncertain Course: Transition and Human Rights Violations in the Congo*, Human Rights Watch, vol. 9, no. 9 (December 1997); Howard French, "Congo's Opposition Pays Price of Defying Kabila," *New York Times*, December 3, 1997.

10. Olivier Lanotte, *Guerre sans frontiers en RDC* (Brussels: Complexe, 2003), 74.

11. Human Rights Watch, *Uncertain Course: Transition and Human Rights Violations in the Congo* (New York: Human Rights Watch, 1997), 41.

12. During the rebellion, the AFDL had an office in charge of nongovernmental organizations.

13. International Crisis Group, *How Kabila Lost His Way*, DRC Report #3, May 21, 1999, 15.

14. Interview with Didier Mumengi, the former minister of information, Kinshasa, November 2007.

15. Laura Myers, "Be Democratic, Albright Tells Congo's Kabila," Associated Press, December 13, 1997.

16. Author's interview with Howard Wolpe, Bukavu, February 2008.

17. Howard French, "In Congo, Many Chafe Under Rule of Kabila," *New York Times*, July 17, 1997.

18. Author's interview with Ministry of Mines official, Kinshasa, July 2009.

19. Author's interview with business official, Kinshasa, July 2009.

20. De Villers and Willame, *Republique democratique du Congo*, 121.

21. Author's interview with Didier Mumengi, Kinshasa, November 2007.

22. Author's interview with Babi Mbayi, Kinshasa, November 2007.

23. Author's interview with Didier Mumengi, Kinshasa, November 2007.

24. Robert Reid, "Security Council Struggles to Get Act Together over Congo," Associated Press, May 29, 1997.

25. Gérard Prunier, *Africa's World War: Congo, the Rwandan Genocide, and the Making of a Continental Catastrophe* (Oxford: Oxford University Press, 2009), 157.

26. Kisangani Emizet, "The Massacre of Refugees in Congo: A Case of UN Peacekeeping Failure and International Law," *Journal of Modern African Studies* 38, no. 2 (2000): 170.

27. Author's interview with Tony Gambino, Washington, DC, July 2007.

28. Prunier, *Africa's World War*, 166.

29. Author's interview with Mabi Mulumba, Kinshasa, January 2008.

30. Author's interview with Mulumba, Kinshasa, November 2007.

31. Author's interviews with Moise Nyarugabo, Kinshasa, November 2007, and Deo Bugera, Johannesburg, March 2008. One can dispute their reliability, as they later fell out with Kabila and went into armed opposition.

32. Author's interview with Nyarugabo, Kinshasa, October 2007.

CHAPTER 13

1. Charles Onyango-Obbo, "Interview with Kagame: Habyarimana Knew of Plans to Kill Kim," *Monitor* (Kampala), December 19, 1997.

2. *Final Report of the International Commission of Inquiry (Rwanda)*, S/1998/1096, November 18, 1998, 5. Other reports, including by the human rights group African Rights, put the figure much higher, at around 30,000–40,000.

3. Author's interview with Paul Rwarakabije, Kigali, March 2008.

4. African Rights, *Rwanda: The Insurgency in the Northwest* (London: African Rights, 1999), 45.

5. Human rights groups differ on whether the killings by the RPA were part of a systematic strategy or due to individuals' indiscipline and abuse. Amnesty International argued for the former in the reports *Ending the Silence* (1997) and *Civilians Trapped in Armed Conflict* (1997), while African Rights does not find evidence for a policy of killing civilians in its 1999 report *Rwanda*.

6. Author's interview with anonymous source, Kinshasa, October 2007.

7. Author's interview with Malik Kijege, Kinshasa, October 2007.

8. Ibid.

9. This section is based on four separate interviews by the author with Didier Mumengi, Kinshasa, October 2007, January 2008, and June 2009.

10. Comer Plummer, "The Kitona Operation: Rwanda's African Odyssey," May 6, 2007, www.MilitaryHistoryOnline.com/20thcentury/articles/kitona.aspx, accessed March 17, 2010.

11. Author's interview with anonymous source, Kinshasa, November 2007.

12. Howard French, "Pilot's Account Seems to Confirm Rwanda Role in Congo Strife," *New York Times*, August 10, 1998.

13. Author's telephone interview with Rwandan intelligence official, January 2008.

14. Author's interview with Didier Mumengi, Kinshasa, October 2007.

15. Author's interview with Todd Pitman, Associated Press correspondent who visited Kitona shortly after these events, Bukavu, July 2006.

16. Gérard Prunier, *Africa's World War: Congo, the Rwandan Genocide, and the Making of a Continental Catastrophe* (Oxford: Oxford University Press, 2009), 189; author's interview with Donald Steinberg, former U.S. ambassador to Angola, New York, July 2007; author's interview with U.S. State Department officials, Washington, DC, July 2007.

17. Interview with Steinberg.

18. Author's interview with Angolan officer, Kinshasa, July 2009.

19. Ian Stewart, "Angolans Seize Congo Rebel Stronghold," Associated Press, August 24, 1998. The same figure was advanced by Gérard Prunier in *Africa's World War*, 421n59, citing an article in the South African magazine *Business Day*.

20. Prunier, *Africa's World War*, 192.

21. Ibid., 189.

22. Mary Braid and Ross Herbert, "Congo Civil War Draws in Rival Neighbours," *Independent* (London), August 23, 1998.

23. Gauthiers de Villers with Jean Omasombo and Erik Kennes, *Republique democratique du Congo: Guerre et politique: Les trente derniers mois de L. D. Kabila, août 1998–janvier 2001* (Paris: L'Harmattan, 2001), 28 (my translation).

24. The decision was made by the Inter-State Defense and Security Commission, an SADC organ that Mugabe was presiding over. Only four of the fourteen members had sent their defense ministers, while other countries had sent lower-level delegates. According to SADC statutes, the decision to send a regional military force would have required an SADC presidential summit.

25. Patrick Lawrence, "Mugabe and Mandela Divided by Personalities and Policies," *Irish Times*, August 21, 1998, quoted by Katharina P. Coleman, *International Organisations and Peace Enforcement: The Politics of International Legitimacy* (Cambridge: Cambridge University Press, 2007), 153.

26. The Congolese government tried to convince the Angolans that Rwanda was backing the UNITA rebels, but it is not clear that this was the case at the time of the Kitona offensive. However, when the Rwandan-led troops withdrew under Angolan fire, they found refuge in UNITA-controlled northern Angola, which fueled speculation about earlier contacts. There is overwhelming evidence, documented in UN reports and elsewhere, that UNITA began trading diamonds through Kigali by 1999 at the latest.

27. Norimitsu Onishi, "Congo Recaptures a Strategic Base," *New York Times*, August 23, 1998.

28. Norimitsu Onishi, "Threat Eased, Congo Leader Arrives Back in His Capital," *New York Times*, August 25, 1998.

29. "Race Charge Against Congo Minister," BBC World Service, July 5, 2000.

30. Author's interviews with Congolese in Masina neighborhood, October 2007.

31. Ross Herbert, "Rebel Suspects Die at Hands of Mob in Congo," *Independent* (London), August 30, 1998. The Rwandan and Ugandan soldiers fled to northern Angola. In order to get back to Rwanda, they had to capture a local airstrip from the Angolan army with the help of UNITA rebels. As the airstrip was small, it took them a month and thirty airplane rotations to evacuate the last of their soldiers, during which time they were under constant attack by the well-armed Angolan army. See Charles Onyango-Obbo, "Daring RPA Raid in Congo, Angola; And a Heroic UPDF Unit," *Sunday Monitor* (Kampala), April 16, 2000.

32. This section is based on interviews with Martin Sindabizera and Colonel Martin Nkurikiye (retired), the former Burundian ambassador to the Congo and the former head of the Burundian intelligence services, respectively, Bujumbura, March 2008.

CHAPTER 14

1. Much of this chapter is based on interviews with Wamba dia Wamba in November 2007 and July 2009. Information on the RCD was also provided by Delly Sessanga, Thomas Luhaka, Mbusa Nyamwisi, Moise Nyarugabo, Benjamin Serukiza, and José Endundo.

2. Randy Kennedy, "His Father Is a Rebel Leader . . . ," *New York Times Magazine*, August 29, 1999.

3. Didier Kazadi Nyembwe, the future head of Kabila's intelligence services, was married to Rashid Kawawa's daughter.

4. Author's interview with Ernest Wamba dia Wamba, Kinshasa, November 2007.

5. Author's interview with former Tanzanian intelligence official, Dar es Salaam, January 2008.

6. Author's interview with Patrick Karegeya, Dar es Salaam, January 2008.

7. Michael Colin Vazquez, "The Guerrilla Professor: A Conversation with Ernest Wamba dia Wamba," *Transition* 10, no. 1 (2000): 146.

8. Ernest Wamba dia Wamba, "On the State of African Philosophy and Development," *Journal of African Philosophy* 2 (2003), www.africanphilosophy.com/issue2/diawamba.html.

9. Author's interview with Moise Nyarugabo, former vice president of the RCD, Kinshasa, November 2007.

10. The commander was General James Kazini. Author's interview with former RCD leader, Kinshasa, October 2007.

11. Author's interview with Thomas Luhaka, November 2007. The story is a version of a parable told about Ethiopian emperor Haile Selassie.

12. Author's interview with Luhaka.

13. Written copy of Ernest Wamba dia Wamba's New Year's speech, December 31, 1998.

14. Author's interview with Moise Nyarugabo, Kinshasa, October 2007.

15. Author's interview with Suliman Baldo, New York, December 2007.

16. This was the case of Desiré Lumbu Lumbu, who was accused of conspiring alternately with the Mai-Mai and with the original RCD and beaten to death in Butembo in December 1999.

17. Gauthiers de Villers with Jean Omasombo and Erik Kennes, *Republique democratique du Congo: Guerre et politique: Les trente derniers mois de L. D. Kabila, août 1998–janvier 2001* (Paris: L'Harmattan, 2001), 79 (my translation).

CHAPTER 15

1. Author's interview with Arnaud Zajtmann, former BBC correspondent, Kinshasa, May 2009.

2. Jean-Pierre Bemba, *Le choix de la liberté* (Gbadolite, D. R. Congo: Editions Venus, 2002), 241.

3. Author's interview with Thomas Luhaka, Kinshasa, May 2009.

4. Christopher Clapham, ed., *African Guerrillas* (Oxford: James Currey; Kampala: Fountain; Bloomington: Indiana University Press, 1998), 5.

5. Bemba himself insists that he was shipping fish through Uganda to Europe on his airline, but many others maintain that it was weapons on the flights, and that they were going from Kampala to the Angolan warlord Jonas Savimbi in exchange for diamonds.

6. Bemba, *Le choix de la liberté*, 10.

7. Author's interview with Colonel Shaban Bantariza, Kampala, December 2007.

8. Bemba, *Le choix de la liberté*, 35–36.

9. Author's interview with a friend of Bemba's, who wished to remain anonymous, Kinshasa, June 2008.

10. Author's interview with a former MLC commander who wished to remain anonymous, Kinshasa, November 2007.

11. Author's interview with José Endundo, Kinshasa, November 2007.

12. This was the case for an attack on Basankusu in 1999, which the Ugandans did not want to carry out.

13. Author's interview with François Mwamba, Kinshasa, November 2007.

14. Author's interviews with Thomas Luhaka and François Mwamba, Kinshasa, November 2007.

15. Tatiana Caryannis, *Elections in the Congo: The Bemba Surprise*, United States Institute of Peace Special Report, February 2008, 7.

16. The second exception was Katanga, the home province of Joseph Kabila, which voted overwhelmingly for him.

17. *Ituri: "Covered in Blood": Ethnically Targeted Violence in Northeastern DR Congo*, Human Rights Watch report, July 7, 2003, 32.

18. Author's interview with MLC leader, Kinshasa, November 2007.

19. Ibid.

20. Ernesto "Che" Guevara, *The African Dream: The Diaries of the Revolutionary War in the Congo*, trans. Patrick Camiller (New York: Grove, 2000), 227.

CHAPTER 16

1. V.S. Naipaul, *A Bend in the River* (London: Vintage, 1989), 27.

2. UN Security Council, *Report of the Inter-Agency Mission to Kisangani*, S/2000/1153, December 4, 2000, paragraph 51.

3. Author's interview with Shaban Bantariza, Kampala, February 2008.

4. The commander of the army was Fred Rwigyema, who was one of thirty soldiers who had begun the NRM rebellion with Museveni; the head of medical services was Peter Bayingana, while the head of military police was Sam Kaka; the best man at Kagame's wedding was Aronda Nyakairima, who later became the commander of the Ugandan army.

5. Author's interview with Colonel James Mujira, acting head of Military Intelligence, Kampala, February 2008.

6. Mahmood Mamdani, *When Victims Become Killers: Colonialism, Nativism, and the Genocide in Rwanda* (Princeton, NJ: Princeton University Press, 2001), 174.

7. Other sources confirm that Kisase was killed by Rwandans, perhaps on Kabila's prodding. A former member of his bodyguard told me that Rwandan security agents had tipped him off regarding the ambush, sparing his life. Gérard Prunier also has an account in his book based on two separate insider accounts, *Africa's World War: Congo, the Rwandan Genocide, and the Making of a Continental Catastrophe* (Oxford: Oxford University Press, 2009), 403n112.

8. Charles Onyango-Obbo, "Kabila Shouts Down Museveni," *Monitor* (Kampala), June 2, 1999. The Ugandans were inspired by their own experience. Museveni's rebellion had originally come to power in 1980, backed by the Tanzanian army, which was intent on overthrowing Idi Amin's dictatorship. When the Tanzanians withdrew, the Ugandan alliance that had been put in place had no internal cohesion, and they broke into factions, forcing Museveni to return to the bush. During his second attempt, Museveni had little external support and over six years of guerrilla warfare was forced to develop grassroots support and strong internal organization. It was this second experience that convinced Museveni, at least on a theoretical level, that too much external influence would cause the rebellion to fail.

9. Author's interview with presidential advisor, Kigali, February 2008.

10. Author's interview with Wamba dia Wamba, Kinshasa, November 2007.

11. Author's interview with Ugandan journalist, Kampala, February 2008.

12. Ibid.

13. Ibid.

14. Levi Ochieng, "Machtpoker am grossen Fluss," *Die Tageszeitung*, June 22, 1999 (my translation).

15. *Report of the United Nations Panel of Experts on the Illegal Exploitation of Natural Resources and Other Forms of Wealth of the Democratic Republic of the Congo*, S/2001/357, United Nations, April 12, 2001, 21.

16. Lara Santoro, "Behind the Congo War: Diamonds," *Christian Science Monitor*, August 16, 1998.

17. Prunier, *Africa's World War*, 215.

18. Author's interview with Kisangani resident, June 2004.

19. Author's interview with MLC leader who was in Kisangani at the time, Kinshasa, June 2009.

20. The "bunch of rebels" is a reference to the Lord's Resistance Army, who had displaced almost a million people in northern Uganda.

21. Author's interview with Levi Ochieng, Ugandan journalist in Kisangani at the time, Nairobi, June 2007.

22. Author's interview with Thomas Luhaka, Kinshasa, November 2007.

23. This section is based on the author's interview with Pastor Philippe, Kisangani, June 2004.

24. Prunier, *Africa's World War*, 240. The students, who had been born in Uganda, were protesting against having to take exams in French, a language they did not speak.

25. David Kibirige, "UPDF Commanders Hooligans," *Monitor* (Kampala), June 11, 2000.

CHAPTER 17

1. Richard Brennen et al., "Mortality in the Congo: A Nationwide Survey," *Lancet* 367, no. 9504 (January 2006): 44–51.

2. Roberts's methodology has been questioned by other researchers, although most concur with his broad conclusions. The initial two studies carried out only surveyed a small, random sample of health zones, raising questions about how representative the study was. Also, the baseline of mortality from 1998, with which they were comparing their results, had not been firmly established.

3. For Rwanda, this included the Congolese Rally for Democracy (RCD), the Union of Congolese Patriots (UPC), the Mudundu 40, as well as several semi-independent local militias affiliated with the RCD, such as Governor Eugene Serufuli's Local Defense Force in North Kivu and Governor Xavier Chiribanya's militia in South Kivu. For Uganda, this included the Patriotic Resistance Forces of Ituri (FRPI), the National and Integrationist Front (FNI), the Congolese Revolutionary Movement (MRC), the Movement for the Liberation of the Congo (MLC), and the Congolese Rally for Democracy-National (RCD-N). The Congolese government was allied to half a dozen Mai-Mai groups, ranging from 8,000 strong to just several hundred, spread throughout the Kivus.

4. This section is based on the author's interviews with residents, Kasika, March 2008. The events have been corroborated by interviews conducted by the United Nations Mapping Team in 2008 and 2009 in Kasika, *Report of the Mapping Exercise Documenting the Most Serious Violations of Human Rights and International Humanitarian Law Committed within the Territory of the Democratic Republic of the Congo between March 1993 and June 2003*, 176. Numerous Congolese NGOs also documented the massacre; their reports include *Massacres de Kasika au sud-Kivu*, CADDHOM, 1998; *Report of 20 November 1998*, COJESKI, 1998; *Report of January 1999*, COJESKI, 1999;

and Jean Migabo Kalere, *Génocide au Congo? Analyse des massacres des populations civiles*, Broederlijk Delen, 2002. See also Ambroise Bulambo, *Mourir au Kivu: Du génocide tutsi aux massacres dans l'est du Congo RCD* (Paris: L'Harmattan, 2001).

5. Interviews with residents, Kasika.

6. His name has been changed to protect his identity.

7. Author's interview with Patrice, Kasika, March 2008.

8. His name has been changed to protect his identity.

9. Author's interview, Bukavu, March 2008.

10. *Report of the Mapping Exercise*, 176.

11. This section is based on the author's interviews in Kilungutwe, March 2008.

12. George Lerner, "Activist: Rape of Women, Girls a Weapon of War in Congo," CNN, October 30, 2009, edition.cnn.com/2009/WORLD/africa/10/24/amanpour .congo.rape.documentary/index.html; *Demographic and Health Survey, 2007*, Ministry of Development and Ministry of Health, Democratic Republic of Congo, August 2008; Kirsten Johnson et al., "Association of Sexual Violence and Human Rights Violations with Physical and Mental Health in Territories of the Eastern Democratic Republic of the Congo," *Journal of the American Medical Association* 304, no. 5 (August 2010): 553–562.

13. Author's interview with Benjamin Serukiza, Kinshasa, November 2007.

14. "Interview with Julius Nyerere," *PBS Newshour*, December 27, 1996.

15. Tatiana Carayannis and Herbert Weiss, "Reconstructing the Congo," *Journal of International Affairs* 58, no. 1 (2004): 134.

CHAPTER 18

1. This description of events is according to the author's interviews with Jean Mbuyu, the national security advisor; Edy Kapend, Kabila's military advisor; and Mwenze Kongolo, minister of interior, Kinshasa, June 2009.

2. Author's interview with a former aide to Kabila, who wished to remain anonymous, Kinshasa, November 2007.

3. The roll call gave a good idea of who had power around the president at the time: Gaetan Kakudji, the interior minister who had been Kabila's representative in Europe during the 1980s; the oil minister Victor Mpoyo, the president's éminence grise for financial deals with multinationals; Yerodia Ndombasi, the eccentric education minister who had known Mzee since his early rebel days; and Edy Kapend, the young military advisor with close links to Angola.

4. Author's interview with Didier Mumengi, Kinshasa, November 2007.

5. Herbert Weiss, *War and Peace in the Democratic Republic of the Congo*, Current African Issues no. 22 (Uppsala, Sweden: Nordiska Afrikaninstitutet, 2000), 15.

6. Gauthiers de Villers and Jean-Claude Willame, *Republique democratique du Congo: Chronique politique d'un entre-deux-guerres, octobre 1996–juillet 1998*, Cahiers Africains 35 (Paris: L'Harmattan, 1998), 233.

7. Interview with Mumengi.

8. International Monetary Fund, *Country Report No 01/123*, July 2001, 29.

9. *Addendum to the United Nations Report of the Panel of Experts on the Illegal Exploitation of Natural Resources and Other Forms of Wealth of DR Congo*, S/2001/1072, United Nations, November 10, 2001, paragraphs 67–68.

10. Author's interview with Jean Mbuyu, Kinshasa, June 2009.

11. Author's interview with Jean-Bosco Ndayikengurukiye, Bujumbura, May 2009.

12. International Crisis Group, *Scramble for the Congo: Anatomy of an Ugly War*, Africa Report no. 26, December 20, 2000, 52.

13. Author's interview with Colonel Maurice Gateretse, Bujumbura, March 2008.

14. Karl Vick, "Desperate Battle Defines Congo's Warlike Peace," *Washington Post*, January 2, 2001.

15. Interview with Ndayikengurukiye.

16. Interview with Mbuyu.

17. Vick, "Desperate Battle."

18. International Crisis Group, *Scramble for the Congo*, 64.

19. Interview with Kabila aide, Kinshasa, June 2009.

20. Interview with two separate Kabila aides, Kinshasa, June 2009.

21. Interview with Mumengi.

22. This description of events is according to my interviews with Jean Mbuyu, the national security advisor, and Edy Kapend, Kabila's military advisor, Kinshasa, June 2009.

23. Stephen Smith and Antoine Glaser, "Ces enfants soldats qui out tué Kabila," *Le Monde* (Paris), February 9, 2001.

24. This tale is recited frequently in Kinshasa. See also Norimitsu Onishi, "Slain Congo Leader Buried to Pomp and Confusion," *New York Times*, January 24, 2001.

25. State Department Report on Human Rights Practices, Democratic Republic of the Congo, 2001; author's interview with former *kadogo*, Kinshasa, October 2007.

26. Smith and Glaser, "Ces enfants soldats."

27. Interview with Mbuyu.

28. Author's telephone interview with former Rwandan security official, June 2010.

29. "Kabila cherche à vendre ses pierres," *La Lettre du Continent*, August 24, 2000; "Dropping Kabila," *Africa Confidential* 41, no. 20, October 13, 2000, quoted in Gérard Prunier, *Africa's World War: Congo, the Rwandan Genocide, and the Making of a Continental Catastrophe* (Oxford: Oxford University Press, 2009), 253nn152, 153.

30. Marie-France Cros, "L'assassinat de Kabila: Un quasi-témoin parle," *La Libre Belgique*, December 24, 2001.

31. Norimitsu Onishi, "Suspects by the Score and, Oh, Such Digressions!" *New York Times*, April 21, 2001.

CHAPTER 19

1. Author's interview with Mwenze Kongolo, Kinshasa, July 2009.

2. Richard Morais, "Friends in High Places," *Forbes*, August 10, 1998.

3. Author's interview with Gécamines official, Kinshasa, July 2009.

4. Andrew Maykuth, "Outside Mining Firms Find Zaire an Untapped Vein," *Philadelphia Inquirer*, May 11, 1997.

5. Ibid.

6. Ibid.

7. "Huge Fortunes at Stake in Zaire," *Business Times* (Johannesburg), April 20, 1997; author's interview with former American Mineral Fields executive, Cape Town, February 2008.

8. Author's interview with Lundin executive, Cape Town, February 2008.

9. Maykuth, "Outside Mining Firms."

10. These companies were not alone. A Canadian company, First Quantum, was also reported to have given a multimillion-dollar advance to the rebels in return for a concession before they arrived in Kinshasa.

11. James G. Stewart, *Corporate War Crimes: Prosecuting the Pillage of Natural Resources* (New York: Open Society Justice Initiative, 2010), 33–36.

12. Ludo de Witte, *The Assassination of Lumumba*, trans. Ann Wright and Renée Fenby (London: Verso, 2001), 31.

13. "Demands and Derailment," Africa Energy & Mining, May 21, 1997.

14. *Special Commission Charged with Examining the Validity of Economic and Financial Conventions Concluded During the Wars of 1996–1997 and 1998: The Lutundula Report*, National Assembly of the Democratic Republic of the Congo, February 26, 2006, 35.

15. Author's interview with Mabi Mulumba, Kinshasa, December 2007.

16. Author's interview with former presidential advisor, Kinshasa, November 2007.

17. Ibid.

18. *Lutundula Report*, 32–33.

19. The commander of the armed forces was General Vitalis Zvinavashe and the minister of defense Sidney Sekeramayi.

20. Author's interview with businessman in Paris, February 2008.

21. "Rautenbach Denies Murder Allegation," South African Press Agency, December 16, 1999.

22. Author's interview with Gécamines official, Kinshasa, July 2009.

23. *Report of the United Nations Panel on the Illegal Exploitation of Natural Resources in the Democratic Republic of the Congo*, United Nations, October 8, 2002, 11; Gérard Prunier, *Africa's World War: Congo, the Rwandan Genocide, and the Making of a Continental Catastrophe* (Oxford: Oxford University Press, 2009), 218.

24. Author's off-the-record telephone interview with a mining executive, May 2009.

25. Confidential South African intelligence report in the author's possession.

26. *Report of the United Nations Panel on the Illegal Exploitation of Natural Resources in the Democratic Republic of the Congo*, United Nations, April 12, 2001, 33.

27. International Monetary Fund, *Democratic Republic of the Congo: Selected Issues and Statistical Appendix*, Country Report 1/123, July 2001, 16.

28. Author's interview with Jean Mbuyu, Kinshasa, November 2007; author's interview with Mwenze Kongolo, Kinshasa, May 2009.

29. Confidential industry intelligence report on Billy Rautenbach, August 10, 2000.

30. Ibid.

31. Cliff Taylor, "Congo Wealth Lures Africa's Power-Players," *Independent* (London), October 31, 1998; Michael Nest, "Ambitions, Profits and Loss: Zimbabwean Economic Involvement in the DRC," *African Affairs* 100, no. 400 (2001): 484.

32. *Report of the United Nations Panel*, 8.

33. Martin Meredith, *Our Votes, Our Guns: Robert Mugabe and the Tragedy of Zimbabwe* (New York: PublicAffairs, 2002), 142.

34. Author's interview with mining officials, Kinshasa, May 2009. There are, unfortunately, almost no legal safeguards in the Congo to prevent such transfer pricing.

35. Author's interview with Dona Kampata, Kinshasa, July 2009.

36. Prunier, *Africa's World War*, 239.

37. His name has been changed to protect his identity.

38. This section is based on several interviews with the pilot in the Eastern Congo, March 2008.

39. The UN panel of experts that was researching the illegal exploitation of natural resources in the Congo at the time was given similar information regarding how long it took to fly the stockpiles to Kigali.

40. According to Global Witness, a kilo of tin was being sold for $6 in Goma in 1998, when the world coltan price was hovering around $60 per kilo of refined tantalum. Coltan sold in Goma usually included around 20 to 40 percent tantalum. See Didier de Failly, "Coltan: Pour comprendre . . . ," in *L'Afrique des Grands Lacs: Annuaire 2000–2001* (Paris: L'Harmattan, 2001), 13, and "Under-Mining Peace," *Global Witness* (June 2005): 28.

41. *Report of the United Nations Panel*, 8.

42. Gauthiers de Villers with Jean Omasombo and Erik Kennes, *Republique democratique du Congo: Guerre et politique: Les trente derniers mois de L. D. Kabila, août 1998–janvier 2001* (Paris: L'Harmattan, 2001), 114–115.

43. Author's interview with Benjamin Serukiza, former RCD vice governor of South Kivu and a prominent member of the Banyamulenge community, Kinshasa, October 2007.

44. Jeroen Cuvulier and Tim Raeymaekers, *Supporting the War Economy in the DRC: European Companies and the Coltan Trade*, International Peace Information Service (IPIS), January 2002, 8.

45. As always, reliable statistics are hard to come by in the region. According to the United States Geological Survey, columbo-tantalite exports for 2000 amounted to 1,011 tons for Rwanda and the Congo combined, while a UN experts panel estimated

exports to be around 1,200 tons for the same period. Rwanda has several, smaller coltan mines, but the bulk of their exports comes from the Eastern Congo. The local price in Goma peaked in the second half of 2000 at $75 per kilo of 20 to 40 percent coltan and $150 for higher-grade product. The world price, however, peaked at around $600 for refined tantalum, so middlemen had handsome profit margins. See George Coakley, *The Mineral Industry of Congo-Kinshasa*, U.S. Geological Survey Country Report, 2002, 10.3, www.usgs.gov.

46. Stephan Marysse and C. Andre, "Guerre et pillage économique en République Democratique du Congo," in *L'Afrique des Grands Lacs*; see also Bjorn Willum, "Purely Beneficial or Contributing to War," PhD diss., October 21, 2001, University of Copenhagen. Willum conducts a comprehensive analysis of gold, coltan, and diamond exports from the Eastern Congo and concludes that the Rwandan army and its business associates were making around $250 million in profits from mineral trade in the Eastern Congo at the height of the war.

47. *Report of the United Nations Panel*, 27.

48. International Institute for Security Studies, *The Military Balance* (Oxford: Oxford University Press, 2002).

49. Author's interview with Colonel Vincent Kitoko, Kinshasa, July 2008.

50. *Rwanda: The Search for Security and Human Rights Abuses*, Human Rights Watch, vol. 12, no. 1(A), April 2000.

51. Author's interview with Patrick Karegeya, Dar es Salaam, January 2008.

52. *Final Report of the United Nations Panel of Experts on the Illegal Exploitation of Natural Resources and Other Forms of Wealth of the Democratic Republic of the Congo*, S/2002/1146, United Nations, October 16, 2002, 15.

53. *World Bank: Doing Business 2009* (Washington: World Bank, 2008), 43.

54. *Final Report of the United Nations Panel*; *Report of the United Nations Panel*; Cuvulier and Raeymaekers, *Supporting the War Economy*.

55. Stewart, *Corporate War Crimes*, 34–36.

CHAPTER 20

1. Gaetan Kakudji was a longtime associate of Kabila, his representative in Belgium during the 1980s, and his interior minister once he came to power; Victor Mpoyo was minister of the state portfolio for several years and handled much of Kabila's financial dealings.

2. According to Edy Kapend, the following people attended this meeting: several of Laurent Kabila's old comrades from his early days as a rebel, namely General Celestin Kifwa, General Sylvestre Lwetcha, General Francois Olenga, Victor Mpoyo, Gaetan Kakudji, and Yerodia Ndombasi; and members of the new vanguard, including Mwenze Kongolo, Didier Mumengi, Nono Lutula, and Henri Mova. Others say the group was smaller but did not include any other names.

3. Author's interview with anonymous presidential aide, Kinshasa, July 2009.

4. Ibid.

5. Danna Harman, "A Shy Son in Congo's Hot Seat," *Christian Science Monitor*, January 23, 2001.

6. Munkana N'Ge and Erik Kennes, *Biographies des acteurs de la transition* (Terveuren, Belgium: Musée Royale de l'Afrique Centrale, 2006), 70. Tanzanian security officials and numerous members of Joseph Kabila's entourage have confirmed this.

7. Author's interviews conducted in Kinshasa in 2007–2009; interestingly, this version is also supported by Laurent Nkunda, who fought alongside Joseph Kabila—albeit as a junior officer—in the AFDL war.

8. Erik Kennes with collaboration by Munkana N'Ge, *Essai biographique sur Laurent Désiré Kabila* (Paris: L'Harmattan, 2003), 300.

9. Colette Braeckman, "Mama Sifa, la mère du president parle," *Le Soir* (Brussels), June 6, 2006 (my translation).

10. Author's interview with Kenyan security official, Nairobi, June 2009; "Portrait: Joseph Kabila," *La Revue* (July/August 2006): 37.

11. "Kabange" denotes the second born of twins in Laurent Kabila's native language, Kiluba.

12. Francois Soudan, "Portrait: Joseph Kabila," *La Revue* (July/August 2006): 41.

13. He had been nominally in charge of some military operations during the AFDL offensive, but according to soldiers serving under him at the time, he worked in the shadow of Rwandan commanders.

14. Gérard Prunier, *Africa's World War: Congo, the Rwandan Genocide, and the Making of a Continental Catastrophe* (Oxford: Oxford University Press, 2009), 258.

15. Ibid.

16. Chris McGreal, "Western Allies Urge Rwanda to Leave Congo," *Guardian* (Manchester, U.K.), February 9, 2001.

17. "Congo Rebels Deny Clearance to U.N. Troops Trying to Land," Associated Press, April 16, 2001.

18. Prunier, *Africa's World War*, 263.

19. Author's interview with UN official, Nairobi, June 2009.

20. Author's interview with American diplomat, Kinshasa, July 2009.

21. Author's interview with foreign journalist, Kinshasa, July 2008. The ambassador in question was Georges Serre.

22. Author's interview with UN official, Nairobi, June 2008.

23. Author's interview with Philip Winter, Kinshasa, June 2008.

24. Netherlands Institute for Southern Africa (NIZA), *The State vs. The People*, 2006, , 41.

25. Author's interview with UN official, Nairobi, June 2008.

26. *Special Commission Charged with Examining the Validity of Economic and Financial Conventions Concluded During the Wars of 1996–1997 and 1998: The Lutundula*

Report, National Assembly of the Democratic Republic of the Congo, February 26, 2006, 63–64.

27. *Final Report of the United Nations Panel of Experts on the Illegal Exploitation of Natural Resources and Other Forms of Wealth of the Democratic Republic of the Congo,* #S/2002/1146, United Nations, October 16, 2002, 7; Toby Heaps, "A Glimpse of the World: Joseph Kabila," Tea with the *FT, Financial Times* (London), April 9, 2006.

28. Brooderlink Delen, "Memorandum to the Attention of the Ministers of Foreign Affairs of the Member States of the International Committee of Support for the Transition in the DRC," Rights and Accountability in Development, 11.11.11, February 20, 2006, 8.

29. "Office Memorandum from Craig Andrews, Principle Mining Specialist, to Pedro Alba, Country Director for the DRC," September 4, 2005, in the author's archive.

30. Author's interview with presidential advisor, Kinshasa, November 2007; author's interview with presidential pilot, Kinshasa, June 2008; Gertler is also named in *Report of the United Nations Panel on the Illegal Exploitation of Natural Resources in the Democratic Republic of the Congo,* United Nations, April 12, 2001.

31. Author's interview with Congolese politician, Kinshasa, July 2009.

32. Author's interview with Congolese mining lawyer, Kinshasa, July 2009.

33. Author's interview with Gérard Gerold, Kinshasa, January 2007.

34. For a study of Laurent Nkunda, see Jason Stearns, "The Emergence of a New Rebellion in North Kivu," in *Afrique des Grands Lacs: Annuaire 2007–2008,* eds. Stefaan Marysse and Filip Reyntjens (Paris: L'Harmattan, 2008); for Rwandan support to Nkunda, see *Final Report of the United Nations Group of Experts on the DR Congo,* S/2008/773, United Nations, December 12, 2008.

35. *We Will Crush You,* Human Rights Watch Report, November 2008.

36. I was speaking with a presidential intelligence officer after an abortive coup attempt by Major Eric Lenge in July 2004.

37. Author's interview with officer in staff headquarters, Kinshasa, July 2009.

38. Author's interview with presidential advisor, Kinshasa, July 2009.

CONCLUSION

1. Philip Gourevitch, "Forsaken," *New Yorker,* September 25, 2000, 65.

2. The International Rescue Committee, in its most recent mortality study in 2007 concluded that 5.4 million people had died as a result of the conflict in the Congo between 1998 and 2007, not counting those who had died between 1996 and 1998, or those who have died since 2007 in the ongoing violence. "IRC Affirms Congo Mortality Findings," January 21, 2010, www.irc.org. Figures of rape are notoriously difficult to estimate, but the United Nations believes that over 200,000 women have been victims of sexual violence since 1998. "Nearly 200 Women and Children Raped in Systematic Attack in Eastern DRC," Medical Foundation for the Care of Victims of

Torture, August 27, 2010, www.torturecare.org.uk/news/latest_news/3173, accessed September 30, 2010.

3. Eve Ensler, "The Beginning of Hope or the End of It," *Huffington Post*, October 30, 2008, www.huffingtonpost.com/eve-ensler/the-beginning-of-hope-or_b_139423.html.

4. Jeffrey Gettleman, "Rape Victim's Words Help Jolt Congo into Change," *New York Times*, October 17, 2008.

5. Author's interview with Sue Hogwood, Bujumbura, March 2008.

6. Author's interview with presidential advisor, Kigali, February 2008.

7. In 1993, a large UN mission (UNOSOM) was deployed to Somalia to secure the distribution of food aid to a starving population. It became embroiled in urban firefights with local militia commanders, leading to the highly publicized death of U.S. soldiers.

8. "Code Cable 00283 from American Embassy in Kigali to Rwanda Collective, Secretary of State, Washington DC," January 6, 1997.

Index

Jaime Windon

Jason K. Stearns has worked on the conflict in the Congo for over ten years, most recently as the head of a special United Nations panel investigating Congolese rebel groups. He first traveled to the Congo in 2001 to work for a local human rights group in the eastern border town of Bukavu. He later worked for the United Nations peacekeeping operation and as a senior analyst for the International Crisis Group. His journalism and opinion pieces have appeared in the *Economist*, *Africa Confidential*, the *Washington Post*, the *Wall Street Journal*, and the *Financial Times*. He is also a regular guest on the BBC, Radio France International, NPR, and CNN. He writes the blog "Congo Siasa" and is completing a PhD at Yale University.